Russia Before and After Crimea

RUSSIA BEFORE AND AFTER CRIMEA

Nationalism and Identity, 2010–17

Edited by Pål Kolstø and Helge Blakkisrud

EDINBURGH
University Press

Edinburgh University Press is one of the leading university presses in the UK. We publish academic books and journals in our selected subject areas across the humanities and social sciences, combining cutting-edge scholarship with high editorial and production values to produce academic works of lasting importance. For more information visit our website: edinburghuniversitypress.com

© editorial matter and organisation Pål Kolstø and Helge Blakkisrud, 2018
© the chapters their several authors, 2018

Edinburgh University Press Ltd
The Tun – Holyrood Road,
12(2f) Jackson's Entry,
Edinburgh EH8 8PJ

Typeset in 11/13 Adobe Sabon by
IDSUK (DataConnection) Ltd

A CIP record for this book is available from the British Library
ISBN 978 1 4744 3385 3 (hardback)
ISBN 978 1 4744 3387 7 (webready PDF)
ISBN 978 1 4744 3388 4 (epub)

The right of Pål Kolstø and Helge Blakkisrud to be identified as the editors of this work has been asserted in accordance with the Copyright, Designs and Patents Act 1988, and the Copyright and Related Rights Regulations 2003 (SI No. 2498).

Contents

List of figures — vii
List of tables — viii
Notes on contributors — ix
Preface — xvii

Introduction: Exploring Russian nationalisms — 1
Pål Kolstø and Helge Blakkisrud

Part I Official nationalism

1. Contemporary Russian nationalism in the historical struggle between 'official nationality' and 'popular sovereignty' — 23
   Emil Pain

2. Imperial and ethnic nationalism: A dilemma of the Russian elite — 50
   Eduard Ponarin and Michael Komin

3. Kremlin's post-2012 national policies: Encountering the merits and perils of identity-based social contract — 68
   Yuri Teper

4. Sovereignty and Russian national identity-making: The biopolitical dimension — 93
   Andrey Makarychev and Alexandra Yatsyk

Part II Radical and other societal nationalisms

5. Revolutionary nationalism in Contemporary Russia — 119
   Alexandra Kuznetsova and Sergey Sergeev

6. The Russian nationalist movement at low ebb — 142
   Alexander Verkhovsky

7. Ideologue of neo-Nazi terror: Aleksandr Sevastianov and Russia's 'partisan' insurgency 163
Robert Horvath

8. The extreme right fringe of Russian nationalism and the Ukraine conflict: The National Socialist Initiative 187
Sofia Tipaldou

Part III Identities and otherings

9. 'Restore Moscow to the Muscovites': Othering 'the migrants' in the 2013 Moscow mayoral elections 213
Helge Blakkisrud and Pål Kolstø

10. Anti-migrant, but not nationalist: Pursuing statist legitimacy through immigration discourse and policy 236
Caress Schenk

11. Everyday patriotism and ethnicity in today's Russia 258
J. Paul Goode

12. Identity in Crimea before annexation: A bottom-up perspective 282
Eleanor Knott

Index 306

Figures

Figure 2.1:	Elite's perception of the United States as a threat to Russian security	56
Figure 2.2:	Scope of Russia's national interests	57
Figure 2.3:	Perceptions of the United States as a threat by the Russian elite and population at large, 1993–2009	58
Figure 2.4:	Dynamics of the masses' attitudes towards the United States and towards people hailing from the Caucasus	60
Figure 11.1:	Budget for State Programme for Patriotic Education, 2001–20	264
Figure 11.2:	Ethnicising by age group	270
Figure 12.1:	Russian language use in Ukraine according to the 2001 Ukrainian census	284
Figure 12.2:	Russian ethnicity in Ukraine according to the 2001 Ukrainian census	284
Figure 12.3:	Language and ethnicity in the 2001 Ukrainian census	285
Figure 12.4:	'In your opinion, what should the status of Crimea be?'	288

Tables

Table I.1:	A typology of Russian nationalisms	5
Table 5.1:	People killed and wounded in neo-Nazi attacks, 2004–16	131
Table 10.1:	Public opinion on migrants in the labour market	242
Table 10.2:	Commitment to multiculturalism	245
Table 10.3:	What kinds of threat do migrants pose?	248
Table 10.4:	Blacklists and deportations	251
Table 11.1:	State Programme for Patriotic Education – budget breakdown	266
Table 11.2:	State Programme for Patriotic Education – activity budgets	267
Table 12.1:	Conceptualising identity in Crimea	294
Table 12.2:	Territorial aspirations, by inductively derived identification category	300

Notes on Contributors

Helge Blakkisrud is Senior Researcher and Head of the Research Group on Russia, Eurasia and the Arctic, at the Norwegian Institute of International Affairs (NUPI), Oslo, Norway. In 2009–10 he was a Fulbright Visiting Scholar at the Institute of Slavic, East European, and Eurasian Studies, UC Berkeley. His research interests include the development of centre–region relations in the Russian Federation, the reform of intra-executive relations in particular, and state- and nation-building in Eurasia. Published books include *Centre–Periphery Relations in Russia* (Ashgate, 2001, co-edited with Geir Hønneland), *Nation-building and Common Values in Russia* (Rowman & Littlefield, 2004, co-edited with Pål Kolstø), *Tackling Space: Federal Politics and the Russian North* (University Press of America, 2005, co-edited with Geir Hønneland), *The Governors' Last Stand: Federal Bargaining in Russia's Transition to Appointed Regional Heads* (Unipub, 2015) and *The New Russian Nationalism: Imperialism, Ethnicity and Authoritarianism, 2000–15* (Edinburgh University Press, 2016, co-edited with Pål Kolstø). Blakkisrud has published peer-reviewed articles in *Communist and Post-Communist Studies*, *Demokratizatsiya*, *East European Politics*, *Ethnic and Racial Studies*, *Europe–Asia Studies*, *Geopolitics*, *Nationalities Papers* and *Post-Soviet Affairs*.

J. Paul Goode is Senior Lecturer (Associate Professor) of Russian Politics at the University of Bath, UK. In 2014–16, he was a Fulbright Research Fellow at Perm State National Research University and Tiumen State University in Russia. Goode is also Associate Editor of *Political Studies Review*. His research interests include nationalism and ethnic politics, authoritarian and hybrid regimes, research methods and regionalism, and centre–region relations in

Russia. He is the author of *The Decline of Regionalism in Putin's Russia: Boundary Issues* (Routledge, 2011), and guest editor of two issues of *Social Science Quarterly* on research methods and fieldwork in the study of nationalism (2015) and authoritarianism (2016). He has published peer-reviewed articles in *Europe–Asia Studies, Journal of Communist Studies and Transition Politics, Perspectives on Politics, Post-Soviet Affairs, Problems of Post-Communism, Russian Politics* and *Social Science Quarterly*.

Robert Horvath is Senior Lecturer in the Department of Politics and Philosophy at La Trobe University in Melbourne, Australia. During 2011–15, he held an Australian Research Council research fellowship. His research interests include the politics of human rights and radical nationalism in post-Soviet Russia. Horvath is the author of *The Legacy of Soviet Dissent: Dissidents, Democratisation and Radical Nationalism in Russia* (Routledge, 2005) and *Putin's 'Preventive Counter-Revolution': Post-Soviet Authoritarianism and the Spectre of Velvet Revolution* (Routledge, 2013); his articles have been published in *Europe–Asia Studies, Russian Review, Nationalities Papers* and *Human Rights Quarterly*. He is currently working on a monograph about the neo-nazi organisation Russian Image (*Russkii obraz*) and its role in Putin's 'managed nationalism'.

Eleanor Knott is an Assistant Professor in the Department of Methodology at the London School of Economics, UK. Her dissertation in Political Science (2016) examined the politics of co-ethnicity and citizenship from the bottom-up, in the cases of Moldova and Crimea, by analysing the meanings of kin–state identification and engagement with kin–state practices (citizenship and quasi-citizenship). Knott has published peer-reviewed articles in *Citizenship Studies, Democratization, East European Politics and Societies, Electoral Studies, Nations and Nationalism* and *Social Science Quarterly*. She is currently working on a book manuscript comparing kin–state politics using the approach of everyday nationalism in Crimea and Moldova.

Pål Kolstø is Professor of Russian Studies at the University of Oslo. His main research areas are nationalism, nation-building, ethnic conflicts and nationality policy in Russia, the former Soviet Union and the Western Balkans. His books include *Nation-building and Ethnic Integration in Post-Soviet Societies* (Westview Press, 1999, editor), *Political Construction Sites: Nation-building in Russia and the Post-Soviet States* (Westview Press, 2000), *National Integration and Violent Conflict in Post-Soviet Societies* (Rowman & Littlefield, 2002, editor), *Nation-building and Common Values in Russia* (Rowman & Littlefield, 2004, co-edited with Helge Blakkisrud), *Myths and Boundaries in South-Eastern Europe* (Hurst, 2005, editor), *Media Discourse and the Yugoslav Conflicts* (Routledge, 2009, editor), *Strategies of Symbolic Nation-building in South Eastern Europe* (Routledge, 2014, editor) and *The New Russian Nationalism: Imperialism, Ethnicity and Authoritarianism, 2000–15* (Edinburgh University Press, 2016, co-edited with Helge Blakkisrud). Kolstø has published roughly forty articles in English-language peer-reviewed journals in addition to numerous publications in other languages. He is a recipient of six large research grants for the study of nation-building and ethnic relations in the post-Soviet world and Eastern Europe.

Michael Komin is a Senior Expert at the Centre for Strategic Research in Moscow, and holds an MA degree in Political Science from the National Research University–Higher School of Economics in St Petersburg, Russia. In 2015–16 he was part of the research and research training group 'Nationalism and national policies in the Soviet Union: quantitative methods', organised by the Laboratory for Comparative Social Research at the Higher School of Economics. His research interests include political identity, political elites as well as institutions and implementation of reform in authoritarian regimes. Komin has published peer-reviewed articles in the Russian-language journals *Politiia*, *Logos* and *Filosofskie nauki*.

Alexandra Kuznetsova is a PhD candidate at the Arthur V. Mauro Centre for Peace and Justice, University of Manitoba, Winnipeg, Canada, and an Assistant Professor at the Department of Social and Political Conflict Studies, Kazan National Research Technological University, Kazan, Russia. Her research interests include nationalism, civil society and critical peace and conflict studies. She has also worked and volunteered in various non-profit organisations and academic institutions in Israel, Russia and Canada. Together with Sergey Sergeev, Kuznetsova won a joint research grant from the Russian Humanitarian Scientific Foundation that resulted in articles on revolutionary nationalism in several peer-reviewed journals, including *Vestnik Permskogo universiteta* and *Kazanskii sotsial'no-gumanitarnyi vestnik*. Her publications also include book chapters in the edited volume *Conflict Studies in Social Life* (KNITU, 2014, edited by Sergey Sergeev, in Russian).

Andrey Makarychev is Guest Professor at the Johan Skytte Institute of Political Science, University of Tartu, Estonia. He is also a Senior Research Associate at the Barcelona Centre for International Affairs (CIDOB), Barcelona, Spain, and a Visiting Professor at the University of Bordeaux, France (2017) and the Free University of Berlin, Germany. His areas of expertise are Russia–European Union relations, post-Soviet countries, cultural and sports mega-events in Eastern Europe and Eurasia, and biopolitics. Previous institutional affiliations include the George Mason University, Fairfax, USA; the Center for Conflict Studies, ETH, Zurich, Switzerland; the Danish Institute of International Studies (DIIS) Copenhagen, Denmark; and Nizhnii Novgorod Linguistic University, Russia. Makarychev co-edited *Changing Political and Economic Regimes in Russia* (Routledge, 2013, with Andre Mommen), and has authored numerous articles published in journals such as *Cooperation and Conflict, Demokratizatsiya, Europe–Asia Studies, Global Governance, European Regional and Urban Studies, International Spectator, Problems of Post-Communism, Journal of Eurasian Studies, Journal of International Relations and Development, Turkish Foreign Policy Review* and *Welttrends*, as well as book chapters in edited volumes published by Ashgate, Palgrave Macmillan and Nomos.

Emil Pain is Director General of the Centre for Ethno-Political and Regional Studies, Moscow, and Professor of Political Science, National Research University–Higher School of Economics, Moscow. He has published thirteen books and more than 300 articles, focusing on nationality politics, ethnic conflict and terrorism in Russia, Caucasus and Central Asia. From 1996 to 1999 Pain served as advisor to President Boris Eltsin on nationality issues. In 2000–1 he was a Galina Starovoitova Fellow on Conflict Resolution at the Kennan Institute, Washington, DC. His publications include *Between Empire and Nation* (Novoe izdatel'stvo, 2004, in Russian), *The Ethnopolitical Pendulum* (Institut sotsiologii RAN, 2004, in Russian), 'Socio-cultural factor and Russian modernization' in *Waiting for Reform under Putin and Medvedev* (Palgrave Macmillan, 2012, edited by Lena Jonson and Stephen White), 'The ethno-political pendulum: the dynamics of the relationship between ethnic minorities and majorities in post-Soviet Russia' in *Managing Ethnic Diversity in Russia* (Routledge, 2013, edited by Oleh Protsyk and Benedikt Harzl) and 'The imperial syndrome and its influence on Russian nationalism' in *The New Russian Nationalism* (Edinburgh University Press, 2016, edited by Pål Kolstø and Helge Blakkisrud).

Eduard Ponarin is Director of the Laboratory for Comparative Social Research at the National Research University–Higher School of Economics in Moscow, and Professor of Sociology at the same institution in St Petersburg. He holds a PhD in Sociology from the University of Michigan (1996). Between 1998 and 2008, he taught at the European University at St Petersburg. In 2005–7, he was an International Policy Fellow at the Open Society Institute, Budapest, Hungary, and in 2009, a Kone Fellow at the University of Helsinki, Finland. Ponarin is Russia's representative in the World Values Survey Association and a member of its Executive Council. He served on the Executive Board of the PONARS network in 2003–6. His research interests include nationalism, religion, modernisation, survey research and applied statistics. He has published peer-reviewed articles in *BMC Public Health*, *Democratization*, *Europe–Asia Studies*, *International Journal of Sociology*, *Journal of Happiness Studies*, *Problems of Post-Communism*, *Social Forces* and *Teaching Sociology*.

Caress Schenk is an Assistant Professor of Political Science and International Relations at Nazarbayev University, Astana, Kazakhstan, with teaching and research specialties related to comparative politics, national identity, immigration control and Eurasian politics. Her research has examined federal vs. regional-level management of migration in Russia, government and civil society responses to migration, human trafficking and labour slavery in Eurasia, migration agency and rights related to corruption and informal practices, and labour migration in the framework of the Eurasian Economic Union. Schenk is a member of the PONARS network and has received research funding from the American Councils for International Education, the Fulbright Scholar Program and Nazarbayev University. Her work has been published in *Demokratizatisya*, *Europe–Asia Studies* and *Nationalities Papers*; she has a forthcoming book *Why Control Immigration? Strategic Uses of Migration Management in Russia* (University of Toronto Press).

Sergey Sergeev is Professor and Head of the Department of Social and Political Conflict Studies at Kazan National Research Technological University and Professor at the Political Science Department, Kazan Federal University, Russia. His research interests include the development of political opposition in Russia, Russian nationalism, youth movements and social and political conflicts in the Republic of Tatarstan. Sergeev serves as an expert in the Kudrin Foundation's Committee of Civil Initiatives. His books include *Political Opposition in the Contemporary Russian Federation* (KGU, 2004, in Russian), *Sociocultural Portrait of the Republic of Tatarstan* (KNITU, 2009, co-authored with Aleksandr Salagaev and Liudmila Luchsheva, in Russian), *New Problems and Contradictions in the Sociocultural Development of the Republic of Tatarstan* (KNITU, 2011, co-authored with Aleksandr Salagaev and Liudmila Luchsheva, in Russian), *Conflict Studies in Social Life* (KNITU, 2014, editor, in Russian) and *The Goth Subculture: Genesis, Style, Influence on Mass Culture* (KNITU, 2016, co-authored with Tatiana Abdullina, in Russian). He has published peer-reviewed articles in journals such as *Politeiia*, *Politeks (Politicheskaia ekspertiza)*, *Sotsis (Sotsiologicheskie issledovainiia)* and *The Soviet and Post-Soviet Review*.

Yuri Teper is an Israel Science Foundation (ISF) postdoctoral fellow at the Department of Political Science at the Hebrew University of Jerusalem, Israel. In 2017, he was also a George F. Kennan Visiting Expert at the Woodrow Wilson Center in Washington DC. In 2014–15 he was a postdoctoral visiting scholar at the Department of Russian and East-European Studies at the School of Arts, Languages and Cultures, the University of Manchester, UK. His PhD dissertation was titled *Nationalism and Political Culture in Symbols and Myths in Putin's Russia: 1999–2010*. Teper specialises in issues of Russian identity politics and nation-building, political mobilisation, regime hybridity and its implications for domestic and foreign policymaking. He has published peer-reviewed articles in *Nations and Nationalism* and *Post-Soviet Affairs*, as well as chapters in several edited volumes.

Sofia Tipaldou is a Marie Curie Research Fellow at the University of Manchester, UK. Before joining the University of Manchester, she was a Visiting Researcher at the Free University of Berlin, Germany, and a postdoctoral researcher at Panteio University, Athens, Greece. She holds a PhD in International Relations and European Studies from the Autonomous University of Barcelona, Spain. Her research focuses on the sociology of the contemporary radical right movement in Russia (emergence, development and outcomes) and in crisis-ridden southern European societies (Greece and Spain). Her broader research interests are nationalism, radical right, social movements and post-Soviet transformation. Tipaldou has published contributions in *Europe–Asia Studies* (2014, co-authored with Katrin Uba) and in the edited volumes *White Power Music: Scenes of Extreme-Right Cultural Resistance* (University of Northampton, 2012, edited by Anton Shekhovtsov and Paul Jackson) and *Eurasianism and the European Far Right* (Lexington Books, 2016, edited by Marlene Laruelle).

Alexander Verkhovsky is Director of SOVA Center for Information and Analysis, Moscow. Research interests include nationalism, religion and politics, and anti-extremism policies in Russia. He has authored several books, including *Political Orthodoxy: Russian Orthodox Nationalists and Fundamentalists, 1995–2001* (SOVA Center, 2003, in Russian), *State Policy Towards National-Radical Organisations, 1991–2002* (SOVA Center, 2013, in Russian) and *Criminal Law on Hate Crime, Incitement to Hatred and Hate Speech in OSCE Participating States* (SOVA Center, 2014, in Russian; English edition 2016). His most recent book chapters are 'Language of authorities and radical nationalists' in *Doublespeak: The Rhetoric of the Far Right since 1945* (ibidem-Verlag, 2014, edited by Matthew Feldman and Paul Jackson), 'Dynamics of violence in Russian nationalism' in *Russia is not Ukraine: Contemporary Accents of Nationalism* (SOVA Center, 2014, edited by Alexander Verkhovsky, in Russian) and 'Radical nationalists from the start of Medvedev's presidency to the war in Donbas: true till death?' in *The New Russian Nationalism* (Edinburgh University Press, 2016, edited by Pål Kolstø and Helge Blakkisrud).

Alexandra Yatsyk is Alexander Herzen Junior Visiting Fellow at the Institute for Human Sciences in Vienna, Austria, and Visiting Researcher at the Centre for Russian and Eurasian Studies, Uppsala University, Sweden. She also serves as Director of the Centre for Cultural Studies of Post-Socialism at Kazan Federal University, Russia. Her works address post-Soviet nation building, sports and cultural mega-events, biopolitics and art. Book publications include *Celebrating Borderlands in a Wider Europe: Nation and Identities in Ukraine, Georgia and Estonia* (Nomos, 2016, co-authored with

Andrey Makarychev), *Mega-events in Post-Soviet Eurasia: Shifting Borderlines of Inclusion and Exclusion* (Palgrave, 2016, co-edited with Andrey Makarychev), *Vocabularies of International Relations After the Crisis in Ukraine* (Routledge, 2016, co-edited with Andrey Makarychev), *Borders in the Baltic Sea Region: Suturing the Ruptures* (Palgrave, 2016, co-edited with Andrey Makarychev) and *Lotman's Cultural Semiotics and the Political* (Rowman & Littlefield, 2017, co-authored with Andrey Makarychev).

Preface

This book emanates from the research project 'Nation-building, nationalism and the new "other" in today's Russia' (NEORUSS) funded by the Research Council of Norway under the Russia and the High North/Arctic (NORRUSS) programme, project number 220599. It is a sequel to *The New Russian Nationalism: Imperialism, Ethnicity and Authoritarianism, 2000–15* (2016), edited by Pål Kolstø and Helge Blakkisrud, likewise published by Edinburgh University Press. Since our research project commenced, major events have taken place that affect Russian nationalism, in particular the annexation of Crimea and the war in Eastern Ukraine. The first volume was well underway when these momentous developments unfolded and we were able to reflect on them only to a limited degree. In this second volume, with more distance to these events, we are better able to incorporate the effects of the Ukrainian crisis on Russian nationalism.

Our research project organised a capstone conference at Tallinn University 28–29 April 2016, and most of the chapters in the current volume were first presented as papers at that conference. We would like to express our sincere gratitude towards the Tallinn University Conference Centre and to Professor Raivo Vetik for their invaluable assistance in organising this conference.

The English language in this book, as everything we publish, has been corrected and improved upon by our indispensable copy editor Susan Høivik.

Pål Kolstø and Helge Blakkisrud, Oslo, May 2017

Introduction: Exploring Russian nationalisms

Pål Kolstø and Helge Blakkisrud

Russia's annexation of Crimea in March 2014 marked a watershed in European history: for the first time since the Second World War, a European state violated the sanctity of international borders and appropriated part of the territory of a neighbouring country. Western states reacted strongly and negatively, and Russia–Western relations may well have been severely damaged for the foreseeable future.

Politicians and scholars alike are struggling to understand how this situation came about. Like all historical turning points, the current breakdown in Russia–Western relations has both immediate triggers and a longer history of gestation. We can choose to focus on the details of the political confrontations in and around Ukraine that led up to this event: Ukraine's parallel negotiations with the European Union (EU) and the Eurasian Economic Union (EEU); President Viktor Yanukovych's abrupt decision not to sign the Deep and Comprehensive Trade Agreement with the EU in November 2013; the massive protest this decision unleashed in the Ukrainian population; and finally, Yanukovych's flight and dismissal. Alternatively, we can broaden the timeframe to include the growing distrust between Moscow and European/North American capitals over the last two decades fuelled by – among other things – NATO's eastward expansion and deployment of ballistic missile defence in former Eastern Europe, on the one hand, and Russia's aggressive policy towards Georgia and other neighbours, on the other. Or we can widen our analytical lens even further to include the more general mental framework within which Russian politicians are acting: the constraints and drivers imposed by perceptions, emotions, self-understanding and world outlook. This book is an attempt to contribute to this latter endeavour by examining and discussing contemporary Russian nationalism in its various incarnations.

Some have interpreted the Putin regime's sudden territorial aggression towards Ukraine in 2014 as a manifestation of deep-seated

Russian imperialism: that the Russians have never been reconciled to the collapse of the Soviet Union, and will exploit any weakness in the neighbouring states to try to re-establish the lost empire (see, for example, Grigas 2016). As is often pointed out, Vladimir Putin is on record as having described the dissolution of the Union of Soviet Socialist Republics (USSR) as 'a major geopolitical catastrophe of the twentieth century' (Putin 2005). Indeed, part of Putin's justification for the annexation of Crimea was that the peninsula was 'Russian' territory. Speaking to an expanded session of the Russian parliament on 18 March 2014 on the occasion of the official accession of Crimea and Sevastopol to the Russian Federation, he argued that 'in people's hearts and minds, Crimea has always been an inseparable part of Russia' (Putin 2014a). 'Russia', then, in the thinking of the Russian leader, seemed to encompass more than the territory of the Russian Federation. This is also the interpretation which Russian imperialists seek to give this event. For instance, immediately after the annexation, high-profile editor-cum-pundit Aleksandr Prokhanov declared: 'this is the beginning of the resurrection of the Russian Empire' (Prokhanov 2014). That view is shared by many of the insurgents in Eastern Ukraine. For instance, in his *The Torch of Novorossiia*, Pavel Gubarev, an early ideologue of the Donbas rebellion, claims: 'we are imperialists: we despise . . . petty, national states' (Gubarev 2016: 286).

Alternatively, the new Russian policy towards Ukraine can be seen as reflecting not 'imperialism' but 'nationalism'. In this interpretive scheme, the emphasis is not so much on the perceived necessity of expanding the Russian state or resurrecting the empire, but the fact that ethnic Russians make up the majority population in Crimea and were allegedly discriminated against by the Ukrainian state. Also this reading can be substantiated by quotations from Putin's March 2014 Crimea speech – as when he bemoaned how ethnic Russians after the fall of the Soviet Union had become 'one of the biggest, if not the biggest divided people in the world' (Putin 2014a). That claim seems to smack less of Russian state patriotism and more of ethnically framed nationalism. And indeed, this is how many Russian ethnonationalists interpret it. For instance, Valerii Solovei, a leading intellectual in the nationalist camp, noted that in his speech, Putin employed the ethnic and cultural word for 'Russian', *russkii*, no less than twenty-seven times. Previously, Putin had used the ethnically neutral and more politically correct word *rossiiskii*, even in speaking about such cultural issues as 'Russian values' (*rossiiskie tsennosti*).[1] The switch to *russkii*, Solovei claimed, was 'an ideological innovation' and signalled that Putin was *not* resurrecting the empire, as the imperialists claimed, but was instead building a Russian national state (Solovei 2014; see also Piper 2014).²

Then again, some observers will deny that we have to choose between these two interpretations. Well-informed authorities on Russian nationalism like Emil Pain maintain that Russian nationalism comes in at least two guises, both imperial and ethnic (as well as in intermediate varieties) (Pain 2016; Pain, this volume). While 'imperial nationalism' might seem a contradiction in terms in other parts of the world, that is not the case in Russia, Pain claims. There is a historical explanation to this: prior to the breakup of the Soviet Union, the Russians had never lived in a nation-state. As soon as the many Russian principalities had been gathered into a unitary state led by the emerging power of Muscovy, the state in the mid-sixteenth century began to expand into territories inhabited by non-Slavic, non-Orthodox peoples, such as the Tatars and other Turkic peoples. Nationally oriented Russians have tended to identify with and feel pride in this state, regarding it as 'their nation-state' even though it was clearly a multinational state and – from the time of Peter the Great – was even officially designated as an 'empire' (Kappler 2001). However, unlike for example the British and French empires, there was no clear demarcation between the metropole and the colonial periphery. Everything was 'Russia', and the number of Russian nationalists who would countenance the truncation of 'their' state could be counted on the fingers of one hand (Szporluk 1989). Before the 1917 Revolution, some Russian nationalists such as Petr Struve could be regarded as 'liberals', and others, like the Slavophiles, as 'conservatives', and yet others, for instance the Black Hundreds, as reactionaries – but they were all 'imperialists' in the sense that they took the empire for granted (ibid.).

After the Revolution, one of the fifteen Soviet republics came to be called the Russian Soviet Federative Socialist Republic (RSFSR), but this entity was not named after the ethnic Russians (*russkie*) living there: it took its name from the former Russian Empire (*Rossiiskaia imperiia*). Millions of ethnic Russians lived outside the RSFSR and felt equally at home wherever they were living – they did not regard the RSFSR as their putative 'own' homeland (Kolstø 1995). Also those Russians who did live in the RSFSR rarely took that republic as their reference point, but would say, as did a popular song from 1978: 'My address is the Soviet Union'. Only when the USSR broke up did the difference between an imperial and an ethnic national identity gradually began to dawn upon many Russians.

Between the French and the German models

Contemporary 'Russian nationalism' is a variegated phenomenon with numerous emphases and possible definitions. The diversity can be quite confusing. In an effort to introduce some sense and order we can start by arranging 'real existing' Russian nationalisms along two axes in a two-by-two matrix (see Table I.1).

The two vertical axes – state-oriented and ethnic – in many respects correspond to the classical distinction between French and German nationalisms as they developed historically. While French nationalists celebrated *la Patrie* and automatically included all inhabitants of the state as French *citoyennes*, German nationalism took the German language and *Kulturnation* as its starting point. Ever since Hans Kohn published his seminal *The Idea of Nationalism* in 1944, historians have regularly presented East European nationalisms as belonging to the German variety (Kohn 1944 [1961]; see also Plamenatz 1976). However, while this designation captures the orientation of most nationalists within smaller East European nations, Russian nationalism is more complex. The reason seems quite straightforward: whereas nationalism among the smaller East European nations developed before they had acquired 'their own' nation-states, a Russian state has existed ever since the Middle Ages, and Russians have had a state to identify with.

Even so, the ethnic understanding of the nation is also widespread in Russia today. Again, the reasons must be sought in history. The Russian state never seriously pursued a 'melting pot' nation-building strategy: no attempt was made to create a common cultural identity among the many linguistic and religious groups residing within the realm. Under the tsars, the non-Russians retained their separate ethnic identities, which were determined primarily by language and religion. Only in the late nineteenth century did the authorities begin to take active steps to subsume White Russians (*belarusy*) and the Little Russians (*malorossy*, today's Ukrainians) into a common Russian ethnic group together with the Great Russians – a policy that eventually failed. Later, under the Bolsheviks, ethnic identities were instead rigidly codified and institutionalised (Slezkine 1994). As a result of this historical legacy, virtually all varieties of Russian nationalism today contain elements taken from both the French state-oriented and the German ethnicity/language/culture-oriented prototypes (Laruelle 2014).[3]

Whereas the two vertical axes in our typology identify the 'in-group' – those who constitute 'the nation' – the two horizontal axes capture

Table I.1 A typology of Russian nationalisms (adapted from Kolstø 2016)

	Primarily state-oriented	Primarily ethnically oriented
'Empire'-oriented	Imperial nationalism	Supremacist nationalism
'Core'-oriented	Russian Federation nationalism	Ethnic core nationalism

the territorial expression of nationhood – which state-formation the nationalists see as their natural 'homeland'. While both France and Germany have waxed and waned in size over the centuries, and the contemporary borders in both states were not fixed until after the Second World War, there is virtually no pressure today for territorial expansion. The situation is very different in Russia, where the multinational empire collapsed as recently as in 1991. As a result, in addition to the distinction between ethnic nationalism and state-focused nationalism, Russian nationalists can be differentiated according to whether they orient themselves towards the current Russian state, the Russian Federation ('core-oriented' nationalism in Table I.1) or towards restoring the borders of one of Russia's larger, imperial historical predecessors – the Russian Empire or the Soviet Union.

Spanning the ideological spectrum

This two-by-two matrix is complemented by an ideological overlay. Russian nationalism can be found across the political spectrum – from the national bolsheviks on the far left, to neo-fascist groupings to the far right. Organisationally, some nationalists, like the right-wing populist Vladimir Zhirinovskii, belong to the political establishment of the Kremlin-loyal 'systemic' opposition. More often, however, nationalists have found an ideological home in various groupings in the 'non-systemic' opposition – or in more marginal, loosely organised intellectual or para-political circles (see Laruelle 2009). The main point is the malleability of Russian nationalism – it is not monopolised by any particular ideological persuasion, but can be found in various constellations ranging from national democrats to anarchists, from parties inside the State Duma to fringe groups that engage in nationalistically motivated terrorism.

Crimea represented a watershed in the structuring of the Russian nationalist field. With the Kremlin adopting many of the former positions of the nationalists, the latter were forced to take a stance for or against the Kremlin's new political line. As we will return to below (see chapter by Alexander Verkhovsky, this volume), after Crimea it might be more pertinent to categorise Russian nationalists ideologically according to whether they are pro- or anti-regime and pro- or anti-Russian Spring (that is, whether they support the pro-Russian uprising in Ukraine), rather than according to a traditional left–right axis. While a pro-regime nationalist stance automatically goes together with support for the Russian Spring – as exemplified by Zhirinovskii's Liberal Democratic Party or State Duma deputy Evgenii Fedorov's National Liberation Movement (*Natsional'no-osvoboditel'noe dvizhenie*) – the anti-regime nationalists are further divided into pro- and anti-Russian Spring. The imperialist Igor Strelkov (Girkin), famed for his role in the war in Donbas and now heading the All-Russian National Movement (*Obshcherusskoe natsional'noe dvizhenie*), falls in the anti-regime, pro-Russian Spring category – whereas, for example, ultranationalist Dmitrii Demushkin and his now-banned *Russkie* (Russians) movement were both anti-regime and anti-Russian Spring.

However, due to the way the Russian political field is structured, most ideological groupings beyond the 'party of power' and the systemic opposition represent rather marginal phenomena. Thus, as argued by Pain in this volume, another at least equally important distinction in the Russian context is *from where* the nationalist impulse originates: from the societal level, or from the state.

Sources of nationalism: State and society

Societal Russian nationalism can be found in various guises: it can be ethnic, state-oriented or imperial, it can be inclusive or xenophobic, and it can be coloured by a range of ideological beliefs. Common to all such variations of Russian societal nationalism is, however, that it emanates from below and is formulated and developed independently of the state. The Russian state has always been extremely sceptical towards all such manifestations of autonomous social initiatives, irrespective of their political message. Societal nationalism is frowned upon by the authorities, and they actively seek to supress it.

For its part, the Russian state has been motivated by a pragmatic *raison d'état*: the state is its own justification and purpose. However, as Pain points out, at certain junctures, the state has elaborated ideological programmes for legitimation in which it resorts to some variety of imperial nationalism. That was the case under Nikolai I when his Minister of Education, Count Sergei Uvarov, developed the ideological doctrine of 'Orthodoxy, autocracy and nationality (*narodnost'*)'. Towards the end of the nineteenth century Aleksandr

III and his son Nikolai II also incorporated elements of such imperial nationalism in their state ideology – and, perhaps more surprisingly, so did Iosif Stalin as General Secretary of the Soviet Communist Party from the mid-1930s until his death in 1953.

We do not have to believe that these rulers were 'convinced' nationalists in any meaningful sense of the word. Most probably, they were simply using nationalism as a tool to mobilise support in the population. In any case, in order to analyse the policies of state nationalism we do not have to look into the hearts and minds of the rulers in order to determine what 'actually', deep down, motivated them: we can focus on their words and deeds. Likewise, from a sociological point of view, a 'nationalist turn' in Russian state policy makes sense only if we can also assume that there exists a pool of nationalist sentiment in the Russian population the rulers believe that they can tap into.

'Crimea is ours' – the revival of state nationalism

Returning to Russia's annexation of Crimea, can this short presentation of the role of nationalism in Russian politics and society help to explain what motivated the Kremlin to break the strong post-Second World War European taboo against territorial enlargement at the expense of a neighbouring state? We believe yes. When various circumstances converged and induced Putin and his team to embark upon an adventurous foreign policy course that they knew would inevitably lead to confrontation with the outside world, they added a nationalistic varnish. Previously in his career, Putin had been very wary of playing with nationalist themes (Hale 2016), but now, when it was imperative to rally the nation around his leadership, strong nationalist tropes crept into his rhetoric.

In this volume, we argue that strong currents of nationalism were evident in Russian society in the decade preceding the Ukrainian debacle; societal nationalism of various ideological persuasions was gaining ground. Furthermore, we see the Kremlin's decision to resort to nationalist rhetoric in connection with the conflict in Ukraine as part of the explanation why Putin could not only annex Crimea and get away with it, but even capitalise on it on the home front. And finally – and perhaps most importantly – we show how societal nationalism has gone into deep decline after Crimea. The champion of democratically oriented Russian nationalism, Aleksei Navalnyi, who made headlines by garnering 27 per cent of the vote in the 2013 Moscow mayoral elections, alienated much of his old constituency due to his principled criticism of the Crimean operation. Similarly, the radical nationalists behind the annual Russian Marches have managed to mobilise only a fraction of the number of people they were able to bring into the streets only a few years earlier.

What we see, then, is a demobilisation of nationalism in Russia at the societal level, at the same time as it is being activated at the state level. This might appear paradoxical, but, as Pain explains, should probably to be regarded as logically interrelated tendencies. The state not only 'taps into' Russian societal nationalism – it also 'drains' it. In times when the state does not feel that it needs nationalism as a legitimation base for its own purposes, various groups of autonomous nationalists can be allowed to operate, thus providing a safety valve for social frustration. However, in times of turbulence and official nationalist ferment, the state tolerates no competitors. Figuratively speaking, state nationalism and societal nationalism in Russia are connected vessels: when the state vessel fills up, the other is being emptied.

'Russian' as simultaneously *russkii* and *rossiiskii*

While we believe the typology described above is helpful in demonstrating the differences between the various main strands of Russian nationalism, it is intended as an analytical model only. The four boxes should be understood as ideal types in a Weberian sense: very few Russian nationalists can be unambiguously pigeonholed into one and only one of the boxes (see Laruelle 2017). This is true also of Russian thinkers and politicians who like to present themselves as purely 'civic' or purely 'ethno-nationalist' in orientation. For instance, during Boris Eltsin's rule, two of his ministers for nationality policy – the ethnic Avar Ramazan Abdulatipov and the ethnic Russian Valerii Tishkov – presented models for a nationality policy for the Russian Federation under a (multi)ethnic and a civic label, respectively (Kolstø 2000: 210–12). The practical differences between the nation-state visions that these two officials promoted, however, were not so obvious (Shevel 2011: 183–84).

Also under Putin, the nation-state model pursued by the Russian state appears to have been, as Oxana Shevel (2011) describes it, 'purposefully ambiguous': to allow Russian policymakers maximum space for manoeuvre, the Kremlin has been vacillating between a civic and an ethno-cultural understanding of the nation. Even today, the signals coming from Putin continue to point in very different, seemingly contradictory, directions. To be sure, from around the onset of his third term Putin appeared to be switching from the Eltsinite *rossiiskii* nation-building terminology to increasingly using *russkii*. The first clear indication of this was his pre-election article on the nationality question, where Putin referred to ethnically Armenian and German citizens of Russia as 'Russian (*russkie*) Armenians' and 'Russian (*russkie*) Germans' (Putin 2012). This was followed up and even accentuated in his various addresses after the Crimean annexation (see Putin 2014a, 2014b). Seemingly, Putin was adopting if not the agenda, then at least the terminology of the ethno-nationalists. However, just as that conclusion seemed logical, Putin gave the go-ahead to drawing up a law defining the *rossiiskii* nation (*rossiiskaia natsiia*) (RIA Novosti 2016).[4] What are we to make of this?

While several interpretations are possible, we suggest that rather than revealing confusion or vacillation in the Kremlin, this can be seen as a strategy for eradicating the difference between *russkii* and *rossiiskii*. That may not be quite as radical as it sounds. Most languages do not make a lexical distinction between an ethnic and civic designation of the nation: neither the paradigmatic 'ethnic' case – German – nor the paradigmatic 'civic' case – French – has more than one word to describe the 'national'. The Russian language, on the other hand, not only *allows* for a distinction between those two aspects, it also makes it impossible for Russian speakers *not* to choose one of the two words, *russkii* or *rossiiskii*, when they talk or write. There is no 'neutral' term to describe Russianness. The only way to fuse those two aspects therefore seems to be to use the two terms interchangeably, until in the end they are understood as expressing the same meaning (as the two designations of the state, 'Russia' and 'the Russian Federation', do in practice).

Seen in this perspective, the language games of the Kremlin's nation-building strategy can be regarded as attempts to make Russia a 'normal' nation-state like Germany and France. While, as pointed out above, German and French nation-building have historically been informed by very different principles, more recently this distinction has been gradually fading. Contemporary French nationalism focuses very much on the need to permeate the entire population with French culture and to teach all citizens to speak proper French; German nationalists created their own unified nation-state in the late nineteenth century – later modified several times – with which they identify keenly (Brubaker 1998). Today, therefore, it is probably more accurate to speak of a common French–German, or simply civic–cultural, 'European' nation model, which, it can be argued, the Russian leadership is attempting to emulate – at least on the rhetorical level.

We should note one major caveat, however: modern European nation-states that identify 'the nation' with the culture, language, citizens and territory of the state no longer question the state borders, not even in cases when compact groups of co-ethnics reside outside the borders of the nation-state. Germany, for example, a country that has experienced dramatic truncations of the state's territory over the last century, does not harbour irredentist aspirations today. For the first couple of decades after the breakup of the Soviet Union, it also seemed as if Russia would follow that path, but the annexation of Crimea belied those expectations. Deeds speak louder than words, and as long as Russia continues to hold on to and justify Crimea's annexation with nationalist rhetoric, it is of minor importance whether this rhetoric is interpreted as 'imperialistic' or 'ethnic': in either case, it is clearly not 'civic'. Therefore, the annexation is not only a watershed in modern European history, but also, we argue, a major barrier to Russia's nation-state transformation.

Structure of the book

The various chapters in this book fit into and lend support to the interpretive framework developed above. In Part I, we study the phenomenon of 'official nationalism' more closely. First comes a background chapter by Emil Pain that further refines this frame. Pain traces the political role and the ideological content of contemporary Russian nationalism against a historical canvas that extends from the late eighteenth century to the present, and explores the understudied and poorly understood relationship between official state nationalism and autonomous societal nationalism. The latter variety appeared in Russia initially as a carrier of ideas of civic and popular sovereignty, drawing on the ideas of the French Revolution. Since the late nineteenth century, however, Russian societal nationalism has been dominated by an anti-liberal tendency.

From its very first appearance, Russian state powers have attempted to neutralise this societal nationalism by replacing it with something ostensibly similar but actually very different: an 'imperial nationalism'. The fact that state-promoted imperial nationalism has no rigid ethnic ties, that it is not transmitted through the channels of cultural tradition but is developed in response to socio-political challenges, might indicate that a radical reprogramming is possible,

Pain argues. However, he concludes that today there are no political forces in Russia that could start the deconstruction of the imperial consciousness. On the contrary: what we see is the continued discrediting of the basic tenets of a civic nation.

Eduard Ponarin and Michael Komin, in keeping with Pain, survey the development of the elite and the masses' attitudes towards nationalism across the post-Soviet period. In the 1990s, new drivers of Russian nationalism appeared on the scene, making possible two alternative scenarios: either, as a reaction to globalisation, a return to an imperial nationalism; or, alternatively, in response to the problems inherited from Soviet federalism and the ensuing ethnic conflict, a rise in ethnic nationalism. Ponarin and Komin analyse the changing balance of imperial and ethnic nationalism and their influence on the choices made by the Russian government.

During Putin's third term, they argue, in a reversal of a long-term post-Soviet trend, the attitudes of the elite shifted dramatically in favour of imperial projects beyond Russia's borders. Another long-term trend has recently accelerated: that of valuing military might over economic power in international relations. Surveys show that the share of elite respondents who see the USA as a threat has now reached an all-time high, standing at more than 80 per cent. The findings of Ponarin and Komin indicate fairly widespread elite support for an imperial scenario, with the West cast as the 'Other' against whom the new Russian identity can coalesce.

Next, Yuri Teper turns to the core of state-level nationalism, to the Kremlin and its post-2012 quest for securing legitimacy, and what he describes as an emerging Russian identity dilemma. His chapter examines the Kremlin's changing attitudes towards nationalism since the onset of Putin's third term, with special emphasis on the post-2014 period. Changes are analysed against two primary factors: regime efforts to sustain popular legitimacy against the backdrop of failure to deliver on output promises, and the perceived popular need for a more articulated national identity.

Teper argues that, since Putin's return to the presidency, the Kremlin's approach to the national issue has undergone a twofold change. First the authorities' mobilisation strategy shifted from being reactive to proactive, with the Kremlin seizing complete control over the nationalist agenda, and the official discourse on identity turning profoundly national. This ethno-national trend peaked around the annexation of Crimea. However, realising the risks such ethno-national rhetoric might pose domestically as well as in relations with the outside world, the Kremlin quickly tempered its message – and cracked down on those nationalists who did not fall in line. The emphasis shifted toward a securitised great-power – or imperial – nationalism, as shown by Russia's subsequent intervention in the Syrian civil war.

Andrey Makarychev and Alexandra Yatsyk round off the first part. They propose a distinct interpretation of the making of Russian national identity by applying the concept of 'biopolitics'. According to Makarychev and Yatsyk, in recent years Russia has taken a biopolitical turn, exemplified by the introduction of regulatory mechanisms aimed at consolidating Russian national identity by disciplining and constraining human bodies. They thus contend that the nationalist turn in Russian state policy during Putin's third period can be regarded as part of a general tendency towards a more authoritarian, intrusive regime type that seeks to control every aspect of the life of the citizens, including their bodies.

Their chapter discusses the concept of biopolitical sovereignty, followed by an examination of specific cases that illustrate practices of biopolitics in legislation on, for example, the penitentiary system, family and reproductive health and gender representations. Makarychev and Yatsyk conclude that a biopolitical agenda currently shapes much of the content and contours of the Kremlin-promoted nation-building project. The regime utilises biopolitical discourses and practices to consolidate its rule, drawing on conservative norms that may be asserted through religious, gender-based or 'Russian World'-grounded discourses. Biopolitics, they argue, offers a specific way of anchoring the uncertain Russian identity in a set of consensually understood nodal points that encapsulate bodily practices of corporeal discipline and control.

The second part of this book, 'Radical and other societal nationalisms', offers a range of perspectives on the societal level, autonomous nationalism. It consists of four chapters that assess the ideological-organisational landscape of the Russian nationalist movement and present key actors.

Alexandra Kuznetsova and Sergey Sergeev examine organisations that combine nationalist principles with propagation of revolution and that advocate the violent dissolution of the existing political regime in the name of the nation (be it civic, ethnic or something else). They identify four main categories of such organisations in Russia today: national bolsheviks, national anarchists, national socialists, and national democrats. The organisations of the 'national bolshevik' category are primarily associated with veteran political activist Eduard Limonov. While continuously modifying their ideological orientation, these organisations have all managed to combine leftist military activism with imperial ideals. The 'national socialist' category, by contrast, consists of proponents of a 'white revolution' who embrace various forms of terror directed against immigrants as well as political rivals. Nationalist and anarchist ideas are combined in the third group, the national anarchists; according to their view, after the demolition of the state, people will live in communities based on ethnic principles. Finally, there are the national democrats, who seek to combine ethnic nationalism with political democracy.

Kuznetsova and Sergeev trace the major actors and dynamics of development within this scene from the early 1990s up to, and including, the Crimean annexation. They conclude that, with increased regime repression in the aftermath of Crimea, Russia's revolutionary nationalists have now lost whatever limited influence they once enjoyed.

In the next chapter, Alexander Verkhovsky examines in detail the changes that have taken place in the Russian nationalist movement in the aftermath of the annexation of Crimea. He provides a broad overview of nationalist activities and initiatives undertaken from below, from the societal level, while also taking into account the complex relationship and interaction between the various groups of nationalists and the powers-that-be.

The Russian nationalist movement had already started to disintegrate before Crimea, Verkhovsky argues. At the time, the decline was not very visible: prior to the onset of the conflict in Ukraine, the Russian ultra-rights looked, if not very strong, then at least rather promising – but they were already suffering from internal rifts. Since 2014, however, the nationalist movement has been torn apart over which side to support in the war in Ukraine. And with the subsequent increase in state repression of the ultra-rights, the whole movement has lapsed into total decline. Verkhovsky's chapter discusses the separate trajectories of the pro-Kremlin and oppositional nationalists, providing a comprehensive overview of the most prominent nationalist organisations and groups in the contemporary landscape of Russian nationalists, assessing their public activism and potential.

Then we move on to individual portraits of prominent figures on the Russian nationalist scene. Robert Horvath traces the career of Aleksandr Sevastianov. A disturbing aspect of current Russian nationalism is the existence of networks of skinheads and neo-Nazi paramilitary groups responsible for violent attacks on migrant labourers and other non-Slavic inhabitants of Russian cities. Horvath examines this phenomenon in relation to the ideology of

Russian nationalism – specifically, to the work of Sevastianov as Russia's leading apologist of ultranationalist revolutionary terror.

Horvath shows how violence has been central to Sevastianov's vision of a Russian national revolution. The chapter outlines the evolution of Sevastianov's revolutionary project. It traces Sevastianov's emerging sympathy for the militant neo-Nazi underground, his compilations of lists of 'enemies of the Russian people' in the early 2000s and his ideological tracts about a global 'racial war'. Next, Horvath examines Sevastianov's interaction with the underground, which reached its apogee during his campaign in defence of Nikita Tikhonov and Evgeniia Khasis, two Russian ultranationalists charged with murdering two prominent human rights activists. And finally, he shows how Sevastianov has recently abandoned the underground, redeploying his arguments to support the 'Russian national revolution' in southeast Ukraine and holding this up as a springboard for the transformation of Russia itself.

In the last chapter in this section, Sofia Tipaldou focuses on the extreme right fringe of Russian nationalism. She presents the Russian societal nationalist scene as a multifaceted social movement network made up of organisations with ideologies ranging from democratic to authoritarian, but with a shared self-understanding of being in opposition to the powers-that-be. Within this network, 'ethno-nationalist' organisations have taken it upon themselves to combat illegal migration, promote Russian ethnic superiority, provide sports and military training, and develop national socialist ideology.

Tipaldou highlights the career of Dmitrii Bobrov and his now-banned National Socialist Initiative (NSI). Together with its close allies, the Movement Against Illegal Immigration and the Slavic Union, the NSI formed the backbone of the *Russkie* (Russians) movement, an umbrella structure aimed at representing the major trends within contemporary Russian societal nationalism. The escalation of the conflict in Ukraine brought these consolidation efforts to a halt, however: Bobrov and the NSI supported the pro-Russian insurrection in Eastern Ukraine, while their closest allies did not. Tipaldou concludes that the conflict in Ukraine exposed the power relations and coalition potential within the Russian extreme right fringe and led to a restructuring of this – now greatly weakened – sector of the Russian nationalist movement.

In the third and final part of the book, we focus on 'identities and otherings' – more precisely, how the Russian 'in-group' is defined in the encounter with its 'others'. Up until Crimea, the growing migrant population provided the nationalists with an easily identifiable 'other', and migrantophobia was on the rise. In their chapter, Helge

Blakkisrud and Pål Kolstø examine the role that migrants – and widespread migrantophobia – play in Russian identity discourse, through the lens of the 2013 Moscow mayoral elections.

On the eve of these elections, Muscovites identified the large numbers of labour migrants in the capital as the most important campaign issue. Blakkisrud and Kolstø explore how 'the migrant issue' was addressed at the candidate level as well as how it was perceived by ordinary Muscovites. First, they trace what images of 'the migrant' the candidates presented; how they assessed the potential for integration into Russian society; and what measures they proposed for regulating the flow of new migrants. Next, drawing on survey data, Blakkisrud and Kolstø discuss to what extent campaign promises reflected the positions of the electorate. They conclude that the Moscow electoral experiment of allowing semi-competitive elections contributed to pushing the borders of what mainstream politicians saw as acceptable positions on migrants and migration policy. In the course of the campaign, incumbent mayor Sergei Sobianin hijacked the anti-migration agenda of the democratically oriented nationalists, represented by the rising star of the non-systemic opposition, Aleksei Navalnyi. As a result, the elections reinforced the idea of 'the migrant' as the new 'Other' in Russian identity discourse.

Next, Caress Schenk, continuing on the migrant theme, discusses how Putin's return for a third presidential term ushered in a period of increasingly securitised migration policy. While the Kremlin's new policies in this area may be framed as anti-migrant, Schenk questions whether they in fact reflect an overt nationalist campaign. To evaluate the extent of nationalist content in the Kremlin's migration-related rhetoric, she structures the discussion around three migration myths: 'migrants take our jobs'; 'they are culturally incompatible with the host society'; and 'they represent a security threat'. While she finds that these myths are to some degree consistent with Russian public opinion, they are not actively utilised by the Kremlin. To the contrary, Schenk concludes that Putin has eschewed a populist course, opting for a migration discourse that seeks to utilise migration for the benefit of the state. Economically, for example, migrants are framed as a tool for development rather than a threat to the native workforce. Though the Kremlin has become more active in addressing issues of national identity, including immigration, Schenk finds that rather than backing a narrowly ethno-political agenda, the state's migration discourse has remained firmly state-oriented.

In his chapter, J. Paul Goode explores the boundary between nationalism and patriotism. Whereas for a long time the Kremlin was reluctant to engage in nationalist rhetoric, ever since the beginning of Putin's first term it has vigorously promoted a multi-ethnic vision of patriotism and patriotic education in all walks of life. The outpouring of public support for the 2014 annexation of Crimea and the subsequent Russian involvement in Donbas in Eastern Ukraine nevertheless demonstrate that such state patriotism and nationalism are not easily distinguished, and that one may easily transmute into the other.

When does patriotism turn into nationalism? Rather than treating the two as categorically distinct, Goode examines how ordinary Russians understand the meaning and implications of patriotism in their daily lives. Based on interviews and focus groups conducted in two Russian regions his analysis reveals the ease with which state patriotism can be ethnicised, such that the practical difference between patriotism and nationalism becomes a matter of political loyalty rather than ethnicity. Goode concludes that the sudden outburst of nationalism in Russia in 2014 may be understood in terms of the ethnicisation of everyday patriotic practices.

In the final chapter, Eleanor Knott addresses the lived experience of Russian identity and nationalism beyond Russia's borders. The chapter focuses on the case of Crimea, a region where the majority of residents have been assumed to identify as ethnically Russian. Using the approach of everyday nationalism, Knott examines the meanings of identifying oneself as ethnically Russian in Crimea before the 2014 annexation, to see how being Russian was articulated, experienced, negotiated and subverted, and opposed to, or combined with, being Ukrainian and/or Crimean.

The annexation of Crimea has often been explained, if not legitimised, by framing the peninsula as a region of strong Russian national identity and support for separatism. Drawing on fieldwork interviews with actors from across the political and social spectrum in the years immediately prior to the annexation, Knott criticises this framing, and argues that a more nuanced understanding of Russian identity is necessary. She problematises what it meant to be ethnically Russian in Crimea and to engage with Russia in terms of identification prior to the annexation. By doing so, she demonstrates how malleable ethnic identity can be, and how the ethnic effervescence among Russians and Russian speakers in Crimea in early 2014 can be seen as largely a product of political engineering.

* * *

The overall aim of this book is to map and examine major developments within the field of Russian nationalism in the crucial years around the 2014 annexation of Crimea. By investigating the interrelationship between official, state-level nationalism and independent societal nationalism, and exploring the internal dynamics involving various actors, identity entrepreneurs and groupings at both levels, we aspire to provide greater clarity to the complex and multifaceted reality of Russian nationalism and national identity at the time around this watershed event.

The annexation of Crimea is likely to have long-lasting implications for the development of Russian nationalism. At the same time, as becomes abundantly clear from the case studies presented in this volume, the field of Russian nationalism is dynamic. Above we have described how the Russian state from time to time 'drains' the vessel of societal nationalism. By the same token, this means that if and when the 'state vessel' for some reason gets emptied of nationalist content, the 'society vessel' may be filled up again. Although at the time of writing (spring 2017) it is too early to conclude on any long-term trajectories, we can note some signs of reappraisal and reversal. By late 2015, the Russian authorities had already seemed to have drawn the conclusion that the potential for pro-regime mobilisation to be derived from the Ukrainian crisis and the Crimean annexation had basically run its course. Coverage of events in Ukraine gradually diminished in regime-controlled Russian media, and the topic virtually disappeared from Putin's speeches. For instance, in his one-hour state-of-the-nation address to the Russian Parliament on 3 December 2015, there was not one mention of the conflict in Donbas – in sharp contrast to the address of the previous year, when Putin referred to Ukraine no less than eighteen times (Putin 2015; Whitmore 2015). Moreover, some triggers of ethnonational mobilisation, like the labour migration issue, seem to have been suppressed rather than permanently removed, and might well reappear on the political agenda. Crimea led to a radical restructuring of the field of Russian nationalism, through a return of the state and a marginalisation of the fledgling pre-Crimea societal nationalism. However, the understanding of who constitutes the Russian nation, and what territorial expression this nation should have, will continue to be the object of contestation and reformulation.

Notes

1. See, for instance, Putin's 'Millennium Manifesto' (Putin 1999).
2. Solovei's article was later removed from the Internet, but Solovei has confirmed the content and that this remains his view. Authors' email communication with Valerii Solovei, 18 December 2015.

3. The dichotomisation of national identity in a French 'civic' and German 'ethnic' model has drawn considerable criticism for its oversimplification of how nation-building processes unfold in the real world (Yack 1996; Kuzio 2002). However, in a post-Soviet Russian context, it makes sense to use the dichotomy as a prism through which to view and understand the Russian nation-building process, as the Russian authorities initially opted for emulating the Soviet practice of simultaneously promoting a civic state identity *and* ethnicising individual identity. To avoid giving the impression that a 'civic' identity is ethnically neutral, however, we refer to what constitutes the main object of reference for the nationalists: *territory* or *group*: hence the use of 'state-oriented' and 'ethnically oriented' in the two-by-two matrix.
4. The *rossiiskii* nation project was soon shelved, however (see Yuri Teper in this volume).

Bibliography

Brubaker, Rogers (1998), *Citizenship and Nationhood in France and Germany*, Cambridge, MA: Harvard University Press.

Grigas, Agnia (2016), *Beyond Crimea: The New Russian Empire*, New Haven, CT: Yale University Press.

Gubarev, Pavel (2016), *Fakel Novorossii* [*The Torch of the Novorossiia*], St Petersburg: Piter.

Hale, Henry (2016), 'How nationalism and machine politics mix in Russia', in Pål Kolstø and Helge Blakkisrud, eds, *The New Russian Nationalism: Imperialism, Ethnicity and Authoritarianism, 2000–15*, Edinburgh: Edinburgh University Press, 221–48.

Kappler, Andreas (2001), *The Russian Empire: A Multi-Ethnic History*, Harlow: Longman.

Kohn, Hans (1944 [1961]), *The Idea of Nationalism: A Study in Its Origins and Background*, London: Transaction Publishers.

Kolstø, Pål (1995), *Russians in the Former Soviet Republics*, London: Hurst.

Kolstø, Pål (2000), *Political Construction Sites: Nation-building in Russia and the Post-Soviet States*, Boulder, CO: Westview Press.

Kolstø, Pål (2016), 'The ethnification of Russian nationalism', in Pål Kolstø and Helge Blakkisrud, eds, *The New Russian Nationalism: Imperialism, Ethnicity and Authoritarianism, 2000–15*, Edinburgh: Edinburgh University Press, 18–45.

Kuzio, Taras (2002), 'The myth of the civic state: a critical survey of Hans Kohn's framework for understanding nationalism', *Ethnic and Racial Studies*, 25, 1: 20–39.

Laruelle, Marlene (2009), *In the Name of the Nation: Nationalism and Politics in Contemporary Russia*, Basingstoke: Palgrave Macmillan.

Laruelle, Marlene (2014), '"Russkii natsionalizm" kak oblast' nauchnykh issledovanii' [Russian nationalism as an object of research], *Pro et Contra*, 1–2: 54–72.

Laruelle, Marlene (2017), 'Is nationalism a force for change in Russia?' *Daedalus*, 146, 2: 89–100.

Pain, Emil (2016), 'The imperial syndrome and its influence on Russian nationalism', in Pål Kolstø and Helge Blakkisrud, eds, *The New Russian Nationalism: Imperialism, Ethnicity and Authoritarianism, 2000–15*, Edinburgh: Edinburgh University Press, 46–74.

Piper, Elizabeth (2014), '"Patriot's handbook" may give insight into Putin's thoughts', Reuters.com, 9 June, <http://www.reuters.com/article/us-russia-putin-ideology-insight-idUSKBN0EK09Y20140609> (last accessed 18 April 2017).

Plamenatz, John (1976), 'Two types of nationalism', in Eugene Kamenka, ed., *Nationalism: The Nature and Evolution of an Idea*, London: Edward Arnold, 23–36.

Prokhanov, Aleksandr (2014), 'Prokhanov: sobytiia v Krymu i na Donbasse – eto vozrozhdenie Rossiiskoi imperii' [Prokhanov: the events in Crimea and Donbas – it is the revival of the Russian Empire], *Pravdoryb*, 31 October, <pravdoryb.info/prokhanov-sobytiya-v-krymu-i-na-donbasse--eto-vozrozhdenie-rossiyskoy-imperii.html> (last accessed 18 April 2017).

Putin, Vladimir (1999), 'Rossiia na rubezhe tysiacheletii' [Russia on the eve of the millennium], *Nezavisimaia gazeta*, 30 December, <http://www.ng.ru/politics/1999-12-30/4_millenium.html> (last accessed 22 May 2014).

Putin, Vladimir (2005), 'Poslanie Federal'nomu Sobraniiu Rossiiskoi Federatsii' [Address to the Federal Assembly of the Russian Federation], Kremlin.ru, 25 April, <http://kremlin.ru/events/president/transcripts/22931> (last accessed 20 April 2017).

Putin, Vladimir (2012), 'Rossiia: natsional'nyi vopros' [Russia: the national question], *Nezavisimaia gazeta*, 23 January, <http://www.ng.ru/politics/2012-01-23/1_national.html> (last accessed 20 April 2017).

Putin, Vladimir (2014a), 'Obrashchenie Prezidenta Rossiiskoi Federatsii' [Message of the President of the Russian Federation], Kremlin.ru, 18 March, <www.kremlin.ru/news/20603> (last accessed 18 April 2017).

Putin, Vladimir (2014b), 'Poslanie Prezidenta Federal'nomu Sobraniiu' [The President's Address to the Federal Assembly), Kremlin.ru, 4 December, <http://kremlin.ru/news/47173> (last accessed 7 March 2015).

Putin, Vladimir (2015), 'Poslanie Prezidenta Federal'nomu Sobraniiu' [The President's Address to the Federal Assembly], Kremlin.ru, 4 December, <www.kremlin.ru/events/president/news/50864> (last accessed 4 May 2017).

RIA Novosti (2016), 'O "rossiiskoi natsii", russkom narode i mezhnatsional'nom sogalsii' [On 'the Russian nation', the Russian people and interethnic accord], 2 November, <https://ria.ru/analytics/20161102/1480543704.html> (last accessed 15 April 2017).

Shevel, Oxana (2011), 'Russian nation-building from Yel'tsin to Medvedev: ethnic, civic or purposefully ambiguous?', *Europe–Asia Studies*, 63, 2: 179–202.

Slezkine, Yuri (1994), 'The USSR as a communal apartment, or how a socialist state promoted ethnic particularism', *Slavic Review*, 53, 2: 414–52.

Solovei, Valerii (2014), 'Natsiia, ne imperiia' [Nation, not empire], 18 March, <http://novayasila.org/lenta/news602> (last accessed 20 May 2014).

Szporluk, Roman (1989), 'Dilemmas of Russian nationalism', *Problems of Communism*, 38, 4: 15–35.

Whitmore, Brian (2015), 'Ukraine!? What Ukraine?' *The Power Vertical*, RFE/RL, 3 December, <www.rferl.org/content/ukraine-what-ukraine/27405286.html> (last accessed 4 May 2017).

Yack, Bernard (1996), 'The myth of the civic nation', *Critical Review*, 10, 2: 193–211.

Part I

Official nationalism

1

Contemporary Russian nationalism in the historical struggle between 'official nationality' and 'popular sovereignty'

Emil Pain

This chapter focuses on the dynamics of the historical role and ideational content of Russian nationalism from the beginning of the nineteenth century to the present.[1] It discusses the under-studied question of the mutual relationship between two manifestations of Russian nationalism: state nationalism and grassroots nationalism. The latter variety has appeared in Russia as a carrier of ideas of civic and popular sovereignty, drawing on the ideologues of the French Revolution. I argue that, throughout history, Russian state authorities have attempted to neutralise civic nationalism by substituting it with something ostensibly similar but actually very different: a paternalistic idea of 'official nationality' in the form of 'imperial nationalism'.

This political technology has been employed repeatedly in Russian history, as seen also during the recent events since 2014. On the other hand, although grassroots Russian nationalism has always had a primarily anti-liberal tendency, this has come to the fore only when a political liberalisation could be observed – during the liberal 'thaws'. When periods of authoritarian reaction returned, Russian nationalism as a societal phenomenon faded away, squeezed out by the ideology of the state.

Russian nationalism: From the Decembrists to 'the Black Hundreds'

Elsewhere I have discussed the evolution of the idea of the 'nation' in the Russian context and the related changes in the ideology of Russian nationalism during 'the long nineteenth century', from 1790 through 1917 (Pain 2015a; 2016b). Several historical stages in this process stand out.

The first stage, 1790–1833, saw the emergence in Russia of a civic conception of the 'nation' as the banner of popular sovereignty, political representation and constitutional order. This interpretation of the nation appeared long before official state nationalism and the ethnic interpretation of nation, and remained dominant in Russia for several decades. This idea was variously defended by the Decembrists – the revolutionaries among the nobility, who in December 1825 demanded the limitation of autocracy in Russia, either through the establishment of a constitutional monarchy, or by the introduction of a republican system. Some experts see the Decembrists as the first representatives of a nationalist ideology in Russia (see Sergeev 2010). In the same civic interpretation, the idea of the nation was used in 1797 by the future emperor Aleksandr I (at that time heir to the throne), who announced that, on becoming tsar, he would grant Russia a constitution and that 'the nation (*natsiia*) will elect its representatives' (quoted in Miller 2012). However, after the Decembrist revolt and the reign of Nikolai I (especially after the Polish uprising 1830–1, with its slogans of national sovereignty), 'the former discourse about the *nation* and *national representation* as a desirable, although difficult, goal to achieve was replaced in official circles by the rejection of a constitution, and national representation was seen as an inappropriate principle for Russia' (Miller 2012, emphasis in original).

In the second stage, 1833–63, came the nationalisation of the idea of nation: the era of official nationality. One of the major strategies to defend the monarchy against the idea of a civic nation was to replace it with other, quasi-similar ideas. In 1833, Minister of Education Sergei Uvarov outlined a formula that became well known in Russia: 'Orthodoxy, autocracy, nationality'. This triad was intended as a bulwark against European freedom of thought, and an antithesis to French revolutionary ideas of 'freedom, equality and brotherhood', which Russian conservatives deemed unsuited for the Russian people. The main innovation in Uvarov's formula was the concept of 'nationality' (*narodnost'*) from which the whole doctrine took the name of 'official nationality'. As opposed to Western models, it emphasised Russia's devotion to its own traditions and distinctness – like the current concept of 'Russia's special path'.

According to Uvarov, the uniqueness of the Russian 'official nationality' consisted in the Russian people's devotion to Orthodoxy and autocracy, rejecting the idea of popular sovereignty. 'Official nationality' was primarily a patriarchal and paternalistic idea which excluded any notion that the people should legitimise the monarch's right to rule. The power of the tsar comes from God; at the same time the principle of nationality prescribes for the tsar the moral obligation to love his people. He is the father of the people – so the children, his subjects, must faithfully honour their autocratic father.

The third stage, 1863–90, brought the first ethnicisation of the idea of the nation and the advent of ethnic Russian nationalism. The concept of 'nationality' had difficulty taking root – not only in the Russian language, but also in political practice. Even the Slavophiles of the 1840s–50s (Konstantin and Ivan Aksakov, Aleksandr Koshelev, Iurii Samarin and others) considered the doctrine of official nationality as 'despotism'. All this encouraged the state ideologists – the guardians of autocracy – to continue their search for terms to replace the seditious concept of the 'nation' (*natsiia*). Count Petr Valuev, one of the most influential state officials under Tsar Aleksandr II (1860s–80s), stressed the importance of replacing the highly politicised concept of the 'nation' (Fr. *nation*) with 'nationality' (Fr. *nationalité*), seen as a purely folk concept reflecting the culture and customs of the people. Over time in Russia, the concept of 'nationality', now *natsional'nost'*, took root in this sense, and in the mid-twentieth century began to be used in academic circles to define 'ethnicity' or 'ethnic identity': a group of people linked together by the myth of a shared origin and with their own self-designation (ethnonym) (Bromlei 1983: 57–58). Valuev also brought into the political language the concept of 'the national question' (using this phrase first in 1863 in a report to the tsar about the situation in Ukraine). Originally, this concept had purely negative connotations, indicating the threat of national (today we would say 'ethnic') separatism. However, when the ethnic nationalism of another group was perceived as negative – what about that of Russia?

With each passing decade in Russian history, the national problem increasingly shifted from its civic roots to something more ethnically coloured. The national topic was interpreted from an essentialist viewpoint as a certain set of characteristics bestowed by fate upon specific peoples (ethnic nations). From the 1880s, Russian Slavophiles, in their disputes with their Westerniser opponents, began actively developing Uvarov's idea of fundamental, everlasting and pre-ordained differences between the Russian people and the Western nations. Moreover, the Slavophiles of the 1880s–90s (such as Nikolai Danilevskii, Konstantin Leontiev and Vasilii Rozanov) rejected the legacy of their predecessors, the early Slavophiles of the mid-nineteenth century. In contrast to them, they adopted the German mystical idea of a 'national spirit', introduced by Johann Gottfried Herder.[2] The late Slavophiles actively developed the idea of Russia's special path, contrasting the national character of the Russians – patient, spontaneous, warm, generous and inclined to *sobornost'* (a preference for collectivism) – to a generic image of a Western mentality, seen as always self-interested, greedy, deceitful and coldly calculating. From the circles of the late Slavophiles there also originated the ideological trend that became known as 'Russian nationalism'. If the late Slavophiles were theorists of nationalism, Mikhail Katkov, who was close to them in spirit, became one of the first nationalists in real politics. Katkov enjoyed substantial influence on state power during the reign of Tsar Aleksandr III – directly, in the capacity of adviser to the tsar, and more indirectly, exercising pressure on the government through the influential newspaper *Moskovskie vedomosti*, which he edited. For example, Katkov sought to eliminate 'foreigners' from the civil service, persons of non-Russian origin, such as Finance Minister Nikolai Bunge or Foreign Minister Nikolai Girs. Like many others, Katkov had begun his activity as a liberal Westerniser, but by the 1880s, he had become a radical Russian chauvinist.

The fourth stage, 1905–17, saw the political formalisation of Russian imperial nationalism and aggressive xenophobia. The first legal party of the Russian nationalists, the Union of the Russian People, emerged in 1905. The service of autocracy and the preservation of the empire were its main goals: 'The Union of the Russian People . . . establishes as its sacred, immutable duty to make any effort to ensure that the land won by the blood of our ancestors remains an eternally inalienable part of the Russian state' (Programma. . . 1905). The programme of action of the radical right-wing of Russian nationalism, which took shape politically at the time, contained ideas of monarchy linked to xenophobia – anti-Semitism in particular. These groups, collectively known as 'Black Hundreds', fomented and organised pogroms against Jews, as well as the murder of two Jewish deputies of the State Duma, Mikhail Gertsenshtein and Grigorii Iollos (Stepanov 2013). It was the Black Hundreds who launched the slogan 'Russia for Russians', which became a common principle held by all Russian nationalists – the political dominance of ethnic Russians, expressed in the demand for preferential rights to ethnic Russians: the *Russian nation*.

Thus, the idea of nation emerged in Russia in the late eighteenth century, with expectations of revolutionary change, centring on the constitution and the limitation of autocracy. By the late nineteenth century, this idea had degenerated into an ideology of defending autocracy and the imperial structure. Russian nationalism has since involved various institutionalised entities promoting national egotism, great-power chauvinism and xenophobia.

State nationalism and grassroots nationalism in the Soviet period

In the Soviet Union, nationalism was officially prohibited as an ideology opposed to the state policy of internationalism. However, the content of Soviet internationalism changed quite radically several times, always bringing a shift in attitudes towards nationalism. Various social and ethnic communities became subsumed under the concept of the 'nation'.

Historian Yuri Slezkine maintains that the founder of the Soviet state, Vladimir Lenin, took an uncompromising stance on the issue of 'nations' and 'national rights': 'it was one of the most uncompromising positions he ever took, his theory of good ("oppressed-nation") nationalism formed the conceptual foundation of the Soviet Union' (Slezkine 1994: 414). I agree with Slezkine as regards the essence of his conclusions, but will challenge his terminology. Indeed, 'good nationalism' is not mentioned in the works of Lenin or his collaborators: to them, nationalism was something extremely negative. In Lenin's view, the ethnic consolidation of national minorities in Russia represented *a national liberation struggle* against Russification. Support for this struggle meant working to establish *real equal rights*, whereas the term 'nationalism' was generally reserved for the activities of political forces defending tsarist power in the name of the ethnic majority – the Russians – or, as they were called at that time, the 'Great Russians'. Such nationalism, which the Bolsheviks referred to as 'Great Russian chauvinism', was sharply denounced by the Communists. In the 1920s, that was the line followed by the entire leadership of the Communist Party.

A noteworthy representative of this line was Iosif Stalin, who was responsible for the nationalities policy of the Party as well as of the Soviet state. His speech at the 12th Party Congress in March 1923 corresponded fully with Leninist doctrine on the national question. Stalin denounced the tsarist Russification policy, supported the struggle of 'dependent nationalities against imperialist oppression', and declared that

> vestiges of great Russian chauvinism, which reflect the privileged position of the Great Russians in the past, can still be found in the Soviet Union. ... Therefore, a decisive battle against the vestiges of Great Russian chauvinism is a first priority task for our party. (Stalin 1923)

However, in 1928–32, during the 'Great Transformation', this policy was radically changed, although initially only in relation to the national minorities. By then, Stalin had started the collectivisation of Soviet agriculture, with massive confiscation of land from the peasantry – mainly ethnic Russians – resulting in deep dissatisfaction among the vast majority of the population. The Soviet authorities then began to whip up xenophobia against national minorities, perhaps seeking to deflect social dissatisfaction into ethnic channels. However, another interpretation is also possible: when state terror was unleashed in the 1930s, it spread, becoming directed against national minorities as well. Whatever the case, ethnic cleansing and deportation of representatives of various national minorities and ethnic groups became a mass phenomenon in the 1930s. In the 1940s, large nations, with hundreds of thousands of members, were deported en masse: Crimean Tatars, Germans, Chechens, Ingushetians, Balkars, Karachais, Kalmyks and others (Polian 2005: 5).

In the 1940s, Stalin revised his own thesis about the unacceptability of the 'privileged position of the Great Russians'. During the Great Patriotic War and immediately afterwards, references to the leading and organising role of the ethnic Russians featured in his rhetoric. His decision to highlight the role of the ethnic majority population immediately gutted the policy of internationalism. Instead of implementing the idea of actual equal rights, the country returned to the imperial principal of a hierarchy of peoples, with the Russians as the 'elder brother', and the Russian republic, the RSFSR, as the 'elder sister' in the family of Soviet republics. In December 1943, the Politburo approved the lyrics of the new Soviet national anthem (replacing 'The Internationale'), which opened with words about how Great Russia (*Velikaia Rus'*) had gathered around her the other republics in an 'unbreakable union'. Yet another sign of the turnabout in Soviet nationalities policy was the new reliance on traditionalism and folkloric Russian nationality: in the mass propaganda, images of Russian heroes like Ilia Muromets from the medieval *bylina*s (epic poems) appeared together with the Kiev-era Prince Aleksandr Nevskii and even the tyrannical Tsar Ivan the Terrible. State awards carrying the names of tsarist military commanders were instituted. All of this was quite alien to Leninist internationalism.

During and after the war, Stalin's policy increasingly included elements of ethnic nationalism. The state ordered the production of artistic works, like films, novels and musical pieces that praised a specific kind of 'Russian character'. At the same time, many artistic works presented negative images of Soviet citizens of other nationalities (German in particular), who were depicted as hidden, masked enemies harmful to Russia (Beliaeva and Mikhailin 2014).

Between 1930 and 1950, Soviet state propaganda fanned phobia against 'traitor-peoples', groups who became subjected to ethnic cleansing and deportation from their traditional territories. In 1948–53, an unmistakable state-orchestrated anti-Semitism appeared in the campaign against 'cosmopolitanism': Soviet Jews were accused of cosmopolitanism, that is, lack of Soviet patriotism – an accusation often accompanied by dismissal from work and even arrest (Fateev 1999).

During this period, Stalin's nationalities policy lost any resemblance to the original version of Soviet internationalism: it simply became a second edition of the imperial ideology of 'official nationality'. All three elements of Uvarov's triad reappeared in some shape. The element of 'autocracy' was clearly discernible, as the new ideology was no less authoritarian or paternalistic than it had been during the times of Nikolai I: Stalin was hailed as 'the Father of the nations'. The 'nationality' (*narodnost'*) of the regime was demonstrated by systematically contrasting Russian Soviet culture with the 'alien' Western culture. And finally, instead of Orthodox Christianity, Marxism – or more precisely, Stalinism – filled the role of official state religion.

The state policy of Soviet-type Russian nationalism ('official nationality') left no room for grassroots societal Russian nationalism – indeed, any manifestations of such nationalism were severely repressed. This situation continued also for some years after Stalin's death. In 1957–58 some underground nationalist circles were broken up: the Russian Popular Party (*Russkaia narodnaia partiia*), the Russian National Party (*Russkaia natsional'naia partiia*) and the Russian National-Socialist Party (*Rossiiskaia natsional'no-sotsialisticheskaia partiia*), as well as Viktor Trofimov's student circle in Leningrad ('Dissidentskie. . .' n.d.). These were all small organisations (fewer than ten members) devoted to the reading and discussion of theoretical questions, but all their members were sent to prison for many years. Other forms of self-organised ethnic and religious communities also continued to be suppressed. The year 1959 was marked by the mass closure of churches, monasteries and religious schools, as well as persecution of priests and pastors.

These repressions eased up in the early 1960s, a time of relative liberalisation known as the 'Khrushchev thaw'. This period saw activity blooming among not only the liberal intelligentsia – the '60's generation' (*shestidesiatniki*) – but also Russian nationalists. As noted by the historian Artem Fomenkov, the preconditions were now created for the semi-legal (non-sanctioned, but not persecuted) political activity of nationalist groups (Fomenkov 2010). In 1964–67 the national-religious All-Russian Social-Christian Union for the Liberation of the People (*Vserossiiskii sotsial-khristianskii soiuz osvobozhdeniia naroda*, VSKhON) operated almost openly in Leningrad. Of all the underground dissident organisations of that time, this probably had the largest membership (twenty-eight members and thirty candidate members). The group was led by Igor Ogurtsov, who held that the state structures should be organised in accordance with Orthodoxy and Dostoevskii-inspired nationalism (*pochvennichestvo*).

Fomenkov concludes that the party organs and the KGB to some degree themselves initiated the activity of the semi-legal nationalist groups, to provoke attacks on the liberally thinking intelligentsia. This was partly accomplished: between 1964 and 1970, denunciations of the so-called bourgeois intelligentsia were quite frequent in the 'literary-patriotic' circle known as Radonezhtsy. Several writers with nationalist attitudes belonged to this circle, including Ivan Shevtsov, Igor Kobzev and Feliks Chuev. Starting from 1963, the journal *Molodaia gvardiia* (*Young Guard*) became the mouthpiece of Russian anti-liberal *pochvennichestvo*-nationalism – in reality, of Russian nationalist thought. From 1968, it was joined by *Nash sovremennik* (*Our Contemporary*). The authorities regarded these two journals and the writers involved (Stanislav Kuniaev, Vladimir Soloukhin, Vadim Kozhinov and others) as ideational fellow travellers. Their activity was tolerated but contained within the framework of the censorship and the norms of 'official nationality'. However, on the crest of this wave, these artists and scholars managed to produce works and actions that were genuinely oppositional and nationalist. This was the case, for instance, with the writer Aleksandr Solzhenitsyn, the historian Lev Gumilev and the mathematician-cum-nationalist publicist Igor Shafarevich.

The KGB did not immediately exert repression against them; as noted, the secret police may have been trying to foment confrontation between the two camps of dissidents – Russian nationalists and Western-oriented liberals. However, in the Soviet period such confrontations, even if they occasionally did take place, were played out in rather unobtrusive forms, mainly in cautious discussions on the pages of books and in journals published abroad.[3] The general refusal of Soviet dissidents to accept totalitarianism was stronger than their points of disagreement, and prevented the latter from erupting into the open. An example was the collaboration between

Igor Shafarevich, who later gained publicity as a fanatical proponent of anti-Semitism, with Mikhail Agurskii, who in the late 1980s became a prominent leader of the Zionist movement in the Soviet Union. In 1974, both of them, together with Aleksandr Solzhenitsyn and others, took part in the preparation of *From Under the Rubble*, an underground anthology of anti-Soviet publicist articles (*samizdat*) – a book that became a symbol of collaborative activity among the various layers of the Soviet dissident movement.

State nationalism and grassroots nationalism in post-Soviet Russia

In the Soviet period, there were numerous examples of mutual support between dissidents who held very different views. After the collapse of the Soviet Union, however, not only ideational but also sharp political disagreements among the various currents of the former dissident movement came to the fore. The new configuration of political groups, and the lines of confrontation, were often quite unexpected.

It might seem paradoxical that in the early 1990s the vast majority of the new organisations of Russian nationalists collaborated not merely with Communists, but with the most conservative phalanx among them – the uncompromising Stalinists, the ideological heirs of those who had repressed earlier generations of Russian nationalists and had replaced the concept of 'Russian' with the concept of 'Soviet'. Some scholars hold that the choice of collaborators was made according to the principle of the 'lesser evil': in the early 1990s, Russian nationalists had to accept either the slogan 'Back to the USSR' or 'forward to the Western world', they had to embrace either Stalinism or Western liberalism – and the great majority opted for Stalinism (Novikov 2012: 263). In my view, this choice came naturally to the ideational heirs of 'the Black Hundreds'. To them, Stalin was not so much the leader of Communists as the ruler of the empire. Moreover Stalin, like the 'Black Hundreds', was radically anti-Western. Finally, Stalin had been the initiator of state-sponsored Soviet anti-Semitism, something highly regarded by xenophobes among Russian nationalists of the 'Black Hundreds' type.

During the twilight of the Soviet Union and in the early post-Soviet years, such Russian nationalists were among the first to create or join political parties, movements, fronts and so on. Following Vladimir Malakhov (2006), I present a general scheme of chief currents in Russian nationalism in the post-Soviet period, while also introducing some minor readjustments in his classification. Malakhov underscores two main sources of contemporary Russian nationalism: the 'Soviet-communist' and the 'traditionalist-*pochvennik*' subcultures (Malakhov 2006). I call the first subculture 'Soviet-imperial', and include in it not only Communists (leftists), but also non-Communist (rightist) ideologues of imperialism.

Leftist imperial nationalists

In this category we find the leading figures of the Communist Party of the Russian Federation (KPRF), headed by Gennadii Ziuganov, as well as more radical leftist groups such as Viktor Anpilov's Working Russia (*Trudovaia Rossiia*). In all these groups, Stalin's hybrid of imperial statism and ethnic nationalism was reborn. A crucial element of the nationalist-Communist propaganda in the 1990s was the image of a 'divided Russian people' resulting from the redrawing of borders between the successor states after the collapse of the Soviet Union. According to Ziuganov, the aim of the 'Russian idea' should be to reunite the divided Russian people (Ziuganov 1994).

Malakhov (2006) also focuses on what he calls a group of 'post-Communists'. Among them, we find Aleksei Podberezkin, leader of the Spiritual Heritage (*Dukhovnoe nasledie*) movement, who hails from Ziuganov's party. Podberezkin was among the first to exploit and romanticise the symbols of the empire. Others in this category are Sergei Kara-Murza, who renounced Stalinism in favour of a more moderate leftist version of a Russian *Sonderweg*; Aleksandr Prokhanov, the main ideologue of the People's Patriotic Union of Russia (*Narodno-patrioticheskii soiuz Rossii*, NPSR), a movement led by Ziuganov between 1996 and 2003; Eduard Limonov, the leader of the National Bolshevik Party (*Natsional-bol'shevistskaia partiia*); and finally, the young author Sergei Shargunov, who since 2016 has represented the Communist Party in the State Duma.

Rightist imperial nationalists

Among the better-known ideologues of rightist imperial nationalism are Vladimir Zhirinovskii and Aleksandr Dugin. The former combines anti-Communist rhetoric with a radically expressed idea of imperial expansion – specifically, the need to re-establish the Russian Empire within its 1913 borders. Since 2003, Zhirinovskii and his party have added a new slogan to their imperial idea: 'We support the poor! We support the [ethnic] Russians!' (LDPR 2003), as well as a demand for the elimination of 'artificial discrimination against

Russians'. What this discrimination against Russians consists of, however, Zhirinovskii does not explain.

Dugin, as the leader of the International Eurasian Movement, is a theoretician of civilisational nationalism. He sees the Russian Empire as a result of a civilisational mutual attraction between the Slavic-Orthodox and the Turkic-Muslim peoples, as well as a geopolitical territory for the confrontation between Russia and the USA.

Traditionalist-*pochvennik* nationalists

The *pochvenniks* are also concerned about the imperial idea, but defence of the empire does not have top priority for them. Instead, they focus more on the interests of ethnic Russians, on the basis of the unique cultural traditions and conditions (*pochva*, or soil) of Russia. The *pochvenniks* trace their Soviet genealogy not to the state nationalists, but to either the Soviet dissident nationalists or the semi-legal literary circles in the 1960s, as well as to the literary milieus around the journals *Molodaia gvardiia* and *Nash sovremennik*. Some *pochvenniks* reject Communism (these are the 'white' *pochvenniks*) whereas the majority of them relate to Communism with equanimity, and some even idolise the figure of Stalin (these are the 'red-browns'). Common to the ideology of all *pochvenniks* is some degree of ethnic nationalism, ranging from moderate expressions of ethnc-nationalism to the most extreme racism. An example of the former would be the adherents of Lev Gumilev, while the latter is represented by the views of Viktor Korchagin, editor of the first Russian translation of Hitler's *Mein Kampf*. In the 1990s Korchagin led the Russian Party (*Russkaia partiia*), a relatively large organisation with more than 5,000 members, promoting the idea of an ethnically pure Russian state. Similarly, in the early 2000s, the co-chairs of the National Great-Power Party (*Natsional'no-derzhavnaia partiia*), Aleksandr Sevastianov and Boris Mironov, represented such radically racist views.

Russian racists are divided, first, between a secular and a religious phalanx; then, within the religious group, between the 'neopagans' (or simply 'pagans') and those adhering to Orthodoxy. The Orthodox *pochvenniks* have established political forces like the Union of Orthodox Banner-Bearers (*Soiuz pravoslavnykh khorugvonostsev*), the Union of Orthodox Brotherhoods (*Soiuz pravoslavnykh bratstv*), the party In Defence of Holy Russia! (*Za Rus' sviatuiu!*) and others. In 2002, the 'pagans' established a Library of Racist Thought (Malakhov 2006), an initiative supported by Andrei Saveliev, who had earlier represented the Motherland (*Rodina*) faction in the State Duma.

Official nationalism and 'official nationality'

The final category concerns the policies of the Russian state authorities aimed at manipulating mass consciousness by evoking artificial traditionalism and a hypersensitive patriotism as a defence against threats (usually imagined) to the independence of the state and its autonomous development. A certain interest in traditionalism was already evident in the administration of the first Russian president, Boris Eltsin. During his time in office, the double-headed imperial eagle again became a state symbol in the state coat of arms, and the imperial tricolour became the official state flag. Public manifestations of the religiosity of the new state authorities were frequent; numerous photographs showed the president together with the patriarch of the Russian Orthodox Church. Nevertheless, in my view, for Eltsin the main purpose of this was not so much to boost his ratings by drawing on the growing popularity of traditionalism, as to use the traditional, historic tsarist symbols as a counterweight to the artificial Communist symbols (see Pain 2015b). In Eltsin's thinking, the resurgence of the Orthodox Church which had been destroyed by the Bolsheviks should also symbolise his strategic line of returning Russia to her 'natural history' which had been interrupted by the Communist takeover.

While Eltsin followed a political course of 'returning Russia to Europe', his successor, Vladimir Putin, resurrected the Stalinist policy of a 'besieged fortress', Cold War-style anti-Western rhetoric and spymania. Eltsin symbolised Russia's break with totalitarianism; under Putin, official notes of protest have gone to the OSCE and to all European countries that have denounced Stalinism and Hitlerism as equally unacceptable versions of totalitarianism (*Argumenty i fakty* 2009; News2.ru 2009). Eltsin underscored the anti-imperial character of his policies; under Putin, the dominant line has been to present Russia as a 'great power' – which essentially means a cult of the empire. The propagandistic mobilisation of Russia's ethnic majority is also based on support for this cult.

The state policy of imperial nationalism in the post-Soviet period has developed in fits and starts. The first phase was heralded by Putin's 2007 Munich speech, regarded by many Western politicians as signalling a return to the Cold War. The second phase commenced with the 2014 annexation of Crimea and the subsequent military activities in the Donbas, severely exacerbating tensions between Russia and the West. The third phase is tied to Russia's military operations in Syria from 2015 onwards. These have led Russia and the Western world to the brink of direct military engagement, giving Russian state nationalism yet another turn.

Each of these new phases in the increasing confrontation with the West has sharpened the harshness of the statements coming from Russian politicians. Even Russian diplomats have appealed more to the emotions of the Russian grandstand than to the international community. Thus, for instance, the Syrian crisis led Minister of Foreign Affairs Sergei Lavrov to draw on Russian ethnic fears, by playing up the threat of US Russophobia (Plavskaia 2016).

In parallel, Stalin-type rhetoric about the unique cultural dignity and superiority of the ethnic Russians is being revived: after Crimea and Syria, the 'fighting spirit' of the Russians has been hailed. In the words of political scientist Sergei Karaganov, who is close to the Kremlin, 'Russians aren't good at haggling, they aren't passionate about business. But they are outstanding fighters' (Karaganov, quoted in Neef 2016).

The Russian state authorities attempt to shield themselves from the world by demonising their enemies and by ostentatious praise of the Russian people. This is nothing new in Russia. Whenever it happens, such official nationalism leads to suppression of grassroots societal nationalism. This is how it was under Nikolai I and under Stalin; now it is being revived under Putin. Just when Putin assumed the presidency, Russian nationalist parties began to be denied official registration. Dozens of leaders of these parties and of their regional branches were taken to court on charges – sometimes trumped-up – of various crimes.

Whenever the state authorities have pursued a policy of liberalisation, this has led to a revival of grassroots nationalism. Such a revival took place during the Khrushchev thaw in the early 1960s, and was repeated in the liberalisation projects of Mikhail Gorbachev (1985–91). At that time, the National-Patriotic Front 'Pamiat' (*Natsional-patriotocheskii front 'Pamiat'*), founded by Dmitrii Vasilev, appeared. The Front was founded in 1987 at a non-sanctioned rally in Moscow against Gorbachev's perestroika and the policy of liberalisation. Pamiat's anti-liberal oppositional stance continued into the first post-Soviet years, but now this policy was even more pronounced in the ultranationalistic splinter organisation Russian National Unity (*Russkoe natsional'noe edinstvo*, RNE). In October 1993, both these political organisations (many of their members bearing arms) opposed the Eltsin administration in the conflict between the Russian president and pro-Communist insurgents in the Russian Supreme Soviet.

Eltsin's supporters won this confrontation, but there were no negative consequences for the above-mentioned Russian nationalist organisations. On the contrary, in 1995 Pamiat acquired legal status (previously, it had been registered in the Ministry of Justice as an interregional organisation only), while RNE in 1999 even tried to register its own candidates in the State Duma elections. In the 1990s – during the Eltsin epoch – more favourable conditions were created for grassroots political self-organisation of the population than ever before in Russian history. The new Russian state authorities refrained from suppressing the activity of most nationalist organisations, even if Russian nationalists at that time stood in fierce opposition to the powers-that-be.

Another period of (limited) liberalisation occurred between 2008 and 2012, during the presidency of Dmitrii Medvedev. In those years, the currents of Russian nationalism described below first emerged (see also Pain 2015a).

The short history of anti-imperial, 'national-democratic' Russian nationalism

Surfing on the wave of political protests in Russia in 2010–12, the contours of a brand-new variety of Russian nationalism appeared. Called 'national-democratic' by its advocates, this variant of Russian nationalism has several specific features.

AN ANTI-IMPERIAL CHARACTER

Konstantin Krylov, one of the most popular theorists of this 'new' nationalism, has emphasised that Russian nationalism proper began to emerge only when it shifted from its obsession with the principles of imperialism and 'great power-ism' to the idea of promoting the interests of the nation. According to Krylov, 'Russian nationalism proper is essentially a new phenomenon. I date its history from around the first decade of the 2000s' (quoted in Nazdem.info 2010). Until the late 1990s, Russian nationalism was conceived of in imperial terms, but this movement, Krylov holds, ought not to be called Russian 'nationalism': 'everything boiled down to fantasies about of "how we can make good the empire".' The national democrats, on the other hand, see consistent nationalism as the opposite of imperial ideology: the latter asserts not the sovereignty of the people, but the sovereignty of the ruler. Nationalism, says Krylov, 'considers the state as being of secondary value. The state exists for the people and not the people for the state' (ibid.).

Anti-Sovietism

Rejecting the idea of empire and reconsidering the role of the state and society led many Russian nationalists to rethink Stalinism, which the Russian nationalists of the 1990s held forward as their banner. Stalin, these statists had declared, 'gathered the Russian lands' and greatly expanded the territory of the Russian Empire. 'When the Soviet state fell apart', says Krylov, 'all ideologically committed Russian forces sided with the Communists. As a result, they could not produce anything but a "red-brown synthesis"' – which, in the opinion of this 'genuine nationalist', led to disaster. But by 2010, the situation had changed radically and the Russian nationalists proposed a new idea: 'Nationalism and democracy are practically the same thing' (ibid.).

A 'democratic turn'

The first sign of what would later be called the 'democratic turn' in Russian nationalism was the formation of an 'anti-Soviet platform', as with the appearance of a separate anti-Soviet section in the 2012 Russian March (Manifest... 2012). After that, many nationalist leaders in their speeches increasingly began to reject not only Stalinism, but also authoritarianism as a political principle. A notable feature of this new Russian nationalism is its demonstrative opposition to those in power. Representatives of the national-democratic opposition began to make appearances and speak at opposition rallies. Thus, the leaders of the National Democratic Party (*Natsional'no-demokraticheskaia partiia*, NDP), including Konstantin Krylov, Vladimir Tor, Rostislav Antonov and Aleksandr Khramov, appeared at the 2011–13 rallies 'For fair elections' in Moscow. Aleksei Shiropaev and Ilia Lazarenko, the ideologists of the National Democratic Alliance (*Natsional-demokraticheskii al'ians*), have promoted the idea of a 'nation-oriented' democracy even more consistently. Valerii Solovei, leader of the New Force party (*Novaia sila*), has also expressed similar national-democratic views in his public speeches.

At the interface between the national-democratic model and the autocratic and imperialist one, the ideas of Egor Prosvirnin – founder of the popular nationalist Internet project *Sputnik i Pogrom* – have evolved. Prosvirnin is one of the most controversial figures among the Russian nationalists. In his programmatic writings in 2010–12, he vehemently criticised the Soviet Communist regime, comparing it to a dark night: 'amidst a clear Russian day, suddenly the dark night of communism fell' (Prosvirnin 2012). He has also focused on the necessity of democratic changes that would, in his view, benefit ethnic Russians: 'Our ideal is a Russian national democratic, law-based state ... with an economic life based on the principles of the rule of law and free competition' (Prosvirnin n.d.; see also 2014a). All this served to draw Prosvirnin close to the national-democratic trend in Russian nationalism. At the same time, the anti-liberal rhetoric in most texts on Sputnik i Pogrom's webpages, with ideas of expansionism and territorial revenge, revealed Prosvirnin's affinity to the ideology followed by the majority of imperial nationalists.

The difference between traditional Soviet imperialists and the new Russian nationalists representing the new national-democratic wing came to the fore in the winter of 2013/14 with the demonstrations organised by the Ukrainian political opposition in Kiev's Maidan Square. At the time, a significant number of Russian national democrats supported the Maidan protesters in one way or another, the National Democratic Alliance most consistently. The leader of this organisation, Aleksei Shiropaev, described the events in Kiev as 'an anticolonial, democratic, European revolution (in terms of its civilisational vector)' (Shiropaev 2014). The Russian nationalists in the NDP assessed the Maidan incidents more cautiously, but without concealing their support for the protests. However, after Russia's annexation of Crimea, the nationalist opposition quickly went into decline. For example, Prosvirnin, who until then had directed caustic criticism at the Russian authorities, now made no secret of his support for the government's actions during the Crimean crisis, and welcomed the inclusion of the peninsula into Russia. He commented on his change of position in a text on his website:

> And the fact that Putin, after decades of surrendering Russian interests everywhere and in every way, suddenly remembered that Crimea is Russian land, is actually good ... It would be strange, to say the least, to criticise Putin for having begun to fulfil a part of our programme. (Prosvirnin 2014b)

The decay of Russian national democracy

When Crimea had been annexed by Russia, even the national democratic elite of Russian nationalists, or at least most of them, proved unable to relinquish the imperial stereotypes. Russian nationalism lost its temporary character of opposition to the government; among its ranks the popularity of President Putin and even of the 'great leader'

Stalin was growing. However, this twist was not tantamount to a rebirth of the leftist Stalinist nationalism of the 1990s. In post-Crimea Russia, nationalists have merged into a single, internally poorly differentiated mass of supporters of the idea of Russia as a great power (*velikaia derzhava*), proud of the actions of the Russian armed forces in Crimea, Donbas and Syria. Anti-Western sentiment has increased significantly. With this ideological dissolution into the general flow of aggressive patriotism, Russian nationalism has lost its ideological originality, its own special niche of political activity – and consequently, the ideological basis even for the consolidation of its former supporters. Except for xenophobia, there is no longer a specific, distinct topic around which the nationalists could converge. For the time being Russian nationalists exhibit one of the lowest levels of not only civic, but also ethnic, solidarity in the entire post-Soviet era.

This conclusion is consistent with the general trend of changes in collective consciousness in the post-Crimea period. First, the interests of the masses are shifting from domestic problems, including ethnic questions, to 'more important' state issues: the annexation of Crimea, the conflict in Donbas and 'the intrigues of the West' in Ukraine. Data from the Levada Centre show that one out of three Russians surveyed (35 per cent) think that after the annexation of Crimea the outside world has begun to fear Russia more than before (Levada 2016); moreover, 63 per cent of the respondents think that domestically Russia also faces more enemies than before (Elkina 2015).

Second, the structure of ethnic phobias is changing. Typical post-Soviet phobias – towards peoples of the Caucasus and Central Asia – have weakened somewhat. In 2014–15 sociologists from the Levada Centre recorded the lowest level of animosity towards 'other nationalities' (defined as people from the Caucasus and Central Asia) over a five-year period. Such hostility was felt 'very often' or 'often' by 13 per cent of the respondents in 2015 and 14 per cent in 2014; prior to 2010, the scores had been 19–20 per cent (Levada 2016: 195).

On the other hand, members of ethnic communities traditionally considered 'insiders' and 'close to' the Russian people have now fallen into the category of 'foreigners'. Against the backdrop of a relative reduction in manifestations of unspecified Russian ethnophobia towards 'other nationalities', there has been a conspicuous rise in negative attitudes towards Ukrainians, whom many Russians until recently referred to as 'brothers' or 'as Russian as we are'. This change is evident from the responses to the question 'Is it necessary to limit the time of stay in Russia for people of the following nationalities?' With regard to Ukrainians, there has been a rapid rise in affirmative answers: in early 2014, 1 per cent of those surveyed answered 'yes', at the end of the same year, 8 per cent, and in 2015, 14 per cent (in previous years, starting from 2004, such scores had always been less than a few percentage points) (Levada 2016). This clearly shows how statist, imperialist attitudes can suppress well-established ethnic stereotypes.

It should be noted that even in those instances when ethnic stereotypes, prejudices and phobias may be prominent in the consciousness of some Russians, this rarely leads to support for autonomous, self-organised nationalist groups. Such groups are regarded as hooligans, extremists or simply as unreliable partners. These same Russians, however, are often ready to embrace Russian chauvinism if it stems from the state itself. Aleksandr Verkhovskii refers to Russian sociological surveys which show that the majority of respondents are in favour of imposing a ban on those nationalist movements (RNE, skinheads and others) that are known to them. At the same time, they are favourably inclined towards those nationalists that enjoy the support of the state (like the Russian Cossacks). 'Consequently', Verkhovskii argues, 'the average Russian citizens continue to tie their hopes to the powers-that-be – it is precisely the state that ought to solve all problems: specifically, it is obliged to chase out the migrants' (quoted in Kuzmenko 2016).

Features of self-identification among the ethnic majority in Russia

Even in a period of social growth and rising popularity of the national-democratic strand of nationalism, its theorists noted that the purification of Russian nationalism from Soviet, imperialist ideology requires a lot of time and effort (Krylov in Nazdem.info 2010). Instead of such purification, however, post-Crimea Russia has shown a growth in the influence of imperialistic ideology among Russian nationalists. Perhaps this might be because, among ethnic Russians (the social basis of Russian nationalists), state identity has traditionally been much stronger than national identity. Ethno-sociological studies conducted in the 1980s, the 1990s, and the 2000s by groups of ethno-sociologists led by Iurii Arutiunian and Leokadiia Drobizheva provide evidence of the correlation between these two identities.

In the twilight of the Soviet era, in 1988, when growing ethnocentrism began to assume a political formalisation and 'national fronts' had appeared in several republics of the Soviet Union, for the majority of ethnic Russians their state-centred identity predominated over their Russian ethnic identity. A sociological survey conducted by the Institute of Ethnology and Anthropology of the Russian Academy of Science showed that 78 per cent of the respondents defined themselves as 'Soviet', and only 15 per cent as 'Russian'. By contrast, in control groups composed of Uzbeks, Georgians and Estonians, the ethnic identity was predominant (reported in Arutiunian et al. 1999: 165). This research also demonstrated how Russians paid significantly less attention to their national culture and history than did other groups. In responding to a question about the most significant problems requiring attention, only 10 per cent of Russians living in the non-Russian republics, and even fewer Russians living in their own ethnic environment within the RSFSR, mentioned 'the development of our own national culture' – whereas 30 to 50 per cent of the Uzbek, Georgian and Estonian respondents saw this as an important issue (Arutiunian 1992: 399). The Russians surveyed also showed less attention to their ethnic group's past, to the idea of a common historical destiny as a factor of ethnic cohesion, to national symbols and to various other points used by sociologists as indicators of ethnic and cultural identity (ibid.: 399–400).

In the first post-Soviet years (1991–93), the growth of ethnic self-awareness and traditionalism took hold also within the Russian Federation. During the so-called 'parade of sovereignties' the elites and the masses in the republics within the Russian Federation (Bashkortostan, Tatarstan, Dagestan, etc.) attempted to gain greater autonomy based on national (ethnic) features. In Chechnya, the national movement declared the republic's independence from the Russian Federation. Even under these conditions, however, Russian self-awareness changed little compared to the Soviet era. More than 80 per cent of the Russians surveyed evinced ethnic nihilism, or indifference, and chose the response, 'I have never thought about what nationality I am'. Only 8 per cent answered, 'I never forget that I am Russian' (Pain 2004: 185).

Between 1994 and 1996, ethnic self-awareness peaked among most ethnic groups in the Russian Federation. The many ethnic conflicts in those years, ethnic separatism and the Chechen War, could not but stimulate the growth of Russian ethnic self-awareness, as evident from several sociological studies. Still, while one quarter of the Russian respondents now clearly emphasised their ethnic identity ('I never forget that I am Russian'), other ethnic groups in Russia showed an even greater increase in ethnic self-awareness: such attitudes were expressed by between half to two thirds of those surveyed (Pain 2004: 185). To a significant degree, growing Russian ethnic self-awareness came as a response to the agitation of the ethnic minorities. Hence, when in the late 1990s the ethnopolitical upsurge began to diminish among most ethnic groups in Russia, the traditional territory- and state-centred identity regained its dominant position among ethnic Russians. In 1999, 79 per cent of Russian respondents defined themselves as 'Russian citizens', as against only 20 per cent among the Yakuts surveyed (Drobizheva 2009: 32).

The Russian ethnic majority do not respond to ethnic traditionalism, but rather to great-power traditionalism: pride in being part of a state with a thousand-year history that includes great military victories and territorial conquests. This is borne out when we consider the heroes in the hall of fame, compiled on the basis of national Internet surveys conducted in the first decade of the new millennium. The list is dominated by the names of tsars, other state leaders and generals such as Petr I, Aleksandr Nevskii, Dmitrii Donskoi, Ekaterina II, Ivan the Terrible, Iosif Stalin and Georgii Zhukov. Only the cosmonaut Iurii Gagarin somewhat redresses the balance among the top ten of this long list of 'state heroes' within the historical consciousness of the Russian people. Likewise, the Great Patriotic War (the Second World War) was chosen as the most significant event in history. One specific feature of the Russian national consciousness, as distinct from, for example, German collective self-awareness, emerges from these evaluations: German society, which engendered Nazism and German totalitarianism, associates the Second World War with national disaster and with defeat in war; by contrast, Russian society, under the influence of propaganda, could associate the Stalinist totalitarian regime with the great victory over fascism.

On the other hand, the predominance of the state-centred identity over ethnic identity is not necessarily an exclusively Russian feature – many people who represented the ethnic majority in the central area of an empire are characterised by this type of identity. For the English, for instance, 'British' overarching identity is much stronger than it is for the Irish, Scottish and Welsh peoples, whose ethnic identities largely figure as the antithesis to the 'British', which is still largely perceived as imperial (Lipkin 2007). In Spain, the ethnic majority, the Castilians (*castellanos*), sacrificed their ethnonym and the name of their language in favour of the national name 'Spaniards' (*españoles*). This pre-eminently state-oriented identification contrasts with the marked predominance of ethnic identity among Spain's minorities, such as the Basques (Kozhanovskii 2007: 241). In France, non-ethnic identities (civic, state and individualistic) have historically prevailed over ethnic identity, although ethnic phobias have erupted also there, as after the French defeat in the 1870-1 war with Germany. More recently, ethnic phobias in French society have intensified towards a new enemy: the immigrants, or rather, *non-European* immigrants. This has somewhat strengthened the ethnic self-identification among many French people – who are nevertheless considered to show much weaker ethnic self-awareness than that of Corsicans, French Basques, French Catalans, and many other ethnic and regional minorities in France (Filippova 2007: 202–10).

All these differences in self-identification among the ethnic majority and the minorities are well explained by the nature of this type of identification itself, which comes to the surface in the relationship between 'us' and 'them'. For minorities surrounded by an ethnic majority, the latter is always the 'constitutive other'. The majority, by contrast, notices the minorities only under certain circumstances – for instance when ethnic conflicts and other incidents occur; when the size of minority populations increases significantly; or when new minorities appear in the country. Ethnic identity is usually not static – it waxes and wanes, especially among the ethnic majority population. But whereas ethnic identity may quickly ignite and fade, the formation of civic consciousness is a long and difficult process that can span several centuries.

Michel Foucault sought to decipher the genealogy of modern power in Western countries, and, through the example of France, analysed the modern forms of control over the people as well as strategies for opposing them (Foucault 2003). For this purpose, he juxtaposed two concepts. The first was the concept of 'population', a passive category, an object of governmental control, a resource for ensuring the security of the country and the development of the territory. The second concept was that of 'society': an active social subject, a source of resistance to paternalism. Precisely such persistence, in Foucault's opinion, leads a country towards another type of government, one which better matches the interests of a civic society and nation. According to Foucault, a French civil nation has not yet been completely achieved, although the idea of popular sovereignty had been proclaimed two centuries earlier. In Russia, the elite began to proclaim the idea of popular sovereignty not much later than in France: even today, in the second decade of the 2000s, there is still no sign of a civic, political nation or of a state subordinated to the interests of the nation.

According to the Levada Centre, no growth in political self-awareness among the people as a source of power could be observed in Russia: between 2006 and 2015, more than two thirds of the respondents (from 67 per cent to 87 per cent, depending on the year) consistently affirmed that they did not believe that they had any influence on the political or economic life of the country (Levada 2016: 58).[4] In fact, aspirations of realising the principle of popular sovereignty have even declined. To the question 'Should we insist (*zastavit*') that the state must serve our interests?' the share of affirmative answers has decreased by as much as 24 percentage points in a quarter of a century: from 37 per cent in 1999 to 13 per cent in 2015 (ibid.: 64). Moreover, in 2015, when the desire of the Russian public to induce the authorities to act in the interests of the people was shown to be at a minimum, a large majority of respondents (60 per cent) did not harbour any illusions regarding the popular character of the Russian government, seeing it as 'mostly not accountable' or 'not accountable at all' to society (ibid.: 62). Only an absolute minority – 9 per cent of those surveyed – believed that 'Our authorities represent the people; they have the same interests as the common people' (ibid.: 65). A further important indicator of the growth in civic consciousness is also lacking in Russia: the aspiration to participate in the governance of the country. During the ten-year period 2006 to 2015, more than half of those surveyed said they were generally 'reluctant to engage in any contact with the authorities' (ibid.: 61).

With historian Geoffrey Hosking, we can say that in Russia 'state-building obstructed nation-building' (Hosking 1997: xxiv). Hosking was writing about Russia's past, but his statement is also applicable to the present situation. In Russia in the early twenty-first century, the state authorities have been imposing on society an ideology very similar to the doctrine of 'official nationality'. Here the regime is supported by the Moscow Patriarchate of the Russian Orthodox Church, which to a large degree is dependent upon the state. This makes it easier to subjugate Russian society under the authoritarian regime. In Russia we find what Foucault would call a 'population' – not a 'society' interested in controlling the state machine and able to realise its leading role.

Concluding remarks

What is today called 'Russian nationalism' can be described as post-imperial consciousness – with nostalgia for the days of the Empire, resentment and various political phobias. This kind of consciousness is characteristic not only of Russian statists, but is also quite widespread among various ethnic communities in Russia. Moreover, it can be found among adherents of different political views, and among people living in other states generally referred to as belonging to 'the Russian World' (Pain 2016a). This is a passive and, to a large extent, virtual community. The vast majority of its members support the slogan 'Crimea is ours!' They admire the 'polite people' and the Donetsk fighters, and follow their activities on television.

If we compare the number of people who participated in the 2015 Russian March with those who took part in the liberal marches of that year, for instance the march in memory of the liberal activist Boris Nemtsov, killed on 27 February 2015 in downtown Moscow, then it appears that the liberal opposition is more ready for self-organisation than are Russian nationalists. Statism essentially paralyses social activism: civic indifference is compensated by the cult of a strong leader and the myth that the individual person is only 'a grain of sand on the beach', a tiny part of the abstract mass of 'our people'.

The fact that imperial consciousness has no rigid ethnic ties, that it is not transmitted through the channels of cultural tradition but is created under the influence of socio-political conditions, would indicate that a radical reprogramming of such a mass psychology is possible. The incentives for such transformation may come not only after a deep historical trauma, as in Germany after the defeat of Nazism, but also as a result of evolutionary changes, as happened in France. Theoretically, this is also possible in Russia. However, today there are no political forces in the country that could start the deconstruction of the imperial consciousness. On the contrary: we find a continued discrediting of the basic tenets of a civic nation – and that undermines the people's desire for, and faith in, the possibility of society ruling the state.

Notes

1. The article was prepared within the framework of a research project funded by the Russian Science Foundation (RSF No. 15-18-00064).
2. This idea had also exerted a strong influence on Uvarov, and later evolved into the doctrine of the 'special German path' (Ger. *Deutscher Sonderweg*).
3. One example of the latter is the Westerniser Andrei Siniavskii's criticism of another dissident, likewise repressed by Soviet power, Aleksandr Solzhenitsyn, for nationalism, in The New York Review of Books (Sinyavsky and Andreyev Carlisle 1979).

4. Based on the sum of the answers 'probably not' and 'definitely not' to the question: 'Do you have any influence on the political and economic life in Russia?'

Bibliography

Argumenty i fakty (2009), 'OBSE priravnivala stalinizm k fashizmu' [OSCE equated Stalinism with fascism], 6 July, <http://www.aif.ru/society/12131> (last accessed 25 November 2016).
Arutiunian, Iurii, ed. (1992), *Russkie. Etnosotsiologicheskie ocherki* [*Russians: Ethno-sociological Essays*], Moscow: Nauka.
Arutiunian, Iurii, Leokadiia Drobizheva and Aleksandr Susokolov (1999), *Etnosotsiologiia* [*Ethnosociology*]. Moscow: Nauka.
Beliaeva, Galina and Vadim Mikhailin (2014), 'Liubopytnyi i zafiksiruiushii glaz: obraz inostrantsa v sovetskom kino' [Curious and fixed eyes: the image of the foreigner in Soviet cinema], *Otechestvennye zapiski* 4, <http://www.strana-oz.ru/2014/4/lyubopytnyy-i-fiksiruyushchiy-glaz> (last accessed 21 November 2016).
Bromlei, Iulian (1983), *Ocherki teorii etnosa* [*Essays on Ethnicity Theory*], Moscow: Nauka.
'Dissidentskie organizatsii 1950-kh–1980 gg v SSSR' [Dissident organisations in the 1950s–1980s in the USSR] (n.d.), <http://biofile.ru/his/27545.html> (last accessed 25 November 2016).
Drobizheva, Leokadiia, ed. (2009), *Rossiiskaia identichnost' v Moskve i v regionakh* [*Russian Identity in Moscow and the Regions*], Moscow: Institut sotsiologii RAN.
Elkina, Mariia (2015), 'Bol'shinstvo grazhdan schitaiut Rossiiu velikoi derzhavoi' [A majority of citizens consider Russia a great power], *Izvestiia*, 24 March, <http://izvestia.ru/news/584415#ixzz3VcJR7jBX%20stia.ru/news/584415> (last accessed 25 November 2016).
Fateev, Andrei (1999), *Obraz vraga v sovetskom propagande, 1945–1954* [*Image of the Enemy in Soviet Propaganda, 1945–1954*], Moscow: ROSSPEN.
Filippova, Elena (2007), 'Chto takoe Frantsiia? Kto takie frantsuzi?' [What is France? Who are the Frenchmen?], in Valerii Tishkov and Viktor Shnirel'man, eds, *Natsionalizm v mirovoi istorii* [*Nationalism in World History*], Moscow: Nauka, 172–226.
Fomenkov, Artem (2010), *Russkii natsional'nyi proekt: russkie natsionalisty v 1960-ye–pervoi polovine 1990-kh godov* [*The Russian National Project: Russian Nationalists from the 1960s to the first half of the 1990s*], Nizhnii Novgorod: Eksprin.
Foucault, Michel (2003), *'Society Must Be Defended': Lectures at the Collège de France 1975–76*, New York: Picador.
Hosking, Geoffrey (1997), *Russia: People and Empire, 1552–1917*, Cambridge, MA: Harvard University Press.

Kozhanovskii, Aleksandr (2007), 'Ispanskii sluchai: etnicheskie volni i regional'nye utesi' [Spanish cases: ethnic waves and regional cliffs], in Valerii Tishkov and Viktor Shnirel'man, eds, *Natsionalizm v mirovoi istorii* [*Nationalism in World History*], Moscow: Nauka, 227–58.

Kuzmenko, Viktoriia (2016), 'Russkii farsh. Kak poiavilis' i kuda idut rossiiskie natsionalisty' [Russian farce: how the Russian nationalists appeared and where they are headed], Lenta.ru, 20 April, <https://lenta.ru/articles/2016/04/20/nationalism/> (last accessed 25 November 2016).

LDPR (2003), *My za bednykh! My za russkikh* [*We Support the Poor! We Support the Russians*], ldpr.ru, <http://ldpr.ru/ldpr_talks/Party_press/Books/?page=40> (last accessed 25 November 2016).

Levada (2016), *Obshchestvennoe mnenie-2015* [*Public Opinion 2015*], Moscow.

Lipkin, Mikhail (2007), 'Dvadtsat' pervyi vek po Grinvichu: Britaniia v poiskakh postimperskoi identichnosti' [Twenty-first century GMT: Britain in search of a post-imperial identity], in Valerii Tishkov and Viktor Shnirel'man, eds, *Natsionalizm v mirovoi istorii* [*Nationalism in World History*], Moscow: Nauka, 122–43.

Malakhov, Vladimir (2006), 'Sovremennyi russkii natsionalizm' [Contemporary Russian nationalism], in Valerii Kurennoi, ed., *Mysliashchaia Rossiia. Kartografiia sovremennykh intellektual'nykh napravlenii* [*Thinking Russia: Mapping Contemporary Intellectual Trends*], Moscow: Nasledie Evrazii, 141–57.

Manifest Antisovetskoi kolonny na Russkom Marshe [Manifesto of the anti-Soviet column at the Russian March] (2012), Legitimist, 1 September, <http://legitimist.ru/sight/politics/2012/09/manifest-antisovetskoj-kolonnyi-na.html> (last accessed 23 November 2016).

Miller, Aleksei (2012), 'Istoriia poniatiia "natsiia" v Rossii' [History of the concept of 'nation' in Russia], *Otechestvennye zapiski*, 1, <http://magazines.russ.ru/oz/2012/1/m22.html> (last accessed 21 November 2016).

Nazdem.info (2010), 'Konstantin Krylov: "Luchshie demokraty poluchaiutsia iz byvshikh fashistov..."' [Konstantin Krylov: 'former fascists make the best democrats...'], 10 May, <http://ru-nazdem.livejournal.com/836129.html> (last accessed 21 November 2016).

Neef, Christian (2016), 'We are smarter, stronger and more determined', Spiegel Online, 13 July, <http://www.spiegel.de/international/world/interview-with-putin-foreign-policy-advisor-sergey-karaganov-a-1102629.html> (last accessed 21 November 2016).

News2.ru (2009), 'MID RF: Iosif Stalin – antifashist, takoi zhe, kak Ruzvel't i Cherchill' [Iosif Stalin was an anti-fascist like Roosevelt and Churchill], <https://news2.ru/story/181554/> (last accessed 25 November 2016).

Novikov, Sergei (2012), 'Russkie natsionalisty: mezhdu liberalizmom i kommunizmom' [Russian nationalists: between liberalism and communism], *Omskii nauchnii vestnik*, 5: 261–64.

Pain, Emil (2004), *Etnopoliticheskii maiatnik. Dinamika i mekhanizmy etnopoliticheskikh protsessov v postsovetskoi Rossii* [The Etnopolitical Pendulum: Dynamics and Mechanisms of Ethnopolitical Processes in Post-Soviet Russia], Moscow: Institut Sotsiologii RAN.

Pain, Emil (2015a), 'Imperskii natsionalizm: vozniknovenie, evoliutsiia i politicheskie perspektivy v Rossii' [Imperial nationalism: emergence, evolution and political prospects in Russia], *Obshchestvennye nauki i sovremennost'*, 2: 54–71.

Pain, Emil (2015b), 'O reversivnykh protsessakh v razvitii postsovetskoi Rossii' [On reverse processes related to Russia's post-Soviet development], *Terra Economicus*, 13, 3: 97–108.

Pain, Emil (2016a), 'Sovremennyi russkii natsionalizm: dinamika politicheskoi roli i soderzhaniia' [Contemporary Russian nationalism: dynamics of its political role and content], *Vestnik obshestvennogo mneniia*, 1–2: 94–97.

Pain, Emil (2016b), 'The imperial syndrome and its influence on Russian nationalism', in Pål Kolstø and Helge Blakkisrud, eds, *The New Russian Nationalism: Imperialism, Ethnicity and Authoritarianism, 2000–15*, Edinburgh: Edinburgh University Press, 46–74.

Plavskaia, Elena (2016), 'Lavrov obviniaet SShA v agressivnoi rusofobii' [Lavrov accuses the USA of aggressive Russophobia], *Izvestiia*, 9 October, <http://izvestia.ru/news/637177> (last accessed 25 November 2016).

Polian, Pavel (2005), 'Deportatsii i etnichnosti' [Deportation and ethnicity], in Nikolai Pobol' and Pavel Polian, eds, *Stalinskie deportatsii. 1928–1953* [Stalin's Deportations, 1928–1953], Moscow: MFD Materik, 5–19.

Programma Soiuza Russkogo Naroda (1905), *Biblioteka Iakova Krotova*, <http://krotov.info/acts/20/1900/1906anti.html> (last accessed 21 November 2016).

Prosvirnin, Egor (n.d.), 'Tsennosti "Sputnika i Pogroma"' [The values of 'Sputnik i Pogrom'], Sputnik i Pogrom, <http://sputnikipogrom.com/mustread/12442/sp-values> (last accessed 4 May 2015).

Prosvirnin, Egor (2012), 'Molitva russkogo' [A Russian's prayer], Sputnik i Pogrom, 11 August, <http://sputnikipogrom.com/russia/1011/russianpraying> (last accessed 4 May 2015).

Prosvirnin, Egor (2014a), 'Fokusy lzhetsa i evnukha' [The magic tricks of a liar and a eunuch], Sputnik i Pogrom, 17 January, <http://sputnikipogrom.com/history/8307/liberaljuggler> (last accessed 4 May 2015).

Prosvirnin, Egor (2014b), 'Zachem "Sputnik i Pogrom" prodalsia Kremliu?' [Why did 'Sputnik i Pogrom' sell out to the Kremlin?], Sputnik i Pogrom, 28 February, <http://sputnikipogrom.com/russia/9581/lets-work-for-our-supreme-leader-putin> (last accessed 21 November 2016).

Sergeev, Sergei (2010), 'Vosstanovlenie svobody: demokraticheskii natsionalizm dekabristov' [Restoring freedom: the democratic nationalism of the Decembrists], *Voprosy natsionalizma*, 2: 78–118.

Shiropaev, Aleksei (2014), 'Ob Ukraine i istoricheskikh sviaziakh. Russkaia Fabula [About Ukraine and historical ties: the Russian plot], rufabula, 31 January, <https://rufabula.com/articles/2014/01/31/about-ukraine-and-historical-ties> (last accessed 21 November 2016).

Sinyavsky, Andrei and Olga Andreyev Carlisle (1979), 'Solzhenitsyn and Russian nationalism', *The New York Review of Books*, 22 November, <http://www.nybooks.com/articles/1979/11/22/solzhenitsyn-and-russian-nationalism-an-interview-/> (last accessed 21 November 2016).

Slezkine, Yuri (1994), 'The USSR as a communal apartment, or how a socialist state promoted ethnic particularism, *Slavic Review*, 53, 2: 414–52.

Stalin, Iosif (1923), 'Natsional'nye momenty v partiinom i gosudarstvennom stroitel'stve' [National factors in party- and state-building], *Pravda*, 24 March, <http://www.hrono.ru/libris/stalin/5-11.html> (last accessed 21 November 2016).

Stepanov, Sergei (2013), *Chernaia sotnia. Chto oni sdelali dlia velichiia Rossii?* [*The Black Hundreds: What They Did for Russian Greatness*], Moscow: Iauza-Press.

Ziuganov, Gennadii (1994), *Drama vlasti* [*Drama of Power*], Moscow: Paleia.

2
Imperial and ethnic nationalism: A dilemma of the Russian elite

Eduard Ponarin and Michael Komin

Nationalism has recently emerged as a significant issue in Russian politics. The 'Russian Marches', the 2011 ban on the Movement Against Illegal Immigration (*Dvizhenie protiv nelegal'noi immigratsii*, DPNI), the persecution of the organisers of the Combat Organisation of Russian Nationalists (*Boevaia organizatsiia russkikh natsionalistov*, BORN) in 2011–15, and the chain of ethnically motivated riots, from Kondopoga in 2006 to Biriulevo in 2013 – all have made clear the increasing salience of nationalist ideas in Russia. Events after the annexation of Crimea and the Donbas rebellion in eastern Ukraine underscore the importance of the issue and its influence on Russia's domestic and foreign policies. The idea of a larger 'Russian World' transcending today's national boundaries to include the territory of other states inhabited by culturally proximate people has been used to legitimise the decision of the Kremlin to include Crimea and Sevastopol among the constituent territories of the Russian Federation.

In our view, however, the idea of the Russian World and the new Russian nationalism associated with it do not correspond to either of the two standard concepts of 'nation' and 'nationalism' widely applied in contemporary social science (see for instance Calhoun 1993). The 'civic nation' is understood as an 'imagined community', a construct of the nation-state, a political myth aimed at unifying the population of a specific territory into a relatively homogeneous group with boundaries that coincide with the physical territory of that state (Anderson 2006). That idea does not correspond to the concept of the Russian World, which is seen as having wider boundaries than those of the current state. On the other hand, 'ethnic nationalism' is based on the (perceived) historical and cultural background of the people, which results in a more rigid, almost fixed, national self-image expressed in the myth of common descent (Smith 2013). This latter variety of nationalism is close to the rather narrow understanding of the Russian (*russkii*) nation that excludes other ethnic groups in the Federation, the kind of nationalism evident among the socially marginalised supporters of the Russian Marches – but it is at least as distant from the 'Russian World' idea as is the civic concept.

In this chapter we focus on a third concept – that of *imperial nationalism*. In our view, it is better suited for describing the phenomenon that has become particularly strong in Russia since 2014, but was present even earlier. Imperial nationalism combines elements of civic nationalism and ethno-symbolism. Like other varieties of nationalism, imperial nationalism constructs an imagined national community. It holds that the national community is not restricted to the territory of the state; rather, it pursues a more global, extraterritorial understanding of the national community subordinated to foreign policy interests. Compared to ethnic nations, such a community is less focused on common descent. Instead, this kind of nationalism appeals to the imperial past of the nation and creates an inimical image of a geopolitical rival – perhaps another imperial nation – against which its own national identity is formed. Imperial nationalism is thus constructed around a geopolitical myth that rallies and consolidates society on the basis of sharp images of a rival nation, an antagonistic 'Significant Other'. This makes imperial nationalism quite distinct from both civic and ethnic nationalism.

The phenomenon of imperial nationalism is not uniquely Russian: it can be traced in several other states that have experienced the processes of post-imperial transformation. For instance, although post-Ottoman nation-building in Turkey was initially formulated in line with the French model of the civic nation (Lewis 1961), more recent developments there look very much like a case of imperial nationalism. In particular, Şener Aktürk has argued that geopolitical instability in Turkey's neighbourhood and the recent inflow of Sunni migrants are dramatically changing the concept of the Turkish nation (Aktürk 2017).

Before turning to the empirical part of our study, let us clarify some other theoretical assumptions that will be important in our further argumentation. We regard nationalism as an element in a deliberate strategy of social engineering which is often pursued by the state (Tishkov 1993). However, contrary to what is often understood in common parlance, we do not see nationalism as an inherently negative phenomenon. For example, as pointed out by Ernest Gellner, nationalism may serve as a constructive force of modernisation, working to build a new social solidarity in a multi-ethnic state in the wake of the decline of traditional social relations (Gellner and Breuilly 2008).

In many contemporary European nation-states, during the early stages of modernisation, new standardised cultures created by nationalism have allowed former strangers to get along in formal contexts. According to Slavoj Žižek (1989), nationalism, as any other ideology, is a part of the interpretation of the modern world and even a means of existing in it. Nationalism creates a comfortable veil that can protect the individual from direct collision with traumatic realities and forces beyond one's understanding and control. The need for this veil, as pointed out by Max Weber (1968), is sharpened by declining social and material status. When realities become uncomfortable, people feel the acute need for something capable of exalting themselves above others. That 'something' need not be based on any actual or measurable (economic) success: it may also be the intangible feeling of belonging to a high-prestige community with special norms and values.

Furthermore, nationalism is often a central component of state ideology, serving to legitimise the very existence of the state. This function of nationalism gains in importance with the disintegration of traditional society, when the individual's belonging to a particular clan is superseded by belonging to the state. For the government, nationalism becomes particularly relevant as a source of ideological legitimacy in times of social and political turmoil (Hobsbawm 2012).

The collapse of the USSR and the loss of the former Soviet identity – further complicated by the legacy of Soviet ethnic federalism, the need for economic modernisation and the plummeting standard of living – created a widespread *anomie* in Russia. Against this backdrop, the rise of Russian nationalism was almost inevitable. Serious research into this process is particularly important at the current stage as the world is now probably witnessing the final stages of the formative period of what may become a new Russian identity. The Russian identity crisis unleashed by the Soviet collapse cannot last forever. After all, as noted by Weber (1968), it took only one generation of politicians to form a new pan-German identity, with that crucial change taking place between 1848 and 1870.

Although national identity is malleable in its formative stages, it becomes a long-term factor in its own right once it has become firmly established. The current events affecting Russia's national identity today (the annexation of Crimea, Russian participation in the global fight against terrorism on the territory of other states – first and foremost in Syria – and Russia's more resolute defence of its foreign policy interests and extraterritorial national interests) will have massive and lasting consequences. Consider, for instance, the historical case of Germany. Napoleon's France was the enemy when the German national identity was formed – and that determined Franco–German relations for more than a century. The identity choices now being made in Russia are likely to have similarly long-term consequences.

The contemporary Russian developments described above point to a change in the thinking of the Russian elite, in the direction of a more purposeful formulation of imperial nationalism. This change is determined by its sources, its mechanisms of proliferation, the preferences of the elite, and the current challenges presented to it. In the following, we analyse various components of this nationalism.

The history of Russian nationalism: An overview

Throughout much of the history of Russia, Russian nationalism was not very widespread. It originated in the late eighteenth century when Russians realised that, despite the radical Westernisation project of Peter the Great, they could not really hope to catch up with Western Europe (Greenfeld 1995). The disappointment with the West felt by the political and cultural elite of the time stimulated a growing interest in native history, language and traditions. This nationalism also took on an anti-Western character, with the West seen as attractive as a way of life but simultaneously hated because of the lingering feelings of inferiority among Russians in a modernised Russia. Liah Greenfeld, following Nietzsche, has referred to this kind of frustration as *ressentiment* (ibid.).

In the late eighteenth century, nationalism could not become a mass phenomenon since the bulk of Russian society were illiterate peasants who lived locally centred lives, were not familiar with the West, and had little interest in Russian high culture. Even so, for most of the tsarist period the history of Russia was used as an instrument in a policy of a symbolic construction of the nation (Malinova 2012). During this period, the history of the state was consistently written as the history of the Russian people and of the Russian elite. Historians such as Nikolai Karamzin, Vasilii Kliuchevskii and others presented the history of Russia as a 1,000-year continuous development, starting from the mid-ninth century. The concept of the 'Russian people', the protagonists of this narrative, consisted of three elements: the Great Russians (*velikorossy*), the Little Russians (*malorossy*, or Ukrainians) and Belorusians (*belorusy*) (Kliuchevskii 1987–90).

Aleksei Miller, who has studied the Russian nationalism of that period, maintains that Russian nationalists implicitly assumed the existence of two Russias: a smaller one consisting of 'the national core' – the territory which was regarded as the Russian lands proper – on the one hand, and the subjugated territories – Poland, the Baltics, the Caucasus and Crimea – on the other (Miller 2008). The nationalists' belief that the subjugation of these territories was historically justified corresponds well with our views on treatment of the current imperial character of Russian nationalism, as presented in this chapter. Furthermore, as many Western studies of the nationality policy of the Russian Empire have shown (see for example Hosking 1997; Kappeler 2001), the imperial bureaucracy deliberately dispatched Russians from Russia proper and elsewhere to indigenous non-Russian territories, or otherwise facilitated their penetration into these areas.[1] Nevertheless, among the masses, Russian nationalism in the early twentieth century remained weak – as could be seen from the defeat of the nationalist White armies by the more cosmopolitan Red Army after the 1917 Revolution.

At the beginning of the Soviet period, the approach to the 'national question' was determined by the Bolsheviks' attitude towards 'the right of nations to self-determination' and their eagerness to secure support among the native elites in the Soviet periphery. With the policy of *korenizatsiia* (indigenisation), the Soviet state at this stage acquired the features of an 'affirmative action empire' (Martin 2001). *Korenizatsiia* was meant to support or create ethnic elites and to promote the languages and cultures of all the peoples of the USSR – with the exception of the Russians, however. Russians were deliberately left without their own specific national institutions, something which was to affect the further development of Russian nationalism (see Bunce 1999).

By the mid-1930s, Russia's former peasant population had achieved mass literacy and some of their children held college degrees. Ethnic Russians in cities all over the USSR formed the basis for Stalin's industrialisation. The communist ideology undertook a sharp turn toward National Bolshevism and the building of communism in a single country. The policy of *korenizatsiia* was readjusted and streamlined in most ethnic autonomies, although it continued basically uninterrupted in the larger union republics (Slezkine 1994). Soviet propaganda began to foist Russian culture and history on the entire population, now presenting it as something common to all Soviet peoples. As David Brandenberger (2002) has noted, it was precisely at this point that Russian nationalism peaked. It was presented under the guise of 'Soviet patriotism' and was distinguished in the official lexicon from 'the Great Russian chauvinism' which the Bolsheviks had fought against until then.

However, the Stalinist nationality policy should not be mistaken for Russian nationalism. At the time, Russians were encouraged to identify with the broad concept of the USSR rather than with 'Russia' as such. Stalin constructed a Soviet people – and if he borrowed many elements of Russian culture for that purpose, that was hardly surprising, given the sheer numbers of Russians in the USSR: Russians in the Soviet Union served as the imperial glue (Vujacic 2007) that joined and kept together the diverse components of the vast Soviet project. This approach might perhaps be seen as a precursor to the current imperial nationalist project. As Russian identity in the Soviet Union had been associated primarily with the entire USSR, the collapse of that polity left the Russians in a state of identity crisis (Lieven 1998), which in turn led to a quest for a new collective identity, a new Russian nationalism.

The dichotomy of Russian nationalism

The imperial legacy and the Russian elite's growing frustration with the West have contributed to the rise of a new Russian nationalism. Members of the elite maintain a contrast between the Russians and the West – primarily the United States of America – which they negatively identify with as Russia's 'Significant Other'. Anti-Western sentiment – and anti-US in particular – is a common form of negative collective identity, typical of late modernisers in many countries, not only Russia.

This identification is consistent with (the bulk of) the Russian elite's vision of reality. They support the call to restore the equal relations of Russia – as the successor state to the USSR – with the countries of the West; further, they support the formation of a hybrid regime with its own understanding of democratic institutions; and the current shift toward conservative and patriarchal values. Moreover, they can base their support, at least partly, on the widespread anti-US sentiment among the population at large.

The last round in the serial surveys of the Russian elite started by William Zimmerman in 1993 (Zimmerman 2002) registered record-high levels of anti-US sentiment (Rivera et al. 2016). In the survey, the Russian elite is divided into seven subgroups: representatives of the executive power, legislative power, business, state-owned companies, mass media, science/education, and the military. The 2016 sample included 243 respondents, distributed among the seven subgroups.

Figure 2.1 shows that anti-US sentiment among the Russian elite is currently at an all-time high. In addition to the intensification of anti-US feelings in 2016, we can note similar rises registered in 1999 and in 2008 – that is, at times when the confrontation with the United States and NATO had escalated to particularly high levels. A graphic expression of such escalation in 1999 was Foreign Minister Evgenii Primakov's famous order, given when he was en route to the USA, for the plane to turn around and fly back to Russia, in protest against NATO's military actions in Yugoslavia. Similarly, in 2008 there was open military conflict between Russia and Georgia over control over South Ossetia, during which the West, and the USA in particular, openly supported the Georgian side.

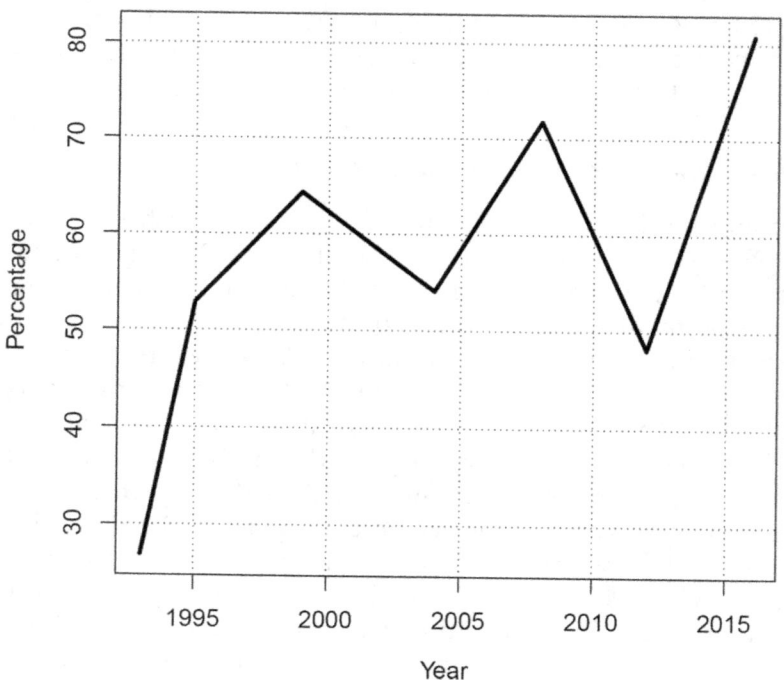

Figure 2.1 Elite's perception of the United States as a threat to Russian security (percentage of respondents who agree that the USA is a threat to Russia)

Russia's reaction to the 2014 revolution in Ukraine, including Russian military involvement in Crimea and in eastern Ukraine, led to confrontation with the West that resulted in economic sanctions and beefing up of NATO forces in Eastern Europe. Because the Russian elite perceives the Ukrainian crisis as caused by the West's desire to prevent Ukraine from participating in Russia's Eurasian project, these events have merely served to reinforce the Russian elite's negative attitudes towards the West in general and towards the USA in particular.

These perceptions are exacerbated by the Russian elite's *ressentiment* – frustration over its failure to Westernise and to be admitted into the club of wealthy and powerful nations. As seen from Moscow, the West's reaction stems from its unwillingness to recognise Russia as an equal power and to take Russia's national interests into serious consideration. Peaceful means failed to bring an equal partnership with the West, so Russia is now relying on military force to make its point. Figure 2.2 shows the recent surge in the share of the elite who displays an imperialist understanding of Russia's national interests, that is, a national interest no longer confined to the current borders of the country.

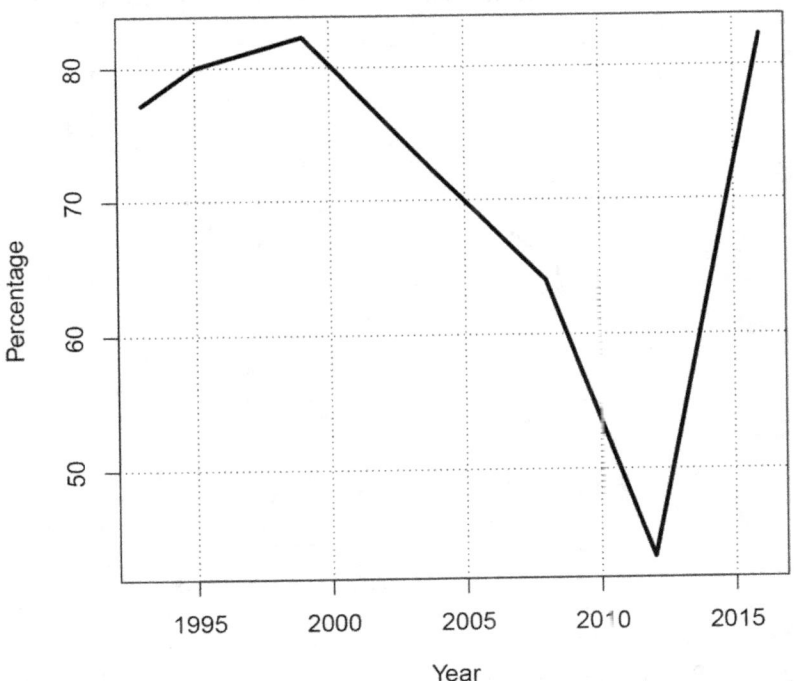

Figure 2.2 Scope of Russia's national interests (percentage of respondents who do not think Russia's interests should be limited to its own territory)

Figure 2.2 shows the recent radical reversal of the long-term trend after the collapse of the Soviet Union towards weaker imperial ambitions. In 2012, most members of the Russian elite had held that Russia's national interests should stop at the state borders. Now, however, the Russian leadership's proactive position on Ukraine and Syria has apparently contributed to a dramatic change. Still, negative perceptions of the United States among the elite are probably at least as important when it comes to explaining this shift.

Interestingly, survey data collected for Richard Rose's New Russian Barometer (NRB) project show that the level of anti-US sentiment among the general population is lower than that found in the elite (based on Zimmerman's surveys) at all points in time (see Figure 2.3).

There are several reasons for the differences in elite and the masses' perceptions. First, frustration with the West had a greater impact on the elite. Although the masses' poverty in the wake of the Soviet collapse was undeniably severe, the elite – who had lost their positions as agents of a superpower – can be said to have suffered no less, in relative terms. Furthermore, due to their greater awareness of international affairs, the elites were more likely to

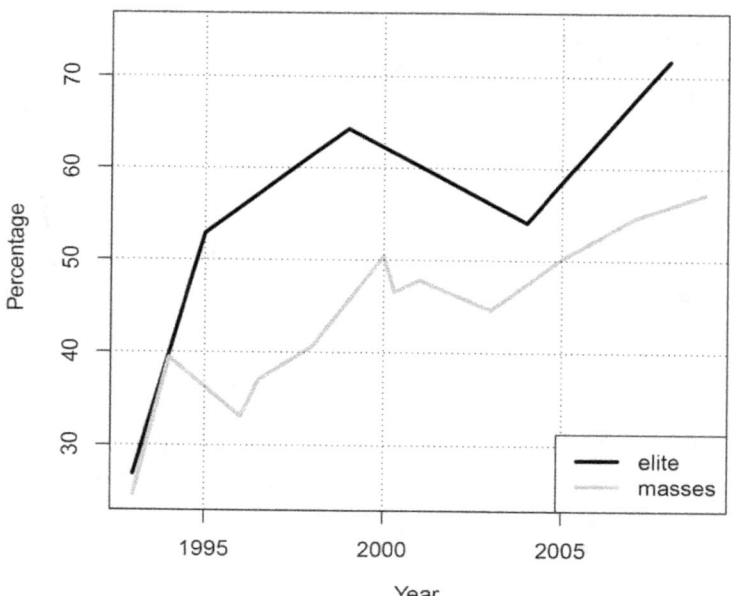

Figure 2.3 Perceptions of the United States as a threat by the Russian elite and population at large, 1993–2009 (percentage of respondents who agree that the USA is a threat to Russian security)

associate the loss of their positions specifically with the United States.

Second, although the elites recognised rather early on that the Westernisation of Russia was failing, the ruling class remained hostage to the pro-Western liberal ideology that had brought them to power. Between 1993 and 1999, they kept reproducing a liberal pro-Western discourse even as they were becoming increasingly frustrated, disappointed and anti-US in their outlook. This is probably why the pace of attitudinal change during this period was greater for the Russian elite than for the masses. The August 1998 financial crisis and the 1999 Kosovo crisis, when Russians felt utterly powerless during the NATO bombardment of Belgrade, made the failure of Westernisation so obvious that public discourse changed quite radically. From 1999 on, the elite and the masses' anti-US sentiments have been in sync.

Third, the elite and the masses may relate to different 'Significant Others'. The masses are somewhat more likely to focus on ethnic neighbours, such as migrants from Central Asia or Russian citizens hailing from the North Caucasus, people whom they encounter and must compete with in their daily lives. By contrast, the elites do not have to compete directly with the migrants. Hence, they are more likely to see the elites of other countries as competitors, foes or friends. This is probably why the elites have always espoused a more anti-US stance than the general public in Russia.

According to data from the Levada Centre, the masses' negative attitudes toward Muslim ethnic groups have become very strong in the course of the past fifteen years.[2] These attitudes are related to violence in the North Caucasus, the influx of Muslim migrants in the central regions of Russia and the financial benefits provided to certain republics within the Russian Federation. At the grassroots level, this economic support has been perceived as a redistribution of resources away from ethnic Russian regions, resulting in mass discontent and nationalist slogans such as 'Stop feeding the Caucasus'.

Importantly, ethnic nationalism among the masses intensifies when anti-US feelings cool down. Conversely, ethnic nationalism subsides at moments of intense disagreement or conflict with the United States, when anti-US sentiment is high (as at the start of the Iraq war in 2003, the Russian–Georgian war in 2008 and during the current Ukrainian crisis).

Indeed, the most significant examples of ethnic unrest in Russia in recent years have coincided with periods of relative calm in

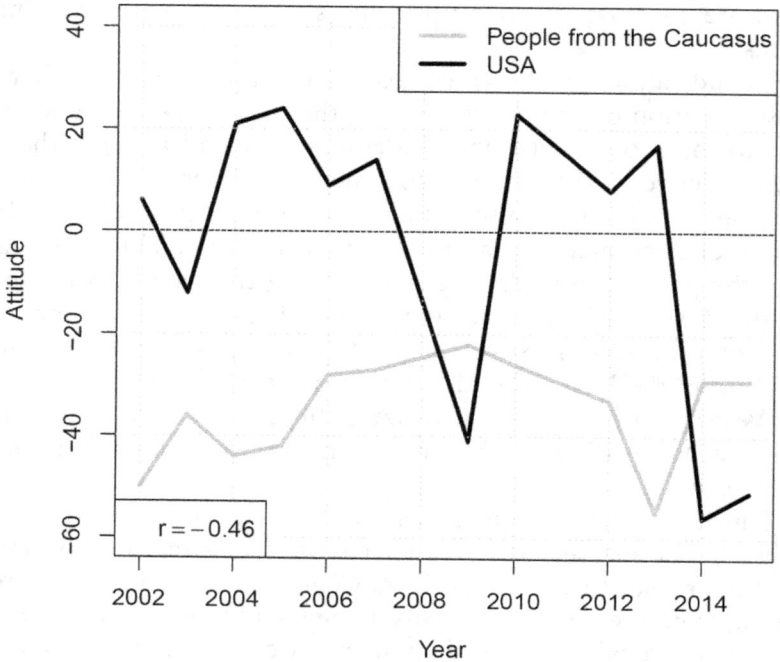

Figure 2.4 Dynamics of the masses' attitudes towards the United States and towards people hailing from the Caucasus (mean responses on a scale from −100 to +100)

US–Russian relations. The major events of ethnic unrest took place in the Karelian city of Kondopoga in 2006, in Manezhnaia Square in Moscow in 2010 and in Moscow's Biriulevo-Zapadnoe district in 2013 – whereas no significant events of this kind took place in 2008, when Russia was fighting against Georgia, or after the start of the Ukrainian crisis in 2014. Figure 2.4 shows the dynamics of the masses' attitudes towards the United States, and towards people hailing from the Caucasus.

Although attitudes toward the United States display considerable variance, we can readily discern a mirror pattern in the two curves. Indeed, the Pearson's correlation coefficient for the two time-series is -0.46, showing that periods of lower anti-US sentiment have coincided with greater anti-Caucasian sentiment.

In our opinion, the negative correlation between ethnic and imperial nationalisms is not a fluke. These two kinds of nationalisms call for diametrically opposing policies domestically and in international relations. For instance, it is hardly possible to pursue Russian projects of Eurasian integration if the Russian populace identifies negatively with Muslims. An anti-Muslim Russian identity does not, however, preclude an alliance with the United States. Conversely, if it is the United States that is the 'Significant Other', then the threat may unite not only the peoples of Russia, but also their neighbours, in an anti-Western coalition.

The choice of the Russian authorities

Before the start of the Ukrainian crisis, the Kremlin's ethnic policy was ambivalent, as it needed to respond to conflicting requests: from elites that had scant taste for ethnic nationalism, and from the masses that did. As a result, the government formulated the idea of an inclusive multi-ethnic nation with a special role reserved for ethnic Russians. This duality can be noted, for instance, in Vladimir Putin's article on 'the national question' published shortly prior to the 2012 presidential elections (Putin 2012).

However, there is in this scheme an essential contradiction that stems from the dichotomy of imperial versus ethnic identities. If Russia were to build an ethnic nation, that would most likely entail strained relations with Muslim and some other minorities within the country, and probably with many former Soviet republics as well. And in such a case, Russia would desperately need the West's benevolence, if not its outright friendship. If, on the other hand, Russia were to opt for an inclusive ('Eurasian') nationalism, that would open up opportunities for post-Soviet integration (to which the West has objected strongly) and would strain Russia's relations with the West.

The Russian authorities were not able to resolve the contradiction between the imperial and the ethnic Russian identities until the events in Crimea and eastern Ukraine. The current crisis can, however, be interpreted as a decision in favour of imperial nationalism – and as a confrontation between Russia understood as an inclusive nation, and the West.

Russian elite perceptions of the United States as a threat and public support for the Russian president are both now up in the 80 per cent range, which would indicate a high degree of national consolidation. Other signs are growing national pride, confidence in political institutions, and general satisfaction and happiness – in spite of economic hardship. The go-ahead for the new imperial nationalism can be used to justify the criminalisation of ethno-nationalist movements, as exemplified by the criminal case brought against the

Combat Organisation of Russian Nationalists and the persecution of the leaders of the *Russkie* (Russians) movement.

This means that we may now see a solution to the dilemma of Russian nationalism that was described by Roman Szporluk at the time of the Soviet collapse: will Russia continue as a multinational empire, or will it become a new nation-state? Szporluk (1989) presciently noted that the Russian bureaucracy might expand its authority beyond the territory of the Russian Federation by playing on ethnic minorities who feel dissatisfied with their situation in the former Soviet republics, now become post-Soviet states.

Our hypothesis that Russia has made a decision in favour of imperial nationalism is corroborated by other research. In her latest book, Agnia Grigas uses the term 're-imperialisation' and interprets the idea behind the 'Russian World' against a long history of support for 'compatriots abroad' (Grigas 2016). She argues that the policy of 're-imperialisation' consists of seven elements or phases: the use of soft power; humanitarian policies; compatriot policies; information warfare; passportisation; protection for Russian-speaking minorities; and finally, annexation (ibid.: 10). The conflict in Ukraine and the annexation of Crimea come as the third example of this chain of events falling under the policy of 're-imperialisation', ultimately leading to actual territorial changes. The two preceding examples were the creation of hot spots in Moldova's Transnistria and Gagauzia regions at the beginning of the 1990s and, in a parallel development, the support to secessionist movements in Georgia's South Ossetia and Abkhazia.

The discourse of imperial nationalism is being employed as an instrument to retain a zone of influence in the former Soviet space. Taking advantage of ethnic or civil conflict in post-Soviet states, the Russian government seeks to prevent these states from escaping Russia and joining the EU or NATO. In addition, the Russian re-imperialisation project exploits the economic weakness of these neighbouring countries, legitimising the powers-that-be as the stability of Russia contrasts favourably against the situation in other former Soviet states.

Our empirical analysis highlights the development of imperial nationalism as distinct from ethnic or civic nationalism. It confirms a hypothesis previously set forth by Emil Pain, with his theory of an imperial syndrome gripping contemporary Russia (Pain 2006). Imperial nationalism makes it possible to solve various urgent political problems while also securing stability for the current political regime. It is therefore probably a deliberate choice of the Russian elite. After all, Russian anti-US sentiment emerged among the elite before it did at among the masses. The elite deliberately promotes the development of anti-US sentiment and anti-Westernism in the masses' consciousness by means of the state-controlled media, thereby also muffling ethnic tensions. The preconditions for such a policy were in place thanks to the 'decomposition of the imperial body', nostalgia for the Empire and the imperial syndrome (ibid.: 301) – sentiments that are widespread not only among the Russian elite but also among the population at large.

Under the conditions of imperial nationalism and the policy pursued by the Russian state today, relations between the elite and the active nationalist groups in the country seem set to remain complicated. The traditional Russian Marches split into two separate events in 2015 and 2016 (Dozhd' 2016). The schism followed attitudes towards the conflict in Ukraine: some nationalist groups endorsed the imperial nationalism and the Russian Spring (*Russkaia vesna*) movement, whereas other groups refused to support the actions of Russian soldiers in Crimea and held on to the discourse of ethnic nationalism. However, both groups of Russian nationalists have taken care to keep their distance from the Russian authorities: the first group because the Kremlin has stopped actively supporting the insurgents in Southeast Ukraine and has failed to bring the patriotic surge in these territories to the desired ending; and members of the second group because they blame the Kremlin for having started the war in Donbas, a war they see as a fight between 'fraternal peoples' (Kolstø 2016). The Kremlin's relations with these groups bring to the fore the contradictions inherent in the political course that Russia's current leadership associates with imperial nationalism – although, as yet, this course seems to have generally been popular among both the elite and the population at large.

Concluding remarks

In addition to the general surge of anti-US sentiment in Russia since 2014, other factors that favour the imperial scenario should also be taken into consideration. First, ever since the start of the Russian actions in Crimea in 2014, Russian media have continued to promote a very clear narrative – and one that resonates well with the audience – about the West's subversive interventions in Ukrainian politics in 2013 in deliberate opposition to Russian interests. Most Russians see Ukraine as their backyard, if not as a room in their own house. Their interest in the Ukrainian crisis (fuelled and sustained, of course, by the state-controlled media) is by far more deeply engrained than, for instance, was the excitement aroused in connection with the Russo–Georgian War in 2008. The consequences are therefore also likely to last longer.

Second, the recent Russian intervention in Syria, which has in effect thwarted US plans to topple the Assad regime, further strengthens the Russian imperial identity. This show of force has served to demonstrate the growing capabilities of the Russian military, which in turn allows Russia to project its power well beyond its borders in defence of its own national interests. Consequently, Russians can again perceive their country as a great power.

Third, Russia's great-power politics has made ethnic divisions *within* the country less salient. Russian citizens from the North Caucasus have fought for the rebel republics in eastern Ukraine. The leader of the Chechen Republic, Ramzan Kadyrov, has repeatedly declared that he and his people are ready to fight against Islamic militants beyond the borders of Russia. Indeed, there is nothing that can unite a people like having a common enemy.

The process of creating a *rossiiskii* (ethnically inclusive Russian) nation was given new impetus in October 2016 when President Putin endorsed the proposal for drafting a law on the *rossiiskaia natsiia* (civic Russian nation) (for further details, see Yuri Teper's chapter in this volume). Such a law may send the Russian nationality policy back in the direction of a civic nation by 'channelling' the imperial discourse and imperial nationalism into a narrower territorial framework. Thus, it might contradict other efforts undertaken by the Russian elite geared towards promoting imperial nationalism. On the other hand, the new initiative does not necessarily preclude further imperial advances – although it will certainly further curb ethnic Russian nationalists. In fact, it may well prove to be another logical step in strengthening the imperial national identity.

In the current situation, with politics taking a conservative turn both in Europe and in the United States, imperialism may take on yet another quality: as further tool for the Kremlin to use in foreign affairs. The conservative, anti-globalist, patriarchal and traditional values that accompany Russia's imperial nationalism may enhance trust in the Russian authorities among some segments of European and US societies – ranging from nationalists and socialists to more traditional conservatives – who have become disillusioned with their own governments and who feel that the political parties, groups and elites that are supposed to represent their interests now treat them with intolerable neglect instead (see Murray 2013).

Russia's emerging new ideology is filling much of the void left by the collapse of the communist system and the communist worldview. Its main purpose is to rally the country's population across ethnic, social and political cleavages, but it may also manage to win some allies and sympathisers in other countries. The Kremlin's current political course enjoys solid support from the masses as well as the elite. Time will show whether it will prove solid enough to cope with the many challenges presented by the current economic crisis and geopolitical competition – but it does appear to have been a successful political strategy thus far. Moreover, as this political course coincides in time with the final stages of the post-Soviet formative period, it is likely to have long-lasting consequences, within the Russian Federation as well as internationally.

Notes

1. Later, these Russian diaspora groups were in some cases to become an instrument of expansion of the Russian World beyond the existing borders of the Russian state, providing the basis for a policy of 'supporting compatriots abroad'.
2. Data from various Levada surveys made between 2001 and 2016, available on <http://www.levada.ru/> (last accessed 20 December 2016).

Bibliography

Aktürk, Şener (2017), 'Post-imperial democracies and new projects of nationhood in Eurasia: transforming the nation through migration in Russia and Turkey', *Journal of Ethnic and Migration Studies*, 43(7): 1101–20.
Anderson, Benedict (2006), *Imagined Communities: Reflections on the Origin and Spread of Nationalism*, London: Verso.
Brandenberger, David (2002), *National Bolshevism: Stalinist Mass Culture and the Formation of Modern Russian National Identity, 1931–1956*, Cambridge, MA: Harvard University Press.
Bunce, Valerie (1999), *Subversive Institutions: The Design and the Destruction of Socialism and the State*, Cambridge: Cambridge University Press.
Calhoun, Craig (1993), 'Nationalism and ethnicity', *Annual Review of Sociology*, 19: 211–39.
Dozhd' (2016) 'Ne russkii marsh: na kakuiu aktsiiu natsionalisty vyidut v Liublino' [Not the Russian March: for what do the nationalists rally in Lyublino], 1 November, <https://tvrain.ru/teleshow/vechernee_shou/ne_russkij_marsh-420198/> (last accessed 14 December 2016).

Gellner, Ernest and John Breuilly (2008), *Nations and Nationalism*, Ithaca, NY: Cornell University Press.
Greenfeld, Liah (1995), *Nationalism: Five Roads to Modernity*, Cambridge, MA: Harvard University Press.
Grigas, Agnia (2016), *Beyond Crimea: The New Russian Empire*, New Haven, CT: Yale University Press.
Hobsbawm, Eric J. (2012), *Nations and Nationalism since 1780: Programme, Myth, Reality*, Cambridge: Cambridge University Press.
Hosking, Geoffrey A. (1997), *Russia: People and Empire, 1552–1917*, Cambridge, MA: Harvard University Press.
Kappeler, Andreas (2001), *The Russian Empire: A Multiethnic History*, London: Routledge.
Kliuchevskii, Vasilii (1987–90), *Sochineniia v deviati tomakh* [*Writings in Nine Volumes*], Moscow: Mysl'.
Kolstø, Pål (2016), 'Crimea vs. Donbass: how Putin won Russian nationalist support – and lost it again', *Slavic Review*, 75, 3: 702–25.
Lewis, Bernard (1961), *The Emergence of Modern Turkey*, Oxford: Oxford University Press.
Lieven, Anatol (1998), 'Lord Salisbury: a model for aspiring imperialists', *The National Interest*, 53: 75–84.
Malinova, Ol'ga (2012), 'Simvolicheskaia politika: kontury problemnogo polia' [Symbolic policy: the contours of the problem], in Ol'ga Malinova, ed., *Konstruirovanie predstavlenii o proshlom kak vlastnyi resurs* [*Construction of Notions of the Past as a Power Resource*], Moscow: INION RAN, 5–16.
Martin, Terry D. (2001), *The Affirmative Action Empire: Nations and Nationalism in the Soviet Union, 1923–1939*, Ithaca, NY: Cornell University Press.
Miller, Alexei (2008), *The Romanov Empire and Nationalism: Essays in the Methodology of Historical Research*, Budapest: Central European University Press.
Murray, Charles (2013), *Coming Apart: The State of White America, 1960–2010*, New York: Crown Forum.
Pain, Emil (2006), 'Imperiia v sebe: o mekhanizmakh vozvratnykh protsessov v sovremennoi rossiiskoi politike' [An empire in itself: on mechanisms of return processes in contemporary Russian politics], *Ab Imperio*, 1: 293–327.
Putin, Vladimir (2012), 'Rossiia: natsional'nyi vopros' [Russia: the national question], *Nezavisimaia gazeta*, 23 January, <http://www.ng.ru/politics/2012-01-23/1_national.html> (last accessed 14 December 2016).
Rivera, Sharon Werning, James Bryan, Brisa Camacho-Lovell, Carlos Fineman, Nora Klemmer and Emma Raynor (2016), *The Russian Elite 2016: Perspectives on Foreign and Domestic Policy*, <https://www.hamilton.edu/documents/russianelite2016final.pdf> (last accessed 14 December 2016).

Slezkine, Yuri (1994), 'The USSR as a communal apartment, or how a socialist state promoted ethnic particularism', *Slavic Review*, 53, 2: 414–52.
Smith, Anthony D. (2013), *Nationalism and Modernism*, New York: Routledge.
Szporluk, Roman (1989), 'Dilemmas of Russian nationalism', *Problems of Communism*, 38, 4: 15–35.
Tishkov, Valerii (1993), 'Etnichnost', natsionalizm i gosudarstvo v post-kommunisticheskom obshchestve' [Ethnicity, nationalism and the state in post-communist society], *Voprosy sotsiologii*, 1–2: 3–38.
Vujacic, Veljko (2007), 'Stalinism and Russian nationalism: a reconceptualization', *Post-Soviet Affairs*, 2, 2: 156–83.
Weber, Max (1968), *Economy and Society: An Outline of Interpretive Sociology*, New York: Bedminster Press.
Zimmerman, William (2002), *The Russian People and Foreign Policy: Mass and Elite Perspectives, 1993–2000*, Princeton, NJ: Princeton University Press.
Žižek, Slavoj (1989), *The Sublime Object of Ideology*, London: Verso.

3

Kremlin's post-2012 national policies: Encountering the merits and perils of identity-based social contract

Yuri Teper

During Putin's third presidential term we have witnessed an unprecedented official preoccupation with identity issues. It has been unrivalled both in the intensity with which the images of Russian national identity were communicated to the public by the authorities and by the specificity of these images. This chapter analyses the Kremlin's changing attitudes towards nationalism since 2012, particularly focusing on the post-2014 period. The described changes are analysed against two primary factors: the regime's efforts to sustain popular legitimacy through concluding a new social contract and the grassroots' perceived need for a more articulated national identity. The analysis suggests an emerging dilemma for the regime between the Russo-centric and great-power elements of Russian national identity.

I first briefly discuss challenges related to national self-determination and self-identification in post-Soviet Russia, presenting the Kremlin's pre-2012 approach to handling the national issue. I then describe how an existing social demand for a more pronounced national identity coupled with Russia's new post-2012 social contract led the Kremlin to take an active and unprecedentedly bold stand in the national identity discourse. Thereafter I examine the changes that took place in the official representation of Russianness during Putin's third presidency. Finally, I discuss the limitations and pitfalls encountered of employing identity as the main base for the regime's legitimacy.

The chapter argues that since 2012 the Kremlin's handling of the national issue has undergone a twofold change: first, the authorities' mobilisation strategy shifted from a reactive approach towards a proactive and initiating mode aimed at seizing firm and complete control over the nationalist agenda. Second, official identity discourse became profoundly national in its orientation, and was significantly ethnicised, up until the when the Kremlin felt the danger of being taken hostage by its own propaganda and the nationalist discourse it had unleashed. Accordingly, after mid-2014 the Kremlin shifted to a more traditional, though greatly amplified, statist great-power discourse, which in turn revealed its own limitations. This has left the Kremlin with newly reconfigured frames of possible identity discourses and dilemmas regarding potential sources of legitimacy.

Russia's national issue and the changing social contract

The Russian Federation was not a product of a demand for national self-determination for its citizens, but the unintended outcome of the economic and administrative collapse of the Soviet system (Cohen 2004: 473–75). During the first years of independence Russia was not much more than the leftover core of the former Soviet state and was not in its essence a nation-state. Consequently, the dissolution of the Soviet Union plunged many Russians into a deep and prolonged identity crisis. Although the newly emerged Russian state had a solid ethnic Russian majority, the combination of ethnic Russians and Russian-speaking minorities being stranded in the neighbouring post-Soviet countries, the existence of ethnic minorities within the new state, and Russia's heavy imperial heritage complicated the task of defining and delimiting the would-be nation (Hosking 1998; Rowley 2000).

The liberal politicians who led the perestroika and Russia's early democratisation efforts did not come up with any meaningful national vision beyond the idea of economic reform and a general need to politically and socially emulate the West (Brudny and Finkel 2011). Eltsin's initial uncertain steps towards forming a civic Russian nationhood later evolved into an equally uncertain quest for a 'national idea' that ended with a gradual shift towards a more familiar national-patriotic direction (Smith 2002). However, the question regarding the nature of the newly emerged Russian state remained unanswered throughout the 1990s, and the country continued to drift between the concepts of an ethnic Russian nation-state and an inclusive civic model.

When Vladimir Putin came to power against the background of the 1998–99 economic and security crises, he seized the opportunity by effectively proposing to Russian citizens a comforting nostalgic statist great-power vision (Laruelle 2009: Ch. 5). However, in national terms this vision was rather vague and inconclusive. Therefore, statist patriotism (*derzhavnost'*) was being increasingly supplemented by Russia's traditional juxtaposition against the 'West', mainly the US. The latter helped to position Russia globally as a major world power and a unique civilisation (Levkievskaia 2005: 179–81; Szaszdi 2008: 9–14; Lucas 2009).

Putin's domestic national policies can be described as 'purposefully ambiguous' (Shevel 2011) and reactive. The Kremlin inconsistently combined civic, ethnic and even some imperial components of Russian identity, without fully committing to any of them. State-patriotism was appropriated as the main vehicle of political mobilisation, while ethnic issues were mainly perceived as an obstacle to societal cohesion and a threat to public order that had to be situationally addressed.

When racially motivated violence grew in the mid-2000s, Putin pushed for more restrictive legislation and repressive policies against the radicals, steps that significantly lowered right-wing violence (Rutland 2010: 127; Laruelle 2013: 2–4). In the field of mainstream politics, radical nationalist and chauvinist expressions were not allowed. Vladimir Zhirinovskii tempered his previously chauvinistic rhetoric, while the electorally successful Motherland (*Rodina*) party was disbanded in 2006 as a result of its nationalist and xenophobic stance. Until 2012 Putin personally was extra careful to adhere to the politically correct inclusive vision of Russianhood and refrained from referencing the ethno-national discourse. For example, he used only the politically correct 'anti-ethnic' term *rossiiskii* to refer to the nation, in contrast to the popularly more common, ethnically connoted *russkii* (Rutland 2010: 122; Malinova 2012: 84–86).

Though Russia's state-aligned media mostly promoted the same image of inter-ethnic patriotic unity, occasionally they were employing ethno-Russian motives aimed at indulging Russian ethno-national sentiments (Hutchings and Tolz 2015: 51–52). The authorities handled the growing grassroots Russian ethno-nationalist and xenophobic movements with extreme caution, while largely denying the existence of a significant inter-communal problem (Teper and Course 2014). For the time being, this policy enabled the Kremlin to maintain broad public appeal without the need to fully confront the highly controversial national issue. Nevertheless, while suppressed and temporarily overshadowed by economic growth and a newly found social stability, the question of Russian national identity remained essentially unresolved.

Underneath the surface, a deteriorating security situation caused by Islamist violence and a growing non-Slav migration to Russia's core regions was gradually widening the gap between the official reluctance to openly address the national issue and the increasingly ethno-cultural popular perception of Russian nationhood (Teper and Course 2014). A steadily growing number of ethnic clashes occurring all across Russia drew widespread public attention and quickly radicalised nationalist discourse. In this respect the major 2010 Manezhnaia Square nationalist riot that took place just outside the Kremlin's walls was a watershed event, which signalled that the social prominence of the issue and the challenge it posed to official nation-building efforts could no longer be ignored.

Furthermore, nourished by the above-mentioned grassroots processes, between 2010 and 2014 a new brand of Russian ethnocentric non-imperial nationalism formed and gradually gained weight (Laruelle 2013: 3; Emil Pain's chapter in this volume). As part of this trend radical nationalist figures such as Konstantin Krylov and Vladimir Tor adopted more democratic rhetoric, while the liberal opposition increasingly drew on nationalist rhetoric. The latter is embodied in the concomitant rise of the national democrat Aleksei Navalnyi and the noticeable nationalisation of the agenda promoted by veteran liberal politician Boris Nemtsov. The national democratic rapprochement became particularly evident when the nationalists took active part in the 2011–12 anti-government protests. Thus, nationalism was not only gaining in potential to destabilise Russia's inter-communal and interregional relations, but also posing a direct threat to the regime.

The system-loyal opposition parties were the first to capitalise on the growing popular demand for a more Russo-centric approach. The 2011 parliamentary election campaign became saturated with ethnically laden appeals. Even the Communist Party could not resist the temptation to run under such an ambiguous slogan as 'Protect ethnic Russians! Revive the fraternity of the peoples!' (*Zashitim russkikh! Vozrodim druzhbu narodov!*) Mounting national pressure from below, which in the course of the campaign was combined with a strong anti-establishment dissent, forced the Kremlin to launch a swift reaction. After years of sitting on the fence, the Kremlin now reinvented itself as an active and initiating player in the field of nationalism. Importantly, this turned out not merely to be a situational campaign manoeuvre, but a fundamental change in the establishment's approach to nationalism.

The strategic nature of this move was related to the regime's underlying sources of legitimacy. Until 2012 the informal social contract between Putin's regime and society had been based on an exchange of political compliance for guarantees of relative economic prosperity, accompanied by a 'strong patriotic consolidation' (Auzan 2009; Makarkin and Oppenheimer 2011). Therefore, when after 2008 the regime started to fail to deliver on its economic promises, it began losing popularity. The 2011–12 protests against electoral fraud in the aftermath of the State Duma elections forced the regime to alter the terms of the social contract. Through its control over the main media and mainstream public discourse, the Kremlin refocused public expectations on the identity aspect of the contract (Gazeta.ru 2014; Auzan 2015; Kolesnikov 2015) and on protecting the population against allegedly rising acute threats to the nation.

The ethno-conservative turn: The Pussy Riot affair and 'morality politics'

In order to comply with the new, self-imposed social contract, the Kremlin embarked on a more active and radicalised identity-based mobilisational strategy, aiming to fully appropriate the national cause. To neutralise potential challenges to the officially promoted visions of Russianness, the Kremlin sought to eliminate competing identity narratives and their proponents from the public sphere. The official preoccupation with identity first became evident with the publication of Putin's lengthy election campaign article dedicated to the 'national question' (Putin 2012). The depth of officialdom's concern with the subject revealed itself at a 2013 state-backed Valdai Discussion Club session fully dedicated to exploring Russia-related identity issues and declaratively aimed at 'defining a competitive identity for Russia'.[1]

At the onset of the 2011 campaign in October, President Dmitrii Medvedev had already demanded from 'all political forces … to refrain from playing the nationalist card and exacerbating xenophobic sentiments' (Kremlin.ru 2011). Putin's above-mentioned article, published in January 2012, acknowledged some of the popular reproaches voiced against immigrants and openly described ethnic Russians (*russkie*) as Russia's 'state-forming people' (Putin 2012). Although some observers have argued that the article is 'eclectic', 'obscure' and highly 'inconsistent', and therefore add little clarity to the issue (Malinova 2012), it unprecedentedly employed the terminology of Russian nationalism, hitherto unacceptable for Russia's top officials. Putin strongly denounced the idea of 'building an ethnic Russian "national" mono-ethnic state', but the intended symbolic accent was transparent to all (Malinova 2012: 85).

Furthermore, as part of his presidential campaign Putin added such nationalistic public figures as the painter Ilia Glazunov and the economist Sergei Glazev, co-founder of the Rodina party, to his supporters' list. Dmitrii Rogozin, former leader of the Rodina party, was appointed deputy prime minister. And at the campaign rally in the Luzhniki stadium on 23 February 2012, nationalist imperial flags were waved while Putin ritualistically proclaimed the unity of the 'Russian multi-national people'. In his speech at the event, which was symbolically held on the Defender of the Fatherland Day, Putin called for the defence of Russia from domestic subversive foreign-oriented forces (RIA 2012).

The so-called Pussy Riot affair formed the immediate backdrop to this call and constituted a turning point in the official identity politics, as well as in Kremlin's reshaping of state–society relations. The controversial anti-Putin punk performance in the Cathedral of Christ the Saviour on 21 February 2012 was used by the authorities to launch a furious campaign aimed at consolidating all patriotic forces of Russian society (labelled 'Putin's majority') around the regime. At the same time, the anti-government protesters were presented as socially marginal yet dangerous, subversive Western agents. In this way the Pussy Riot affair was used by the Kremlin to 'strengthen public support for its policies', in large by modelling 'the Russian nation as ethnically and religiously homogeneous' (Yablokov 2014: 622).

Although 'Putin's majority' was not outwardly defined in ethnic terms, the campaign publicly installed the Russian Orthodox Church and the Orthodox faith as *the* foundation of Russian nationhood and the state (Hutchings and Tolz 2015: Ch. 8). This implied an unprecedented ethnicisation of the official identity discourse. The ethnic appeal was aimed at Russia's nearly 80 per cent self-described Christian Orthodox majority, for whom Orthodoxy served primarily as an ethnic and cultural marker of their Russianness (Burgess 2009: 7–8).[2] Although by 2012, Putin and the authorities had for several years increasingly associated themselves with the Russian Orthodox Church (Malashenko and Filatov 2012), the Pussy Riot affair discursively established its official paramount status.

After Putin's successful re-election and pro-government Russo-centric mobilisation, the anti-Pussy Riot campaign, which threatened to alienate Russia's ethnic and religious minorities, particularly the Muslims, was curtailed and then terminated by autumn 2012. Instead, the emphasis of the Kremlin's conservative 'morality politics' shifted to a more general – and domestically unifying – direction (Sharafutdinova 2014). The focus on ethnically connoted Christian Orthodoxy was partially relaxed in favour of a more inclusive agenda that positioned Russia as a world champion of traditional core values, confronting the danger arguably posed by the degenerative Western liberalism.

This stance was most boldly manifested in Putin's 2013 Valdai speech (Putin 2013), where he declared that 'many Euro-Atlantic countries have moved away from their roots', specifically from their 'Christian values', which suggested a 'direct path to degradation', 'primitivisation' and 'profound demographic and moral crisis'. Moreover, this liberal agenda was allegedly 'aggressively imposed all over the world'. Contemporary Europe was stigmatised, ridiculed and labelled as the hotbed of moral and societal degradation, which according to the official narrative particularly manifested itself in the accommodation of the lesbian, gay, bisexual and transgender (LGBT) agenda.

Domestically this morality politics resulted in adopting a series of new restrictive laws, including banning the adoption of Russian children by citizens of the US and other Western countries, the 'Dima Iakovlev law' (2012); banning 'gay propaganda', which in practice meant excluding all gay-related subjects from the public discourse (2013); toughening up the punitive measures associated with insulting the religious feelings of citizens (2013); and banning the use of profane language (2014). The conservative campaign also spurred the intimidating, officially backed activity of various 'moral crusaders' among politicians and conservative 'social activists'. Irina Iarovaia from the United Russia Party and especially Elena Mizulina from A Just Russia are, for example, known for their role in formulating conservative and restrictive legislation, while Minister of Culture Vladimir Medinskii actively propagated conservative-patriotic values. Among the many conservative 'grassroots' activists that have suddenly emerged in the post-2012 era, the pro-Kremlin patriotic-Orthodox biker Aleksandr Zaldostanov, also known as 'Khirurg' ('the surgeon'), rose to the status of a semi-official ideological figure. And Dmitrii Enteo (Tsorionov) and his grouping God's Will (*Bozh'ia volia*) enjoyed the authorities' tacit support in sabotaging LGBT events, rock performances, theatrical productions and art exhibitions that in their view offended the Church and the believers' feelings. Importantly, in contrast to past practices, a major concern of the regime has become to directly and indirectly control the cultural sphere and tasking it with instilling ultra-patriotic, militantly conservative and isolationist values (Jonson 2016).

Thus, while the conservative 'morality politics' initially was meant to provide a moral response to the public outcry over the pervasive corruption of the ruling establishment (Rutland 2014: 580), in the longer run it created a societal atmosphere and legal pretext that were used to further curtail the personal and political freedoms of Russian citizens. It also provided Putin's anti-Westernism with a previously missing ideological backing, with which he could counter the Western liberal-democratic appeal and produce a familiar 'rally-around-the-anti-Western-flag' effect. Finally, the morality politics' universal claim favourably positioned Russia as a major global player set on a noble mission of protecting the world's traditional moral-cultural pillars. This in turn contributed to Russian national self-esteem and the regime's popularity at home. Indeed, whereas according to Putin regaining the status of a geopolitical superpower might be still beyond Russia's reach (RBK 2016), claiming the role of a world moral leader made propagandistic sense and was perfectly in line with Russia's historical tradition.

The ethno-national appeal: The anti-immigrant campaign and the annexation of Crimea

After the Kremlin had consolidated popular support for the continuation of the political status quo, done away with the liberal opposition and claimed absolute monopoly over the identity discourse, it proceeded to take control over part of the agenda of the increasingly popular non-systemic nationalists. Thus, while the authorities' initial conservative, Russo-centric turn capitalised on the popular craving for a more pronounced Russian identity and a latent anti-Western sentiment, the Kremlin's next move was aimed at taking advantage of anti-immigrant and Russian ethno-nationalist sentiments. Eventually, this made it possible to neutralise the ethno-nationalist subversive potential.

The anti-immigrant issue was approached first. Seemingly this happened on the Kremlin's own initiative; the anti-immigrant campaign was not triggered by any particular incident and included fully staged or pre-planned media events. Up until this point – with the brief exception of the 2006 anti-Georgian campaign that entailed the extradition of several thousand Georgian citizens – the official rhetoric on migration issues had remained within the bounds of the politically correct. In May 2012, however, Russian television embarked on an anti-immigrant campaign that was aimed not only against Muslim newcomers from Central Asia and the South Caucasus, but also internal migrants originating in Russia's own North Caucasian republics. The latter was particularly striking, as it essentially marked some Russian citizens as outsiders.

During the campaign, news and talk shows aired calls to close Russia's borders with the Central Asian states, allegedly to avoid the spread of crime, illnesses and cultural backwardness. At the same time internal migration from the North Caucasus to Russia's core regions was portrayed as an 'invasion' fraught with devastating consequences for the 'indigenous [ethnically Russian] population' (Tolz and Harding 2015: 452, 473). In contrast to previous coverage, migration and inter-ethnic issues in Russia were no longer positively contrasted to the situation in Europe, but shown as a common problem (although liberal incompetence in handling migration was still highlighted) (Tolz and Harding 2015: 469–70). The call for a need to preserve Europe's and Russia's traditional character effectively linked the immigrant issue to the parallel conservative discourse.

During the 2013 Moscow mayoral elections, even the Kremlin-backed candidate, Sergei Sobianin, chose to focus his campaign on the issue of illegal immigration. Sobianin was running against Aleksei Navalnyi, who was well known for his critical stance on the subject. Devoid of much concrete content, Sobianin's campaign to a significant degree consisted of demonstrative actions taken against Moscow's various immigrant groups and untypically firm declarations on the need to fight illegal immigration (Arkhipov and Kravchenko 2013; Golosov 2014: 240; Malakhov 2014: 1075). Sobianin's campaign by far outdid Navalnyi's in its emphasis on the migration issue, thus marking an unprecedented official endorsement of the anti-immigrant agenda (see Helge Blakkisrud and Pål Kolstø in this volume).

The anti-immigrant campaign stoked Russia's already existing inter-ethnic tensions and greatly contributed to the outburst of a wave of high-profile inter-ethnic clashes in the fall of 2013. The peak was reached in October with Moscow's Biriulevo riots (Laruelle 2013: 3; Maloverian 2013). The danger of a full-fledged inter-communal anti-establishment conflict now seemed real and, accordingly, the anti-immigrant campaign was swiftly aborted.

Although inter-communal violence was halted, the campaign had introduced xenophobe appeals into mainstream politics, and Putin was faced with a tough dilemma: he could stick to the anti-immigrant agenda and authorise at least some of the practical measures associated with it, such as introducing a visa regime for several Commonwealth of Independent States (CIS) countries or adopting a new approach to Russia's North Caucasian republics. Alternatively, to preserve Russia's aspirations for regional leadership and domestic status quo, he would have to cede the anti-immigrant issue to the opposition. However, soon a new opportunity for a powerful ethno-nationalist (and seemingly internally safer) outward-looking mobilising appeal presented itself in the form of the Ukrainian crisis. The Ukrainian adventure, which the Kremlin probably believed it could get away with internationally, indeed relieved it from the need to solve the anti-immigrant dilemma – but simultaneously presented Russian authorities with new threats and challenges.

The issue of Russian national unification, whether through annexation of territories or repatriation, had not been an important part of Russia's domestic or foreign policy agenda. On the contrary, the Kremlin had pushed the issue of unification of ethnic Russians to the margins of the political discourse (Zvelev 2008; Shevel 2012; Malakhov 2014). The official ethno-national irredentist identity discourse that developed around the Ukrainian crisis therefore substantially departed from all previous practice.

Russia's case for unification with Crimea was based on a claim of having a moral obligation to actively support and protect *russkie* brethren beyond Russia's borders, and, subsequently, the need to unite the divided *russkii* people in one state. Remarkably, this classical ethno-national rhetoric and the nearly exclusive use of the ethnically laden word '*russkii*' to refer to the Russian nation were universally adopted by the official media and Russia's top officials, including the hitherto cautious Putin (Teper 2016).

Putin's 18 March speech celebrating Russia's 'unification' with Crimea (Putin 2014a) represents a hallmark of officialdom's endorsement of Russian ethno-nationalism. In this speech, Putin stressed Crimea's predominantly *russkii* population, described the peninsula as 'native *russkii* soil' and compared Crimea's unification with Russia to the unification of the divided German nation in 1989. Putin's use of the term *russkii* did not go unnoticed. On the Channel One's *Politika* talk show, the nationalist commentator Egor Kholmogorov stressed that *russkii* was used twenty-nine times, contrasting this with the usual two or three references in Putin's previous speeches (*Politika* 2014a). This led Kholmogorov to triumphantly conclude that 'Putin has de facto announced the birth of a real *russkii* nation-state'. Given the overall tenor of the official rhetoric at the time, this was not necessarily a far-fetched exaggeration or a nationalist's wishful thinking. In the heydays of the Crimea events, Russia was all but explicitly proclaimed as the nation-state of the ethnic Russians.

A few of the regime's last remaining red lines of national ambiguity were still preserved. In most instances when the term *russkii* was used in official propaganda or by the Kremlin's officials, it was not explicitly explained. The vagueness undeniably imparted a blood/ethnicity meaning to official identity discourse (Laruelle 2015: 126), but most often the context in which the word was used nevertheless conveyed a more lingua-cultural sense of Russianness. *Russkie* were referenced as a community of native Russian speakers, people who adhere to a certain set of culturally conditioned historical myths. For example, among the main triggers behind Russia's actions in Crimea, Putin mentioned Ukraine's attempts 'to deprive *russkie* [in Ukraine] of their historical memory, and sometimes even of their native language' as tools of Ukrainian 'forced assimilation' (Putin 2014a). The *Politika* talk show similarly aired an outcry from Denis Pushilin, the head of the self-proclaimed Donetsk People's Republic, and the above-mentioned Kholmogorov, on no less than a lingua-cultural 'ethnocide' of Russians allegedly taking place in eastern Ukraine (*Politika* 2014b).

It is likely that such a relatively inclusive definition of Russianness, that – using Blakkisrud's (2016: 265) distinction could be described as 'Russo-centric' rather than purely 'ethnic' – owes to the fact that during the Crimean crisis, Russianness was primarily defined in contrast to the Ukrainians, who like the Russians are both Slav and mostly Christian Orthodox. Hence, whereas a more distant Other might have led to a more exclusive national definition, at this stage there was little sense in highlighting blood descent or religion in order to characterise Russian nationhood. Even this implied lingua-cultural national formula favoured the nation's Slavic core, and therefore essentially relegated Russia's other ethnic and religious groups to a second-class status. Still, the vagueness in the definition of *russkie* along with the neo-Slavophil civilisational motifs that were sometimes employed to reference the nation helped to soften the overall radical ethnicisation of the official discourse.

The Slavophil motifs, so dominant in Putin's 2012 article on the national question (see Yanov 2012), were now largely sidelined or put at the service of *russkii* nationalism. Indeed, during the Crimea events the Russian nation replaced the state as the main focal point of the official identity construction. Russia was shown as undergoing an internal rebirth that entailed the realisation of its national self, which, in the words of talk show host Vladimir Solovev (*Voskresnyi vecher* 2014) consisted of the 'way of life', 'culture', 'language' and 'faith' of the *russkie*. This internal makeover was supposedly the factor that allowed Russia to regain its national dignity and true sovereignty versus the West during the Crimea crisis.

The official rhetoric generally conveyed that Russia emerged out of this crisis as an unprecedentedly consolidated and spiritually strong nation. The alienated minority of oppositionists was labelled 'national traitors' and a 'fifth column' by both Putin (2014a) and the state-controlled media (*Vesti nedeli* 2014; *Voskresnoe vremia* 2014). Thus 'Putin's majority' was now extended to all patriotically oriented members of society, remaining passive sceptics and non-systemic nationalists included. Support for Putin was identified with the support for Russia, and vice versa.

As could be noticed from Solovev's description of the Russian national 'self' cited above, the ideas of the conservative morality campaign were not fully abandoned, but sometimes reappeared as secondary elements in the ethno-national discourse. In the same vein, religious motifs were sometimes used to highlight Russia's historical links to Crimea, particularly in connection with the revival of the legend that Prince Vladimir, the purported founder of the Russian state and baptiser of Rus, was baptised in Crimea. Based on this, Putin in his 2014 annual address to the Federal Assembly described Crimea as 'sacred' to the Russian people in the same way as the Temple Mount is for the Muslims and Jews (Putin 2014b). Furthermore, in the midst of the Ukrainian crisis, after Russia's involvement in Eastern Ukraine had already been exposed by international media and experts, Russia's Foreign Minister Sergei Lavrov echoed Putin's 2013 Valdai speech: Western antagonism to Russia was explained by Russia's return to the Orthodox faith and the West's detachment 'from its own Christian roots' and insistence on imposing its worldview on others (Interfax 2014).

After fighting broke out in Eastern Ukraine in late April 2014 and it became evident that events there would not follow the smooth Crimean scenario, the Kremlin stopped referring to Donetsk and Luhansk as *russkie*, as it initially had done (these regions had together with Crimea been labelled *Novorossiia*, literally 'New Russia'). Thus, the Kremlin discursively withdrew Russia's ethno-national claims to Eastern Ukraine. It is logical to assume the change was meant to avoid creating public expectations of Russia intervening in the fighting or annexing embattled fraternal *russkie* territories, as Russian hardcore ethno-nationalists demanded (Laruelle 2015). Besides, a change in the official rhetoric was also needed to calm down Russia's closest allies, Belarus and Kazakhstan, who due to their significant Russophone populations saw themselves as potential next victims of Russia's new pretentions. All factors combined, by late spring of 2014 an unmistakable change had taken place in Moscow's course.

A statist retreat? From the Ukrainian affair to the intervention in Syria

In May 2014, the Kremlin openly distanced itself from the Novorossiia project by opposing Crimean-style referenda on the status of the two rebellious Eastern Ukrainian regions. Towards the end of the month, when addressing the St Petersburg Economic Forum, Putin did not even mention Novorossiia or any other issues pertaining to the unity of the Russian people (Baunov 2014). Although Russia carried on clandestinely supporting the separatist forces and Russian television continued with its close coverage of the fighting, in both official rhetoric and the state-aligned media a national focus on the Ukrainian events was dropped in favour of a more geopolitically dominated outlook: the new Ukrainian regime was demonised and the danger of Ukraine falling under full Western domination highlighted. As a result, henceforth among the Russian public an anti-American framing started to predominate in the understanding of the conflict in Ukraine (Cottiero et al. 2015: 534–35).

The rationale for the annexation of Crimea continued to be framed in ethno-national terms, while in general Russian–Ukrainian national differences were downplayed and blurred (see Kremlin.ru 2014; Putin 2014b; 2015). As compared to the previous discourse this new position ironically undermined the rationale for Russia's further territorial annexations. Those, mostly non-systemic, nationalists who did not comply with the new change in the official discourse and who continued to push for Russian action in Ukraine and unequivocal support for the Novorossiia project were persecuted.

In June 2014, the well-known leader of the radical Eurasianist movement, Aleksandr Dugin, who during the Crimea events had enjoyed increased media attention, was fired from his position as Chair of Sociology of International Relations at the Moscow State University after voicing demands for the killing of all perpetrators of 'the atrocities in Ukraine' (*Vedomosti* 2014). In light of the changing policy toward Ukraine, his radical calls were probably considered too extreme. Reactions against other, less servile nationalists, soon followed. In October, Egor Prosvirnin, the editor of the influential nationalist website Sputnik i Pogrom announced that he had been interrogated by the police for disseminating extremist messages (Grani.ru 2014). Prosvirnin attributed this to his tough criticism of the Kremlin's reluctance to seize control over the entire Southern and Eastern Ukraine. Nearly a year later his house was searched on allegations of incitement of hatred – again in his opinion because of his uncompromising stance on Novorossiia (Kozyrev 2015).

Similarly, in October 2014, Aleksandr Belov (Potkin), the former leader of the Movement Against Illegal Immigration (*Dvizhenie protiv nelegal'noi immigratsii*), was arrested, and later, in 2016, sentenced to 7.5 years in jail for extremist activity, incitement of hatred and money laundering (Vasilchenko 2016). Belov's associates linked his arrest to his refusal to assist Russian security services in their attempts to get rid of Russian ultranationalists by inducing them to fight on the pro-Kievan side in Ukraine, so as to discredit them at home (Tumanov 2014). Another prominent nationalist, Dmitrii Demushkin, conversely claimed that the reason for Belov's prosecution was the nationalists' overall refusal to support the authorities' clandestine efforts to mobilise volunteers to fight against the Ukrainian forces in Donbas, and the Kremlin's fear of a nationalist–liberal alliance (Nekhezin 2016).

In 2016 Demushkin, who since 2014 had been arrested numerous times, stated that 'the political movement of Russian nationalists was crushed by the security services on the orders of the Kremlin' (Volchek 2016). He described the movement's dire condition: 'Everybody is jailed, the organisations are closed, the media have stopped writing [about us]. . . . Nowadays there is no major city [in Russia] where the leaders of the nationalists would not be jailed' (Sheremet'eva 2016).

By seizing the ethno-nationalist agenda from the anti-system nationalists and cracking down on their organisations, Putin tried to clear the entire political field of any potential rivals, aspiring to become the sole representative of the Russian nationalist cause. Suppressing the nationalists also allowed the authorities to neutralise any potential public criticism directed at the swift curtailing of the ethno-irredentist agenda. The Kremlin made it abundantly clear that it was the only actor authorised to employ nationalist appeals, as well as to decide *when* and *how* to apply such appeals. By late 2015, after this task seemingly had been accomplished, however, the Kremlin decided it was time to retreat to the familiar safety of great-power statist mobilisation, and to reorient the public agenda towards international affairs.

As noted above, both the domestic and international pitfalls of employing a strong ethno-national appeal quickly became clear to the Russian authorities. Moreover, polls showed that since mid-2015 the Russian public was losing interest in the Ukrainian issue (Levada 2015; FOM 2015). In other words, the mobilising potential of the

Crimea events was exhausting itself. Hence, the Russian intervention in the Syrian civil war became the new focus of identity-based mobilisation: the operation was used to yet again readjust the identity discourse to the changing political circumstances and the regime's current needs.

The discourse that was developed around the Russian operation in Syria conveyed a clear great-power, anti-Western message. Whatever it lacked in national accent, it strived to compensate for with dramatic images and maximalist rhetoric. As one commentator noted, the Syrian operation was 'Russia's first American-styled' war (Li 2016). It was very 'American' in its military aspects, and no less in its media component. Real-time footage of precision bombardment by Russian planes, and pictures of Russian cruise missiles shot from a distance at assumed terrorist targets were repeatedly broadcast on Russian TV, thus referencing familiar images of US overseas operations. These imagery associations were aimed at demonstrating Russia's cutting-edge military and a technological might, appropriate for a first-rank global power.

According to Putin's initial declarations on the operation's rationale (*Vremia* 2015), as well as subsequent Russian media broadcasts, by taking on the Islamic State (IS) Russia was both addressing its own potential problems with home-grown Islamists and taking care of an acute global threat. The fact that by then the IS has gained an extreme media prominence both in Russia and worldwide turned Russian actions in Syria into a highly prestigious and noble mission, which was further framed by intense patriotic bravado and anti-Westernism. The official media bragged unrestrainedly about Russian achievements in fighting the IS and contrasted them with US incompetence and maliciousness. Hence, in Syria Russia ostensibly stood up to not only the Islamic terrorists but also to US global hegemony. Kremlin propagandist Sergei Markov expressed the general spirit of the argument on Russia's Channel One *Politika* talk show, when saying that 'for the US, Russia is a much more formidable enemy than ISIS' and that Americans 'are afraid that in Syria the rebirth of Russia as a great power will take place' (*Politika* 2015).

This great-power discourse was mainly aimed at boosting Russian national pride, but accentuating geopolitical anti-Westernism also helped in defining Russian identity within the constraints of a non-ethnic discourse. After standing up to US expansionism in Crimea, the televised show-off of Russia's achievements in the prestigious Middle Eastern arena was intended to upgrade Russia to the status of a truly global power, one which in certain aspects were superior even to the USA. This inclusive non-ethnic discourse formally aligned with the government's promise to safeguard Russian society against alleged arising security threats and the enhanced identity component that was part of Russia's post-2012 social contract.

The new great-power discourse resembled pre-2012 statist patriotism, but the turnaround was incomplete. Above all, in order to satisfactorily compensate for the lack of a meaningful definition of 'the nation', the outside threat and anti-Westernism elements of the message had to be greatly amplified in comparison to what had been the case with statist patriotism. Additionally, as before, elements of the previous identity formulations were ingrained in the currently predominating rhetoric. In the Syrian case, these were religion-based and therefore ethnically connoted. For example, on the eve of the operation, Dmitrii Kisilev's weekly news programme featured an item that accentuated Western indifference to the tragic plight of Middle Eastern and particularly Syrian Christians (*Vesti nedeli* 2015). The next weekend, Semen Bagdasarov, the in-house Middle East expert of Vladimir Solovev's talk show, explained Russia's deep commitment to Syria by Russia's predominately Christian Orthodox character, which allegedly turned Syria into Russia's 'holy land' (*Voskresnyi vecher* 2015).

Despite its mostly non-divisive character and substantial public support, the Syrian operation failed to attract significant attention among the Russian public (Levada 2016a). Hence, not surprisingly, Putin tried to scale down Russian involvement, first in March 2016 and then, after a new period of intensified activity, in December 2016, after the conclusion of yet another ceasefire. Whatever the eventual fate of this latest 'withdrawal', the situation poses the question of what possible future moves the Kremlin might take to sustain its identity-based legitimacy.

Summing up: A 'trial and error' approach to nationalism

The new, identity-based post-2012 social contract led the Russian regime to continuously present society with new formulations of national identity. The main manifestation of these agendas was discursive, channelled through the state-controlled media. Throughout the period in question, the identity subjects and emphases were constantly changed. One possible explanation for this may be that the Kremlin wanted to avoid pursuing – or at least only partially implement – the policies prescribed by the presented agendas.

Second, the frequent changes in the official identity discourse can also be explained by the need to retain the attention and emotional involvement of the Russian public with the Kremlin's predominately media-based identity campaigns. Since the campaigns were virtually devoid of any meaningful popular participation or governmental actions, the audience quickly grew weary and bored with each new promulgated theme. This tendency could be seen in the popular assessment of the current state of affairs in the country, which soared around the height of each of the described campaigns, but then returned closer to its previous level after several months at the most (Levada 2016b). The above-mentioned figures on the level of popular attention to the Ukrainian events and the Syrian operation similarly support this proposition.

Finally, the seemingly erratic tactic can also be related to the desire to sideline all nationalist alternatives to the official identity discourse. In contrast to its more 'democratic' English analogue, the Russian proverb suggests that one should lead rather than just join those whom you cannot beat (*Ne mozhesh borot'sia, togda vozglav'*). This was exactly the Kremlin's approach to the nationalist challenge during Putin's third presidency. The Kremlin capitalised on nationalist issues that posed potential threats to its rule, diverted the chosen agendas in its favour and then did away with the neutralised opponents – only, as for now, to return to the comfort zone of a renewed version of great-power patriotism.

This tactic fits the broader historical pattern depicted by Emil Pain in his contribution to this volume. However, the establishment's success may not be as definite and complete as it might seem at first glance. History teaches us that this tactic worked well for a long time in tsarist Russia and the Soviet Union, but in the end both regimes nevertheless failed spectacularly. Though the Kremlin's main national competitors were defeated during Putin's third presidency, in the future pro-regime identity mobilisation will have to be performed against a backdrop of worsening economic conditions and narrowing agenda options.

Most underlying challenges essentially persist. Some have even been aggravated. The problems related to Russian national identification as well as inter-communal tension have not been resolved, only temporarily overshadowed by the Crimean and Syrian events. The deteriorating economy is likely to dampen the appeal of pursuing great-power external agendas, and revive domestic, xenophobic and Russo-centric sentiments, which in the meantime have been further exacerbated and legitimised by the official propaganda.

Furthermore, despite the remarkable receptiveness of the Russian public to the changing agendas, gaining sufficient levels of mobilisation by reusing old messages while at the same time largely refraining from acting upon these agendas might turn out to be extremely difficult. To achieve previous levels of mobilisation, messages would have to be radicalised and become more concrete, and inconvenient actions would have to be taken to support the credibility of the official message. For example, convincingly applying ethno-national or anti-immigrant agendas without taking substantial actions over time on these subjects would be extremely difficult. Therefore, despite having achieved discursive hegemony, during the next legitimacy crisis the Kremlin may be deprived of some of the vital manoeuvring space related to identity discourse. And as the Kremlin has learnt during the period in question, consistently applying specific identity formulation (any identity formulation) for political mobilisation inevitably entails acute costs and threats to the regime.

Hence, the Kremlin faces a serious dilemma, which it most probably is aware of but still is unsure how to tackle. Putin's October 2016 enigmatic suggestion to introduce a law that would define the civic Russian nation (*rossiiskaia natsiia*) may be part of a search for a solution. Experts' assessments on the nature of the initiative vary. Some, like Professor Valerii Solovei, contend the proposal is aimed at uniting the people under a civic nationhood model in response to 'noticeable signs of emerging cleavages in the masses' and the 'anxiety' of the latter (BBC 2016a). Others, like Aleksei Chesnakov, director of the Centre for Current Politics, and Kirill Martynov from the Higher School of Economics, see the initiative in the light of approaching presidential elections as 'cementing' the support of the conservative electorate or, conversely, mobilising the whole public under the 'national unity' banner (BBC 2016b).

Based on an analysis of the writings by one of the initiative's authors, Viacheslav Mikhailov, Konstantin Gaaze (2016) speculates that under the proposed new law the concept of the 'Russian nation' will be reformulated as a sort of inclusive, albeit Russo-centric community. At the same time, Gaaze points out that such a move will require significant constitutional amendments and could endanger society's stability. He thus wonders whether the Kremlin's real interest in the initiative is constitutional reform. Aleksandr Verkhovskii suggests three simultaneously possible rationales behind the proposal: intra-governmental bureaucratic struggles for power; the Kremlin's desire to reassert its current overarching yet Russo-centric national vision; and the authorities' plans for making a 'symbolic [propagandist] act to strengthen the political unity of the nation against its enemies' in the West, devised to sustain post-Crimea patriotic outburst (Verkhovsky 2016).

The subsequent lack of public discussion of the initiative's contents and goals lead to the puzzlement of the expert community. The authorities' disoriented work on the law project (Gorodetskaia 2016) may testify to the Kremlin's uncertainty about what course the official identity politics should take.[3] Replacing the current social contract by a profound change in the regime's promise of securing the nation against acute threats or changing the contract's identity component may require substantial changes to the Russian political system.

Notes

1. Email from the organisers of Valdai conference to the participants ahead of the 2013 forum.
2. By 2009, only 50 per cent of Russians considered themselves to be religious (and just 7 per cent said that religion was 'very important' to them). When asked which institutions should shape their moral values, only 4 per cent mentioned the Church (Burgess 2009: 7–8).
3. In March 2017, the working group preparing the draft law announced that due to 'society's unpreparedness to accept the idea of a unified nation' uniting all nationalities, it was decided to drop the reference to the *rossiiskaia natsiia*. Instead, it would move forward with a law 'On the fundamentals of state nationality policy' (Gorodetskaia 2017)

Bibliography

Arkhipov, Ilya and Stepan Kravchenko (2013), 'Putin's men targeting migrants as Moscow mayor race heats up', Bloomberg.com, 15 August, <https://www.bloomberg.com/news/2013-08-14/putin-s-men-crackdown-on-migrants-as-moscow-mayor-race-heats-up> (last accessed 11 December 2013).

Auzan, Alexander (2009), 'Dynamics of a social contract', *Russia in Global Affairs* 2, <http://eng.globalaffairs.ru/number/n_13026> (last accessed 27 November 2015).

Auzan, Aleksandr (2015), 'Lovushka "kolei"' [The track trap], GAIDPARK Summer Discussions School, <http://www.colta.ru/articles/society/8428> (last accessed 15 November 2015).

Baunov, Aleksandr (2014), 'Pochemu Putin sdast Donbass. No na etom ne konchitsia' [Why Putin is giving up the Donbas. But this is not over], Slon, 27 May, <http://slon.ru/world/pochemu_putin_sdast_donbass-1103680.xhtml> (last accessed 10 May 2015).

BBC (2016a), 'Politolog Valerii Solovei: vlasti Rossii komprometiruiut poniatie patriotizma' [Political scientist Valerii Solovei: Russian authorities compromise the concept of patriotism], 1 November, <http://www.bbc.com/russian/features-37353946> (last accessed 17 January 2017).

BBC (2016b), 'Komu nuzhen "zakon o rossiiskoii natsii"' [Who needs the 'law on the Russian nation'], 1 November, <http://www.bbc.com/russian/features-37834616> (last accessed 15 January 2017).

Blakkisrud, Helge (2016), 'Blurring the boundary between civic and ethnic: the Kremlin's new approach to national identity under Putin's third term', in Pål Kolstø and Helge Blakkisrud, eds, *The New Russian Nationalism: Imperialism, Ethnicity and Authoritarianism, 2000–15*, Edinburgh: Edinburgh University Press, 249–74.

Brudny, Yitzhak M. and Evgeny Finkel (2011), 'Why Ukraine is not Russia: hegemonic national identity and democracy in Russia and Ukraine', *East European Politics and Societies*, 25, 4: 813–33.

Burgess, John P. (2009), 'Orthodox resurgence: civil religion in Russia', *Religion in Eastern Europe*, 29, 2: 1–14.

Cohen, Stephen F. (2004), 'Was the Soviet system reformable?', *Slavic Review*, 63, 3: 459–88.

Cottiero, Christina, Katherine Kucharski, Evgenia Olimpieva and Robert W. Orttung (2015), 'War of words: the impact of Russian state television on the Russian Internet', *Nationalities Papers*, 43, 4: 533–55.

FOM (2015), 'Interes k sobytiiam na Ukraine: monitoring' [Interest in the events in Ukraine: monitoring], <http://fom.ru/mir/11929> (last accessed 30 December 2016).

Gaaze, Konstantin (2016), 'Leviafanu ne snilos: chem mnogonatsional'nyi narod meshaet rossiiskoii natsii' [Leviathan couldn't even imagine: how a multinational people stands in the way of the Russian nation], Carnegie.ru, 3 November, <http://carnegie.ru/commentary/?fa=65029> (last accessed 16 January 2017).

Gazeta.ru (2014), 'Svoboda i kolbasa v obmen na Krym' [Freedom and sausage in return for Crimea], 31 March, <http://www.gazeta.ru/comments/2014/03/31_e_5970485.shtml> (accessed 25 November 2015).

Golosov, Grigorii V. (2014), 'The September 2013 regional elections in Russia: the worst of both worlds', *Regional & Federal Studies*, 24, 2: 229–41.

Gorodetskaia, Natal'ia (2016), 'Zakon o rossiiskoi natsii spuskaiut na regional'nyi uroven'' [The law on the Russian nation descends to the regional level], *Kommersant*, 16 December, <http://kommersant.ru/doc/3171483> (last accessed 6 January 2017).

Gorodetskaia, Natal'ia (2017), 'Edinstvo natsiia ne vyderzhalo kritiki' [The unity of the nation could not stand the criticism], *Kommersant*, 7 March, <http://www.kommersant.ru/doc/3235995> (last accessed 21 March 2017).

Grani.ru (2014), '"Sputnik i Pogrom": FSB proveriaet nas na ekstremizm ['Sputnik i Pogrom': FSB interrogates us for extremism], 3 October, <http://grani.ru/Society/Law/m.233626.html> (last accessed 22 June 2015).

Hosking, Geoffrey (1998), 'Can Russia become a nation-state?', *Nations and Nationalism*, 4, 4: 449–62.

Hutchings, Stephen and Vera Tolz (2015), *Nation, Ethnicity and Race on Russian Television: Mediating Post-Soviet Difference*, London: Routledge.

Interfax (2014), 'Zapad otdaliaetsia ot Rossii iz-za ee vozvrata k pravoslaviiu, schitaet Lavrov' [The West is moving away from Russia because of its return to Orthodoxy, Lavrov thinks], 5 June, <http://www.interfax-religion.ru/?act=news&div=55525> (last accessed 2 September 2014).

Jonson, Lena (2016), 'Post-Pussy Riot: art and protest in Russia today', *Nationalities Papers*, 44, 5: 657–72.

Kolesnikov, Andrei (2015), 'Putin thrives on Russian passivity', *Newsweek*, 4 November, <http://www.newsweek.com/putin-thrives-russian-passivity-321066> (last accessed 7 December 2015).

Kozyrev, Makar (2015), 'U sozdatelia "Sputnika i Pogroma" proveli obysk po povodu ekstremizma' [The creator of 'Sputnik i Pogrom' was searched because of extremism], *MK*, 17 September, <http://www.mk.ru/social/2015/09/17/u-sozdatelya-sputnika-i-pogroma-proveli-obysk-po-povodu-ekstremizma.html> (last accessed 20 December 2016).

Kremlin.ru (2011), 'Vstrecha s rukovodstvom Soveta Federatsii' [A meeting with the leadership of the Federation Council], 17 October, <http://kremlin.ru/news/13073> (last accessed 24 October 2012).

Kremlin.ru (2014), 'Vserossiiskii molodezhnyi forum "Seliger–2014"' [The 'Seliger–2014' All-Russian Youth Forum], 29 August, <http://kremlin.ru/events/president/news/46507> (last accessed 15 May 2015).

Laruelle, Marlene (2009), *In the Name of the Nation*, New York: Palgrave Macmillian.

Laruelle, Marlene (2013), 'Anti-migrant riots in Russia: the mobilizing potential of xenophobia', *Russian Analytical Digest*, 141: 2–4.

Laruelle, Marlene (2015), 'The Ukrainian crisis and its impact on transforming Russian nationalism landscape', in Agnieszka Pikulicka-Wilczewska and Richard Sakwa, eds, *Ukraine and Russia: People, Politics, Propaganda and Perspectives*, Bristol: E-International Relations Publishing, 123–28.

Levada (2015), 'Rossiisko-ukrainskie otnoshenia v zerkale obshestvennogo mneniia' [Russian–Ukrainian relations in the mirror of the public opinion], 5 October, <http://www.levada.ru/2015/10/05/rossijsko-ukrainskie-otnosheniya-v-zerkale-obshhestvennogo-mneniya-sentyabr-2015/> (last accessed 27 November 2016).

Levada (2016a), 'Siriiskii konflikt' [The Syrian conflict], 31 October, <http://www.levada.ru/2016/10/31/sirijskij-konflikt/> (last accessed 29 December 2016).

Levada (2016b), 'Iiulskie reitingi odobrenia i doveria' [July ratings of approvement and trust], 27 July 2016, <http://www.levada.ru/2016/07/27/iyulskie-rejtingi-odobreniya-i-doveriya-7/> (last accessed 1 February 2017)

Levkievskaia, Elena (2005), 'Russkaia ideia v kontekste istoricheskikh mifologicheskikh modelei i mekhanizmi ikh obrazovaniia' [The Russian idea in the context of historic mythological models and the mechanisms of their formation], in Mariia Akhmetova, ed., *Sovremennaia rossiiskaia mifologiia* [*Contemporary Russian Mythology*], Moscow: Izdatelskii tsentr RGGU, 175–206.

Li, Robert (2016), 'Voennye aspekty rossiiskoi operatsii v Sirii' [Military aspects of the Russian operation in Syria], *Nezavisimoe voennoe obozrenie*, 15 January, <http://nvo.ng.ru/wars/2016-01-15/8_aspects.html> (last accessed 22 November 2016).

Lucas, Edward (2009), *The New Cold War: Putin's Russia and the Threat to the West*, New York: Palgrave Macmillan.

Makarkin, Alexei and Peter M. Oppenheimer (2011), 'The Russian social contract and regime legitimacy', *International Affairs*, 87, 6: 1459–74.

Malakhov, Vladimir S. (2014), 'Russia as a new immigration country: policy response and public debate', *Europe–Asia Studies*, 66, 7: 1062–79.

Malashenko, Aleksei and Sergei Filatov, eds (2012), *Pravoslavnaia tserkov pri novom patriarkhe* [*The Orthodox Church Under the New Patriarch*], Moscow: Carnegie Moscow Center.

Malinova, Olga (2012), 'Simvolicheskoe edinstvo natsii?' [Symbolic unity of the nation?], *Pro et Contra*, 16, 3: 76–93.

Maloverian, Iurii (2013), 'Pogrom v Biriulevo: protiv migratsii i protiv vlastei' [The pogrom in Biriulevo: against migration and against the authorities], BBC, 14 October, <http://www.bbc.co.uk/russian/society/2013/10/131014_biryulyovo_aftermath_ comments.shtml> (last accessed 23 December 2014).

Nekhezin, Viktor (2016), 'Turemnyi srok Potkina sochli mest'iu za otkaz voevat v Donbasse' [The imprisonment of Potkin was considered as retaliation for refusing to fight in the Donbas], BBC, <http://www.bbc.com/russian/features-37177481> (last accessed 10 December 2016).

Politika (2014a), 18 March, <http://www.1tv.ru/shows/politika/vypuski/politika-1-chast> (last accessed 15 May 2015).

Politika (2014b), 23 April, <http://www.1tv.ru/shows/politika/vypuski/politika-vypusk-ot-23-04-2014> (last accessed 15 May 2015).

Politika (2015), 14 October, <http://www.1tv.ru/shows/politika/vypuski/politika-vypusk-ot-14102015> (last accessed 28 December 2016).

Putin, Vladimir (2012), 'Rossiia: natsionalnyi vopros' [Russia: the national question], *Nezavisimaia gazeta*, 23 January, <http://www.ng.ru/politics/2012-01-23/1_national.html> (last accessed 17 April 2015).

Putin, Vladimir (2013), 'Zasedanie mezhdunarodnogo diskussionogo kluba "Valdai"' [Session of the international Valdai discussion club],

Kremlin.ru, 19 September, <http://kremlin.ru/news/19243> (last accessed 9 October 2014).

Putin, Vladimir (2014a), 'Obrashchenie Prezidenta Rossiiskoi Federatsii [Message of the President of the Russian Federation], Kremlin.ru, 18 March, <http://kremlin.ru/events/president/news/20603> (last accessed 10 April 2015).

Putin, Vladimir (2014b), 'Poslanie Prezidenta Federal'nomu Sobraniu' [Address of the President to the Federal Assembly], Kremlin.ru, 4 December, <http://kremlin.ru/events/president/news/47173> (last accessed 10 May 2015).

Putin, Vladimir (2015), 'Vladimir Putin: my v Rossii vsegda schitali, chto russkie i ukraintsy – odin narod' [Vladimir Putin: in Russia we have always considered that Russians and Ukrainians are one people], *Kommersant*, 18 March, <http://www.kommersant.ru/doc/2689175> (last accessed 11 May 2015).

RBK (2016), 'Putin nazval SShA edinstvennoi sverkhderzhavoi' [Putin called the USA the only superpower], 17 June, <http://www.rbc.ru/politics/17/06/2016/5763fd629a79474315e898d7> (last accessed 16.12.2016).

RIA (2012), 'Vystuplenie Vladimira Putina na mitinge v Luzhnikakh' [Vladimir Putin's speech at a rally in Luzhniki], 23 February, <https://ria.ru/vybor2012_putin/20120223/572995366.html> (last accessed 15 January 2017).

Rowley, David G. (2000), 'Imperial versus national discourse: the case of Russia', *Nations and Nationalism*, 6, 1: 23–42.

Rutland, Peter (2010), 'The presence of absence: ethnicity policy in Russia', in Julia Newton and William Tompson, eds, *Institutions, Ideas and Leadership in Post-Soviet Russia*, Houndmills: Palgrave Macmillan, 116–36.

Rutland, Peter (2014), 'The Pussy Riot affair: gender and national identity in Putin's Russia', *Nationalities Papers*, 42, 4: 575–82.

Sharafutdinova, Gulnaz (2014), 'The Pussy Riot affair and Putin's demarche from sovereign democracy to sovereign morality', *Nationalities Papers*, 42, 4: 615–21.

Sheremet'eva, Svetlana (2016), 'Dmitrii Demushkin: Putin pomog postroit "samostiinuiu" Ukrainu i nauchil nenavidet "rusniu"' [Dmitrii Demushkin: Putin helped to build independent Ukraine and taught to hate the Russians], Apostrof, 30 May, <http://apostrophe.ua/article/society/1970-01-01/dmitriy-dmushkin-putin-pomog-postroit-samostiynuyu-ukrainu-i-nauchil-nenavidet-rusnyu/5290> (last accessed 15 December 2016).

Shevel, Oxana (2011), 'Russian nation-building from Yel'tsin to Medvedev: ethnic, civic or purposefully ambiguous?', *Europe–Asia Studies*, 63, 2: 179–202.

Shevel, Oxana (2012), 'The politics of citizenship policy in post-Soviet Russia', *Post-Soviet Affairs*, 28, 1: 111–47.

Smith, Kathleen (2002), *Mythmaking in the New Russia*, Ithaca, NY: Cornell University Press.

Szaszdi, Lajos F. (2008), *Russian Civil-military Relations and the Origins of the Second Chechen War*, Lanham, MD: University Press of America.
Teper, Yuri (2016), 'Official Russian identity discourse in the light of the annexation of Crimea: national or imperial?', *Post-Soviet Affairs*, 32, 4: 378–96.
Teper, Yuri and Daniel D. Course (2014), 'Contesting Putin's nation-building: the "Muslim other" and the challenge of the Russian ethno-cultural alternative', *Nations and Nationalism*, 20, 4: 721–41.
Tolz, Vera and Sue-Ann Harding (2015), 'From "compatriots" to "aliens": the changing coverage of migration on Russian television', *The Russian Review*, 74, 3: 452–77.
Tumanov, Grigorii (2014), 'Aleksandr Potkin planiroval pokinut' Rossiiu pered zaderzhaniem' [Aleksandr Potkin planned to leave Russia before the arrest], *Kommersant*, 16 October, <http://www.kommersant.ru/doc/2590673> (last accessed 20 December 2016).
Vasilchenko, Elena (2016), 'Osuzhdennyi na 7.5 let Belov-Potkin nazval prigovor "trishkinym kaftanom"' [Belov-Potkin sentenced to 7.5 years called the verdict 'a sham'], *MK*, 24 August, <http://www.mk.ru/social/2016/08/24/osuzhdennyy-na-75-let-belovpotkin-nazval-prigovor-trishkinym-kaftanom.html> (last accessed 15 December 2016).
Vedomosti (2014) 'Politolog Dugin uvolen iz MGU, na postu zavkafedroi ego smenit Zhirinovskii' [Political scientist Dugin fired from MGU, Zhirinovskii replaces him as chair], 28 June, <http://www.vedomosti.ru/politics/news/2014/06/28/zhirinovskij-smenit-dugina-na-postu-zavkafedroj-sociologii> (last accessed 22 June 2015).
Verkhovsky, Alexander (2016), 'What's behind the proposed law on the Russian nation?', *The Moscow Times*, 1 November, <https://themoscowtimes.com/articles/putin-supports-law-on-russian-nation-55976> (last accessed 15 January 2017).
Vesti nedeli (2014), 14 September, <http://www.vesti.ru/doc.html?id=1970071> (last accessed 15 January 2017).
Vesti nedeli (2015), 27 September, <https://russia.tv/video/show/brand_id/5206/episode_id/1232935/video_id/1333925/> (last accessed 15 January 2017).
Volchek, Dmitrii (2016), 'Generaly poiaviatsia na ulitse' [Generals will appear on the streets], Radio Svoboda, 23 January, <http://www.svoboda.org/a/27504150.html> (last accessed 10 December 2016).
Voskresnoe vremia (2014), 7 December, <https://www.1tv.ru/news/2014/12/07/30572-chast_poslaniya_adresovannaya_igrayuschim_na_valyutnom_rynke_protiv_rublya _smotrelas_dostatochno_zhestko> (last accessed 15 January 2017).
Voskresnyi vecher (2014), 18 March, <https://russia.tv/video/show/brand_id/21385/episode_id/975021/video_id/981731/> (last accessed 20 April 2015).

Voskresnyi vecher (2015), 30 September, <https://russia.tv/video/show/brand_id/21385/episode_id/1233851/video_id/1385296/> (last accessed 22 December 2016).

Vremia (2015), 30 September, <http://www.1tv.ru/news/issue/2015-09-30/21:00> (last accessed 21 December 2016).

Yablokov, Ilya (2014), 'Pussy Riot as agent provocateur: conspiracy theories and the media construction of nation in Putin's Russia', *Nationalities Papers*, 42, 4: 622–36.

Yanov, Alexander (2012), 'Putin's cheat sheet', Institute of Modern Russia, 14 February, <http://imrussia.org/en/?option=com_content&view=article&id=199%3Aputins-cheat-sheet&catid=45%3Aconversationswithayanov&Itemid=94&lang=ru> (last accessed 15 October 2014).

Zvelev, Igor (2008), 'Sootechestvenniki v rossiiskoi politike na postsovetskom prostranstve' [Compatriots in Russian politics at post-Soviet space], *Russia in Global Affairs*, 1, <http://www.globalaffairs.ru/number/n_10265> (last accessed 17 May 2013).

4

Sovereignty and Russian national identity-making: The biopolitical dimension

Andrey Makarychev and Alexandra Yatsyk

Biopolitical practices have increasingly come to the fore in Russian political life.[1] In only a few years, what started as a marginal series of speech acts expressing concerns about human bodies entered the mainstream of Russian political discourse. Some examples: as in Soviet times, punitive psychiatry is again in focus as one of the repressive instruments the state uses against dissenters (Nikitin 2013). Corporal discipline has become pervasive (Pavlovskii 2016). The Public Chamber has proposed to introduce a new school subject called 'Moral basics of family life', with separate classes for boys and girls; virginity would be promoted, and there would be regular lie-detector tests of teachers concerning their morals (Chernykh 2015). In medicine, the Russian government has issued a much-discussed regulation on limiting the public release of information concerning cases of suicide among terminally ill patients (Maetnaia and Evstifeev 2015). Some politicians, including Deputy Prime Minister Arkadii Dvorkovich, have indicated that Russians eat too much in times of economic crisis (Znak.com 2015), while the mayor of Vologda has suggested his fellow citizens should 'eat nettles' (Gazeta.ru 2015).

Here we are dealing not with sporadic episodes, but with a new and growing trend affecting the whole system of power relations, with nation-building at its core. A possible explanation for this proliferation of biopolitical discourses lies in the dysfunctionality of other forms and practices of political subjectivities. Russia's national sovereignty cannot be based on, or express itself through, an economic rationale: modernisation, central under Medvedev's presidency, has clearly been sidelined. Contrary to what Carl Schmitt maintained (Schmitt 2005), sovereignty cannot rely solely on legal practices: corruptive unlawfulness has become a structural characteristic of power relations in Russia. Internationally, sovereignty cannot be geopolitically grounded, since Russian geopolitical preferences – with spheres of influence at their core – are rejected by most foreign partners. With the global crisis of 'grand narratives', national sovereignty cannot count on ideological resources, which have become largely discredited in Russia. Against this backdrop, in claiming uncompromised and undivided sovereignty, the state must resort to a depoliticised type of organicist discourse, with biopolitical categories of 'family' and 'nation' as a collective body at its centre. Biopower has become one of the most effective and feasible forms for generating bounded political roles and statuses pertinent to nation-(re)building.

In a wider sense, the rapidly growing importance of biopolitical arguments in debates on Russian national identity can be explained by an ontological void: post-Soviet Russian identity has in many respects become an empty signifier, a concept not attached to any fixed set of socially recognised meanings (Makarychev 2013). The crisis of ideologies and grand narratives has been instrumental in elevating the otherwise deeply private issues of sexuality, natality, lifestyles and patterns of reproductive behaviour to the top of the identity agenda in Russia. Biopolitics offers a specific way of anchoring the increasingly dispersed and uncertain Russian national identity in a traditionalist understanding of social roles within a highly patriarchal matrix of hegemonic masculinity (see, for instance, Rutten 2012; Bernstein 2013; Goscilo 2013; Rutland 2014; Sperling 2015).

In the following, we examine these points in detail. We start with the concept of biopolitical sovereignty, emphasising its complex structure and the precarious role of the state in its functioning. Then we turn to specific cases that illustrate different practices of biopolitics in Russian legislation, gender representations, and so on. While the state may strengthen its capacity for appropriating and instrumentalising biopolitical discourses and the ensuing practices as the foundation for its conservative project-on-the-move, we argue that the biopolitical momentum might strike back, producing forces of biopolitical resistance to and contestation of the hegemonic discourse that could shake its foundations.

Conceptualising biopolitical normalisation

Biopolitics can be understood as a relatively soft (but fairly pervasive) technology of power and governance targeted at such areas as health, sanitation, birth rates and sexuality (Finlayson 2010: 97). Biopolitical reasoning sees human life as part of the political calculations and mechanisms underlying the exercise of power and the provision of security (Dillon and Lobo-Guerrero 2008: 266).

Of the various ways of applying the idea of biopolitics in multiple social, cultural and political contexts, particularly important is the conflict between two interpretations of the essence of this concept. One dates back to the works of Michel Foucault, the other is associated with Giorgio Agamben.

Foucault sought to draw a semantic line between sovereign power and biopower – the first as power to take lives, the second as power to streamline people's productive capacities. He admitted that the two forms of power might coexist, but this would presume a 'devitalisation of sovereignty' (see Butler 2004: 52). Foucault's distinction between sovereign power and biopower can be understood as involving at least two important aspects: biopower has population rather than territory as its object (Joseph 2009), and in certain contexts it is connotative with 'a politics of the body – the (self-)disciplines applied to wo/man-as-body' (Merlingen 2006: 183).

Arguably, Foucault is retelling one old story of security (geopolitics) and paralleling this with 'his novel account of the other (biopolitics)' (Dillon and Lobo-Guerrero 2008: 274). In this sense, biopolitics is less about possessing territories, and more about managing human beings and their bodily lives, as well as disciplining and supervising human bodies for the sake of survival. Second, sovereignty presupposes the 'power of death' (Singer and Weir 2006: 458), whereas biopolitics 'promotes the life and efficiency of the body politic' (Widder 2010: 422). Put differently: in the name of the sovereign power the state sends its citizens to die on the battlefield – whereas biopolitical mechanisms help people to survive. These mechanisms of biopower function at the micro level, entangled in a web of bodily relations, largely alienated from 'the political order proper [which is] . . . inscribed in the constitution, laws, institutions' (Finlayson 2010). Thus, the hegemonic conception of identity is based largely on corporeal practices of Self–Other distinctions, without necessarily implying a state-based ideology.

Agamben (1998), for his part, assumes that biopolitical strategies of including 'bare life' (human biological existence) within the political realm always constitute the hidden centre of sovereign power. Indeed, he views the production of a specifically biopolitical body as 'the original activity of sovereign power' (see Vogt 2005: 77). This stands in contrast to Foucault's denial of the significance of sovereign power 'in opposition to a supervening and tentacular biopower' (Fitzpatrick 2005: 56).

Here we take the side of Agamben and his many followers, who see biopolitical regulation as 'produced immanently by sovereign power and for sovereign power' (Vaughan-Williams 2009: 741) by introducing exceptional regulatory mechanisms that gradually become routine and extend from certain groups to the whole nation. While not going so far as to accept Agamben's idea of 'the camp' – a metaphor he uses to depict the evolution of the modern state into a comprehensive model of total surveillance and coercive control (Agamben 1998) – we do assume that countries with strong totalitarian traditions, like Russia, represent terrains for the practical implementation of the mechanisms of biopolitical regulation and totalisation described by Agamben.

Russia's biopolitical turn

We propose a distinct interpretation of recent developments on the Russian political scene, applying the concept of biopolitics at the centre of analysis. This approach constitutes a departure from dominant schools of thought which view contemporary Russian political and social concepts through traditional lenses, including institutional change, state–society relations, centre–periphery controversies and so on. By contrast, our approach scrutinises the phenomenon of the biopolitical turn in Russia, as exemplified by the application of a set of regulatory mechanisms aimed at solidifying the national identity by disciplining and constraining human bodies.

For centuries in Russia, not only living spaces, but also the very lives of human beings did not fully belong to the people. This can account for the biopolitical explanation of power mechanisms in a country where human bodies have increasingly become subject to state regulatory intervention. What people eat, drink and smoke, what they do with their sexuality, how many children they are expected to have – the state offers ready answers to many of these issues. 'Deviant' practices – like homosexuality – are to be either punished or disciplined, by various regulatory mechanisms. Normalisation procedures as practised by the state are not about educating, but about possessing and controlling human bodies as the biopolitical assets of the state. It is in this sense that sovereignty – the underlying concept of the Putin regime – is largely manifested through biopolitical means of control and supervision that unfold beyond the increasingly dysfunctional political institutions of the state.

Agamben (1998) describes a transformation of politics into biopolitics as a move from the rule by and through institutions, to the application of techniques of control deriving basically from sovereign will rather than from established rules or norms. It is in this context that we must understand Agamben's idea of the 'bareness of life' as 'life without mediation', that is, without institutional intermediaries between the political class and the population. This is precisely the kernel of Putin's 'vertical of power': an unmediated system of one-way communication between the holder(s) of sovereign power and the populace. It is this 'bare life' of ordinary citizens manipulated from the top of the power hierarchy that makes representational institutions or civil society organisations redundant and ultimately disavows politics as a sphere of normative contestation.

Explaining power relations through a biopolitical prism might seem neither new nor unusual. What makes the Russian case peculiar is the drastic turnabout – from almost total neglect of bodily aspects in politics in the early post-Soviet years, to their elevation to the pinnacle of the political agenda under the presidency of Vladimir Putin, whom we see – at least during his first two terms in office (2000–8) – as being more a technocrat than an ideologue. That the state should maintain an explicitly permissive attitude to the plethora of issues of corporeality and body politics could be seen as an essential part of its informal social contract with society, and a precondition for a relative balance between the two during the first two post-Soviet decades. And then, that balance was undermined by the new conservative trend in Kremlin policy that came as a reaction to the growing demands for social and political change emerging in the autumn of 2011 (Remizov 2013).

Biopolitics gained popularity among Russian opinion-makers because it offered a series of nodal points for cementing the dispersed discourse on Russian identity without resorting to straightforward ideological clichés. The traction of biopolitics lies in its role as a trans-ideological and post-political substitution for politics as a sphere of struggles and contestations. Since the fall of the Soviet Union, among Russian elites 'politics' had connoted something manipulative, artificial and alienated from society: members of the ruling class were greatly predisposed to post-political thinking, with ideologies seen as discredited constraints and not incentive boosters. However, this post-political mentality would require some nodal points for anchoring the fragmented and unfixed set of discourses beyond traditional ideological (left–right, conservative–liberal, democratic–autocratic) dichotomies.

Biopolitics fits this niche ideally, and meets the demands for a substitute to ideologies. With its references to the individual and collective body as the core of a new 'regime of truth', biopolitics can be placed within the post-political register, appealing to something allegedly well-established and traditional, and defining itself in opposition to emancipatory attempts to challenge the 'natural state of affairs'. Moreover, biopolitics is trans-ideological, because it transcends ideological divides and reconciles them, adapting to liberal (according to Foucault's logic) or conservative expectations. That being said, however, the functionally 'natural', 'evident', 'indisputable' characteristics of the alleged normality of human beings constituting the national self are in fact illusions, because of the socially and culturally constructed nature of all biopolitical concepts.

In Russia, biopolitics not only gives an additional set of power tools to the authorities, it is also an intrinsic element in debates on the essence and borders of the political community. Russian biopolitics is a set of instruments that defines belongingness to the 'imagined' community on the basis of loyalty to official policies, while ostracising those who do not fit with the standards set by biopolitics. Biopolitical regulations, bans and restrictions have become a main tool for articulating the rules shaping the national political community of Russia, drawing its political boundaries by establishing biopolitical distinctions with other communities. With their many restrictive effects, these bans entail mechanisms of 'inclusive exclusion': 'if someone is "banned' from a political community, he or she continues to have a relation with that group: there is still a connection precisely because they are outlawed' (Vaughan-Williams 2009: 734). Cases in point here are the practices of political incarceration, ostracising LGBT people and fuelling anti-migrant feelings among the populace.

Biopolitical instruments have become indispensable elements of nation-building in Russia. From a biopolitical perspective, national identity-making necessarily implies disciplinary practices of controlling and regulating human lives as a precondition for aggregating the population into a single collective body, the nation. The ultimate goal is to create the nation as a socially coherent community, based on a biopolitical understanding of national identity as a shared set of norms requiring submission of the individual to the group. Consolidation of biopower goes hand in hand with the making of collective communities and the ensuing distinction between the outside and the inside, which implies the (re)drawing of the boundaries of the collective national body.

Certain structural factors have facilitated the proliferation of biopolitical practices. One is the crisis of territorial conceptualisations of power: geography has ceased to be the dominant prism for tackling political issues, which are increasingly seen as related to human beings and their everyday lives. A second factor is the crisis of 'grand narratives' and the concomitant ideological void which has made human life a major universal category grounded in seemingly ideologically neutral issues like nutrition, healthcare and reproductive behaviour.

How can a biopolitical frame be useful in studying the making of national identities and national communities? Biopolitical regulations set the rules for belonging to as well as disciplining the population; as a major source of establishing and implementing norms, they define mechanisms of inclusion and exclusion, as well as the inside/outside dynamics. Moreover, the idea of biopolitical norms as a basis for national consolidation has strong moral/religious underpinnings. This can explain the biopolitical understanding of conservatism, with anti-LGBT, anti-same-sex-marriage and anti-immigrant discourses and practices at its core.

The exercise of biopower is feasible in a disciplinary society that legitimises state surveillance of people's lives through various regulatory mechanisms aimed at motivating and constraining human bodies. Biopolitical reasoning sees human life as part of political calculations and mechanisms for the exercise of power and providing security. However, biopower is not simply a technique of governance: it *produces* its objects and differing modalities of actor subjectivities which are never 'pre-given' and do not exist before – or beyond – biopolitical discourses. In Russia, many concepts of the hegemonic discourse derive from a biopolitical understanding of social reality: for instance, the concept of family as the constitutive background for social relations translates into a family-based understanding of 'the Russian world' as a trans-territorial biopolitical community. Biopower is constitutive to Putin's conservative project that revives the traditional understanding of social and cultural roles and corporeal practices. Russia's conservative identity produces a boundary between a 'conservative'/ 'holy' Russia and a 'liberally emancipatory'/ 'sinful' Europe, with harsh attacks on multiculturalism and moral support for multiple homophobic actions. Here the great-power rhetoric necessarily includes a biopolitical component, since biopolitical norms require an opposite, a deviation/perversion. In the Russian discourse, that deviant opposite is liberal emancipatory Europe ('the Big Other'). In line with this reasoning, the Russian civilisational discourse (in particular, 'the Russian World') is grounded in the biopolitical distinction between Russia and the West, and EU enlargement is seen as the expansion of the sphere of 'gay culture'.

Against this backdrop, the proliferation of biopolitical ideas and practices in Putin's Russia should be understood as a specific instrument for stabilising a hegemonic discourse which, since the fall of the Soviet Union, has lacked coherence and has been intrinsically fragmented. This discourse was not functioning effectively, it lacked the necessary 'quilting' points, which led to its decomposition into culturally divergent and often competing narratives of Russia's collective self. The idea of biopolitical normalisation, essential to Putin's version of conservatism, is meant to solidify and consolidate this discourse as the pivotal hegemonic strategy of power.

The biopolitical strategy of nation-building is grounded in victimising certain groups of citizens and restricting their freedoms. A former Chief Sanitary Inspector of Russia, Gennadii Onishchenko elevated issues of sanitation and hygiene to the level of national security, regularly slapping import bans on products from countries with which Moscow had unresolved problems, like Georgia, Moldova and Ukraine. In an overtly biopolitical move, Nikolai Patrushev, the head of the Russian Security Council, included 'family values' among the highest security priorities (Bekbulatova et al. 2013). Elena Mizulina, head of the State Duma Committee on Family, Women and Children Affairs, has referred to artificial conception, including surrogate maternity, as analogous to nuclear weaponry that destroys Russia as a nation (Gazeta.ru 2013). She has also admitted that when the Duma voted for the 'Dima Iakovlev bill' – which prohibits adoption of Russian orphans by US citizens – that was an act of asserting sovereignty (Mizulina 2013b). Thus, the sovereign power reinstalls itself domestically and internationally through control over human beings, with biopolitics at its core.

The elevation to the top of the political agenda of a whole set of issues related to the body of the Russian President – from public displays of his stamina to rumours of illnesses – also testifies to the pre-eminence of biopolitical discourses (Medvedev 2015). The nexus of biopolitics with sovereign power is evident in the multiple public exposures of Putin's body as an object of 'sexualized gaze' (Sperling 2015). Putin's divorce in 2013, at the zenith of the Kremlin-patronised campaign for strengthening the institution of the family, can be understood only within the paradoxical logic of sovereign exceptions: the leader of the nation is above the rules of the polity he cements and incarnates. Putin is displayed as a

> youthful, energetic, sexually active expert in judo, who, like Mussolini, is happy to bare a powerful torso at the first opportunity. Completing the picture is a war in Ukraine, in which the virile, potent Russia, like Nazi Germany and Fascist Italy before it, confidently expects to kick the butt of those weak, divided, effeminate democratic states. (Bayer 2015)

Anything that could be seen as a sign of weakness or femininity within this logic of biopolitical sovereignty is rejected – including liberalism and homosexuality. Typically, it is these negative qualities that get projected onto the imagery of 'enemies' crafted by Kremlin propaganda (Iampolski 2015).

Illustrative is Putin's occasional usage of medicalised language, involving biopolitical metaphors with strong authoritarian potential – like the threatening promise to 'send a doctor' to the head of a state corporation who missed an important meeting with the president, to avoid being told off (Krichevskii 2008). A metaphor coined by a Russian policy analyst – 'a sick world in anticipation of healing procedures' (Galkin 2012: 5) – can be applied as a biopolitical interpretation of Putin's foreign policy, with its rising neo-imperial momentum and implicit denial of freedom of choice for many of Russia's neighbouring countries.

The state and biopolitical sovereignty

Biopolitical mechanisms for sustaining national unity and solidarity compensate for a deficit of effectively operating state-promoted and sustained norms and/or ideologies. This model of power relations is 'biopolitical' in the sense that the state, being neither its engine nor key reference point, has taken advantage of the potential for mobilising the population and selectively utilising it for political purposes. In this, Russia resembles other countries where 'loyalty to nation qua biopolity is occasioned simply by the fact that, for most people, there is no alternative source of life-security, no matter how bad their state may be in absolute terms' (Kelly 2010).

The biopolitical kernel of Russian patriotism, devoid of references to rational categories and deeply traumatic, is explained by Zakhar Prilepin in his novel *Sankia* (2006). The protagonist, a young Russian nationalist, avers: 'I am ready to live under any type of authority should it secure the maintenance of territory and the regeneration of population. Today this is not the case', and then adds an even stronger biopolitical statement:

> There is no ideology nowadays; it is instincts that are ideological . . . The soil, honour, victory, justice – none of those fundamentals needs an ideology. Love necessitates no ideology . . . There is only a sense of kinship, that's it. The comprehension of what is going on in Russia is based neither on a certain volume of knowledge nor on intellectual casuistry that can be used to deconstruct everything, but on the feeling of cognation. It grows in human beings from childhood, and it is impossible to get rid of it. If you feel that Russia is tantamount to your wife, as in Aleksandr Blok's poetry, then you treat it as your wife. In a biblical sense – as someone with whom you are deeply involved and pledged to live with until death . . . And in this case you have no choice . . . All that is genuine denies the very idea of choice. (Prilepin 2006)

This reasoning might be called 'a practical ideology' (Rubtsov 2014) – a set of instrumental ideas that defy public dialogue, instead favouring 'uncompromised moral condemnation . . . that reduces the comprehension of issues to a metaphysical fight of good against evil' (Morozov 2010). It is against the backdrop of this ideological void and 'lack of a foundational substance' (Cerella 2012) in Russia (see, for instance, Storch 2013) that Prilepin's vision of biopolitical patriotism – leaving no room for making individual decisions based on conventional wisdom or rationale – surged with the massive public support for the annexation of Crimea and the instigation of pro-Russian separatism in eastern Ukraine. This type of national-patriotic narrative does not need the idea of a modern, effective, rational and socially caring state as a condition for its functioning. The idea of a well-governed nation-state is supplanted by a biopolitical reasoning that sees the nationalist discourse as self-constituting on the basis of its belonging to the mentally constructed and valorised community of like-minded compatriots.

We find a key condition for the expansion and implementation of a biopolitical agenda in the blurred boundaries of the state, and the subsequent creation of a grey zone between legality and illegality as well as between private rights and public morals. One example would be the practice of paramilitary Cossack units inspecting gay clubs; a spokesperson for the Cossacks in St Petersburg claimed that their brigades would be checking nightclubs for their 'compliance with ethics and Orthodox traditions' (RuFabula 2015). Indeed, the state intentionally outsources some biopolitical functions of disciplining and normalising to non-state groups: that gives the Kremlin the advantage of being able to cultivate the social base for homophobia without the state itself being directly involved. It is the expansion of this grey zone between legality and its disregard that constitutes the most fertile ground for Putin's biopolitical sovereignty.

Realms of biopolitical power

We now turn to some issues that are widely debated as crucial elements of biopolitical regulation in Russia. These range from the use of the penitentiary system, LGBT controversies, and to adoption, reproduction and gender representations – all unified by the regulatory mechanisms of a state that uses biopolitical strategies to vitalise sovereign power.

PRISON AS A BIOPOLITICAL INSTITUTION

Prison is the most radical embodiment of the state's control over human bodies, which makes it a quasi-political institution in Russia. Indeed, it is hard to understand Russian politics without reference to the widespread use of incarceration. The Khodorkovskii trial, the Magnitskii affair, the Pussy Riot verdict and the lawsuit against Aleksei Navalnyi are perhaps the best-known recent examples here.

The Kremlin's policy of putting the most active protestors in the May 2012 mass demonstrations in Moscow in jail – a case known as the 'Bolotnaia affair' after the square in Moscow where the demonstrations took place – also fits in the logic of biopolitical regulation based on practices of incarceration on political grounds. In October 2013, a district court in Moscow sentenced Mikhail Kosenko, a participant in the mass riots in Bolotnaia Square, to an indefinite term of forced psychiatric treatment. The court relied on the recommendations of the Serbskii Centre[2] specialists, marking a clear return to Soviet practices of punishing people for their political activity by sending them to mental hospitals (Davidoff 2013). The following month, the State Duma authorised such enforced hospitalisation for psychiatric treatment.

A highly publicised example of the biopolitical function of the Russian prison system was the ruling of a local court in Mordovia, where Nadezhda Tolokonnikova, a Pussy Riot artist, served her two-year sentence. The court turned down Tolokonnikova's request for parole on the grounds of her refusal to take part in a beauty contest in prison. In an illuminating comment from Sergei Medvedev, this decision is seen as de facto making participation in sexist rituals an obligation for female prisoners – a clear illustration of the 'camp mentality' of the whole system of biopolitical governance in Russia (Medvedev 2013).

Actually, the biopolitical role of the prison in Russia can be described as 'inclusive exclusion', since the physical isolation of the Kremlin's opponents does not necessarily imply their political insulation. Articles by and interviews with the imprisoned Mikhail Khodorkovskii (Khodorkovsky 2013) and Nadezhda Tolokonnikova (2013) constitute a specific genre and segment of Russian political discourse. The speaking positions of both have been strengthened by their personal experiences of being persecuted by the regime. Tolokonnikova has taken up several socially important issues relating to prisoners' rights, as well as physical and material conditions within the penitentiary system (Degot' 2013) – prompting a response from a key figure within the Russian Orthodox Church, Archpriest Vsevolod Chaplin, who defended the idea of punishment as necessarily related to physical deprivation (Chaplin 2013). Tolokonnikova's appeals from prison triggered a deeply political effect of further differentiation of liberal and conservative discourses, thereby playing an important role in publicly articulating the narrative of resistance to the regime.

The ban on homosexual propaganda

The Kremlin's attitude towards homosexuality reveals an understanding of democracy as the rule of the majority over minorities, leading to the goal of socially and normatively homogenising the political community. Anti-gay legislation has made clear the general atmosphere of suppressing minorities in Putin's Russia and has unleashed highly parochial sentiments in society.

Formally, the June 2013 law banning propaganda for non-traditional sexual relations was aimed solely at shielding minors from (homo)sexually explicit information. But the imprecise definition of 'propaganda' raised concerns that its implementation could be arbitrary. Thus, the problem is not only the law itself, but its spillover effects. After all, a broad interpretation of 'gay propaganda' as any sort of public exposure of homosexuality-related issues might imply banning books or films with homosexual context (Brooke 2013). Opinions on revoking parental rights on the grounds of homosexuality were seriously considered by a group of Russian legislators (Dozhd' TV 2013a). Russia's anti-gay legislation has also provoked homophobic assaults against LGBT people (Gutterman 2013). In Zabaikal *krai*, a local lawmaker proposed giving paramilitary Cossack units the right to punish gay people physically (Chita.ru 2013).

It is not only the state but also vigilante groups within society that fuel anti-gay sentiments. The Russian Mothers movement (*Russkie materi*) has advocated complete bans on foreign adoption and on homosexuality (Dozhd' TV 2013b). Leonid Roshal, head of the National Medical Chamber, openly admitted that he hates homosexuals (*Metro* 2013). A group of Orthodox believers sued the singer Madonna for gay propaganda after her August 2012 concert in St Petersburg. Russian social media also extensively covered the case of schoolteacher Ilia Kolmanovskii, who was fired from his job at the request of the parents' committee after he had been spotted at a protest meeting against anti-gay legislation (Kichanova 2013).

However, it is unlikely that the regime will ultimately prove capable of controlling the effects of the biopolitically centred discourse it has unleashed. The anti-gay campaign has been shown to have provoked an upsurge of interest in the topic on the Internet (Klishin 2013). Ironically, the state-controlled TV channels, which are supposed to thwart 'gay propaganda', are full of entertainment shows that display pop stars known to be gay (Ioffe 2013). When Anton Krasovskii, a well-known TV personality, publicly confessed to being gay, and added: 'I am a human being, just like Putin', he ended up being ousted – but he also received widespread publicity and support, mainly within the new social media (Krasovskii 2013).

Anti-adoption law

A law passed in 2013 forbidding US families from adopting Russian orphans was rhetorically substantiated by reference to twenty cases of tragic deaths of Russian adoptees in the USA (statistically a tiny percentage against the backdrop of about 60,000 Russian children adopted by US families). The so-called Dima Iakovlev Bill, named after one of the victims, is an illustrative case of a biopolitical ban based on the assumption that the bodies of 'our' children belong to the nation.

The narrative of the victimisation of Russian children adopted abroad disregards most rational arguments – the miserable prospects for most of the one million orphans in Russia, the diminishing number of Russian families willing to adopt abandoned children (Rabkor.ru 2013), and the incomparably higher (thirty-nine-fold) risks associated with living in adopted families in Russia in comparison to the USA (Tolkovatel' 2013). Supporters of the law also choose to ignore the fact that in a great many cases US families have willingly adopted sick orphans in need of expensive medical treatment unavailable in Russia (Boitsova 2013).

Again, as in the cases mentioned above, the anti-adoption law ended up publicly raising various inconvenient and potentially troublesome questions for the Kremlin – from conditions in Russian orphanages to the reasons for the enormous number of abandoned children across the country. This shows that biopolitical regulations come with a certain price and entail social responsibilities that the state is hardly capable of performing effectively.

Family and reproductive behaviour

The draft concept of a new family policy, first published in 2013, is perhaps the best illustration of 'biopolitical totalisation' as applied to the whole set of family-related matters. The document, edited by State Duma representative Elena Mizulina, contains explicitly religious connotations by claiming that the family is a 'small church' that sustains the idea of immortality. It proposes to give the Russian Orthodox Church the right to interfere in matters of the state's family policies, including allowing priests to participate in local commissions on juvenile delinquency and drawing on the clergy's expertise in acts of legislation (Mizulina 2013a). The draft attempts to introduce a model of 'the normal family' as one with at least three children and two generations living in a common household. Apart from this, Mizulina and associates proposed revising the legal norm of equality of divorced spouses in favour of mothers staying with children, and favoured a drastic increase in paternal alimony.

This bill is only part of a wider array of initiatives aimed at regulating the intricacies of family relations. A local legislator in a provincial city proposed limiting the number of possible marriages to three (RBK 2013). Another member of a regional legislature aired the idea of conscripting young women who are childless after age twenty (*AiF* 2012). At the 2013 All-Russian People's Front convention, Olga Kryshtanovskaia, a sociologist and Kremlin loyalist, proposed mandatory DNA tests for potential fathers of children born outside official marriage upon the mother's request (Rozhkova 2013). There were figures in the State Duma lobbying for a ban on abortion as well (Podrabinek 2013). It is not incidental that in 2012 Putin compared street protestors wearing the white ribbons that became the symbol of the 2011/12 mass protests with vendors of contraceptives – people who, in his view, could be associated with things inappropriate as regards biopolitical stimulation of the birth rate. All these measures are pivotal points in Russia's newfound conservative agenda, marked by explicit conflict with liberal emancipation in general and feminist ideology in particular.

However, in response the Kremlin faces a counter-reaction from social groups that are unhappy with – and thus challenge – Kremlin-orchestrated biopolitical bans. What makes the state's family policy a particularly uneasy issue is the controversy over juvenile justice, a policy area where the state is challenged by even more conservative and religious groups who contest the state's right to take children away from their families, even in cases of parental abuse. To these groups, children are 'family property' (Baunov 2013) and the state has no moral right to interfere in such matters – the whole idea of juvenile justice being attributed to the effects of Western-driven liberalism.

Gender representations

Apart from the state, other generators of biopolitical activity include the mass media, advertising and the fashion industry. By and large, the Russian media industry reproduce biopolitical images and messages. Scholars have noted sexist and patriarchic patterns of femininity propagated in the Russian mass media through hedonistic, nationalistic or even liberal discourses (Tartakovskaia 2000).

In its turn, post-Soviet hegemonic masculinity proclaims autonomy, professionalism, affluence, independence, aggression, dominance in the private and public spheres, patriarchal inclinations and the fetishisation of consumption (Tikhonova-Iatsyk 2009). Some basic patterns of post-Soviet masculinity build on the imagery of pre-Soviet and Soviet times – for example, soldier and defender, noble aristocrat, hussar and intellectual (Zdravomyslova and Temkina 2002). But they also reveal a dominant form of Western masculinity with its heterosexuality, material abundance and commitment to 'manly work', all of which make the man's world very different from the world of women, emotions and family (Chernova 2002). Other authors draw political parallels to dominant attitudes towards sexuality (Zherebkin 1999) and between traditional notions of masculinity and nationalist discourses (Marsh 2013: 204).

Representations of President Putin in the Kremlin-loyal media are a clear example of constructing the visual imagery of a virile and masculine political leader (Goscilo 2013). The many photos of Putin as a bare-chested horseman, as a swimmer, motorcycle rider, jet pilot, judo expert, ice hockey player, diver, huntsman and so on, attest to the biopolitical grounds of his leadership style. Ostensibly, a series of 'Putin's kisses' (Putin kissing children, different animals and even fish) could be interpreted as the construction of an image of Putin as King of Nature/King of the Beasts, strengthening his hegemonic masculinity (Mikhailova 2013).

Complementing Putin's image as a superhero is a feminised 'Russian people' (Rutten 2012: 576). Examples here include an erotic calendar with half-naked Russian women and the logo 'We Love You!', along with a series of pop songs with self-explanatory titles like 'I'd like to be your Conny' (the name of Putin's dog) (2011), and 'A man like Putin' (2008).[3]

However, biopolitical mechanisms are not necessarily hierarchically top down. Many alterations in sexual patterns are grounded in the increasing social activism of 'sexual minorities' who are fighting for their rights, sustained by a market that seeks to explore new groups of consumers as a resource. Sexuality as a key component of biopolitics is a cornerstone of consumerist ideology, with the media industry at its core. Sexual representations in pop culture gradually expand contexts of bodily canons and gender habits; in particular, commercial messages appealing to the gay audience use 'hidden advertisements' to commodify LGBT people with tools understandable only to insiders (Clark 1995).

Banning is the key biopolitical instrument for the state, whereas for the cultural production industry, biopolitics is about setting/framing corporeal standards and norms – of private life, sexuality, reproductive behaviour, family relations and canons of beauty – and inciting corresponding models of social relations. The biopower of officialdom is based on conservative principles of surveillance, whereas the counter-biopolitics of actionist/performative art is grounded in the idea of the emancipated body as an object of hegemonic discourses and a subject of resistance. Take, for example, the Pussy Riot group's lyrics in 'Putin wet himself', venting dissatisfaction 'with the culture of male hysteria' and the 'sexist regime' (ECHR 2012: 16). Another example could be Petr Pavlenskii's bodily art actions against the regime, as represented by the public nailing of his scrotum to the cobblestone paving of Red Square in 2013 in a gesture of solidarity with protesters in Ukraine, sewing his mouth shut to express support for Pussy Riot in July 2012, or wrapping himself naked in wire in St Petersburg in May 2013 to protest against unjust laws, including anti-LGBT legislation.

Concluding comments

We have argued that a *biopolitical agenda* shapes much of the content and contours of the Kremlin-promoted nation-building project. The concept of a sovereign Russia is in many respects based on biopolitical grounds as nodal points for stabilising the regime and preventing fragmentation and dispersal. The regime utilises biopolitical discourses and practices for consolidating its rule, drawing on conservative norms that may be asserted through religious, gender-based or 'Russian World'-grounded discourses. Biopolitics offers a specific way of anchoring the uncertain Russian identity in a set of consensually understood nodal points that encapsulate bodily practices of corporeal discipline and control.

This biopolitical regime distinguishes Russia markedly from the West. The calls for boycotting the 2014 Sochi Olympic Games because of the rise of anti-LGBT attitudes in Russia, or global reactions to the imprisonment of the Pussy Riot artists, call into doubt the prospects of harmony between Russia and the European normative order. Since the autumn of 2011 the Kremlin has set about building its domestic political capital on a clearer dissociation of Russia from the West. At stake is the very essence of Putin's attempts to recreate a conservative majority as the biopolitical basis of his reign and formulate a biopolitical agenda for national community-building. However, biopolitical practices also serve to fuel resistance to what is seen as unwarranted encroachment in the private sphere and a revival of parochial practices of controlling human bodies. By employing biopolitical tools of governance for the sake of sovereignty, the regime is in fact creating the preconditions for questioning the key tenets of the Putin-centred sovereignty discourse, and thereby its subsequent erosion.

Notes

1. This work was supported by institutional research funding (IUT 20–39) of the Estonian Ministry of Education and Research.
2. The Serbskii State Scientific Centre for Social and Forensic Psychiatry is a psychiatric hospital and Russia's main centre of forensic psychiatry. In the past, this institution, then known as the Serbskii Institute, attracted negative publicity because many Soviet dissidents were examined here and then committed to psychiatric hospitals.
3. 'Ia khocu byt' tvoei Konni' [I'd like to be your Conny], performed by Devochki za Putina, is available at <http://www.youtube.com/watch?v=7TC_N9qQLJ8> (last accessed 16 September 2014) and 'Takogo kak Putin' [A man like Putin], performed by Shpilki, is available at

<http://www.youtube.com/watch?v=_OFOPd6pgjI> (last accessed 16 September 2014).

Bibliography

Agamben, Giorgio (1998), *Homo Sacer: Sovereign Power and Bare Life*, Stanford, CA: Stanford University Press.
AiF (2012), 'Cheliabinskii deputat predlozhila obiazat' rossiianok rozhat' do 20 let' [Cheliabinsk deputy proposed to oblige Russian women to give birth by 20], 28 December, <http://www.chel.aif.ru/society/news/76344> (last accessed 8 March 2014).
Baunov, Aleksandr (2013) 'S"ezd zaputavshikhsia roditelei' [Convention of confused parents], Slon, 11 February, <http://slon.ru/russia/sezd_zaputav-shikhsya_roditeley-885732.xhtml> (last accessed 8 March 2014).
Bayer, Alexei (2015), 'Building fascism', *Kyiv Post*, 8 March, <http://www.kyivpost.com/opinion/op-ed/alexei-bayer-building-fascism-382918.html> (last accessed 10 August 2015).
Bekbulatova, Taisiia, Il'ia Safronov and Maksim Ivanov (2013), 'Na strazhe dukhovnoi bezopasnosti' [Safeguarding spiritual security], *Kommersant*, 25 April, 2.
Bernstein, Anna (2013), 'An inadvertent sacrifice: body politics and sovereign power in the Pussy Riot affair', *Critical Inquiry*, 40, 1: 220–41.
Boitsova, Marina (2013), 'Sleza Timofeia' [Timofey's tear], Rosbalt, 5 April, <http://www.rosbalt.ru/piter/2013/04/05/1114405.html> (last accessed 8 June 2014).
Brooke, James (2013), 'Russia prepares law to ban "gay propaganda"', Voice of America, 6 May, <http://www.voanews.com/content/russia-law-gay-propaganda/1655417.html> (last accessed 1 February 2014).
Butler, Judith (2004), *Precarious Life: The Power of Mourning and Violence*, New York: Verso.
Cerella, Antonio (2012), 'Religion and political form: Carl Schmitt's genealogy of politics as critique of Jürgen Habermas' post-secular discourse', *Review of International Studies*, 38, 5: 975–94.
Chaplin, Vsevolod (2013), 'Mir s Bogom i liud'mi dast tol'ko pereotsenka sovershennogo' [Peace with God and people is achievable only with rethinking of the past], Pravoslavie i mir, 23 September, <http://www.pravmir.ru/prot-vsevolod-chaplin-o-nadezhde-tolokonnikovoj-mir-s-bogom-i-lyudmi-dast-tolko-pereocenka-sovershennogo/> (last accessed 7 September 2014).
Chernova, Zhanna (2002), 'Normativnaia muzhskaia seksual'nost': (re) prezentatsii v mediadiskurse' [Normative male sexuality: (re)presentations in media discourse], in Elena Zdravomyslova and Anna Temkina, eds, *V poiskakh seksual'nosti* [*Looking for Sexuality*], St Peterburg: Dmitrii Bulanin, 527–49.

Chernykh, Aleksandr (2015), 'Uchebnik devstvennosti i mnogodetnosti' [A textbook on virginity and many children], *Kommersant*, 27 May, <http://www.kommersant.ru/doc/2734779> (last accessed 18 December 2015).
Chita.ru (2013), 'Zabaikal'skii deputat predlozhil priniat' kraevoi zakon o telesnykh nakazaniiakh dlia geev' [Transbaikal representative proposed to adopt regional law on corporal punishment for gays], 20 June, <http://news.chita.ru/50394/> (last accessed 6 September 2014).
Clark, Danae (1995), 'Commodity lesbianism', in Gail Dines and Jean M. Humez, eds, *Gender, Race and Class in Media: A Text-Reader*, Thousand Oaks, CA: Sage, 142–51.
Davidoff, Victor (2013), 'Soviet psychiatry returns', *The Moscow Times*, 13 October, <http://www.themoscowtimes.com/opinion/article/soviet-psychiatry-returns/487761.html#ixzz2hgACD8fw> (last accessed 10 July 2014).
Degot', Ekaterina (2013), 'Vzorvat' Bastiliiu' [Blow up the Bastille], *Vedomosti*, 27 September, <http://www.vedomosti.ru/lifestyle/news/16831861/ekaterina-degot-vzorvat-bastiliyu> (last accessed 10 July 2014).
Dillon, Michael and Luis Lobo-Guerrero (2008), 'Biopolitics of security in the 21st century: an introduction', *Review of International Studies*, 34, 2: 265–92.
Dozhd' TV (2013a) 'Peskov: V Rossii net problem s gomoseksualizmom, est' problema s ego propagandoi' [Peskov: there is no problem with homosexuality in Russia, there is a problem with its propaganda], 5 September, <http://tvrain.ru/articles/peskov_v_rossii_net_problem_s_gomoseksualizmom_est_problema_s_ego_propagandoj-351561> (last accessed 1 February 2014).
Dozhd' TV (2013b), '"Russkie materi" ne platiat den'gi za miting' ['Russian mothers' do not pay money for meeting], 28 February, <http://tvrain.ru/articles/russkie_materi_ne_platjat_dengi_za_mitingi-337678/> (last accessed 1 June 2014).
ECHR (2012), Application no. 38004/12: Mariya Vladimirovna ALEKHINA and others against Russia. Lodged on 19 June 2012, <http://hudoc.echr.coe.int/eng?i=001-139863#{%22itemid%22:[%22001-139863%22]}> (last accessed 10 July 2014).
Finlayson, J. Gordon (2010), '"Bare Life" and politics in Agamben's reading of Aristotle', *The Review of Politics*, 72, 1: 97–126.
Fitzpatrick, Peter (2005), 'Bare sovereignty: *Homo Sacer* and the insistence of law', in Andrew Norris, ed., *Politics, Metaphysics, and Death: Essays on Giorgio Agamben's* Homo Sacer, Durham, NC: Duke University Press, 49–73.
Galkin, Aleksandr (2012), 'Zakhvoravshii mir v ozhidanii lechebnykh protsedur' [A sick world in anticipation of healing procedures], *Politiia*, 2: 5–19.
Gazeta.ru (2013), 'Mizulina predlozhila zapretit' surrogatnoe materinstvo, sravniv ego s iadernym oruzhiem' [Mizulina suggested banning

surrogate maternity, comparing it with nuclear weapons], 10 November, <http://www.gazeta.ru/politics/news/2013/11/10/n_3314749.shtml> (last accessed 16 September 2014).

Gazeta.ru (2015), 'Vlasti Vologdy ob"iasnili shutkoi prizyv mera est' krapivu' [Vologda's authorities said mayor's recommendation to eat nettles a joke], 6 February, <http://www.gazeta.ru/social/news/2015/02/06/n_6899629.shtml> (last accessed 10 August 2015).

Goscilo, Helena, ed. (2013), *Putin as Celebrity and Cultural Icon*, New York: Routledge.

Gutterman, Steve (2013), 'Killing in Russia adds to concerns over treatment of gays', Reuters, 11 May, <http://www.reuters.com/article/2013/05/11/us-russia-killing-idUSBRE94A0F720130511> (last accessed 1 June 2014).

Iampolski, Mikhail (2015), 'Putin's Russia is in the grip of fascism', *Newsweek*, 9 March, <http://www.newsweek.com/putins-russia-grip-fascism-312513> (last accessed 10 August 2015).

Ioffe, Julia (2013), 'Russia's past is ever present: the "homosexual propaganda" ban is traditionalism at its worst', *New Republic*, 8 February, <http://www.newrepublic.com/article/112362/russias-gay-propaganda-ban-putin-brings-past-present#> (last accessed 10 July 2014).

Joseph, Jonathan (2009), 'Governmentality of what? Populations, states and international organizations', *Global Society*, 23, 4: 413–27.

Kelly, Mark G. E. (2010), 'International biopolitics: Foucault, globalization, and imperialism', *Theoria*, 57, 123: 1–26.

Khodorkovsky, Mikhail (2013), 'Ten years a prisoner', Khodorkovsky, 25 October, <http://www.khodorkovsky.com/writings-and-interviews/mikhail-khodorkovsky-ten-years-a-prisoner-the-new-york-times-opposite-the-editorial-page/> (last accessed 16 September 2014).

Kichanova, Vera (2013), 'Roditeli trebuiut uvolit' uchitelia Il'iu Kolmanovskogo za "propagandu gomoseksualizma"' [Parents demand teacher Ilia Kolmanosvkii be fired for 'homosexual propaganda'], Slon, 30 January, <http://slon.ru/russia/roditeli_khotyat_uvolneniya_uchitelya_vtorogo_litseya_igorya_kolmanovsko_za_propagandu_gomoseksualiz-880889.xhtml> (last accessed 6 September 2014).

Klishin, Il'ia (2013), 'Kto na samom dele "propagandiruet gomoseksualizm"' [Who really 'propagates homosexuality'?], *Vedomosti*, 30 January, <http://www.vedomosti.ru/opinion/news/8535221/glupost_ili_izmena?full#cut> (last accessed 10 July 2014).

Krasovskii, Anton (2013), 'Ia gei, i ia takoi zhe chelovek, kak prezident Putin' [I am a gay, and I am a human being like President Putin], Snob, 6 February, <http://www.snob.ru/selected/entry/57187> (last accessed 6 September 2014).

Krichevskii, Nikita (2008), 'Zanimatel'naia putinomika. Vypusk XII (metallurgicheskii)' [Entertaining Putinomics. Volume 12 (metallurgical)], APN, 28 July, <http://www.apn.ru/publications/article20438.htm> (last accessed 16 September 2014).

Maetnaia, Elizaveta and Dmitrii Evstifeev (2015), 'Utseleli formulirovki chinovnikov' [Officials' wording has survived], Gazeta.ru, 19 March, <http://www.gazeta.ru/social/2015/03/19/6605913.shtml> (last accessed 5 August 2015).
Makarychev, Andrei (2013), 'Ontologicheskaia depressiia i otsutstvuiushchii tsentr ideologii: Rossiia glazami zarubezhnykh ekspertov' [Ontological depression and the missing centre of ideology: Russia through the eyes of foreign experts], *Neprikosnovennyi zapas*, 6, 92, <http://magazines.russ.ru/nz/2013/6/18m.html> (last accessed 10 August 2015).
Marsh, Rosalind (2013), 'The concepts of gender, citizenship, and empire and their reflection in post-Soviet culture', *The Russian Review*, 72, 2: 187–211.
Medvedev, Sergei (2013), 'Lagernoe defile: pochemu v Rossii tak populiarny konkursy krasoty' [Camp defile: why beauty contests are so popular in Russia], Forbes, 24 September, <http://www.forbes.ru/mneniya-column/protesty/245114-sotsialnyi-lift-pochemu-v-rossii-tak-populyarny-konkursy-krasoty> (last accessed 10 July 2014).
Medvedev, Sergei (2015), 'Telo korolia: kak zdorov'e Putina stalo glavnoi temoi rossiiskoi politiki' [The body of the king: how Putin's health became key topic for Russian politics], Forbes, 25 March, <http://www.forbes.ru/mneniya-column/tsennosti/283581-telo-korolya-kak-zdorove-putina-stalo-glavnoi-temoi-rossiiskoi-polit> (last accessed 10 August 2015).
Merlingen, Michael (2006), 'Foucault and world politics: promises and challenges of extending governmentality theory to the European and beyond', *Millennium: Journal of International Studies*, 35, 1: 181–96.
Metro (2013), 'Leonid Roshal' priznalsia, chto nenavidit geev' [Leonid Roshal confessed that he hates gays], 26 February, <http://www.metronews.ru/novosti/leonid-roshal-priznalsja-chto-nenavidit-geev/Tpombz—G6NnRrEc6Zzk/> (last accessed 1 December 2014).
Mikhailova, Tatiana (2013), 'Putin as the father of the nation: his family and other animals', in Helena Goscilo, ed., *Putin as Celebrity and Cultural Icon*, New York: Routledge, 65–81.
Mizulina, Elena (2013a), 'Kontseptsiia gosudarstvennoi semeinoi politiki Rossiiskoi Federatsii na period do 2025 goda (Obshchestvennyi proekt)' [The concept of the state family policy of the Russian Federation until 2025 (Public project)], <http://elenamizulina.ru/pdf/Book_1_preview.pdf> (last accessed 10 October 2016).
Mizulina, Elena (2013b), 'Moe golosovanie za zakon Dimy Iakovleva – politicheskoe' [My voting for the Dima Iakovlev law was political], *Pervyi Kanal*, 24 February, <http://www.1tv.ru/sprojects_edition/si5756/fi21739> (last accessed 10 August 2015).
Morozov, Aleksandr (2010), 'Sem' novostei rossiiskoi vnutrennei politiki: kak umiraet politicheskoe' [Seven news items about Russian domestic politics: how the political dies], Slon, 10 October, <http://slon.ru/russia/sem_novostey_rossiyskoy_vnutrenney_politiki_kak_umiraet_politicheskoe-1002865.xhtml> (last accessed 10 August 2015).

Nikitin, Vadim (2013), 'Putin's punitive psychiatry and other flashbacks', Foreign Policy Association, 9 October, <http://foreignpolicyblogs.com/2013/10/09/putins-punitive-psychiatry-and-other-flashbacks/> (last accessed 18 December 2015).

Pavlovskii, Gleb (2016), 'Kreml: ot konservativnoi politiki – k revoliutsii' [The Kremlin: from conservative politics to revolution], *Russkii Zhurnal*, 30 May, <http://russ.ru/Mirovaya-povestka/Kreml-ot-konservativnoj-politiki-k-revolyucii> (last accessed 18 December 2015).

Podrabinek, Aleksandr (2013), 'Dorodovaia khvatka' [Prenatal grip], Grani.ru, 3 June, <http://grani.ru/opinion/podrabinek/m.215270.html> (last accessed 8 March 2014).

Prilepin, Zakhar (2006), *San'kia*, <http://sankya.ru/> (last accessed 12 September 2015).

Rabkor.ru (2013) 'Vse men'she rossiian khotiat stat' priemnymi roditeliami' [Fewer Russians want to be adoptive parents], 22 March, <http://rabkor.ru/news/2013/03/22/children-in-russia> (last accessed 6 September 2014).

RBK (2013), 'V Dume prokommentirovali initsiativu ob ogranichenii chisla brakov' [Comments in Duma on initiative on limitation of number of marriages], 26 June, <http://top.rbc.ru/society/27/06/2013/863689.shtml> (last accessed 1 December 2014).

Remizov, Mikhail (2013), 'Konservatizm i sovremennost'' [Conservatism and contemporaneity], *Svobodnaia mysl'*, 5, <http://www.svom.info/entry/281-konservatizm-i-sovremennost> (last accessed 10 July 2014).

Rozhkova, Natal'ia (2013) 'ONF predlagaet dlia "mal'chikov" vvesti otvetstvennost' za seks s "devochkoi"' [ONF proposes to make 'boys' responsible for sex with a 'girl'], *Moskovskii Komsomolets*, 28 March, <http://www.mk.ru/politics/article/2013/03/28/832922-onf-predlagaet-vvesti-dlya-malchikov-otvetstvennost-za-seks-s-devochkoy.html> (last accessed 10 July 2014).

Rubtsov, Aleksandr (2014), 'Novyi kul'turnyi kod: poluchite, raspishites'' [New cultural code: get it, sign it], *Vedomosti*, 14 April, 6.

RuFabula (2015), 'Pravoslavnye kazaki budut inspektirovat' peterburgskie kluby' [Orthodox Cossacks to inspect Petersburg clubs], 26 April, <http://rufabula.com/news/2015/04/26/inspectors> (last accessed 10 August 2015).

Rutland, Peter (2014), 'The Pussy Riot affair: gender and national identity in Putin's Russia', *Nationalities Papers*, 42, 4: 575–82.

Rutten, Ellen (2012), 'Putin on panties: sexing Russia in late Soviet and post-Soviet culture', in Rene M. Genis, Erick de Haard, Janneke Kalsbeek, Evelin Keizer and Jenny Stelleman, eds, *Between West and East: Festschrift for Wim Honselaar on the Occasion of his 65th Birthday*, Amsterdam: Pegasus: 567–95.

Schmitt, Carl (2005) *Political Theology*, Chicago, IL: University of Chicago Press.

Singer, Brian and Lorna Weir (2006), 'Politics and sovereign power: considerations on Foucault', *European Journal of Social Theory*, 9, 4: 443–65.
Sperling, Valerie (2015), *Sex, Politics and Putin: Political Legitimacy in Russia*, New York: Oxford University Press.
Storch, Leonid (2013), 'Bezydeinost' kak sovremennaia "Russkaia ideia"' [A lack of ideas as the contemporary 'Russian idea'], Ekho Moskvy, 28 August, <http://echo.msk.ru/blog/kritikator/1145264-echo/?=last> (last accessed 10 August 2015).
Tartakovskaia, Irina (2000), '"Sil'naia zhenshchina plachet u okna": gendernye reprezentatsii v postsovetskoi massovoi kul'ture' [A strong woman crying at the window], in Sergei Kukhterin and Aleksandr Sogomonov, eds, *Aspekty sotsial'noi teorii i sovremennogo obshchestva* [*Aspects of Social Theory and Contemporary Society*], Moscow: Institut sotsiologii RAN, 155–76.
Tikhonova-Iatsyk, Aleksandra (2009), '"Glamurnyi podonok" i "surovyi gei", ili postsovetskie reprezentatsii maskulinnosti v televizionnoi pop-kul'ture: "Nasha Russia" na TNT' ['Glamour scumbag' and 'tough gay', or post-Soviet representations of masculinity in TV popular culture: 'Nasha Russia' on TNT], in Pavel Romanov and Elena Iarskaia-Smirnova, eds, *Vizual'naia antropologiia: nastroika optiki* [*Visual Anthropology: Turning the Lens*], Moscow: TsSPGI, 256–75.
Tolkovatel' (2013) 'Zhit' v priemnoi sem'e v Rossii v 39 raz opasnee, chem v SShA' [Life in adoptive family in Russia is 39 times more dangerous than in the USA], 21 March, <http://ttolk.ru/?p=10148> (last accessed 8 June 2014).
Tolokonnikova, Nadezhda (2013), 'Ia sebe ne smogu prostit' do kontsa zhizni, esli ia ne poprobuiu khotia by chto-to izmenit" [I would not forgive myself until the end of my life if I did not try to change something], Slon, 26 September, <http://slon.ru/russia/nadezhda_tolokonnikova-996833.xhtml> (last accessed 10 July 2014).
Vaughan-Williams, Nick (2009), 'The generalised bio-political border? Re-conceptualising the limits of sovereign power', *Review of International Studies*, 35, 4: 729–49.
Vogt, Erik (2005), 'S/Citing the camp', in Andrew Norris, ed., *Politics, Metaphysics, and Death: Essays on Giorgio Agamben's Homo Sacer*, Durham, NC: Duke University Press, 74–106.
Widder, Nathan (2010), 'Foucault and power revisited', *European Journal of Political Theory*, 1, 4: 411–32.
Zdravomyslova, Elena and Anna Temkina (2002), 'Krizis maskulinnosti v pozdnesovetskom diskurse' [Crisis of masculinity in late Soviet discourse], in Sergei Ushakin, ed., *O muzhe(N)stvennosti* [*On Mascul(femin)inity*], Moscow: NLO, 432–52.
Zherebkin, Sergei (1999), 'Muzhskie i zhenskie fantazii: politiki seksual'nosti v postsovetskoi natsional'noi literature' [Male and female fantasies:

politics of sexuality in post-Soviet national literature], *Gendernye issledovaniia*, 3: 275–96.

Znak.com (2015), 'Dvorkovich prizval rossiian men'she est' i bol'she rabotat" [Dvorkovich suggested Russians should eat less and work harder], 19 June, <http://www.znak.com/urfo/news/2015-06-19/1041530.html?from=post_fb> (last accessed 10 August 2015).

Part II

Radical and other societal nationalisms

5
Revolutionary nationalism in contemporary Russia

Alexandra Kuznetsova and Sergey Sergeev

At first glance, nationalism and revolution would hardly seem to be connected with each other.[1] Consider the associations that these notions commonly evoke: nationalism targets primarily local or regional problems, with the goal of maintaining the status quo or imitating the past; by contrast, the major features of revolution are often innovation and universal change (together with violence). Shmuel Eisenstadt noted the revolutionaries' belief in 'creating a new order – total, cultural, social' (1978: 685) and listed the consequences of revolution, including the radical break with the past and the far-reaching transformation of all spheres of social life. Contemporary revolution scholars, such as Jack Goldstone, see the use of violence for establishing new institutions as a main element of revolution (Goldstone 2013: 1–9). However, Goldstone admits that, in some revolutions of the late twentieth century and the beginning of this century, violence has not played such a prominent role (ibid.: 104–16). Martin Malia has compared revolutions from the fifteenth to the twentieth centuries and comes to the rather pessimistic conclusion that the nature of revolution could never fit into a single, coherent model (Malia 2006: 287–301). Indeed, if we look at the conservative revolution movement in Germany in the 1920s and 1930s or the Iranian revolution in 1978–79, these were hardly consistent with an understanding of revolution as an innovative and international phenomenon. Still, the connection between nationalism and revolution is far from simple and straightforward, whether in a historical or in a cross-national perspective.

This chapter examines the connection between nationalism and revolution in contemporary Russia. In doing so, we briefly discuss some general trends in the mutual development of these two phenomena and the impact they have had on contemporary Russian nationalistic revolutionaries. We then proceed to outline the sub-scenes of Russian national revolutionaries, discussing the development among national bolsheviks, national anarchists, national socialists and national democrats, before offering some conclusions on the status of Russian national revolutionaries of today.

Trends in the mutual development of nationalism and revolution

In connection with the first great modern revolutions (1789–1848), nationalism and revolution developed as a consistent unity. Later, however, they separated as many revolutionaries declared internationalism, and conservative nationalism emerged as a counterweight to revolutionary nationalism. Thus, if we imagine revolutionary nationalism of the eighteenth to nineteenth centuries (from Jean-Jacques Rousseau to Giuseppe Mazzini) as our thesis, conservative nationalism became the antithesis. In the twentieth century, various ideologues and politicians once again began to link nationalism with revolution. One such attempt was the conservative revolution, or the 'revolution from the right', which occurred in Germany in the 1920s–30s, represented for instance by the writings of Arthur Moeller van den Bruck.

The Russian national revolutionaries of the 1990s and 2000s were influenced by the conservative revolution movement. The German conservative revolution has been particularly important as a source of inspiration, but also the Western European 'new right', with its attempt to reconcile racism with anti-imperialism and anti-capitalism, has wielded considerable influence (Griffin 2003: 30–34). From the 1990s to the beginning of the 2010s, the national revolutionary 'scene'[2] in Russia developed several sub-scenes: the national bolsheviks, the national anarchists, the national socialists (proponents of a white racist revolution) and the national democrats (the proponents of creating a Russian political nation and ethnic democracy).

National revolutionaries are nationalists who believe that revolution or radical political restructuring is both necessary and desirable. They include corresponding provisions in their manifestos. Russian national revolutionaries are diverse: the ideological spectrum ranges from the almost democratic national democrats to open neo-Nazis and thus mirrors virtually every branch of the Russian extra-parliamentary opposition – nationalists, leftists and democrats are represented both in the extra-parliamentary opposition and in the nationalist revolutionary organisations. In addition, the evolution of national revolutionary groups is closely linked with the transformation of Russian public feeling. The *ressentiment* of the 1990s, which later resurfaced in 'the Crimea syndrome', triggered the emergence of national bolsheviks. The rise of xenophobia after the turn of the century instigated a call for a racist 'white revolution'. And the upsurge of civic activity at the beginning of the 2010s stimulated the formation of national anarchists and national democrats. Overall, while national revolutionaries in Russia are marginal political groups that have been left to their own devices, they can nevertheless be said to have responded quickly to any change in the Russian political process.

National bolsheviks

The origins of the first national revolutionary organisations in Russia date back to 1992. The ideologists behind these organisations were motivated by the frustration and bitterness caused by the collapse of the Soviet Union, the breakup of the former Warsaw Pact, the diminishing international role of Russia, falling living standards and growing social inequality. The most prominent among these new national revolutionary organisations was the National Bolshevist Party (NBP), headed by Eduard Limonov (real name: Savenko).

In 1993, the year of its inception, the NBP was a small radical group with only several dozen members. By the end of the 1990s, it had grown to have branches in over fifty regions and a total of 5,000–7,000 members. The bold actions of NBP activists have been in the public spotlight[3] – and NBP activists have increasingly experienced the brutality of expanding authoritarianism in today's Russia.

Limonov as a charismatic yet radical leader has played a significant role in developing and expanding the NBP. Nevertheless, his leadership is not the whole explanation of the NBP's success (the NBP continued to operate while Limonov was incarcerated between 2001 and 2003). There are several reasons behind the effectiveness of the NBP (Sergeev 2004: 157–59). First, Limonov made youth the social base for the NBP: 'Our Russia is old. Every city is divided by the *nomenklatura*. Youth has no place for itself in the city . . . The originality of our party derived from the decision to recruit youth, not the local opposition' (Limonov 2002a: 113, 118). Thus, the NBP sought to position itself as a channel of social mobility for youth: 'Revolutions have always been accomplished by youth; reaction is the job of middle-aged and older people' (Limonov 2003a: 46).

Second, when most media channels were inaccessible to the party, the NBP managed to establish its own channel through which it could address its constituencies directly: the newspaper *Limonka*, which has been published since 1994, and is subtitled *The Direct Action Newspaper*. From 1994 to 1998, this newspaper became the NBP's major party-building tool. According to Limonov, 'some months after a "Limonka" had been dropped somewhere,[4] first a group and later a *natsbol* [national bolshevik] cell appeared there. These boys met, discussed the paper, and then wrote to us ... In this way we established our first organisations' (2002a: 90).

Third, the NBP attracted many Russian counterculture activists, such as avant-garde composer Sergei Kurekhin, the poet Alina Vitukhnovskaia and several rock artists, including Aleksandr Nepomniashchii, Egor Letov (of the rock band Grazhdanskaia Oborona) and Sergei Troitskii (of the rock band Korroziia Metalla). According to Ilia Kukulin, the NBP and its *Limonka* were 'from the onset envisioned not simply as political institutions, but as an art project' (2008: 303). This view is supported by Limonov, who has described the party as 'a cultural phenomenon in the first place, and not political. [The party possesses] the unique aesthetics of a revolt' (Limonov 2002b: 333).

The NBP managed to create a unique cultural style represented by skinny guys with short hair and black clothes who looked 'similar to the popular type of inner-city teenage boys: black jeans, boots, a jacket and a cap – at the same time being different from this type by their extreme asceticism ... nothing excessive, nothing rich or fancy in their outfits' (Limonov 2002a: 238–39). The NBP did not invent this style itself: it adopted and adapted it, drawing on existing cultural models.

At the same time, this style was closely connected to ideological guidelines. In his 2002 biography, Limonov elaborates on this. There he writes that political forces in Russia have always borrowed from earlier models: monarchists and *chernosotniks* (Black Hundreds) associated themselves with models presented by the pre-revolutionary Union of the Russian People, whereas Aleksandr Barkashov's Russian National Unity (*Russkoe natsional'noe edinstvo*) and Nikolai Lysenko's People's Republican Party (*Respublikanskaia narodnaia partiia*) adopted the Nazi storm-trooper model of the 1920s and 1930s. Viktor Anpilov and his Labour Russia (*Trudovaia Rossiia*) used as a template the late Stalinist Soviet Union, and the Communist Party of the Russian Federation, the Brezhnev Soviet regime (Limonov 2002a: 126, 169). The NBP saw themselves as the only modern party: 'We have created our party based on counter-culture and opposition politics.

We collected all the heroes who were fighting against the system, from both the left and the right' (Limonov 2002a: 169).

In 1999, the NBP underwent a transformation, redirecting its focus to public actions with symbolic implications. There were two major types of such actions. The first were attacks on 'moral targets' (Limonov 2002a: 213), in which activists publicly insulted the political and cultural establishment. NBP activists threw tomatoes and eggs and poured mayonnaise and ketchup on officials, or slapped them with flower bouquets. All these actions were decidedly nonviolent: when, for example, activists would slap their target with flowers, they used carnations, not roses, since the former have no thorns (ibid.). From 1999 to 2002, the moral targets were politicians and intellectuals who, according to the NBP, had harmed Russia and ethnic Russians (for example, Mikhail Gorbachev or film-maker Nikita Mikhalkov). Starting in 2003, the NBP also attacked politicians who were part of the political regime or were supportive of it. During the 2003 State Duma election campaign, the NBP carried out 'moral attacks' on the chairman of the Central Election Commission Aleksandr Veshniakov, on Prime Minister Mikhail Kasianov, on St Petersburg governor Valentina Matvienko and on several United Russia party leaders (NBP 2003).

The second type of action involved symbolic takeovers of public offices. Initially, in 1999 and 2000, the NBP conducted such takeovers in the 'Near Abroad' (Limonov 2002a: 214–17, 246–51). In Russia, the most notorious of these actions, which also grabbed international attention, were the takeover of the Ministry of Health and Social Development on 2 August 2004 in protest against the monetisation of social welfare, and the takeover of the Presidential Administration on 14 December 2004, with demands to free the activists arrested during the previous takeover.

In parallel, radical shifts took place in the ideological orientation of the NBP. Initially, the party's founding fathers – Eduard Limonov and Aleksandr Dugin – had seen the NBP as imperialstatist. According to the original party programme, the goal was to unite all ethnic Russians in one state, to be followed by the creation of a 'gigantic continental empire' spanning from Vladivostok to Gibraltar (NBP 1994). The programme combined 'an iron Russian order' with a prioritisation of the rights of the nation (including total cultural freedom). Its orientation toward 'traditionalist, hierarchical society' (ibid.) was, however, clearly in conflict with the party slogan 'for modernity, modernisation and avant-garde'. The relationship between state-nationalist and socialist ideas in the programme was also (perhaps intentionally) left unclear. On the whole, the NBP programme did not resemble the programme of an organisation whose ideological worldview was located in the counterculture.

Limonov gradually became disillusioned about the prospects for collaboration with members of the nationalist establishment. In his 2003 book *The Other Russia*, he radically transformed his ideology and moved from right–left statism toward anarchism, replacing the idea of a 'total empire' with a stateless society and a war of all against all, further rejecting both city life and the idea of the monogamous family: 'The primary principle of the new civilisation must be a full heroic life in armed nomadic communes, free communities of men and women based on brotherhood, free love and the communal upbringing of children' (Limonov 2003a: 267). Limonov's description of this 'new civilisation' is reminiscent of the Republic of Pirates, Makhno's anarchist republic,[5] and a post-apocalyptic *Mad Max 2* entourage:

> The armed communes will look like primordial tribes ... One should not be afraid of potential conflicts between the armed communes, nor should one be afraid of a fight. The creative aggression of separatism is preferable to the globalist prison order. (Ibid.: 269)

There is a connection between this new utopia and the counterculture: both emphasise the role of youth, marginalised groups and sexual freedom. However, even after changing his key principles, Limonov continued to synthesise rightist and leftist ideologies. He gave the fighting instinct a central place in his utopia, demonstrating the relationship of his ideology with the radical right and with Social Darwinist doctrines.

Despite this reorientation, after his release from prison in 2003, Limonov did not insist on adopting a new party programme. He maintained that the old one had already become sacrosanct and should therefore be preserved – adding, however, that it could be interpreted in different ways, with *The Other Russia* being one such possible re-interpretation (Limonov 2003b). All the same, in 2004 a new NBP programme was adopted. It contained hardly any ideas from the initial programme or from *The Other Russia*: it was democratic and socialist in orientation, with certain elements of egalitarianism and populism (see NBP 2004). The programme thus represented yet another transformation of Limonov and the NBP. After suppressing its anarchist and nationalist motives, the NBP now moved closer to democratic and leftist extra-parliamentary organisations. In order to challenge the authoritarian regime and support democratic civil rights, the party joined the Other Russia coalition. After NBP was banned by the authorities in 2007, the national bolsheviks have thus operated under the 'Other Russia' appellation – since 2010 as the (still) unregistered Other Russia party.

The NBP's public actions have also changed. From 2005 to 2008, NBP organised unauthorised public rallies called Dissenters' Marches. Since 2009, it has held meetings on the thirty-first of each month which has thirty-one days (an action known as Strategy-31). The thirty-first is symbolic: Article 31 of the Russian Constitution guarantees freedom of assembly and public meetings. These walks, meetings and picket protests have brought together from a few hundred to some 3,000 people, and have always provoked an immediate and severe reaction from the authorities. Almost every protest has been dispersed by the police and the Special Purpose Mobility Unit (*Otriad mobil'nyi osobogo naznachenia*, OMON), and the participants detained and prosecuted.[6]

In 2011–12, Limonov and the Other Russia activists participated in the mass political protests for fair elections. Limonov represented the most radical wing of the opposition, demanding that the regime be dismantled. He criticised the 'bourgeois' opposition leaders (Gennadii Gudkov, Sergei Parkhomenko and Vladimir Ryzhkov) for changing the meeting place on 10 December 2011 from Revolution Square to Bolotnaia Square, for making compromises with the government and undermining the protests:

> If the bourgeois leaders had not taken dozens of thousands of protesting citizens away from the city centre, the citizens would have been protesting inside the State Duma or the CEC [Central Election Commission] tonight . . . Achieving freedom for the country is possible only [by] talking vigorously: from the position of citizen power knocking on the doors of their buildings with thousands of fists. (Limonov 2011)

In 2014, after the annexation of Crimea, Limonov for the first time in his political career declared approval of the policies of Vladimir Putin (Limonov 2014). Later, he called for further steps to annex the Donetsk and Luhansk regions as well as the rest of Novorossiia (Limonov 2015a; 2015b). Volunteers from Limonov's Other Russia party participated in the military conflict against the Ukrainian army, and two are reported having been killed.

Some *natsbols* disapproved of Limonov's reorientation and opposed the new policy, which they claimed represented 'treason against national bolshevist ideas and the future Russian revolution' (NBP 2014). A splinter group thus announced the establishment of the National Bolshevist Platform, but then proceeded to ally with other national revolutionary groups in the new National Revolutionary Bloc (*Natsional-revoliutsionnyi blok*).

National anarchists

The national anarchists, or national revolutionaries, have a shorter history and are less infamous than the national bolsheviks. Their first groupuscules emerged in Russia around 2008/2009 in the midst of a fierce struggle between anti-fascist groups and neo-Nazi skinheads. The ideological trajectories that produced nationalist and national revolutionary groups mirrored each other: the nationalists emerged from a left-to-right shift and the partial acceptance of rightist ideology by anarchists and autonomists, while the national revolutionaries came as the result of a right-to-left shift and the partial acceptance of leftist ideology by some nationalists.

The ideology of national anarchism does not fit neatly into the established trichotomy of Russian nationalism – imperial, civilisational and ethnic (Pain 2007; Verkhovskii 2007). Imperial nationalism promotes the creation of a big multi-ethnic state, to encompass, according to various approaches, the territory of the former Russian Empire or the Soviet Union. Civilisational nationalism identifies a state model with a dominant role for ethnic Russians, while ethnic nationalism advocates the creation of a state exclusively for ethnic Russians.

The *natsbols* are an example of imperial nationalism, whereas national democrats support Russian ethnic nationalism. National anarchists, however, refute the concept of a state per se. Their vision is of ethnically 'clean' communes as the model for the future organisation of humanity (Sunshine 2008), and this links them to the ethnic nationalists. According to the national anarchists, ethnic communes will evolve naturally, as most people prefer to live with ethnically similar neighbours. These communes will then unite in federations of ethnically related peoples, each commune remaining autonomous. A person who chooses to live with another ethnic group would have to respect that group's culture and traditions. The national anarchists may have borrowed this idea of separate living and ethno-cultural homogeneity from the New Right, from the writings of the French academic and philosopher Alain de Benoist in particular (*Telos* 1993–94).

One of the first national anarchist groups to appear was *Volnitsa*. This group was established in 2009 by Kirill Banshantsev, a nationalist activist from St Petersburg. Prior to this, Banshantsev had been a member of the Slavic Community (*Slavianskaia obshchina*) organisation. Some sources claim that Banshantsev also had been an activist in the Movement Against Illegal Immigration (pn14.info 2012b; KRAS-MAT 2013). However, Banshantsev himself denies any such involvement (Sobeskii 2014).

The Volnitsa manifesto was clearly influenced by Marxism and Marxist discourse, incorporating concepts like the 'alienation of labour', 'exploitation', 'surplus product' and others. The language used in describing an ideal society is, however, closer to the West European Third Way of the 1950s and 1960s. This was an option in-between 'classical liberal capitalism and the Marxist-Leninist state capitalism, between imperial chauvinism and anti-nationalist cosmopolitanism' (Vol'nitsa 2012). According to the manifesto, an anti-globalist and anti-cosmopolitan revolution would lead to 'direct democracy', to 'a Republic of people's councils (*soviets*)' (ibid.). Citizens of this new republic would elect representatives for short-term positions with an imperative mandate that could be revoked at any point.

The authors of the manifesto concede that different peoples may share the same territory if these peoples are 'complementary' (Vol'nitsa 2012). In addition, 'representatives of every nation should have an opportunity to occupy a separate piece of land and establish there the rules that correspond with its culture'. Further, 'consumption culture' is considered 'degenerative', and is contrasted 'original folk culture', which they associate with 'spiritual development, [and] respect for and preservation of the diversity of ethnic identities' (ibid.).

The manifesto speaks against tolerance – also typical of the Russian political right. An armed militia should preferably replace the army and police. This militia would conduct ethnic and racial cleansings whenever necessary and would thus 'rapidly dominate over any violators, oppressors and aggressors, fighting evil only with evil and with no tolerance' in order 'to become a master on its own land' (Vol'nitsa 2012).

For its pantheon of heroes, Volnitsa made an unusual choice. It excluded not only tsars, generals, statists and bureaucrats but also the internationalist revolutionaries. Instead, it honoured the heroes of popular uprisings against tsarism and Bolshevism, from Stepan

Razin to the Kronshtadt sailors, as well as Russian revolutionary anarchists and the *narodniki*.[7]

Through its political actions Volnitsa has attempted to highlight its symbolic unity with the left. In November 2012, several dozen Volnitsa activists participated in a demonstration organised by the Left Front in Moscow to mark the ninety-fifth anniversary of the October Revolution. The Volnitsa slogans demonstrated continuity with anarchist traditions – 'The state is an enemy of people', 'Raise the black flag high' – but also with revolutionary traditions: 'For a Russia without noblemen and slaves', 'For Soviets without Bolsheviks'. In addition, the slogan 'Glory to the heroes' echoed Ukrainian nationalist ideals, while other slogans highlighted the synthesis of nationalist and socialist ideas (Sobeskii 2012). That same month, Volnitsa activists also took part in a Polish Independence Day march in Warsaw organised by autonomous nationalists, which ended in clashes with police and anti-fascist groups (Vesna narodov 2012).

In March 2013, Volnitsa voluntarily disbanded, due to a combination of disagreements within the organisation and growing external pressure from the authorities. Some activists led by Banshantsev continued the leftist traditions and joined a socialist revolutionary group called Autonomous Action (*Avtonomnoe deistvie*), an anarchist-communist, anti-authoritarian organisation established in 2002.[8] The same year as Banshantsev joined Autonomous Action, this organisation split into two groups, one focusing on class struggle and the second holding that the left must also counter homophobia, sexism and racism.

Those national anarchists who had disagreed with Banshantsev went on to establish a new organisation, *Narodnaia Volia* (Popular Will), which filled the political-ideological niche formerly occupied by Volnitsa. However, Narodnaia Volia is not preoccupied with the usual wars between different subcultures or the traditional enmity between the right and left and between Nazis and anti-fascists, opting instead to focus on 'opposition to the growing state terror in Russia' (Volin 2015).

The new organisation takes a pessimistic view of the possibilities of a world revolution – according to Narodnaia Volia, one should not have 'any illusions about the possibility of a world revolution and building the ideal community globally' (Volin 2015). However, it sees the Maidan revolution in Kiev as 'an example of the possibility of collective revolutionary creativity by the public', something which could pave the way for popular control over the bureaucracy (ibid.). Narodnaia Volia has been critical of both the Russian and the

Ukrainian authorities; according to one of its ideologists, both have benefitted from the war:

> As a result of the Russian aggression, the potential avant-garde of the new revolution is dying at the frontline as members of volunteer battalions, betrayed by the corrupt authorities of the Ministry of Internal Affairs and the General Staff of Ukraine. (Ibid.)

While condemning the Ukrainian authorities, Narodnaia Volia holds that Ukraine has the right to self-defence. Russia's involvement, by contrast, is regarded as extremely negative: 'There is a real threat that the imperial forces could use the revolutionary processes in Kiev to restore Putin's Russia's control over Ukraine' (ibid.). To show its opposition, Narodnaia Volia activists took part in the September 2014 All-Russian March for Peace, a protest against the war in Ukraine.

Narodnaia Volia takes a different approach to inter-ethnic relations from other national anarchists. It accepts the equality of various ethnic groups on the condition that these groups live separately, govern themselves and preserve their own ethnic identity. According to its manifesto,

> Each nation shall have the right to defend its ethnic and racial identity, as well as a right to self-defence against encroachments on its rights by any hostile forces ... Thus, taking current conditions into consideration, we are reviving the ancient traditions of popular self-governance. (Narodnaia Volia 2013)

In 2014, Narodnaia Volia, the Nationalist Bolshevist Platform (*Natsional-bol'shevistskaia platforma*) and the Russian Socialist Movement (*Russkoe sotsialisticheskoe dvizhenie*, RSD)[9] created the Nationalist Revolutionary Bloc (*Natsional-revoliutsionnyi blok*). The RSD had been established in the early 2010s by autonomous nationalists. The main difference between Volnitsa and the RSD had been the latter's socialist, rather than anarchist, orientation. However, the degree of nationalist identification also varies. For example, Narodnaia Volia does not use the 'Celtic' cross (or short sun-cross) among its official symbols, although one of its ideologues admits that this symbol can 'convey a meaning of national liberation in contrast to the reactionary, conservative, imperial nationalism. Besides, this cross was used in the Novgorod Republic, which many consider as an alternative to the despotic Muscovy' (Volin 2015). The RSD, for its part, uses the Celtic cross both as a separate symbol and in combination with the red and black five-pointed star. And although it does not explicitly mention the separation of ethnic groups in its programme, it underlines the necessity of 're-ethnicisation' and the deportation of all illegal immigrants (Russkoe sotsialisticheskoe dvizhenie 2015).

National socialists

The third group of national revolutionaries are the supporters of a white revolution: radical skinheads (or boneheads). In 1995, there were only about 150 skinheads in Moscow, and even smaller numbers in other cities. By 2003/2004, there were 50,000 skinheads at the national level with 5,000–5,500 in Moscow and its suburbs and up to 3,000 in St Petersburg (Tarasov 2004).

Whereas in the USA, Great Britain and other Western European countries skinheads became racist and xenophobic in the 1970s (Hebdige 1987: 54–59), the skinhead movement in Russia was pro-Nazi from the outset (Tarasov 2004). The emergence of mass xenophobia in the early 2000s stimulated the rapid development of the skinhead movement. According to public opinion polls, the share of respondents who express full or partial support for the slogan 'Russia for Russians' in 1999 exceeded 50 per cent – and it has not declined since (Levada 2014). Most likely, an atmosphere of resentment and jealousy created such a change in public opinion. The social and economic crisis of 1998 and the onset of the Second Chechen War added to the xenophobic atmosphere in Russian society. For the ordinary citizen, the growing number of immigrants from Central Asia and the Caucasus demonstrated the humiliation and decline of Russia. Immigrants had been common in the Soviet era as well; however, their presence did not have the same effect as now. At home, sitting in their kitchens, older people would complain that 'before, they used to respect and be afraid of Russians, now they despise us'. The younger generation of skinheads, however, were not sitting idle in the kitchens – they were trying to re-establish *Russian* order in the streets.

According to the SOVA Center, after 2004 there was a steady growth in violent ethnically motivated crimes. First, gangs attacked people of non-Slavic appearance and members of youth subcultures (including punks, goths and rastas). In 2004, there were 268 such attacks, in which fifty people were killed. In 2006 and 2007, the number of attacks continued to grow, peaking in 2008 with more than 100 deaths. In 2009, attacks began to decrease, although eighty-four people were killed and 443 wounded that year. From 2011 the level of violence started to decrease markedly, and this trend has continued to this day (Table 5.1). This change can be attributed to the

Table 5.1 People killed and wounded in neo-Nazi attacks, 2004–16

Year	Number of deaths as a result of neo-Nazi attacks	Number of people wounded or beaten in neo-Nazi attacks
2004	50	218
2005	49	419
2006	66	522
2007	89	618
2008	166	499
2009	84	443
2010	42	401
2011	25	195
2012	19	191
2013	23	203
2014	36	133
2015	11	82
2016 (8 months)	4	34

Source: Adapted from the SOVA Center annual reports, <www.sova-center.ru> (last accessed 20 October 2016).

transformation of the political situation, but also to the fact that many prominent neo-Nazi activists have been arrested and convicted.

Another radical nationalist organisation is the Combat Organisation of Russian Nationalists (*Boevaia organizatsiia russkikh natsionalistov*, BORN), established in 2008. The BORN fighters have been picking their targets among persons known for their political views: in particular, they have organised the assassinations of several well-known anti-fascists, including Fedor Filatov, Ilia Dzaparidze and Ivan Khutorskoi. On 19 January 2009, BORN members killed the prominent Russian lawyer and moral leader of the anti-fascist movement Stanislav Markelov and *Novaia gazeta* journalist Anastasiia Baburova on the streets of Moscow. The perpetrators, Nikita Tikhonov and Evgeniia Khasis, were arrested in November that year. Tikhonov was sentenced to life and Khasis to eighteen years in prison (Tumanov and Kozlov 2014).

BORN fighters committed yet another notorious murder in April 2010, killing Judge Eduard Chuvashov. He had twice presided over trials of neo-Nazi gangs: of the White Wolves gang of Aleksei Dzavakhishvili and of the gang of Artur Ryno and Pavel Skachevskii, in both cases handing out long-term sentences. In 2012–13, the assassins as well as the plotters behind this murder were arrested and sentenced to life in prison (Afonskii 2015).

Some BORN members were simultaneously members of a legal nationalist organisation called Russian Image (*Russkii obraz*), established by Ilia Goriachev. During the trial against Tikhonov and Khasis, Goriachev's testimony proved central to the guilty verdict. In 2015, however, Goriachev too was arrested and sentenced to life imprisonment (Nazaretz and Muradova 2015).

The National Socialist Society–North (*Natsional-sotsialisticheskoe obshchestvo–Sever*, NSO–Sever) was another neo-Nazi group motivated by ideas of a white supremacy revolution. This group, established in 2004, sprang out of the National Socialist Society, a neo-Nazi organisation with cells in several Russian cities, including Murmansk, Nizhnii Novgorod, Riazan, Samara and St Petersburg. Its goal was to build a Russian nation-state based on the ideas of national socialism. NSO–Sever was led by Maksim Bazylev (also known as Adolf) and Lev Molotkov. The organisation used existing legal mechanisms: its members participated in municipal elections and held picket protests and meetings where they distributed neo-Nazi newspapers, brochures and books. But they also engaged in extra-legal activity: NSO–Sever members committed twenty-seven murders, twenty-four of which were classified as hate crimes. One of the perpetrators characterised these deaths as 'collateral damage of the nationalist revolution' (Fal'kovskii 2014: 6–7). In 2010, the activity of the National Socialist Society was banned, and the following year, twenty-four members of NSO–Sever were sentenced to various terms in prison, including five life sentences.

The defeat of the radical nationalist underground led to confusion among Russian nationalists. To consolidate, national socialist groups in 2012 published a joint manifesto on 'The Problems of the Nationalist Movement and the Ways to Overcome Them' (pn14.info 2012a). According to the manifesto, the primary goal of the Russian nationalist movement is 'to break down the contemporary political and economic system and establish an order that will benefit the development and prosperity of the Russian nation and the White race'. The Russian nation is defined in racial terms: 'the fight against the anti-popular regime and against Jewishness is our major goal'. The manifesto condemns liberalism, capitalism and Marxism, and tries to reconcile the priorities of the Russian nation with German-style national socialism. Finally, the manifesto rejects democracy and general elections and asserts that seizure of power must be violent.

National democrats

Towards the end of the first decade of the new millennium, the Russian ethno-nationalist movement gave birth to a new national democratic movement. The image of Russian nationalism as anti-liberal, anti-Western and supportive of the authoritarian regime seemed to have become outdated: national democracy became a new trend of the Russian nationalist movement.

The National Russian Liberation Movement (*Natsional'noe russkoe osvoboditel'noe dvizhenie*, NAROD)[10] was one of the first national democratic organisations. It was founded in 2007 by Sergei Guliaev and Aleksei Navalnyi, the latter turning into a leader of the protest movement from 2011 to 2013. The major goal of the NAROD movement was to protect and develop the Russian nation by dismantling the current political regime and building a modern democratic state. Nationalists who promoted xenophobia were declared 'national provocateurs' (NAROD 2007).[11] At approximately the same time, Professor Valerii Solovei – a scholar and supporter of Russian ethno-nationalism – began to draw attention to the revolutionary potential of Russian nationalism (Solovei and Solovei 2009: 405–35).

In 2010, several members of the defunct National Front party, including Ilia Lazarenko and Aleksei Shiropaev, established the National Democratic Alliance (*Natsional-demokraticheskii al'ians*, NDA). In the 1990s, some future NDA members had positioned themselves as racist national revolutionaries. For instance, the Russian Union of Youth created by Ilia Lazarenko in 1991 had transmuted into the Russian Union of Youth–National Revolutionary Action (*Soiuz russkoi molodezhi–Natsional-revoliutsionnoe deistvie*, SRM–NRD) and later the National Revolutionary Action Front (*Front natsional-revoliutsionnogo deistviia*, FNRD). The FNRD leaders understood 'nationalist revolution' as the 'revolution of the white man' aimed at worldwide white racial supremacy (Verkhovskii et al. 1996: 137–40). In 1994, the FNRD was recast as the National Front party – and then soon disappeared from the political scene.

By 2010, Lazarenko and Shiropaev had radically changed their racist views. They began to advocate the creation of a new Russian democratic state, to be achieved by reformatting the territory of the present-day Russian Federation and establishing seven ethnically Russian republics based on Russian *krais* and *oblasts*. They further declared that a new federal agreement would have to be signed with the non-Russian ethnic republics (except for in the North Caucasus). The political regime of the new Russian Federation would be democratic but with harsh immigration laws for persons from the Caucasus, Asia and Africa (Natsional-demokraticheskii al'ians 2010).

In November of 2010, Anton Susov and Aleksandr Khramov, former members of the Movement Against Illegal Immigration (*Dvizhenie protiv nelegal'noi immigratsii*, DPNI), established the Russian Civic Union (*Russkii grazhdanskii soiuz*, RGS) movement. The main principles of this movement are basically consistent with the ideas of NAROD and NDA: the promotion of a democratic state, free and fair elections, and restrictions on immigration. The RGS manifesto talks about a Russian 'political nation' which should be built around 'the Russian ethnic core' (APN 2010). The document does not directly exclude the North Caucasus from the Russian state, but insists on cutting off funding, renegotiating borders and establishing strict border controls. At the same time, RGS renounces fascism, racism and religious fundamentalism. Instead, it promotes democratic nationalist traditions, drawing on such symbols as the Novgorod Veche, the Cossacks and the Decembrists (ibid.).

The RGS manifesto is not unambiguous, however: although it condemns racism, it proclaims support and protection primarily for ethnic Russians, including the Russian diaspora abroad. Its views on the status of ethnic minorities within the Russian Federation that are unwilling to join the Russian political nation and to assimilate remain unclear. The manifesto notes only that their rights will be 'considered' (rather than 'protected') 'in accordance with international treaties' (ibid.).

In March 2012, two important national democratic organisations – the Russian Civic Union and the Russian Public Movement (*Russkoe obshchestvennoe dvizhenie*) – merged into the National Democratic Party (*Natsional'no-demokraticheskaia partiia*, NDP) led by Konstantin Krylov. According to the manifesto adopted in connection with the founding of the new party, the National Democratic Party denounced authoritarianism, and confirmed its democratic orientation: democracy was understood as the responsibility of the state to protect the principles of democratic rights and freedoms. The authors of the manifesto tried to combine such democratic values with an ethnocentric understanding of the Russian nation: 'Russia must become the native home for all Russians (*russkie*)' and adherence to hard-line migration policies (Natsional'no-demokraticheskaia partiia 2012: 3–5).

The national democrats also use the concept 'national revolution'. However, they speak about 'national democratic' and 'democratic' revolutions (Khramov 2011: 44, 46, 67). The goal of such a revolution is to create a Russian nation-state – a federation of Russian territories – although existing ethnically non-Russian republics would be allowed to join. Ideally, this revolution should be legitimate and nonviolent:

> [Russians] just need to come and vote in the parliamentary elections and in the elections to the Constitutional Assembly [which is intended to re-introduce a state based on national democratic principles]. If they are deprived of this opportunity, Russians will take it back in the streets. (Ibid.: 69)

Accordingly, the national democrats welcomed the 2009–10 mass protests in Vladivostok and Kaliningrad,[12] which they saw as the beginning of 'an emerging anti-authoritarian revolution' (ibid.: 206–7). Likewise, they actively participated in the For Fair Elections movement of 2011–12.

The 2011–12 protest movement served to unite nationalist movements and parties, such as the Other Russia, the *Russkie* (Russians) movement, the Russian Civic Union, the Russian Public Movement and the Russian Image. Unexpectedly, during the protests a coalition of liberal, leftist, civil society and nationalist organisations was also established. In some cities, for example Kazan, national democrats were in charge of organising the protests. At the national level, five nationalist representatives were elected to the Russian Opposition Coordination Council. Leonid Byzov (2012) notes that nationalists who opposed imperial tradition joined the opposition. Although he labels these activists 'leftist' and 'revolutionary', the national democrats are in fact supporters of a market economy (Natsional'no-demokraticheskaia partiia 2012: 4).

Among those arrested after the Bolotnaia Square protests on 6 May 2012 were some national democrats, although they were not numerous. Among the thrity-three protesters arrested, three were nationalists: two NDP members, Iaroslav Belousov and Ilia Gushchin, and one member of the *Russkie* movement, Rikhard Sobolev. A fourth, Oleg Melnikov, also took part in nationalist activities but did not consider himself a nationalist. In comparison, nine activists from various leftist organisations were arrested, as well as five civic activists, five liberal activists and ten ordinary citizens.[13]

After the annexation of Crimea, the national democrats split. Since 2014, Krylov's National Democratic Party has been demanding that the Russian state give stronger support to the separatists in Donetsk and Luhansk, although as a general line, the party has maintained a negative attitude toward Kremlin policies. Writer and party activist Maksim Veletskii describes the separatist movements in Donetsk and Luhansk as the 'democratic revolution of the Russian people', whereas Putin's policies are denounced as anti-national, supportive of the oligarchy and 'filthy *ordynshchina*'.[14] Such standpoints have led to the emergence of slogans like 'the government must resign' and 'Novorossiia must join Russia' (Veletskii 2015). Other national democratic leaders, including Shiropaev, condemn the 'post-Crimea' policies of the Russian government (Shiropaev 2016). However, these national democratic leaders have no independent political platform; the organisations they established have not succeeded.

Conclusions

Nationalism, in Russia as well as in general, has two distinct faces. Conservative nationalism often has the goal of maintaining the status quo and protecting the existing regime. By contrast, revolutionary nationalism is commonly opposed to the regime and seeks to achieve its radical transformation. Until recently, Russian nationalists identified themselves with conservative nationalism, and revolutionary nationalism found itself in the shadow of its twin – national revolutionaries were seen as weirdos and freaks. However, in the early years of the twenty-first century, Limonov's national bolsheviks established themselves as a regular and steadfast opponent of the existing political system in Russia, and Nazi-inspired revolutionaries (the proponents of the white revolution) introduced street terror to Russian cities.

At the end of the first decade of the new millennium, new types of revolutionary nationalists began to appear. National anarchists have envisioned a way out of the neo-Nazi versus anti-fascist confrontation by amalgamating these two opposing perspectives. National democrats have sought to integrate Russian nationalism and democracy. This revival of oppositional nationalism has apparently worried the regime. Targeted repressions in 2012 and 2013 intimidated the opposition, including the nationalists, and the rise in jingoism after the 2014 annexation of Crimea has deprived the opposition of mass support. In addition, the annexation split the revolutionary nationalist movement into supporters and opponents of the official Kremlin policy. As a result, Russia's revolutionary nationalists have lost whatever limited influence they once enjoyed. Nevertheless, in a time of regime crisis, a revival of nationalist ideas in new shapes and forms is still possible.

Notes

1. This chapter was prepared with financial support from the Russian Foundation for Humanities, project number 15-03-00223: The Role of Nationalism in the Revolution Processes (A Comparative Analysis).
2. In describing the national revolutionaries, the term 'scene' is more appropriate than the term 'movement'. In cultural sociology, 'scene' is broadly defined as a complex of the social institutions and cultural practices of a subcultural community.
3. Pro-regime Russian youth organisations such as Nashi would later copy the NBP's style and methods for public actions.
4. Wordplay: *limonka* is slang for 'hand grenade', but also a pun on the name of the NBP leader, Limonov.
5. From 1918 to 1921, during the Russian Civil War, Nestor Makhno led an anarchist rebel army – and a republic – based in Eastern Ukraine (today's Zaporizhia oblast).
6. Such open use of force against the extra-parliamentary opposition can be seen an entirely rational elite strategy: the internally insecure elite saw organisationally independent groups as a potential threat, so such groups had to be co-opted or suppressed before becoming too dangerous (Gel'man 2010).
7. The *narodniki* was a revolutionary socialist movement within the Russian intelligentsia in the second half of the nineteenth century.
8. The Russian anti-fascist movement, which aims to resist nationalists physically, was established through Autonomous Action (Sergeev 2013).
9. This organisation should not be confused with *Rossiiskoe sotsialisticheskoe dvizhenie*, which is closely connected with the Fourth International.
10. The abbreviation of the movement, NAROD, also means 'the people'.
11. Later Navalnyi would begin to advocate civic nationalism 'based on the unity of civil rights and freedoms' (Mikhnik and Navalnyi 2015: 58–59).
12. Protests in Vladivostok (2008–10) and Kaliningrad (2009–10) were motivated by socioeconomic reasons. In Vladivostok, the population was worried about an increase in automobile import tariffs. Many people there are engaged in trade in second-hand cars from Japan, and the rise in tariffs made this business unprofitable. In Kaliningrad, the protests were sparked by increases in utility payments and vehicle taxes. The number of protestors varied from several hundred to several thousand people.
13. For information on the Bolotnaia case and the prisoners of Bolotnaia, see <http://rosuznik.org/arrests> (last accessed 7 December 2016).
14. *Ordynshchina* was a tax collected by the Mongols from the Russian lands during the rule of the Golden Horde (from 1237 to 1480).

Bibliography

Afonskii, Aleksei (2015), 'Figuranty dela BORN poluchili ot 24 let do pozhiznennogo zakliucheniia' [Persons involved in the BORN case sentenced to from 24 years to life in prison], RAPSI, 21 April, <http://www.rapsinews.ru/judicial_news/20150421/273587891.html#ixzz3Zp4bIFp4> (last accessed 26 March 2016).

APN (2010), 'Manifest ob obrazovanii natsional-demokraticheskogo dvizheniia Russkii grazhdanskii soiuz' [Manifesto on establishing the national-democratic movement Russian Civic Union], 19 November, <http:// www.apn.ru/special/article23357.htm> (last accessed 25 March 2016).

Byzov, Leonid (2012), 'Politicheskie tsveta novorusskogo protesta' [The political colours of the new Russian protest], *Monitoring obshchestvennogo mneniia: ekonomicheskie i sotsial'nye peremeny*, 1: 27–32.

Eisenstadt, Shmuel (1978), *Revolution and the Transformation of Societies*, New York: Free Press.

Fal'kovskii, Il'ia (2014), *Nezametnye ubiistva* [*Unnoticed Murders*], Moscow: Common Place.

Gel'man, Vladimir (2010), 'Porochnyi krug repressii' [The vicious circle of repressions], Slon.ru, 7 June, <https://slon.ru/russia/porochnyy_krug_repressiy-403429.xhtml> (last accessed 25 March 2016).

Goldstone, Jack (2013), *Revolutions: A Very Short Introduction*, Oxford: Oxford University Press.

Griffin, Roger (2003), 'From slime mould to rhizome: an introduction to the groupuscular right', *Patterns of Prejudice*, 37, 1: 27–50.

Hebdige, Dick (1987), *Subculture: The Meaning of Style*, New York: Routledge.

Khramov, Aleksandr (2011), *Katekhizis natsional-demokrata* [*Catechism of a National Democrat*], Moscow: Skimen.

KRAS-MAT (2013), 'Natsionalizm kak narkotik' [Nationalism as a drug], 28 February, <http://www.aitrus.info/node/2750> (last accessed 26 March 2016).

Kukulin, Il'ia (2008), 'Reaktsiia dissotsiatsii: legitimatsiia ul'trapravogo diskursa v sovremennoi rossiiskoi literature' [Dissociative reaction: legitimising the ultra-right discourse in modern Russian literature], in Marlene Laruelle, ed. *Russkii natsionalizm: sotsial'nyi i kul'turnyi kontekst* [*Russian Nationalism: Social and Cultural Context*], Moscow: NLO, 257–338.

Levada (2014), Natsionalizm, ksenofobiia i migratsiia [Nationalism, xenophobia, and migration], 26 August, <http:// www.levada.ru/26-08-2014/natsionalizm-ksenofobiya-i-migratsiya> (last accessed 25 March 2016).

Limonov, Eduard (2002a), *Moia politicheskaia biografiia* [*My Political Biography*], Moscow: Amfora.

Limonov, Eduard (2002b), *V plenu u mertvetsov* [*In the Captivity of the Dead*], Moscow: Ul'tra.Kul'tura.
Limonov, Eduard (2003a), *Drugaia Rossiia. Ochertaniia budushchego* [*The Other Russia: Outlines of the Future*], Moscow: Ul'tra.Kul'tura.
Limonov, Eduard (2003b), 'O praktike i teorii Partii i sostoianii Rossii' [On the practice and theory of the Party and the state of Russia], *Limonka*, 234.
Limonov, Eduard (2011), 'Moe ofitsial'noe zaiavlenie' [My official announcement], *Zhivoi zhurnal*, 10 December, <http://limonov-eduard.livejournal.com/2011/12/10/> (last accessed 26 March 2016).
Limonov, Eduard (2014), 'Nekhorosho. Dazhe kak-to ottalkivaiushche vygliadit' [Not good. It even looks somewhat repulsive], *Zhivoi zhurnal*, 20 May, <http://limonov-eduard.livejournal.com/483257.html> (last accessed 16 October 2016).
Limonov, Eduard (2015a), 'Trebuem interventsii!' [We demand intervention!], *Zhivoi zhurnal*, 3 January, <http://limonov-eduard.livejournal.com/587184.html> (last accessed 26 March 2016).
Limonov, Eduard (2015b), 'Est' opaseniia' [There are concerns], *Zhivoi zhurnal*, 19 January, <http://limonov-eduard.livejournal.com/595175.html> (last accessed 26 March 2016).
Malia, Martin (2006). *History's Locomotives: Revolutions and the Making of the Modern World*, New Haven, CT: Yale University Press.
Mikhnik, Adam and Alexander Navalnyi (2015), *Dialogi* [*Dialogues*], Moscow: Novoe izdatel'stvo.
NAROD (2007), 'Manifest Natsional'nogo russkogo osvoboditel'nogo dvizheniia "NAROD"' [Manifesto of the National Russian Liberation Movement 'NAROD'], APN, 27 June, <http:// www.apn.ru/publications/article17321.htm> (last accessed 25 March 2016).
Narodnaia Volia (2013), Manifest [Manifesto], <http://ru.narvol.org/manifest/> (last accessed 26 March 2016).
Natsional-demokraticheskii al'ians (2010), 'Manifest Natsional-demokraticheskogo al'iansa' [Manifesto of the National Democratic Alliance], Natsional-demokratiia v Rossii, 15 March, <http://ru-nazdem.livejournal.com/767252.html> (last accessed 28 March 2016).
Natsional'no-demokraticheskaia partiia (2012), 'Manifest o sozdanii Natsional'no-demokraticheskoi partii' [Manifesto on the establishing of the National Democratic Party], *Voprosy natsionalizma*, 10: 3–5.
Nazaretz, Evgeniia and Mariia Muradova (2015), 'Delo Goriacheva: verdikt' [Goriachev's case: the verdict], Radio Svoboda, 14 July, <http://www.svoboda.org/content/article/27126734.html> (last accessed 25 March 2016).
NBP (1994), 'Programma NBP' [The NBP programme], <http://theory.nazbol.info/index.php?option=com_content&view=article&id=64:-1994-&catid=31:general&Itemid=27> (last accessed 25 March 2016).
NBP (2003), 'Rasstrel'nyi spisok NBP' [Hit list of the NBP], *Limonka*, 203.

NBP (2004), 'Programma NBP' [The NBP programme], <https://rg.ru/2005/01/19/nbp-dok.html> (last accessed 25 March 2016).
NBP (2014), 'Zaiavlenie natsional-bol'shevikov' [Announcement of the National-Bolsheviks], <https://vk.com/wall47971091_979> (last accessed 25 March 2016).
Pain, Emil' (2007), 'O fenomene imperskogo natsionalizma' [On the phenomenon of imperial nationalism], in Marlene Laruelle, ed., *Russkii natsionalizm v politicheskom prostranstve* [*Russian Nationalism in the Political Space*], Moscow: Franko-rossiiskii tsentr gumanitarnykh i obshchestvennykh nauk, 336–55.
pn14.info (2012a), 'Manifest Russkogo natsional'nogo dvizheniia' [Manifesto of the Russian Nationalist Movement], 27 June, <http://pn14.info/?p=116439> (last accessed 27 March 2016).
pn14.info (2012b), Kirill Banshantsev, rulevoi piterskoi Vol'nitsy [Kirill Banshantsev, helmsman of the Petersburg Volnitsa], 7 September, <https://pn14.info/?p=119914&cpage=29> (last accessed 26 March 2016).
Russkoe sotsialisticheskoe dvizhenie (2015), 'Perekhodnaia programma Russkogo sotsialisticheskogo dvizheniia' [The transitional programme of the Russian Socialist Movement], 18 January, <http://rus-soc.blogspot.ru/2015/01/blog-post_18.html> (last accessed 27 March 2016).
Sergeev, Sergei (2004), *Politicheskaia oppozitsiia v sovremennoi Rossiiskoi Federatsii* [*Political Opposition in the Contemporary Russian Federation*], Kazan: Kazanskii gosudarstvennyi universitet.
Sergeev, Sergei (2013), 'Levye radikaly v rossiiskoi provintsii: dvizhenie "antifa"' [The radical left in the Russian countryside: the anti-fa movement], *Politeks*, 1: 38–50.
Shiropaev, Aleksei (2016), 'K forumu Svobodnoi Rossii v Vilniuse' [To the Free Russia forum in Vilnius], *Russkaia fabula*, 8 March, <https://rufabula.com/author/alexey-shiropaev/1061> (last accessed 15 September 2016).
Sobeskii, Maksim (2012), 'Levye natsionalisty otprazdnovali godovshchinu Oktiabrskoi revoliutsii [Leftist nationalists celebrated the anniversary of the October revolution], RuPolitika, 17 November, <http://rupolitika.ru/rusvopros/maksim-sobeskiy-levyie-natsionalistyi-otprazdnovali-godovshhinu-oktyabrskoy-revolyutsii/> (last accessed 25 March 2016).
Sobeskii, Maksim (2014), 'Kak leveli natsionalisty' [How nationalists became leftist], Avtorskii blog, <http://zavtra.ru/content/view/kak-leveli-natsionalisty/> (last accessed 25 March 2016).
Solovei, Tat'iana and Valerii Solovei (2009), *Nesostoiavshaiasia revoliutsiia* [*The Revolution that Didn't Happen*], Moscow: Feoriia.
Sunshine, Spencer (2008), 'Rebranding fascism: national-anarchists', *Public Eye*, 23, 4, <http://www.publiceye.org/magazine/v23n4/pdf/v23n4.pdf> (last accessed 25 March 2016).
Tarasov, Aleksandr (2004), 'Natsi-skiny v sovremennoi Rossii: doklad dlia Moskovskogo biuro po pravam cheloveka' [Nazi skinheads in

contemporary Russia: report to the Moscow Human Rights Bureau], *Skepsis*, <http://www.scepsis.ru/library/id_605.html> (last accessed 25 March 2016).
Telos (1993–94), 'Three interviews with Alain de Benoist', 98–99: 173–207.
Tumanov, Grigorii and Viacheslav Kozlov (2014), 'Vskrytie BORNa' [Uncovering BORN], Lenta.ru, 17 February, <https://lenta.ru/articles/2014/02/17/born> (last accessed 25 March 2016).
Veletskii, Maksim (2015), 'NDP. Protiv vlasti i liberal'noi oppozitsii' [The NDP: against the regime and the liberal opposition], Natsional'no-demokraticheskaia partiia, 28 February, <http://rosndp.org/ndp-protiv-vlasti-i-liberaljnoj-oppozicii.htm> (last accessed 29 March 2016).
Verkhovskii, Aleksandr (2007), 'Ideinaia evoliutsiia russkogo natsionalizma: 1990'e i 2000'e gody' [The ideological evolution of Russian nationalism in the 1990s and 2000s], in Aleksandr Verkhovskii (ed.), *Verkhi i nizy russkogo natsionalisma* [*The Upper and Lower Echelons of Russian Nationalism*], Moscow: SOVA Center, 5–32.
Verkhovskii, Aleksandr, Anatolii Papp and Vladimir Pribylovskii (1996), *Politicheskii ekstremizm v Rossii* [*Political Extremism in Russia*], Moscow: Institut eksperimental'noi sotsiologii.
Vesna narodov (2012), 'Varshava v ogne' [Warsaw on fire], 18 November, <http://vk.com/wall-33042756_42096> (last accessed 25 March 2016).
Volin, Veniamin (2015), 'Narodnaia Volia: "Nas postoianno pytaiutsia zapisat' v tot ili inoi lager"' [Narodnaia Volia: 'They are always trying to link us to one or the other camp'], *Sensus novus*, 16 March, <http://www.sensusnovus.ru/policy/2015/03/16/20402.html> (last accessed 25 March 2016).
Vol'nitsa (2012), 'Manifest natsional-anarkhistov' [The manifesto of the National Anarchists], <http://www.democratia2.ru/group/f025ffaa-f3dc-4ddb-b4f9-3ce4ea23dcae/content> (last accessed 26 March 2016).

6

The Russian nationalist movement at low ebb

Alexander Verkhovsky

In discussions on Russian nationalism 'after Crimea' it is widely held that the authorities have hijacked the nationalist agenda,[1] that Russian nationalism has migrated from the Russian March to the offices of the Kremlin ideologues, in short, that Russian nationalism has ceased to be an oppositional phenomenon and become political mainstream. I argue that the picture might not be that simple.

An adequate assessment of the situation requires analysis along at least four dimensions. We need, first, to assess the objectives and actions of Russia's political leadership (and that is not a unified political entity); second, to analyse popular and (presumably) influential ideological texts reflecting this alleged shift as well as texts that do not support it; third, to study the mood of the masses through the lens of sociological surveys; and finally, to assess the actions and situation of the groups and organisations that can collectively be labelled as the 'nationalist movement'. Such a complex analysis is impossible in one article – indeed, hardly possible for a single author. Here I concentrate on the last of the above-mentioned dimensions: a review of nationalist activities at the grassroots – while also taking into account the whole spectrum of relations between the nationalists and the powers-that-be.

Decline of the traditional nationalist movement

The Russian nationalist movement is diverse, but since the beginning of the new century it has been dominated by organisations and groups whose activists (but not necessarily leaders) have come either from the Nazi-skinhead environment or directly from the ranks of successive radical youth groups that depart only marginally from neo-Nazi ideals. The leader and symbol of this dominant part of the nationalist movement was Aleksandr Belov's Movement Against Illegal

Immigration (*Dvizhenie protiv nelegal'noi immigratsii*, DPNI). This was accompanied on the flanks by smaller national democratic groups (we will return to these below) and by openly neo-Nazi groups and organisations, like Dmitrii Demushkin's Slavic Union (*Slavianskii soiuz*). If the old nationalists of the 1990s wanted to remain relevant, they too could not do without these same activists, as shown by the infusion of new members into Sergei Baburin's Russian All-People's Union (*Rossiiskii obshchenarodnyi soiuz*, ROS).

From 2012, the Russian nationalist movement entered a phase of deepening crisis. I have described this process in detail in a previous publication within the framework of the NEORUSS project, covering the development up to 2015 (Verkhovsky 2016). Here I will therefore only summarise a few fundamental observations regarding this process, supplemented with an update on recent developments, up until the end of 2016.

The decline of the nationalist movement is very noticeable, even when measured by simple quantitative indicators. There have been far fewer public actions, and those that are still organised draw considerably fewer participants and are held in fewer cities than before (Alperovich and Yudina 2016; Iudina and Al'perovich 2016). To the general public, this decline has been made evident by the dramatic decline in the number of participants in the annual Russian Marches on 4 November – the only nationalist event that is widely covered in the media. At its peak, in 2011 and 2013, the Russian March (or rather, the two rival marches) gathered more than 6,000 people in Moscow alone, but in 2015 the three separate marches in the capital were attended by less than 1,500 people altogether (not counting the participants in the official 'We Are United' march). That year marches were organised in twenty-four cities, only half the number of a few years earlier. In 2016 the level of participation in Moscow remained the same as the previous year, but marches were held in only eleven cities (SOVA Center 2016b).

In addition to rallies, an important form of public activity for nationalists has been 'raids': actions aimed at disrupting the work or residency of migrants who lack the necessary documentation; supressing the sales of semi-legal drugs; identifying and 'punishing' paedophiles and homosexuals; and so on. The raids are characterised by three main features: first, they are directed at a goal that is deemed justifiable by the overwhelming majority of Russians as well as by the state. Second, they are often carried out in full agreement with the police (or the Migration Service), and conducted with the participation or at least the clear acquiescence of these agencies.

Third, the raids involve acts of arbitrariness accompanied by violence or the explicit threat of violence, but this violence almost always remains within limits that ensure that the police are not given any reason to interfere, or at least, bring the participants to justice. Such raids had already become familiar in the 1990s, but became much more systematic and widespread after the police in 2011 had jailed hundreds of neo-Nazis for more severe forms of violence. The number of raids peaked in 2013, and has since declined.

There are several reasons for this decline. First, from 2013, the authorities began to clamp down on the activities of groups that crossed the line of open, demonstrative violence. Among the groups that were broken up by the authorities were the Shield of Moscow (*Shchit Moskvy*), which was associated with the pro-Kremlin organisation Young Russia (*Rossiia Molodaia*); the purely neo-Nazi movement Restrukt!, and its breakaway group Attack (*Ataka*) (the latter being somewhat less brutal in its actions). Second, from the onset of the military operations in Donbas in 2014, some groups switched their focus from conducting raids, to participating in the war. The most striking example here is Bright Rus (*Svetlaia Rus'*), from which the group E.N.O.T. Corp. emerged. This group not only assisted the Donetskaia Narodnaia Respublika (DNR) and Luganskaia Narodnaia Respublika (LNR), but also had a permanent active combat unit stationed in Donbas. Third, from 2015 onwards, groups associated with the *Russkie* (Russians) movement, the National Social Initiative (previously the National Socialist Initiative, *Natsional-sotsialisticheskaia initsiativa*, NSI) and others, were subjected to heavy repression (see below). As a result, their raiding activities were sharply reduced or stopped altogether.

Even racist street violence began to decline, even though this kind of action is mainly carried out by participants of small groups not directly linked to publicly prominent nationalist organisations. Whereas in 2011–13 the SOVA Center could report about twenty to thirty murders and around 200 other victims of hate crimes annually, in 2014 it registered thirty-six murders, but fewer than 140 other victims, and in 2015 no more than eleven murders and eighty-five other victims. These statistics are of course not complete, but they accurately reflect the overall trend. The even less complete data for the first half of 2016 only confirm these observations (Iudina and Al'perovich 2016).

The nationalists themselves tend to attribute the decline to state repression, and this explanation is not unfounded: repression is not a chimera of the nationalists, but a reality. To be sure, in recent years the number of convictions for racist violence has declined, but this can in part can be explained by the reduction in violence itself. The number of convictions for hate propaganda and similar crimes has, however, increased from year to year; in 2015 this growth accelerated noticeably, and statistics from the first half of 2016 indicate that this growth will continue (Iudina and Al'perovich 2016).[2] Of course, Russian nationalists were not the only ones convicted for 'crimes of an extremist nature'. Still, we can safely say that most of these convictions were connected to ethno-religious xenophobia in forms inherent to Russian nationalists. This enforcement practice therefore represents a real pressure on the Russian nationalist movement.

Part of the decline can also be attributed to the drain caused by the conflict in Ukraine. Many radical activists have set off to fight there, and those who have participated in military action on the Ukrainian side can obviously not return to Russia (this particularly concerns groups belonging to the radical rightist Misanthropic Division). Others have simply emigrated, fearing persecution.

There is also a change in approach by the authorities: since the second half of 2014 there have been many more instances of criminal cases against defendants who are not just ordinary activists or simply randomly selected individuals, but prominent leaders of the nationalist movement. As mentioned, the neo-Nazi movement Restrukt! was suppressed in 2014: its leader Maksim (Tesak) Martsinkevich was put behind bars, and later several activists were also convicted. The same fate befell the breakaway group Attack. At about the same time, the best-known leader of the Russian nationalists, Aleksandr Belov, head of the *Russkie* movement and earlier of the DPNI, was arrested.[3] Criminal charges have also been brought against the leaders of the St Petersburg-based Russian Cleansing (*Russkaia zachistka*), Nikolai Bondarik and Dmitrii 'Beshenyi' Evtushenko (the latter also an important figure in the St Petersburg branch of the *Russkie* movement). Even though both received lenient sentences, Russian Cleansing subsequently became more peaceable.

In 2015 more prominent figures among the national radicals were arrested, including Aleksei Kolegov, leader of the Komi-based Russian nationalist organisation Northern Boundary (*Rubezh severa*). Among those who escaped arrest in 2015/2016, several were suspected or accused of breaking the law, sometimes in more than one individual instance: Dmitrii Bobrov, leader of the NSI; Dmitrii Demushkin, the only prominent leader of the *Russkie* movement still at large; Egor Prosvirnin, founder of the popular (among nationalists) website Sputnik i Pogrom, and others (Alperovich and Yudina

2015; 2016; Iudina and Al'perovich 2016). In August 2016, Belov was sentenced to a term of 7.5 years – unprecedented for such cases.

The new pressure also affected organisations not usually perceived as nationalistic. The entire leadership of the national Stalinist initiative group for conducting a referendum 'For Responsible Power' (*Za otvetstvennuiu vlast'*) was arrested.[4] In June 2016, Iurii Ekishev, a prominent activist in the national Stalinist movement Minin and Pozharskii's People's Militia (*Narodnoe opolchenie imeni Minina i Pozharskogo*, NOMP) was likewise arrested.[5] New charges were announced against former Colonel Vladimir Kvachkov, the leader of NOMP, who was already serving a prison sentence. In 2016 problems also began to pile up for Eduard Limonov's Other Russia (*Drugaia Rossiia*).

The pressure was felt not only by the opposition, but also by supporters of Novorossiia and the uprising in Donbas. Most prominent among these was Igor Strelkov, the hero of the separatist rebellion. In January 2016 a criminal case was launched against one of the members of Strelkov's Committee of 25 January (*Komitet 25 ianvaria*, K25), also known as the All-Russian National Movement of Igor Strelkov (*Obshcherusskoe natsional'noe dvizhenie pod rukovodstvom Igoria Strelkova*). Another member of this committee was investigated in connection with the above-mentioned Ekishev case.

Previously, judicial bans on organisations were performed practically 'post-mortem' (as was the case for instance with the National Socialist Society), or had no practical effect (for instance, in the case of the DPNI or the Slavic Union). However, the banning of the *Russkie* movement in 2015 – by the way, on questionable grounds – led to the termination of the activity of this crisis-ridden organisation. In other cases, such as the ban on the NSI, a similar effect was not achieved, although the activity of the NSI was reduced to a minimum.

But repression cannot convincingly be regarded as the only, or even the most important, explanation for the decline of the nationalist movement. For example, the level of activity of Konstantin Krylov's National Democratic Party (*Natsional'no-demokraticheskaia partiia*, NDP) and Baburin's ROS was reduced drastically, even though pressure on these organisations, especially on ROS, was minimal. Moreover, despite the absence of external pressure, ROS failed in its attempt to take part in the 2015 regional and local elections (Alperovich and Yudina 2016).

Of course, the nationalist movement had already been undermined back in 2012 by the decision of its leaders to join the liberal opposition in the mass protests, a move highly unpopular among the neo-Nazi majority, and by the 2014 schism caused by diverging views on the events in Ukraine (Kolstø 2016). But even in the interval between these two years, in 2013 – that is, in the period when an anti-migrant campaign was conducted from above, and there were increasingly frequent anti-migrant riots – the Russian nationalist movement failed to expand its membership. Neither xenophobic participants in local riots nor people with oppositional leanings who attended protest meetings were prepared to join the movement.

I have elsewhere put forth some explanations for this failure: the unacceptability of the neo-Nazi style to members of the general public, the refusal to support extra-systemic grassroots violence, and, as a whole, the tendency of the majority of the population to orient themselves predominantly towards the authorities and officially approved initiatives, rather than towards some independent, oppositional activity (Verkhovsky 2016).[6] The strengthening of the position of the central government after Crimea, it appears, has dashed any expectations that this relationship between the public and the authorities will change anytime soon. The decline in the activity of the nationalist movement seems to a large extent to be a result of the disillusionment caused by recognition of this state of affairs.

National democrats

The sector of the Russian nationalist scene usually termed 'national democratic' has experienced no less of a decline. This sector is to a lesser extent related to the neo-Nazi skinhead environment and traditions; it has emphatically distanced itself from violence, and is generally more intellectual in orientation. The national democrats have attracted considerable attention from researchers (see, for example, Laruelle 2014), and among some, this sector has inspired hopes of a new Russian nationalism that could play a progressive role in Russian history, akin to that played by nationalism in a host of European countries in the nineteenth and part of the twentieth centuries.[7] We should also note that the national democrats themselves have understood their role in this way (Nazdem.info 2010), thereby implicitly falling victim to anachronism.

Towards the end of the first decade of the new millennium, national democracy as a distinct trend within Russian nationalism indeed became noticeable. The most prominent organisations and groups within this sector were the above-mentioned National Democratic Party of Konstantin Krylov; the New Force (*Novaia sila*) party, founded in early

2012, that is, at the peak of the protest movement, by Moskovskii gosudarstvennyi institut mezhdunarodnykh otnoshenii (MGIMO) Professor Valerii Solovei; Vladimir Milov's Democratic Choice (*Demokraticheskii vybor*), which broke away from the liberal Solidarity movement in 2009; and finally, the tiny National Democratic Alliance (*Natsional-demokraticheskii al'ians*), led by two veterans of the ultra-right movement, Aleksei Shiropaev and Ilia Lazarenko. Some other organisations also played significant roles in the development of national democratic camp, like the Russian Civil Union (*Russkii grazhdanskii soiuz*), and of course, Aleksei Navalnyi's project NAROD, which was founded in 2007 but lasted for less than two years. Navalnyi's subsequent political activities have also been linked to the national democratic camp, but it is impossible to characterise his own organisations as such.

Even at their peak, the national democrats constituted only a small portion of the nationalist movement. At any march in Moscow they could gather perhaps 200 people at the most.[8] Of course, Navalnyi has turned out to be a very successful opposition politician – but more in the guise of a liberal democrat and an anti-corruption fighter than in the role of a national democrat. Among most nationalists, he remains extremely unpopular and, over time, the amount of nationalist rhetoric in his speeches has decreased (Pain 2014). Nationalist themes were addressed, of course, during the very xenophobic 2013 Moscow mayoral election campaign, but Navalnyi did so no more than most other candidates (see chapter by Blakkisrud and Kolstø in this volume). Thus, up to now, Navalnyi has not formed any specific political movement that could be characterised as 'national democratic'.

The crisis of the nationalist movement had a detrimental effect on the already small national democratic organisations. The National Democratic Party, as noted, has curtailed its activity significantly;[9] the New Force party simply ceased to exist in 2014; and the Democratic Choice split in December 2015 (Gorbachev 2016), and is now totally invisible, while the National Democratic Alliance remains marginal. By the beginning of 2015 it was difficult not to notice the national democrats' glaring lack of success:[10] with a few local exceptions, all these organisations had not developed beyond being mostly clubs of bloggers.

As to the reasons for the failure of the national democrats, we may generally exclude the problem of *style*, which first caught the public eye in connection with the DPNI and then with the *Russkie* movement. Still, it cannot be entirely ruled out: the negative reputation of the *Russkie* movement did trouble the National Democratic Party, for example, which marched together with the *Russkie* and which by many were considered to be the 'intellectual wing' of this movement. It is not surprising that Valerii Solovei wanted to accept only *new* activists into his party; those who were already members of the nationalist movement had clearly exhausted their potential.[11] However, sufficient numbers of new people were not found. As a result, Solovei simply liquidated the party and returned to his career as a professor. For others, however, there was no such alternative.

On the other hand, the *statist orientation* of most of the Russian public obviously impacted on the national democrats as well. However, the failure of the national democrats is also partly rooted in their very ideology. Like their more radical partners in the nationalist movement, the national democrats were all opposed to imperialist nationalism and understood nationalism in ethnic terms. However, their anti-imperial orientation does not mean that their nationalism can be considered as 'civic' in the modern sense of this word: for this, they put too strong an emphasis on the ethno-cultural (if not racial) aspect in their definition of a nation (Pain 2016). It can be argued that the Russian national democrats have been firmly following the pattern of German romantic nationalism of the mid-nineteenth century, and not than that of British or French nationalism of the same era, paying scant attention to the changes that have occurred since then in the nation-building process.

This focus on the older romantic ideals of ethno-nationalism also has another fundamental flaw: historically, this nationalism was focused on putting together a state on the basis of the fragments of feudalism, or liberation from a foreign imperial power. However, Russia has a long history as a unified country. And it is still an empire, even though not as large as before. Ever since Soviet times, Russian ethno-nationalists have therefore insisted on interpreting 'the state' as something foreign to them. Concepts like the existence of an 'occupation government' in Russia are often used to underline this point. Or the empire is explained as a mechanism for supporting the peripheral regions at the expense of the metropolitan centre, and the imperial leadership as an agent (witting or unwitting) of the ethnic minorities, or even of migrants. Such assumptions do not correspond to the everyday experience of the average Russian, and are accepted only by like-minded people – or by those receptive to conspiracy theories, but in Russia the latter very rarely espouse democratic values.

Thus, those who are ready to oppose the powers-that-be and are attracted by the idea of 'Russia for Russians' joined the *Russkie* movement rather than the national democrats. And, with few exceptions, those who put more emphasis on freedom and democracy did not want to join the ranks of the nationalists. This state of affairs has been stable for a long time. Whereas some new groups that have arisen on the ruins of the *Russkie* movement may possibly be regarded as national democratic in orientation (see below), they do not refer to themselves as such – and, most importantly, they are very small.

What is the oppositional nationalist movement today?

Many observers have the impression that the space once occupied by the oppositional nationalist movement in the political expanse is now empty. That is not entirely correct, but there has certainly been a sharp decline in activity, with many organisations having completely or almost completely ceased their activities, and the sector has been transformed into new and as yet unfamiliar groups.

In order to better grasp the current activity of the Russian nationalist movement we may divide the current membership in this movement according to three criteria: relationship with the authorities, approach to Novorossiia, and the tendency to set up their own political organisations. Obviously, not all of the eight possible combinations of these three criteria are represented in the real world (for instance, one can hardly be completely loyal to the Kremlin *and* also speak out against Novorossiia), and a specific group may not always easily fit into the given combinations. Still, this approach can be helpful in guiding us through the ideological landscape.[12]

As of 2016, leadership within the oppositional nationalism sector has shifted from the opponents of Novorossiia to its supporters. The latter group includes several hubs around which activists unite, the most important being Strelkov's K25. K25 was founded as a club of well-known nationalists with highly differing convictions: the monarchist Strelkov is found together with the moderate national democrat Krylov and the radical national democrat Prosvirnin, the national Stalinist Vladimir Kucherenko (alias Maksim Kalashnikov), the national Bolshevik Eduard Limonov and the officious nationalist publicist Egor Kholmogorov. With its considerable internal pluralism, K25 focuses on 'the Russian World' (*Russkii mir*). It portrays itself as being in opposition, but in practice tries to avoid conflict with the government, and its rhetoric repeats much of the propaganda presented on state TV. Judging from its activity during the first months of its existence, there is no reason to believe that the K25 will become the basis for an influential movement. Yes, it was responsible for the action that attracted the largest number of nationalists in the first half of 2016 – the rally in memory of those killed in Odessa on 2 May 2014 – but even at this rally only around 300 people participated. A joint rally with the NDP on National Unity Day (4 November) 2016 drew only 200 persons (SOVA Center 2016b).

When K25 began to transform itself from a club into an organisation, Limonov left (as could be expected), and his Other Russia is now competing for exactly the same ideological niche. After the cessation of active combat in Donbas, Other Russia lost some of the former enthusiasm, and relations with the authorities soured, but Limonov's party remains quite active. When on 5 April it organised the Day of the Russian Nation (*Den' russkoi natsii*) in several cities, these demonstrations were attended by representatives of other nationalist organisations, both oppositional and pro-Kremlin. But even this comparatively successful action was not very impressive, measured by quantitative indicators.

A much weaker competitor to the K25 is a long-standing coalition of Novorossiia supporters, the Russian National Front (*Russkii natsional'nyi front*, RNF). The RNF is also highly pluralistic, as it is based on a coalition of Andrei Saveliev's radical ethno-nationalists in Great Russia (*Velikaia Rossiia*), Stanislav Vorobev's more conservative Russian Imperial Movement (*Russkoe imperskoe dvizhenie*) and the earlier-mentioned national Stalinist group For Responsible Power. Unlike K25, the RNF is undeniably in opposition to the authorities. In 2016 it was the only organisation that managed to organise a 'Russian 1 May' (*russkii pervomai*) in Moscow. Even in the absence of competitors, however, barely 100 people participated in the event. Mention can also be made of another, still weaker coalition of Novorossiia supporters: the National Conservative Movement 'Russian World' (*Natsional'no-konservativnoe dvizhenie 'Russkii mir'*), which has enjoyed even less success than the RNF.

Another hub around which supporters of Novorossiia has gathered is the Battle for Donbas (*Bitva za Donbass*), created in 2014 by fairly radical groups. The main participants in this grouping nevertheless emphasise their loyalty towards the authorities: the Right-Conservative Alliance (*Pravo-konservativnyi al'ians*, PKA), led by Aleksei Zhivov and Evgenii Valiaev,[13] and Aleksandr Dugin's better-known Eurasian Youth Union (*Evraziiskii soiuz molodezhi*).

In the Battle for Donbas, Zhivov and Valiaev also collaborate with far less loyal groups, such as the internet project Sputnik i Pogrom. By the end of 2014, members of this coalition were no longer invited to talk shows on state TV, and the coalition had clearly fallen out of favour. Today, the coalition has shrunk to the size of the PKA. It still seeks to make itself heard, but due to lack of activists and, apparently, fears of persecution, these attempts have been reduced to publishing materials and organising discussions.

The PKA is not the only example of this trend. Some other former radical activists now also prefer the role of experts. Here we may note the People's Diplomacy (*Narodnaia diplomatiia*) foundation, whose publications are actively promoted at the international level, and, it seems, not without the support of the authorities.[14] These people, together with more moderate nationalists, are gradually forming a new intellectual milieu. At the personal level this milieu also includes representatives of pro-Kremlin organisations, such as members of the Motherland (*Rodina*) party. Thus, the pro-Novorossiia majority of the nationalist opposition is now less publicly visible, focusing – not necessarily voluntarily – on organising conferences and club discussions, while clearly gravitating away from an oppositional stance.

In the September 2016 federal, regional and local elections these organisations were hardly noticeable. The vast majority either demonstratively ignored the elections or called for a boycott. And the reason is clear: the pro-Kremlin parties that took part in the elections did not feel they needed the support of such organisations; the opposition parties could not accept the Novorossiia supporters; and the organisations themselves lacked resources to field their own candidates. Therefore, some activists from the ultranationalist part of the political spectrum joined the candidate lists of parties that clearly had no chance of gaining seats in the parliament, such as the Patriots of Russia (*Patrioty Rossii*) and the Greens (*Zelenye*). The only ultra-rightist who made a noticeable appearance was Valentina Bobrova from the National Conservative Movement, who ran for the Greens in a single-mandate district in Voronezh and finished as number five out of ten (SOVA Center 2016a).

Within this pro-Novorossiia majority there are also groups that are somewhat more removed from politics. These are entities of various kinds that were established during the war in Donbas as fighter groups or combat training groups. Over the past few years, nationalists of all hues have of course been actively involved in combat training, but Novorossiia supporters clearly outnumber the opponents, who have very limited resources. Among such pro-Novorossiia groups, mention should first of all be made of the Imperial Legion (*Imperskii legion*), set up by the Russian Imperial Movement, and its training club Reserve (*Rezerv*), and the group E.N.O.T. Corp., which has grown out of the Orthodox nationalist movement People's Assembly (*Narodnyi sobor*) and Bright Rus. The national radicals naturally come into contact with Donbas war veterans who hold other views, but it is still too early to come to a conclusion about the impact this may have.

The opponents of the Novorossiia project are much more disorganised and, moreover, deprived of opportunities to speak in public. The numerical strength of their organisations is difficult to estimate, but they have been unable to retain their former support levels and have most likely shrunk to a size similar to the pro-Novorossiia organisations, or become even smaller.

The former leader of the *Russkie* (Russians) movement, Dmitrii Demushkin, has decided not to set up a new organisation, as the three previous organisations he led have all been banned. He is now competing for the legacy of the *Russskie* with Vladimir Basmanov, who has established the Committee 'Nation and Freedom' (*Komitet 'Natsiia i svoboda'*, KNS). However, Basmanov has left Russia (and competes with various nationalist émigré groups), while Demushkin has a strong a reputation for working under the control of the police. As for the key political differences between the two, Basmanov, although never ceasing to act as an ethno-nationalist, has been striving for convergence with the liberal opposition. To this end, he organised the participation of nationalists in the open primaries of the liberal People's Freedom Party (*Partiia narodnoi svobody*, PARNAS). Thanks in part to this campaign, Viacheslav Maltsev, a Saratov non-partisan right-populist blogger, ended up as number two on the PARNAS party list (Aleksandr Belov, who was under arrest, won fifth place in the primaries, but was not included on the ticket by the PARNAS party congress). A few other organisations also take the same line as KNS: these include the new organisations Free Russia (*Svobodnaia Rossiia*), the Russian Joint National Alliance (*Russkii ob"edinennyi natsional'nyi al'ians*, RONA) and Honour and Freedom (*Chest' i svoboda*); the old Russian Right Party (*Rossiiskaia pravaia partiia*); and the above-mentioned National Democratic Alliance. They are capable of bringing out one, and occasionally two, dozen people onto the streets of Moscow.

All these groups actively supported PARNAS in the September 2016 elections – which came as an extremely unpleasant surprise to the traditional liberal supporters of this party. Maltsev included in his campaign apparatus several ultra-rightists like Demushkin and the well-known anti-Semite Boris Mironov (federal minister of the media 1993–94). Maltsev's open and unsanctioned racist attacks attracted not only the support of nationalists but also condemnation: many, both among opponents and supporters of Novorossiia – including Igor Strelkov – regarded him as an agent provocateur. It is hard to say how many ultra-rightists voted for PARNAS, but it is clear that they did not influence the overall result, which proved extremely disappointing for PARNAS: with no more than 0.7 per cent of the overall vote, it finished eleventh out of fourteen parties. Ultra-rightist candidates running on a PARNAS ticket in single-mandate districts also failed to get elected. Aleksei Samokhin, for instance, finished as number eight out of ten candidates in his district. With hindsight we can note that this experiment of creating an open alliance between liberals and ultra-rightists was a failure, and PARNAS even found itself on the brink of a schism.

Finally, the neo-Nazi majority among the radical nationalists is increasingly being forced out of politics. As mentioned, some organisations have been closed down, others were directly involved in the Ukrainian conflict on the side of Kiev government, thereby ruling out the possibility of a role for themselves in Russian politics. The majority of those who remain no longer engage in any kind of activity, not even in hate crimes. The minority, still active, is represented by several small groups: the Black Bloc (*Chernyi blok*), the Unappeasable League (*Neprimirimaia liga*) and finally, the raiding project Citadel (*Tsitadel'*), which, however, shows almost no signs of life today. At the 2015 Russian March these groups were represented by two columns with a total number of less than 100 people. From that point on, they have been cut off from any legal activity, and the number of supporters can be assumed to have dwindled even further.

Also among the groups categorised as opponents of Novorossiia there is a tradition of engaging in martial arts/combat training. For example, Demushkin has apparently been refocusing his efforts on his network of knife-fighting clubs. Politically, these clubs recruit many more than just the opponents of Novorossiia and ultra-rightists. Some minor clubs may display a somewhat higher degree of ideological purity, but these are definitely smaller.

Pro-Kremlin nationalist organisations

Moving from 'nationalism from the bottom-up' to 'nationalism from above' – more precisely, to how 'nationalism from above' can be supported by some movements from below – a great deal has already been written about official or semi-official Putinist nationalism in the aftermath of Crimea (see, for example, Kolesnikov 2015). Clearly, the part of official rhetoric that can be attributed to nationalist discourse is directed not only against the main opponent constructed through this rhetoric – the West and Western liberal ideas – but is also contrasted to the message of the ethnic nationalists of the 'street'.[15] First, it accords primacy to state, empire and civilisation, not race or ethnicity. Second, the role of enemy and 'significant other' is filled by the West, not by the South or the East. Third, emphasis is placed on moral conservatism ('traditional values') and tradition as such – although this is already no longer in explicit opposition to Russian nationalism.

In 2014 it seemed that the unprecedented growth of patriotic enthusiasm could generate a new and far from marginal nationalist movement based on the theses put forward in official rhetoric – not least since the 'street' ethno-nationalism of the early 2000s was already on the decline and had 'vacated the place'. But this did not occur.

The first and most obvious reason is that the political leadership of the country does not need such a movement to hold on to power. Moreover, the authorities can safely assume that an active grassroots movement would not be completely predictable and might consequently become a source of future problems – as indeed was the case with the Motherland party between 2003 and 2006 (Baunov 2016).

A less obvious reason is that the official rhetoric is pure propaganda, not ideology, and is intended for passive consumption. It is obviously difficult to say with certainty what is ideology and what is not, but in this case there are several indications that no official ideology as such has been consolidated. First, the rhetoric remains too volatile. Second, while some ideology-producing centres exist (Laruelle 2016), they have not been developing into a unified whole. Third, there are no authoritative ideological leaders in sight: unlike the case of some highly pragmatic TV propagandists like Dmitrii Kiselev and Vladimir Solovev, people who have clear convictions either enjoy insufficient authority (as is the case with Aleksandr Dugin or Maksim Shevchenko), or they present propaganda in their capacity as cultural leaders, and not as ideologists (even though some, such as Patriarch Kirill, may aspire to the role of ideologist). Moreover, none of these figures can be said to represent the official position.

The biggest initiative in 2014/2015 was the Anti-Maidan movement, but this soon fizzled out. This is not the only pro-Kremlin grassroots initiative that has disappeared from the surface of public life. Pro-Kremlin-oriented public figures tend to understand very well when they can expect support from the top, and when not, and are usually not prepared to act without such official support.

Some organisations remain afloat and ready to continue operations, even without substantial regime support but with calculations about the future (Alperovich 2016). The first to be mentioned in this category should be the Motherland party. It cannot boast of electoral successes, and in most Russian cities, including Moscow, its party organisations have remained weak,[16] but it still has some clout. In St Petersburg, for instance, it was Motherland that organised the 2013 and 2014 Russian Marches – and not the oppositional nationalists, who had been sent packing home or to Moscow (in 2015 no march at all was held in this city). Not surprisingly, within the nationalist movement Motherland is regarded as a spoiler, as the Liberal Democratic Party of Russia (LDPR) had previously been. In 2016 Motherland largely moved away from the ethno-nationalist agenda, and, as is the case with the majority of the KPRF and the LDPR, it combines mild criticism of the authorities with total agreement with the official patriotic agenda. Ethno-nationalism is generally presented at the level of cautious hints: for example, in the 2016 elections the party presented itself as the 'National Front' (*Natsional'nyi front*). Some of the party's candidates in single-mandate districts were ultra-rightist football hooligans.

In recent years, two other, closely related, organisations – the Great Fatherland Party (*Partiia velikoe otechestvo*), led by pop-historian Nikolai Starikov, and the National Liberation Movement (*Natsional'no-osvoboditel'noe dvizhenie*, NOD) led by Evgenii Fedorov, a State Duma deputy from United Russia – have emerged from previously marginal positions. Both espouse utterly paranoid forms of anti-Westernism and contempt for ethno-nationalist themes. The NOD, together with its closely allied group, SERB,[17] is known mainly for its numerous hooligan attacks on activists from the non-nationalist part of the opposition. Those taking part in these attacks almost always go unpunished – so it appears that these organisations are needed not for the sake of their ideas, but as instruments for exerting pressure against the genuinely oppositional groups.

The practice of 'limited violence' in the pro-Kremlin sector of the nationalist movement is not limited to attacks on the opposition, however. While for example the anti-immigrant raids by Motherland appeared to have halted completely, vigilante initiatives by nationalists have acquired a noticeable boost. These initiatives are at the same time completely depoliticised – they tend to take the form of anti-alcohol campaigns (in the spirit of the 'healthy lifestyle' popular among young nationalists). Especially noticeable here are Sober Courtyards (*Trezvye dvory*) and Lion Against (*Lev protiv*), whose activities are constantly linked with the use of limited violence.

In the pro-Kremlin sector of Russian nationalism there also exists another format of club activity. Ambitious projects such as the Izborsk Club have not produced any significant results – but they have not disappeared either. Also some other organisations function primarily as clubs, as regards size as well as type of activities. This is the case for instance with the youth organisation of the Motherland party, Tigers of the Motherland (*TIGRy Rodiny*), which was created in 2015 in an unsuccessful attempt at expanding the party into the far-right field. The borderline between these clubs and former oppositionists, such as members of the earlier-mentioned People's Diplomacy, has been blurred to the extent that it makes sense to speak of a unified club environment of pro-Novorossiia nationalists.

The pro-Kremlin nationalist environment thus contains elements that could serve as a basis for future expansion: clubs, vigilante initiatives, party structures and so on. It is still too early to speak of any actual growth, however. The September 2016 State Duma elections served to confirm this. NOD simply supported the United Russia party, and NOD activist Mariia Katasonova finished as number eight among thirteen candidates in a single-seat constituency in Moscow. The Anti-Maidan movement did not take part in the elections at all, while the Great Fatherland Party was barred from participation and supported 'patriotic' candidates from various other parties. ROS supported only its own leader Sergei Baburin, who ran for the KPRF and finished as number four among eleven candidates in a Moscow single-seat constituency (SOVA Center 2016a). In these 'managed elections' even pro-Kremlin activists clearly stood no chance of winning if they did not fit into the scheme designed from above – but it is also worth underlining that, as we have seen, none of the nationalist candidates was even among the front-runners in their respective districts. Also well known and more or less nationalistically oriented public figures with no party affiliation did poorly. No such figures were accorded a 'secure' spot on the tickets of the leading parties. Likewise, no such candidates were promoted by United Russia in single-mandate districts – nor, for that matter, by any other party in districts where United Russia had decided not to run in order to let other parties win (Zuev 2016).

The only nationalist candidate who made it into the State Duma was therefore the leader of Motherland, Aleksei Zhuravlev, who ran in Voronezh in a district where United Russia deliberately did not field a competitor against him. In the party race, Motherland garnered no more than 1.5 per cent of the vote. We can also note that Vladimir Zhirinovskii's LDPR took a remarkably high per cent of the vote – with 13.1 per cent, finishing third, right behind the KPRF. However, there is no reason to believe that the LDPR will act as a nationalist party in the State Duma: this party has long since lost whatever independent ideological orientation it might once have had.

Conclusions

There can be no doubt that the Russian nationalist movement will experience a new rise: if for no other reason simply because it cannot fall any deeper, and because Russian nationalism as such is unlikely to disappear from the ideological map of the country. In theory, the federal government can monopolise this space on the ideological map, but this would be possible only under a significantly more authoritarian regime than the present one. Instead, what we are likely to see is the emergence of new grassroots initiatives based on new configurations of ideas (including some of the same as we see now), but most importantly, with new activists in their ranks.

What is clear is that this will not happen anytime soon. Support for the Russian regime's authoritarian and anti-Western policies remains high in society; moreover, these policies are less and less perceived as problematical (Kozlov and Nosonov 2016). We are not talking about fiery support for the regime, but of passive acceptance, as demonstrated by the low turnout at the September 2016 elections – including among the traditionally loyal sector of the electorate (Churakova and Mukhametshina 2016). As a result, there appears to be no basis for a new protest movement recruited from among the pro-Putin part of the populace – and without the support of this segment, the Russian nationalists will not be able to recruit a fresh pool of activists.

The most important questions, the answers to which will define the face of tomorrow's Russian nationalist movement, nevertheless remain open. First, will migrantophobia return to top place in the nationalist agenda? While the level of migrantophobia has declined since the onset of the conflict in Ukraine (Pipiia 2016), there are reasons that indicate that this may increase again. Second, what of the place of violence within the nationalist movement? In particular, how will the current structures focused on violence – the training clubs, the military formations and the raids – develop? Third, how will the relationship between imperialist and ethno-nationalist ideas develop? Will the ideas about 'getting rid of the Caucasus' and/or opposition to 'Islamic expansion' be re-actualised (for instance, in the case of a deterioration of the situation in the North Caucasus)? Will the majority in the nationalist movement support further territorial expansion of the Russian state, or will it turn more toward isolationism? Finally, which will prevail among nationalists – the focus on 'traditional values' and the Russian Orthodox Church, or the desire to 'save Russia' through modernisation? Many questions can be asked, but at this stage there are no conclusive answers available.

Notes

1. It is interesting to see how even a prominent pro-Kremlin political analyst such as Konstantin Kostin from the Foundation for the Development of Civil Society defends this view (NSN 2014).
2. In 2015 there was also again a slight increase in the number of convictions for hate crimes.
3. Belov's brother, Vladimir Basmanov, had already emigrated by then.
4. This group was the successor to the banned Army of the People's Will (*Armiia narodnoi voli*).
5. In February 2015, NOMP was banned by the authorities, after which the group was renamed the People's Militia of Russia (*Narodnoe opolchenie Rossii*).
6. According to a June 2016 Levada survey, just 9 per cent of respondents said they felt fully or largely responsible for what was happening in the country, and only 5 per cent thought that they could somehow influence the situation (Levada 2016).
7. Emil Pain has probably been the main proponent of this idea. See for example his discussion with other experts and with the national democrats themselves at Radio Svoboda (Fanailova 2012).
8. All quantitative assessments in the chapter are based on observations made by members of the SOVA Center team.
9. The current weakness of the party can be illustrated by the fact of its 2016 attempt to organise a network action on the anniversary of the 2 May 2014 tragedy in Odessa, which basically failed.
10. This was also recognised by Pain, who earlier had held great hopes for this sector (SOVA Center 2015).
11. Personal conversation with the author.
12. The following description of nationalist organisations builds on the results of monitoring conducted by the SOVA Center, summarising the situation up until the summer of 2016. For an extended version, see Alperovich (2016).

13. Valiaev had been a prominent activist in Russian Image (*Russkii obraz*), a movement that competed with the DPNI between 2007 and 2009 (Horvath 2014).
14. See the foundation's publications on the site <www.publicdiplomacy.su> (last accessed 20 October 2016).
15. There is nothing new in this: the same opposition was officially recorded in documents adopted in 2011–12 (Verkhovsky 2014).
16. At the official march on 4 November 2014, in the columns of Motherland there were little more 100 people.
17. The South East Radical Block – a group founded by a pro-Russian activist from Zaporizhia, Ukraine, Igor Beketov (also known as Gosha Tarasevich), who later fled to Russia.

Bibliography

Alperovich, Vera (2016), 'Transformation of the Russian nationalist movement: 2013–2016', SOVA Center, 23 August, <http://www.sova-center.ru/en/xenophobia/reports-analyses/2016/08/d35252/> (last accessed 1 September 2016).

Alperovich, Vera and Natalia Yudina (2015), 'Calm before the storm? Xenophobia and radical nationalism in Russia, and efforts to counteract them in 2014', in Alexander Verkhovsky, ed., *Xenophobia, Freedom of Conscience and Anti-Extremism in Russia in 2014*, Moscow: SOVA Center, 5–66.

Alperovich, Vera and Natalia Yudina (2016), 'The ultra-right movement under pressure: xenophobia and radical nationalism in Russia, and efforts to counteract them in 2015', in Alexander Verkhovsky, ed., *Xenophobia, Freedom of Conscience and Anti-Extremism in Russia in 2015*, Moscow: SOVA Center, 7–66.

Baunov, Aleksandr (2016), 'Khozhdenie v narod i obratno. Rossiiskaia vlast' mezhdu professionalami i entuziastami' [Going to the people and back: the Russian government between professionals and enthusiasts], Moskovskii Tsentr Karnegi, 24 October, <http://carnegieendowment.org/files/CP_Baunov_web_Rus.pdf> (last accessed 15 November 2016).

Churakova, Ol'ga and Elena Mukhametshina (2016), 'Iavkoi na vybory ozabotilis' vse politicheskie sily' [All political forces are worrying about the turnout in the elections], *Vedomosti*, 19 September, <http://www.vedomosti.ru/politics/articles/2016/09/19/657671-pobedu-edinorossam> (last accessed 20 December 2016).

Fanailova, Elena (2012), 'Natsionalizm i demokratiia' [Nationalism and democracy], Radio Svoboda, 19 August, <http://www.svoboda.org/content/transcript/24682869.html> (last accessed 1 September 2016).

Gorbachev, Aleksei (2016), '"Demvybor" raskalyvaetsia vse glubzhe' ['Demvybor' is breaking apart even more], *Nezavisimaia gazeta*, 12 January.

Horvath, Robert (2014), 'Russkii Obraz and the politics of "managed nationalism"', *Nationalities Papers*, 42, 3: 469–88.
Iudina, Nataliia and Vera Al'perovich (2016), 'Evoliutsiia i devoliutsiia: Ksenofobiia i radikal'nyi natsionalizm i protivodeistvie im v Rossii v pervoi polovine 2016 goda' [Evolution and devolution: xenophobia, radical nationalism and efforts to counteract them in Russia during the first half of 2016], SOVA Center, 13 July, <http://www.sova-center.ru/racism-xenophobia/publications/2016/07/d35018/> (last accessed 1 September 2016).
Kolesnikov, Andrei (2015), 'Russian ideology after Crimea', Carnegie.ru, 22 September, <http://carnegie.ru/2015/09/22/russian-ideology-after-crimea/ihzq> (last accessed 1 September 2016).
Kolstø, Pål (2016), 'Crimea vs. Donbas: how Putin won Russian nationalist support – and lost it again', *Slavic Review*, 75, 3: 702–25.
Kozlov, Viacheslav and Dmitrii Nosonov (2016), 'Rossiiane ne khotiat mirit'sia' [Russians do not want to make peace], RBK, 21 September, <http://www.rbc.ru/newspaper/2016/09/21/57e11fb89a7947659 69f5414> (last accessed 16 October 2016).
Laruelle, Marlene (2014), 'Alexei Navalny and challenges in reconciling "nationalism" and "liberalism"', *Post-Soviet Affairs*, 30, 4: 276–97.
Laruelle, Marlene (2016), 'Russia as an anti-liberal European civilisation', in Pål Kolstø and Helge Blakkisrud, eds, *The New Russian Nationalism: Imperialism, Ethnicity and Authoritarianism, 2000–15*, Edinburgh: Edinburgh University Press, 275–97.
Levada (2016), 'Otvetstvennost' i vliianie' [Responsibility and influence], 13 July, <http://www.levada.ru/2016/07/13/otvetstvennost-i-vliyanie/> (last accessed 1 September 2016).
Nazdem.info (2010), 'Konstantin Krylov: "Luchshie demokraty poluchaiutsia iz byvshikh fashistov..."' [Konstantin Krylov: 'Former fascists make the best democrats...'], <http://nazdem.info/texts/110> (last accessed 25 April 2015).
NSN (2014), 'Patriotizm perekhvatil povestku u radikal'nogo natsionalizma' [Patriotism intercepted the agenda of radical nationalism], 10 November, <http://nsn.fm/policy/ekspert-russkie-marshi-ugasayut-proizoshel-perelom-natsionalizma-v-patriotizm.php> (last accessed 20 December 2016).
Pain, Emil' (2014), 'Sovremennyi russkii natsionalizm v zerkale runeta' [Contemporary Russian nationalism in the mirror of Runet], in Aleksandr Verkhovskii, ed., *Rossiia – ne Ukraina: sovremennye aktsenty natsionalizma* [*Russia is not Ukraine: Contemporary Accents of Nationalism*], Moscow: SOVA Center, 8–31.
Pain, Emil (2016), 'The imperial syndrome and its influence on Russian nationalism', in Pål Kolstø and Helge Blakkisrud, eds, *The New Russian Nationalism: Imperialism, Ethnicity and Authoritarianism, 2000–15*, Edinburgh: Edinburgh University Press, 46–74.

Pipiia, Karina (2016), 'Intolerantnost' i ksenofobiia' [Intolerance and xenophobia], Levada, 11 October, <http://www.levada.ru/2016/10/11/intolerantnost-i-ksenofobiya/> (last accessed 16 October 2016).

SOVA Center (2015), 'Diskussiia "Natsional-demokraty v Rossii – nastoiashchee i budushchee"' [The discussion 'National Democrats in Russia – the present and future'], 3 July, <http://www.sova-center.ru/racism-xenophobia/discussions/2015/07/d32339/> (last accessed 1 September 2016).

SOVA Center (2016a), 'Racism and xenophobia in September 2016', 12 October, <http://www.sova-center.ru/en/xenophobia/news-releases/2016/10/d35588/> (last accessed 16 October 2016).

SOVA Center (2016b), 'Russian March – 2016', 15 November, <http://www.sova-center.ru/en/xenophobia/news-releases/2016/11/d35822/> (last accessed 16 November 2016).

Verkhovsky, Alexander (2014), 'Language of authorities and radical nationalism', in Matthew Feldman and Paul Jackson, eds, *Doublespeak: The Rhetoric of the Far Right since 1945*, Stuttgart: ibidem-Verlag, 271–300.

Verkhovsky, Alexander (2016), 'Radical nationalists from the start of Medvedev's presidency to the war in Donbas: true till death?', in Pål Kolstø and Helge Blakkisrud, eds, *The New Russian Nationalism: Imperialism, Ethnicity and Authoritarianism, 2000–15*, Edinburgh: Edinburgh University Press, 75–103.

Zuev, Ivan (2016), '"Patrioticheskii revansh" na vyborakh v Gosdumu ne sostoialsia' [The patriotic revenge at the State Duma elections failed], Nakanune.ru, 23 September, <http://www.nakanune.ru/news/2016/9/23/22448146> (last accessed 16 October 2016).

7

Ideologue of neo-Nazi terror: Aleksandr Sevastianov and Russia's 'partisan' insurgency

Robert Horvath

One of the most disturbing developments in post-Eltsin Russia has been the proliferation of xenophobic violence and its mutation into revolutionary terrorism.[1] Vladimir Putin's first two terms (2000–8) in the Kremlin witnessed a steady increase in racist attacks against migrant labourers and other non-Slavic inhabitants of Russian cities. During the Medvedev–Putin 'tandemocracy', some neo-Nazi fighters expanded their range of targets to include prominent public figures, state functionaries and members of the judiciary. This turn towards terror provoked intense discussion in Russian nationalist circles. One influential group of publicists took up the cause of the terrorists, whom they celebrated as precursors of a national revolution against the rule of foreign occupiers and a cosmopolitan oligarchy. Members of this group also campaigned in defence of arrested fighters, whom they portrayed as innocent victims of a Russophobic state.

This chapter examines the career of the most outspoken ideologue of this tendency, Aleksandr Sevastianov. A prolific author and a leading representative of racist ethno-nationalism, Sevastianov achieved prominence first as leader of a major nationalist party and then as a propagandist of revolutionary violence. In 2009, he triggered a major controversy by publishing an elaborate vindication of the racist killers in the 'Russian underground', whom he extolled as morally healthy adolescents and heirs of wartime partisans. In a series of statements, he contended that this 'children's crusade' threatened to become a national uprising against a regime that was facilitating the influx of racial outsiders.

Despite his prominence, Sevastianov's relationship to ultranationalist violence has attracted little academic attention.[2] Most scholarly references to his career revolve around his contributions to anti-Semitism, white supremacist ideology and the pseudo-science of *rasologiia* ('raciology').[3] By comparison with the extensive corpus of scholarship dedicated to the neo-Eurasianism of Aleksandr Dugin, Sevastianov is a neglected figure. There is no systematic study of his public career or his revolutionary project. This oversight has been reinforced by the fact that analyses of the rise of Russian skinheads and neo-Nazi youth have paid little attention to the influence of the public intellectuals who have incited and justified racist violence.[4]

This chapter seeks to shed light on Sevastianov's emergence as the leading Russian ideologue of ultranationalist revolutionary violence. It traces four phases in the evolution of his public stance on violence since the collapse of the Soviet Union. During the first phase (1992–97), which was dominated by his involvement in the campaign to prevent the repatriation of 'trophy art', he avoided overt statements on violence. During the second phase (1998–2003), when he became a leader of a radical nationalist party, he constantly reaffirmed his commitment to legality but hinted that violent militants had a role to play in the party's rise to power. During the third phase (2004–12), which coincided with a wave of violence committed by neo-Nazi gangs, he glorified these killers as precursors of a national revolution. During the latest phase (2013–16), he shifted this framework to the separatist insurgents in the Donbas, whom he extolled as the creators of a revolutionary state that would become a springboard for the transformation of Russia itself.

The rise of a radical nationalist

Aleksandr Sevastianov's early career offered few signs of his future as a radical nationalist. Born in 1954, he seemed destined for the life of a minor Soviet scholar, living in the cloistered world of lecture theatres, libraries and museums. After graduating from the Moscow State University, Sevastianov earned his candidate's degree for a thesis on eighteenth-century literature (Sevast'ianov 1983). During the final decades of the Soviet regime, he taught at the Moscow Region Pedagogical Institute, and contributed articles about the visual arts to specialist journals. In the 1980s, he served as a consultant to museums, libraries and galleries across the Soviet Union (Antikompromat 2012). This academic background contributed to Sevastianov's authority as a nationalist ideologue in two ways. First, it developed the writing skills that enabled him to become a prolific and versatile publicist. Second, it endowed him with the literary flair, erudition and connections that made it possible to speak to wider audiences than a narrow circle of committed militants.

No less important for Sevastianov's career were the racial prejudices that he had developed under the Soviet regime. By his own admission, his understanding of 'the intricacies of Russian–Jewish fundamental incompatibility' was shaped by the trauma of his first, failed marriage to a Russian woman of Jewish origin (Sevast'ianov n.d.[a]). These prejudices helped Sevastianov to identify with the nascent nationalist movement, which embraced anti-Semitism both as a marker of allegiance and as a mobilising passion. During the 1990s, anti-Semitism provided a framework for nationalist ideologues to explain both mass impoverishment and the rise of the oligarchs. Sevastianov became one of those ideologues.

Sevastianov played a minor role in the political struggles that accompanied the terminal crisis of the Soviet Union. His transition from cultural scholarship to the battlefield of post-Soviet ideology was precipitated by the controversy over the repatriation of 'trophy art', cultural artefacts that had been confiscated by Soviet armies during their defeat of Nazi Germany. In the early 1990s, the issue became a cause célèbre for Russian nationalists. Exploiting his knowledge of art and museums, Sevastianov became a standard bearer of the campaign against repatriation. In a series of articles in the liberal and nationalist press, he contended that the confiscated treasures were important for the edification of a society that had been culturally impoverished by the devastation inflicted by the Nazis. If Russians did not master the European legacy, he argued, 'we will never join the family of European peoples as an equal' (Sevast'ianov 1995). To rally support in the intelligentsia, Sevastianov created the League for the Defence of the National Heritage of Russia, an ephemeral structure launched in 1992 by an open letter signed by such pillars of the cultural establishment as academician Dmitrii Likhachev and the director of the Hermitage Museum, Vitalii Suslov (Sevast'ianov 1997). The triumph of this campaign was signalled by a protest against the return of medieval manuscripts from the German Gotha Library. An article by Sevastianov triggered a demonstration by militants who burned an effigy of the minister of culture (ibid.).

Sevastianov's first experience of political activism was in the Congress of Russian Communities (*Kongress russkikh obshchin*, KRO), one of the crucibles of post-Soviet Russian nationalism. Founded in 1992 as a network of Russian organisations across the former Soviet space, KRO became both a discussion forum and a training ground for nationalist activists. After the defeat of the 'red-brown' coalition in October 1993, KRO briefly became the principal vehicle of Russian ethno-nationalism. It attracted nationalist ideologues like Sevastianov as well as major institutional figures like Iurii Skokov and General Aleksandr Lebed. The tension between these two groups reached crisis point during the 1996 presidential election campaign, when the KRO candidate, Lebed, colluded with the Kremlin to ensure Eltsin's victory. This manipulation of the electorate provoked outrage amongst rank-and-file militants. Sevastianov would later reflect that it was 'impossible to convey the utter revulsion which all honest members of KRO felt at this dirty game' (Sevast'ianov 2000). Alongside many other members of KRO's Moscow branch, Sevastianov abandoned the compromised organisation.

In the aftermath of this debacle, Sevastianov became a leading propagandist of ultranationalist ideas. In 1997, he became editor of *Natsional'naia gazeta*, a newspaper that was widely distributed among nationalist organisations around the country. As a platform for biological racism and the proponents of eugenics, it clearly spoke to the obsessions of an ultra-rightist readership (see, for example, Goncharov 1996). No less important were its efforts to convince this readership of the value of political violence. One article held up Latin American death squads as a model for emulation. Hailing their 'boldness and decisiveness, responsibility and duty, faithfulness to order and tradition', the article drew attention to how death squads had decimated the ranks of 'democratic' activists, a target that suggested obvious parallels with Sevastianov's own adversaries in Russia. The article explained how one of the most important death squad organisers in El Salvador, Roberto d'Aubuisson, had combined close involvement in paramilitary activity with participation in electoral politics that had brought his party to power (Sh 1997).

The party of vengeance

The plateform for Sevastianov's first venture into electoral politics was Spas, an alliance of radical nationalist groupings that was founded by two deputies from Vladimir Zhirinovskii's LDPR in late 1998 (*Panorama* n.d.). Having achieved official registration, the bloc sealed an alliance with Russian National Unity (*Russkoe natsional'noe edinstvo*, RNE), a neo-Nazi organisation whose paramilitary fighters had played a prominent role in the 'red-brown' uprising in October 1993. Despite its notoriety, the RNE enjoyed close links with an array of local government structures. It had planned to compete in the 1999 parliamentary elections, but its efforts to achieve registration were blocked by the Moscow city government. Spas offered an alternative path to the State Duma. In a deliberately provocative move, Spas's election list was headed by the RNE leader, Aleksandr Barkashov. Although relegated to ninth position, Sevastianov was poised to become the ideologue of the bloc, which was dominated by party functionaries (Spas 1999). In the end, his hopes of a seat in the State Duma were dashed by the Eltsin administration, which was clearly alarmed at the possibility of a red-brown resurgence (Kalinin 1999; Mikhailova and Khamraev 1999). Sevastianov took part in the protracted court proceedings which culminated in the de-registration of Spas less than a month before the elections (Sevast'ianov n.d.[b]; Sukhova 1999).

The demise of Spas paved the way for Sevastianov's most serious bid for power. In February 2002, he joined Stanislav Terekhov to create the National Great-Power Party of Russia (*Natsional'no-derzhavnaia partiia Rossii*, NDPR). Terekhov, a combatant in the 1993 red-brown uprising, embodied the left-wing, neo-Stalinist strain in Russian radical nationalism. Soon the leadership group was joined by Boris Mironov, a former minister of the press and a notorious anti-Semite. Each member of the triumvirate made a particular contribution to the new party. As a leader of the Union of Officers (*Soiuz ofitserov*), Terekhov brought military connections and a cohort of army veterans. As a former cabinet minister, Mironov was responsible for cultivating sympathetic state functionaries. As the party's leading intellectual, Sevastianov undertook the formulation of the party's ideology (Sevast'ianov 2003).

The rapid growth of NDPR was made possible by the disarray in nationalist ranks in the early Putin era. With its war in Chechnya, the Kremlin appeared to have reclaimed the ground of patriotism. At the same time, the election cycle of 1999–2000 was a rout for nationalist forces. Under these conditions, two groups of militants converged in NDPR. The first came from the existing nucleus of Terekhov's Union of Officers. The second was made up of militants from the collapsing monolith of Barkashov's RNE, which was torn apart by a succession of schisms in late 2000 (Verkhovskii and Kozhevnikova 2009). By December 2002, there were fifty-three NDPR branches around the country, and the party claimed 13,000 members (Vasil'ev 2002).

From its inception, the NDPR was Janus-faced. Its formal programme, composed for the purpose of registration at the Central Electoral Commission, was an anodyne document that avoided incitements to violence and racial hatred (see NDPR 2002). By contrast, NDPR statements addressed to the nationalist milieu were shockingly explicit in their advocacy of racial inequality. The 'Unification Platform', one of the party's founding documents, stipulated that Judaism and Zionism were to be proscribed 'as doctrines propagandising national exclusiveness' (Soiuz ofitserov 2001). Another manifesto proposed the exclusion of non-Russians from high governmental posts and a requirement for political candidates to document their racial ancestry for three generations. Illegal migrants were to be declared 'outside the law': 'no one will bear responsibility for their life, health and property' (Agafonov 2002b; NDPR.ru 2011).

No less ominous was the party's barely concealed embrace of armed struggle. In his address to the NDPR founding congress on 26 February 2002, Sevastianov drew attention to the paramilitary fighters in its own ranks. Coining a phrase that would resonate in the media, he proclaimed that the NDPR was 'the party of vengeance':

> The contradiction today between legal and illegal methods of struggle is as great as ever ... But, dear friends, illegal methods of struggle are not publicly discussed ... Here sit a multitude of representatives of the RNE. These are tough nationalists, and we understand that we have succeeded in doing what our enemies fear so much and what was so difficult to do – we are creating a united movement, a united platform, and we sit here today, representatives of different ideologies, but representatives of Russian blood. The National Great-Power Party of Russia is the party of vengeance. This is the crucial word which the people expect from us. That is, when we speak on the scale of Russia. And if we speak on a world scale, then we are a detachment of the global intifada. (Agafonov 2002a)

Sevastianov's inflammatory language was echoed by his two co-leaders. Warning that the political struggle might quickly assume 'other forms', Terekhov declared that 'the party had been created not to formulate and declare principles, but as a fighting unit' (Agafonov 2002a). In a similar vein, Mironov scorned 'the futility of the parliamentary path' and exhorted his listeners 'to exterminate this Jewish democratic interior [*nutro*]' (ibid.).

Despite the menacing tone of its Congress, the NDPR was registered by the Ministry of Justice as a legal political party on 26 September 2002 (Khamraev 2002). The result was a major public scandal, which gradually spread from liberal newspapers to the radio station Ekho Moskvy and major television stations. Liberal journalists and human rights activists drew attention to the NDPR's racist ideology, the anti-Semitic utterances of its leaders, and their incitements to violence (Agafonov 2002a; Brod 2002; Deich 2002; Popova 2002). Indignation in liberal circles was exacerbated by the passage, only two months earlier, of anti-extremism legislation that was publicly justified as a barrier to neo-Nazism.[5] Others criticised the double standards of the Ministry of Justice, which had shown no qualms about denying registration to the Liberal Russia party (*Liberal'naia Rossiia*), an initiative that posed no obvious threat to constitutional order (Agafonov 2002a). The climax of the controversy was an appearance by Sevastianov and his co-leaders on *Vremena*, the popular current affairs programme hosted by Vladimir Pozner on Channel One, Russia's main state television station (see Pozner 2002).

The scale of the furore evidently took the authorities by surprise. Minister of Justice Iurii Chaika complained that the media had failed to alert him to the danger posed by the NDPR before its registration (Agafonov 2002b). In fact, officials of his own ministry's Department for Public and Religious Associations had attended the NDPR founding congress (Agafonov 2002a). Under mounting pressure, the ministry now prepared to correct its oversight. A pretext was provided by Boris Mironov, who used a newspaper interview to demand the disenfranchisement of Russian Jews (Vasil'ev 2002). Less than one month later, the NDPR received a formal warning from the Ministry of Justice, which claimed that Mironov's call to deprive citizens of their constitutional rights constituted 'an incitement to national discord' (Chernega 2003). Under the terms of the new anti-extremism legislation, the NDPR was required to repudiate the offending statements within three days (ibid.). Instead, Sevastianov and his co-chairmen asserted in their response that Mironov's words had been 'purely personal' and that the party proposed not the denial of constitutional rights but changes to the constitution itself – a perfectly legal form of political activity (Gul'ko 2003). Unimpressed by this sleight of hand, Chaika left the warning in force and passed evidence about Mironov's statement to the Prosecutor's Office (Agafonov 2003). The mounting administrative pressure culminated in a ruling by the Ministry of Justice that disqualified the membership lists of fifteen NDPR branches (Tsygankov 2003).[6] As a result, the party fell below the legislative threshold of branches in forty-five subjects of the Federation. On 19 May, the NDPR was formally de-registered, a decision confirmed by a court ruling in September (Kolesnichenko 2003).

In the aftermath of this defeat, Sevastianov's support for violence became more overt. At the party's next congress in September 2003, he offered an implicit endorsement of political terrorism. Henceforth, he declared, the Russian movement would diverge into two separate paths – the legal path and the illegal path, 'as was done by Irish fighters for independence' (Sevast'ianov 2004a). In an effort to preserve the NDPR as a presence in the legal sphere, Sevastianov and Terekhov created a parallel interregional movement with an identical acronym, National Great-Power Path of Rus (*Natsional'no-derzhavnyi put' Rusi*, NDPR). But in neither of its manifestations did the NDPR become an organising centre of 'the Russian movement'. Overshadowed by network-based structures like the Movement Against Illegal Immigration (*Dvizhenie protiv nelegal'noi immigratsii*, DPNI), the NDPR became one of the many tiny organisations crowding the far-right fringes of Russian politics. Although its militants participated in the 2005 inaugural Right March and the next Russian March, NDPR relations with other parties were complicated by Sevastianov's propensity to impugn the integrity of political rivals and his condemnation of the Jewish ancestry of leading Russian Orthodox clerics.[7] By November 2008, when Sevastianov formally resigned his NDPR membership (Sevast'ianov 2008), the organisation had virtually disappeared from the political landscape.

As his party withered, Sevastianov moved from abstract theorisation of political violence to endorsement of specific crimes. He attracted a storm of criticism for his response to the murder of Nikolai Girenko, a prominent St Petersburg ethnographer who was shot dead in his flat by members of the Borovikov-Voevodin skinhead gang on 19 June 2004. As an expert witness, Girenko had helped to convict numerous ultra-right militants accused of inciting ethnic enmity (Kostiukovskii 2004). One of his most notable successes had been the trial of Pavel Ivanov, head of the NDPR Novgorod branch and editor of the anti-Semitic newspaper *Russkoe veche*, who was banned from journalistic activity for three years (Kostiukovskii 2004). The case brought Girenko face to face with Sevastianov, who appeared as an expert for the defence and used the case as a pretext to stand for the regional governorship (Iakovleva 2003; Ivanova 2003).

Defeated in court and in the election, Sevastianov responded to the news of Girenko's murder with a menacing declaration that hailed the perpetrators of this 'just act of vengeance' and pilloried their victim as 'the most abominable *shabes-goi*' (here: a gentile serving Jewish interests). According to Sevastianov, the death of Girenko marked 'the beginning of a new era for the Russian national-liberation movement', a time of reprisals that would not be confined to inveterate enemies like Girenko. Potential targets included high state officials:

> the death of the scoundrel will undoubtedly force many to ponder, particularly those (beginning with Kremlin puppet-masters like [Vladislav] Surkov or [Vladimir] Khinchagoshvili), who are implicated in the judicial persecution of Russian national-patriots and our exclusion from the field of legal politics. (Sevast'ianov 2004a)

The first blueprint for this revolutionary project was a list of the forty-nine 'most outstanding enemies of the Russian people', which Sevastianov published in *Natsional'naia gazeta* in August 2004. To deter legal action, Sevastianov claimed that the list was merely a response to the lists of promoters of racial intolerance compiled by human rights activists (Kolesnichenko 2004). This disclaimer was difficult to reconcile with the accusatory tone of the compilation and its obvious connection to the murder of Girenko. Sevastianov had promised to assemble such a list in his panegyric to Girenko's killers, and publication of the list was a clear signal to those who aspired to emulate that deed (Girenko was identified in the list as an 'executed traitor'). The list was also an act of intimidation against the forty-nine 'enemies'. The 'enemies' included liberal political figures like Andrei Kozyrev, journalists like Anna Politkovskaia and Nikolai Svanidze, scholars like Valerii Tishkov and Emil Pain, and human rights activists like Iurii Dzhibladze and Evgenii Proshechkin. Their alleged transgressions spanned the gamut of Sevastianov's ideological obsessions. Many had been involved in the monitoring or prosecution of far-right militants. Some had advocated the repatriation of 'trophy art'. Others were tainted with 'Russophobia' or the subversion of gender norms through the promotion of family planning or tolerance for homosexuality. Special condemnation was reserved for Vladislav Surkov, the deputy head of the presidential administration, who was stigmatised not only as 'half-Jew, half-Chechen' but also as a 'Russophobe' who had blocked the registration of the NDPR and had tried to transform the Russian movement into a Kremlin project (Sevast'ianov 2004b).

In March 2005, the NDPR's reputation for violence was reinforced by the attempted assassination of Anatolii Chubais, a symbol of market reform and an object of loathing in nationalist circles. Leading suspects in the investigation included Ivan Mironov, the son of the NDPR's former co-chairman, Boris Mironov, who was already in hiding to avoid prosecution on charges of inciting ethnic hatred (Pankov 2005). Ivan Mironov followed his father into hiding, and was arrested in late 2006. In its coverage of the affair, the newspaper *Izvestiia* drew attention to Sevastianov's inflammatory brochure about the 'party of vengeance', in which he had vowed that 'I will not rest until I see the corpse of Gaidar', another symbol of liberal reform (Filimonov 2005). In his usual fashion, Sevastianov retaliated with threats of legal action against those who suggested that his intention was anything but legal retribution (Sevast'ianov 2005).

Ideologist of the 'partisans'

The decline of the NDPR coincided with a surge in xenophobic violence. During 2004–8, the SOVA Center tracked a steady increase in the numbers of persons killed or injured in racially motivated assaults (Kozhevnikova 2009). This bloodshed reached a climax during the 2007–8 election cycle. In the first quarter of 2008, there were some eighty-six assaults, which claimed forty-nine lives. This death toll was double the figure for the same period in the previous year, and was comparable the annual total of racially motivated killings in 2004–5 (Deriabin 2008).

Sevastianov made no secret of his support for the killers. In early 2006, *Natsional'naia gazeta* published a long list of racially motivated murders, assaults and acts of vandalism, which had been compiled by the Moscow Bureau for Human Rights. In an unsigned explanatory note that prefigured themes of Sevastianov's later writings, the newspaper hailed this violence as a 'people's war' against immigration, which was nothing less than 'conquest, invasion, occupation' (*Natsional'naia gazeta* 2006). Lambasting state functionaries who expected Russians to submit to this onslaught, the author proclaimed with undisguised enthusiasm that 'the Russian people are alive!' Having lost hope in their government, the Russian people 'are rising up against the occupiers in any way they know', just as their ancestors had fought earlier invaders. In a veiled warning to the authorities, the author concluded that until the government declared war on the occupiers, 'the indignant people will not give up the fight' (ibid.).

Sevastianov's hopes for this insurgency were boosted by the bombing of Moscow's Cherkizovskii Market, a trading centre dominated by non-Slavs, in August 2006. The blast killed fourteen and injured sixty-one (Lokotetskaia 2008). The perpetrators were neo-Nazi activists from the military-patriotic club Spas, an organisation unrelated to the electoral bloc of the same name. As the police rounded up Spas members, Sevastianov's NDPR collected donations for the families of the detainees. He also lent historic significance to their deeds, declaring to the newspaper *Novye Izvestiia* that the bombing was 'only the first stage' of a process in which 'the underground will become more conspiratorial and more consolidated'. If the authorities continued to deny nationalists the right to participate in political life, then 'you can expect an intensification of illegal activity' that would make the Ku Klux Klan look like a storm in a teacup (Kolesnichenko 2006).

Despite his enthusiasm, Sevastianov's first attempts to reach out to this milieu were unsuccessful. In the spring of 2007, he delivered a lecture about race and ethnogenesis to militants of the neo-Nazi gang Slavic Union (*Slavianskii soiuz*, SS). His audience was baffled by his erudition and pseudo-scientific jargon. To one observer, it seemed that Sevastianov 'had taken the wrong door':

> The terms 'monogenism', 'polygenism', and 'morphology' dismayed the young Nazis. At the words 'negrification' and 'mestizisation' they become a little animated, but on hearing the phrase 'the culture of Mohenjo-daro', they rushed for the exit. They returned when the lecturer had departed. (Stepenin 2007)

What enabled Sevastianov to bridge this divide was the security forces' crackdown on the neo-Nazi underground. In highly publicised trials during 2008–10, Russian courts convicted a series of fighters accused of racially motivated murders. The proceedings provided Sevastianov with considerable information about the defendants, which he used as raw material for a series of statements in support of the underground.

The most important of these articles, titled 'The Russian underground: reality, myths, prospects', appeared on the mainstream nationalist website APN on 13 March 2009. Almost 24,000 words in length, this article offered a description of the neo-Nazi underground, a rationalisation of its deeds and an evaluation of its prospects. Feigning scholarly detachment, Sevastianov claimed that his aim was not to justify the mounting violence but 'without anger and passion, to find and explain its real roots, in order to avoid a dangerous escalation of the rising tendencies'. Anticipating steps to prosecute him, he warned 'all enemies of the Russian people and other witch-hunters' that they would find in his text none of the crimes proscribed by anti-extremism legislation (Sevast'ianov 2009b).

Nevertheless, Sevastianov's sympathies clearly lay with perpetrators of this violence, not with the authorities. His central contention was that the neo-Nazi underground was a normal phenomenon. Racist serial killers like Artur Ryno and Pavel Skachevskii were not renegades or freaks but 'normal, physically and morally healthy children of our Russian people'. Indeed, the ranks of the combatants included many promising youths, prize-winning students whose patriotic sensibilities had inspired them to become 'the insurgent part of the young generation of the state-forming people'. They had taken up arms in a struggle that had been shirked by their complacent and disillusioned elders. Drawing on the theory of aggression popularised by the German zoologist Konrad Lorenz, Sevastianov attributed the racist violence of these youths to the workings of the same natural instincts that led various animal species to defend their territory against interlopers. This primordial struggle was proof of national vigour. What was unnatural was the campaign against aggressive instincts that was waged by proponents of ethnic tolerance, who were 'cripples in the field of instincts' (Sevast'ianov 2009b).

In political terms, Sevastianov conceptualised the disparate and scattered forms of skinhead violence as a war waged by Russian youth against the enemies of the nation. Citing official statistics, he argued that this war was growing in intensity and in geographical scope. One turning point was the bomb blast in Cherkizovskii Market in August 2006. 'Never before', reflected Sevastianov, 'had the child-partisans used a weapon of mass destruction' (Sevast'ianov 2009b). This war had two distinguishing characteristics. First, Sevastianov endorsed the self-description of some skinhead fighters as 'partisans' and suggested that their struggle was comparable to the guerrilla war waged by Soviet partisans against Nazi invaders during the Second World War. Second, this was an 'ethnic war', a struggle waged by one people against other peoples. For Sevastianov, the corollary was that 'these youths are the people', not the entire people, but a growing part of it (ibid.).

The underlying message of Sevastianov's article was that the 'partisans' represented a threat not merely to the ethnic enemy but also to the Putin regime. By building a multi-ethnic empire rather than a national state, by denying Russian nationalist parties access to the electoral process and by persecuting nationalist militants, this regime was inviting a confrontation with the partisan insurgents. Carefully choosing his words, Sevastianov insinuated that high state functionaries might one day become targets: 'It is one thing to kill a hundred Tajik janitors; it is quite a different thing to kill those two or three people whose decisions allow millions of immigrants to enter the country' (Sevast'ianov 2009b). Indulging his penchant for compiling death lists, Sevastianov indicated that the victims might also include other adversaries of the national liberation struggle: human rights activists and journalists who instigated the persecution of skinheads; political scientists who formulated the 'anti-Russian' conception of state nationality policy; lawmakers who drafted draconian laws and set the law-enforcement organs against Russian nationalists; and political technologists who inoculated a trusting people with the ideology of toleration and political correctness (ibid.).

To magnify the political potential of the 'partisans', Sevastianov repeatedly likened them to the revolutionaries who had toppled the tsarist regime. Recalling two landmarks in the progress of revolutionary terrorism, he suggested that the verdict in the Ryno-Skachevskii trial 'would enter the history textbooks of coming centuries', just like the shot fired at Tsar Aleksandr II by Dmitrii Karakozov and the first trials of the People's Will. The use of riot police against ethnic Russian students demonstrating against ethnic quotas for university places showed that 'the experience of Bloody Sunday, 9 January 1905, which predetermined the collapse of the Romanov empire and the Bolshevik revolution, has taught nothing to the Russian authorities' (ibid.). The growing numbers of partisans serving long prison sentences would ensure that 'prisons and camps in the near future will become an academy of the Russian national revolution, just as they had once been an academy of the socialist revolution'. In the more distant future, predicted Sevastianov, a Russian national state will erect monuments to Artur Ryno, Pavel Skachevskii, Dmitrii Borovikov, Nikolai Korolev and other skinhead killers as 'outstanding fighters, partisans, heroes and martyrs of the victorious Russian idea' (ibid.).

In the summer of 2009, Sevastianov lent his erudition to a major propaganda initiative in support of the 'partisans'. *Russian Resistance* (*Russkoe soprotivlenie*) was a two-hour documentary film produced by three ultra-rightist groups involved in the defence of imprisoned fighters: Russian Image (*Russkii obraz*), Russian Verdict (*Russkii verdikt*) and White Memory (*Belaia pamiat'*). Available on the Internet, the film purported to be a 'journalistic investigation', but it served the interests of the neo-Nazi underground and its sympathisers. It glorified murderers of immigrants as defenders of the Motherland. It set out information to help them in their struggle with the repressive apparatus. And it provided a platform to publicise the debate about the relative merits of anti-migrant terror and revolutionary violence directed against the state.

Sevastianov made two notable contributions to the film. First, he glorified anti-immigrant violence by likening it to previous patriotic uprisings. In a relaxed, didactic tone, he explained that 'partisans' were a traditional defence mechanism of Russian society in times of troubles:

> There were as many partisans in Russia as there were invaders ... And whenever the state, the principality could not defend itself ... the people rose up ... It was so under the Polovtsians, the Pechenegs, the Tatars ... Remember the cudgel of people's war described by Tolstoi in *War and Peace*. To say nothing of the last war, from 1941 to 1942 ... It is a normal phenomenon in our history. (*Russkoe soprotivlenie* 2009)

Sevastianov's second contribution was to offer a prophetic vindication of the revolutionary path. In the closing section of the film, which presented different viewpoints about the future of the struggle, Sevastianov took the side of those who sought to redirect neo-Nazi violence from immigrants to the regime. Adopting his customary pose of a concerned citizen, he warned of a series of assassinations of state functionaries that would culminate in a revolutionary upheaval:

> The ones who suffer might be those people who order the importation of a foreign workforce here, those people who create laws under which partisans are prosecuted, those people who implement punitive policies, and further up the ascending ladder ... to the very top. (*Russkoe soprotivlenie* 2009)

He reminded viewers that Russia had experienced such assassinations during the Socialist Revolutionary terror of the early twentieth century, which claimed the lives of two interior ministers and the tsar's uncle. If the current 'wave of mutual terror' were not stopped in time, concluded Sevastianov, 'there will be an escalation of violence that will gradually spread into a very real civil war' (*Russkoe soprotivlenie* 2009).

Sevastianov's pronouncements did not pass unnoticed in 'partisan' circles. In late 2009, he was praised in *Strategiia-2020*, a kind of national revolutionary manifesto that appeared on the website of the neo-Nazi organisation *Blood&Honour/Combat88*. Its authors included Nikita Tikhonov, a young neo-Nazi intellectual who had founded BORN (*Boevaia organizatsiia russkikh natsionalistov*), a paramilitary group that waged a campaign of high-profile assassinations between late 2008 and 2010. The victims included a federal judge, a prominent lawyer, a journalist, symbolic racial targets and prominent Antifa (leftist anti-fascist) militants. *Strategiia-2020* was conceived both as a vindication of this terror and as a guide to revolutionary strategy. Its central contention was that 'direct action' – arson, killings and acts of terrorism – was both the essence of the nationalist movement and a road to power. The paramilitary fighters of the neo-Nazi underground, 'those of us who are engaged in the physical extermination of occupiers and traitors', were the prime movers of the struggle (*Strategiia-2020* n.d.[a]). In order to become a revolutionary force, the insurgents needed to fulfil two tasks. First, fighters had to 'devote maximum attention to improving their military skills'. Second, propagandists were to wage 'an information war' to glorify the fighters and offer 'active approval and moral support'. Sevastianov's article about the partisans was extolled as 'the best model of this agitational work' (*Strategiia-2020* n.d.[b]).

The arrest of Tikhonov and his girlfriend, Evgeniia Khasis, offered Sevastianov a new opportunity to celebrate the partisans. Both defendants were charged with the murder of the lawyer Stanislav Markelov and the journalist Anastasiia Baburova. Sevastianov assiduously attended their trial, and produced a stream of articles that reduced the case to a Manichean struggle between heroic, morally pure defendants and a Russophobic cabal of security officials, lawyers and journalists. The tone of his commentary is exemplified by a long article titled 'The case of Tikhonov and Khasis: ascent into legend', which appeared within days of the guilty verdict. It extolled Tikhonov and Khasis as incarnations of patriotic virtue. Both had endured the ordeal of arrest and mistreatment without compromising their ideals or betraying their comrades. Whilst insisting on the defendants' innocence, Sevastianov portrayed Tikhonov as a kind of superman 'amongst a sick, degenerating tribe'. Khasis was the perfect match for this titan: 'a beauty, an intelligent mind, reacting swiftly and precisely, passionate in every word and movement'. Displaying his penchant for biological racism, Sevastianov reflected that 'the appearance of such people after twenty years of hopelessness and defeat tells us that the resources of the Russian gene pool are not yet depleted' (Sevast'ianov 2011a).

Sevastianov prophesied that Tikhonov and Khasis were destined to become symbols of the coming insurrection. Both had 'dreamed of a Russian revolution, a struggle for our national rights and interests'. Far from being the bloodthirsty killers vilified by the liberal press, Tikhonov and Khasis were 'national heroes, innocent victims of an anti-Russian regime and martyrs of the Russian idea'. At liberty, they may have been 'worth entire movements', but in prison they were exemplars of courage and principle, who would inspire others to take up their fallen banner. These followers 'will make that very Russian revolution which will fling open prison doors and set free Nikita and Zheniia and thousands of our other comrades'. For the present, Sevastianov exulted that 'our movement has its first icons'. These, he noted sarcastically, were a gift from the Kremlin and its henchmen: 'By taking from us living people, priceless in their uniqueness, they have given us in return a legendary image, to which generations of Russian nationalists will pray and begin to imitate' (Sevast'ianov 2011a). In fact, this cult proved short-lived. Seven months after Sevastianov's panegyric, Tikhonov and Khasis began to collaborate with the investigators (Sokopov 2014). By then, Sevastianov was hard at work on his final statement on the matter, a book about the trial (Sevast'ianov 2013).

Putin's 'national, anti-liberal revolution'

The crushing of the neo-Nazi 'partisans' coincided with a remarkable change in Sevastianov's political position. One month before the 2011 Duma elections, as liberals and moderate nationalists converged in opposition to the regime, Sevastianov exhorted his supporters to vote for Zhirinovskii's LDPR, a pro-Kremlin party that had long served as an instrument for co-opting the nationalist vote (Sevast'ianov 2011b). When mass demonstrations against election fraud erupted in December, Sevastianov excoriated the liberal standard-bearers of the protest movement and expressed horror that some of his erstwhile nationalist comrades were prepared to collaborate with these 'enemies of the people' (Sevast'ianov 2012a; 2012d). Full of hope, he elaborated a nationalist agenda for Putin's return to the presidency (Sevast'ianov 2011d). For a time, Sevastianov discerned a 'Russian national, anti-liberal revolution' in Putin's moves to repatriate offshore capital and in the appointment of Dmitrii Rogozin to head the military-industrial complex (Sevast'ianov 2012b). Such intercession on behalf of an apparently tottering regime evoked some criticism in nationalist circles (Malai 2012).

Sevastianov's faith in Putin quickly dissipated, however. Unlike Rogozin, Sevastianov was infuriated by Putin's pre-election statement on the national question (Sevast'ianov 2012c). Nevertheless, the two veterans found common ground in their rejection of coalitions between nationalists and their liberal enemies.[8] During the presidential election campaign, Sevastianov lambasted the leaders of the protest movement and their nationalist allies (Sevast'ianov 2011c). Despite his attacks on the regime's opponents, Sevastianov did not escape the post-election crackdown. In April 2012, he was interrogated and his flat was searched in connection with an investigation of extremist materials (Sevast'ianov 2012e; 2012f).

Sevastianov's wavering position towards the Putin regime continued during the Russo–Ukrainian conflict of 2014. On the one hand, he applauded the annexation of Crimea and echoed official propaganda against 'fifth columnists' who had sided with the Ukrainian enemy (Sevast'ianov 2014a). On the other, he shifted his revolutionary hopes from the neo-Nazi partisans to the separatist insurgents in the Donbas. In the place of non-Slavic 'occupiers' from Central Asia and the Caucasus, Sevastianov now identified Ukrainians as an ethnic enemy that threatened the survival of the Russian people. In a long programmatic article, he contended that Ukrainians were waging an ethnic war against Russia, that their hatred of Russians was incurable 'like leprosy', and that the 'ethnocide' of Russians was imminent (Sevast'ianov 2014b). In the place of the 'partisans' and their 'children's crusade', Sevastianov now hailed the insurgents as precursors of a Russian national revolution. Their feats were shaping the 'ethnogenesis' of a new people and a new state, which would become a springboard for the revolutionary transformation of Russia itself (ibid.).

Conclusions

Violence has been central to Sevastianov's revolutionary project. During two decades in public life, Sevastianov has repeatedly justified racist violence. None of the other major ideologists of contemporary Russian nationalism has written so much about the neo-Nazi underground and its campaign of terror. None has worked so tirelessly to defend its 'prisoners of war' and to portray its fighters as heirs of earlier generations of patriotic warriors. None has argued so clearly and consistently for racist violence as a path to national revolution.

It is difficult to gauge Sevastianov's influence upon the killers from BORN and other paramilitary groups, although some of them clearly valued his talents as a propagandist. What is undeniable is that Sevastianov was cultivated for many years as an authoritative opinion-maker and commentator by leading nationalist forums and publications. His prestige in these circles is evidence of an enduring conspiracy of silence in legal nationalist circles. In 2015, Nataliia Kholmogorova reflected about the moral failure of prominent nationalists, including herself, to speak out 'clearly and stridently about the unacceptability of violence as a political method' (Kholmogorova 2015). This reticence has serious implications for the future. Until Sevastianov's ideas are discredited, until mainstream nationalists dissociate themselves from his inflammatory ideology, his brand of revolutionary nationalism will remain a threat to civil peace in Russia.

Notes

1. This chapter was funded by Australian Research Council Grant FT110100690.
2. One sign of this lack of attention is that Sevastianov is incorrectly described as a parliamentary deputy in a major article on ultranationalists and the internet (Zuev 2011: 138). Sevastianov himself has enumerated numerous errors in the brief account of his career in a major reference work, *Radikal'nyi russkii natsionalizm* (Verkhovskii and Kozhevnikova 2009) (see Sevast'ianov 2009a).
3. On Sevastianov's racist ideas, see particularly Viktor Shnirel'man (2007; 2011) and Marlene Laruelle (2014: 97–98). For a discussion of one of Sevastianov's anti-Semitic tracts, see Aleksandr Ianov (Yanov 2014).
4. Sevastianov is not mentioned in studies of far-right violence in Russia by Richard Arnold (2010) and Martin Laryš and Miroslav Mareš (2011).
5. For the anti-extremism law, see Federal'nyi zakon (2002); for the linkage of this law to radical nationalism, see Rodin et al. (2001). For liberal criticism of the contradiction between the recent law and the registration of the NDPR, see Vyzhutovich (2002).
6. Sevastianov attributed this disqualification to a directive from the Ministry of Justice ordering regional offices not to register NDPR (Sevast'ianov 2009a).
7. In October 2006, Sevastianov provoked a scandal in the organising committee of the Russian March by attacking the Patriarch as a non-Russian (Frolov 2006).
8. See Rogozin's theses at a meeting of nationalist activists on 4 February 2012 (Mikhailov 2012).

Bibliography

Agafonov, Sergei (2002a), 'Miniust registriruet natsistov' [Ministry of Justice registers Nazis], *Novye Izvestiia*, 26 September, 1.
Agafonov, Sergei (2002b), 'Miniust ne zametil poteri litsa' [Ministry of Justice did not notice loss of face], *Novye Izvestiia*, 12 November, 1.
Agafonov, Sergei (2003), 'Ot uchastkovogo do genprokurora' [From the local police to the public prosecutor], *Novye Izvestiia*, 17 January, 1.
Antikompromat (2012), 'SEVAST'IANOV Aleksandr Nikitich', <http://web.archive.org/web/20120404013404/http://anticompromat.org//sevastyanov/sevastbio.html> (last accessed 14 December 2015).
Arnold, Richard (2010), 'Visions of hate: explaining neo-Nazi violence in the Russian Federation', *Problems of Post-Communism*, 57, 2: 37–49.
Brod, Aleksandr (2002), 'Otkrytoe pis'mo Moskovskogo Biuro po pravam cheloveka Prezidentu RF V.V. Putinu, general'nomu prokuroru RF V.V. Ustinovu, Ministru iustitsii Iu.Ia. Chaike' [Open letter from the Moscow Bureau for human rights to President V. Putin, Public Prosecutor V. Ustinov and Minister of Justice Iu. Chaika], *Novye Izvestiia*, 26 September, 2.
Chernega, Iurii (2003), 'Miniust ulichil Natsional'no-derzhavnuiu partiiu v ekstremizme' [Ministry of Justice accused the National Great-Power Party of extremism], *Kommersant*, 10 January, 3.
Deich, Mark (2002), 'Miniust predpochitaet...' [Ministry of Justice prefers...], *Moskovskii Komsomolets*, 18 October, 4.
Deriabin, Aleksandr (2008), 'Vesennee probuzhdenie britogolovykh' [Spring awakening of skinheads], *Nezavisimaia gazeta*, 1 April, 21.
Federal'nyi zakon (2002), 'O protivodeistvii ekstremistskoi deiatel'nosti' [On countering extremist activity], *Rossiiskaia gazeta*, 30 July, <http://www.rg.ru/2002/07/30/extremizm-dok.html> (last accessed 15 January 2016).
Filimonov, Dmitrii (2005), '"Partiia vozmezdiia" prigovorila Chubaisa ot imeni naroda' ['Party of vengeance' sentenced Chubais in the name of the people], *Izvestiia*, 28 April, <http://izvestia.ru/news/302110> (last accessed 12 April 2016).
Frolov, Kirill (2006), 'Antipravoslavnye – eto antirusskie antinatsionalisty i destruktory' [The anti-Orthodox – they are anti-Russian anti-nationalists and destructors], *Votserkovlenie politiki*, 4 October, <http://kirillfrolov.livejournal.com/49124.html> (last accessed 14 March 2016).
Goncharov, Aleksandr (1996), 'Evgenika: vchera, segodnia, zavtra' [Eugenics: yesterday, today, tomorrow], *Natsional'naia gazeta*, 1, <http://web.archive.org/web/20050217212038/http://ncpr.ru/publication/?pid=702&part=101> (last accessed 13 November 2016).
Gul'ko, Nikolai (2003), 'Natsional'no-derzhavnaia partia otvetila Miniustu' [National Great-Power Party answered Ministry of Justice], *Kommersant*, 13 January, 3.

Iakovleva, Elena (2003), 'V nachale bylo slovo. Rugatel'noe' [In the beginning was the word. An abusive one], *Rossiiskaia gazeta*, 18 July, 3.
Ivanova, Svetlana (2003), 'Redaktor gazety obviniaiut v antisemitizme' [Newspaper editor accused of anti-Semitism], *Kommersant*, 6 November, 6.
Kalinin, Nikolai (1999), 'Vybory-99. Spasut li "Spas"?' [Elections-99: will 'Spas' be saved?], *Trud*, 4 November.
Khamraev, Viktor (2002), 'Vybirai! Pravila dlia golosuiushchikh' [Choose! Rules for voters], *Politbiuro*, 7 October.
Kholmogorova, Natal'ia (2015), 'O dele BORN' [On the case of BORN], *Livejournal*, 27 July, <http://nataly-hill.livejournal.com/2191614.html> (last accessed 30 July 2016).
Kolesnichenko, Aleksandr (2003), 'Nedoregistrirovannye' [De-registered], *Novye Izvestiia*, 18 September, 2.
Kolesnichenko, Aleksandr (2004), 'Spisok Sevast'ianova' [Sevastianov's list], *Novye Izvestiia*, 24 August, 2.
Kolesnichenko, Aleksandr (2006), 'Ul'trarusskie' [Ultra-Russians], *Novye Izvestiia*, 8 September, 5.
Kostiukovskii, Viktor (2004), 'Fashisty ego nenavideli' [Fascists hated him], *Russkii kur'er*, 21 June, 1.
Kozhevnikova, Galina (2009), 'Osennii renessans-2009: Ot RNE do Kolovrata' [Autumn renaissance 2009: from RNE to Kolovrat], SOVA Center, 19 December, <http://www.sova-center.ru/racism-xenophobia/publications/2009/12/d17583> (last accessed 16 September 2015).
Laruelle, Marlene (2014), 'Russia's radical right and its West European connections: ideological borrowings and personal connections', in Mats Deland, Michael Minkenberg and Christin Mays, eds, *In the Tracks of Breivik: Far Right Networks in Northern and Eastern Europe*, Berlin: LIT Verlag, 87–104.
Laryš, Martin and Miroslav Mareš (2011), 'Right-wing extremist violence in the Russian Federation', *Europe–Asia Studies*, 63, 1: 129–54.
Lokotetskaia, Mariia (2008), 'Chetyre pozhiznennykh sroka' [Four life sentences], *Gazeta*, 16 May, 10.
Malai, Sergei (2012), 'Bez paniki, tovarishchi!' [Do not panic, comrades!], APN, 5 January, <http://www.apn.ru/publications/article25673.htm> (last accessed 11 April 2016).
Mikhailov, Aleksei (2012), 'Natsional'nyi vopros. Russkii otvet' [The national question: the Russian answer], Russkii obraz, 4 February, <http://web.archive.org/web/20120207210727/http://rus-obraz.net/activity/258> (last accessed 19 November 2015).
Mikhailova, Svetlana and Viktor Khamraev (1999), '"Spas" na vyborakh' ['Spas' at the elections], *Vremia MN*, 3 November.
Natsional'naia gazeta (2006), 'Idet voina narodnaia' [A national war is going on], 3–5, <http://www.nationalka.ru/2006-3-5-93-95-/idet-voyna-narodnaya.html> (last accessed 23 March 2016).

NDPR (2002), 'Osnovye polozheniia programmy Natsional'no-derzhavnoi partii Rossii' [Main provisions of the programme of the National Great-Power Party of Russia], *Rossiiskaia gazeta*, 26 March, 12.

NDPR.ru (2011), 'Otryvok iz Programmy Natsional'no-derzhavnoi partii Rossii' [Excerpt from the programme of the National Great-Power Party of Russia], <http://ndpr.ru/index.php/2011-07-25-15-59-35/259-2011-07-28-18-32-08> (last accessed 26 September 2016).

Pankov, Andrei (2005), 'Klub patriotov' [Club of patriots], *Novye Izvestiia*, 25 April, 6.

Panorama (n.d.), 'Spas' [Spas], <http://www.panorama.ru/works/vybory/party/spas.html> (last accessed 5 February 2016).

Popova, Tat'iana (2002), 'Natsisty podbiraiutsia k Dume, schitaiut pravozashchitniki' [Nazis are selected for the Duma, human rights activists believe], *Kommersant*, 2 October, 8.

Pozner, Vladimir (2002), 'Vremena' [Times], *Pervyi Kanal*, 9 November, <http://vladimirpozner.ru/?p=6809> (last accessed 12 January 2016).

Rodin, Ivan, Lidiia Andrusenko and Vladimir Tikhomirov (2001), 'Nuzhen ne tol'ko zakon, no i politicheskaia volia' [You need not only the law, but also political will], *Nezavisimaia gazeta*, 7 May, 3.

Russkoe Soprotivlenie (2009), *Dokumental'nyi film Russkoe Soprotivlenie* [*Documentary on Russkoe Soprotivlenie*], <https://www.youtube.com/watch?v=gPPQio-nG3Q> (last accessed 13 November 2016).

Sevast'ianov, Aleksandr (n.d.[a]), 'Avtobiografiia' [Autobiography], sevastianov.ru, <http://www.sevastianov.ru/index.php?option=com_content&task=view&id=7&Itemid=56> (last accessed 25 January 2016).

Sevast'ianov, Aleksandr (n.d.[b]), 'Politicheskaia biografiia' [Political biography], sevastianov.ru, <http://www.sevastianov.ru/politicheskaya-biografiya/politicheskaya-biografiya.html> (last accessed 14 January 2016).

Sevast'ianov, Aleksandr (1983), *Soslovnoe rassloenie russkoi khudozhestvenno-publitsisticheskoi literatury i ee auditorii v poslednei treti XVIII veka* [*Social Stratification of Russian Fictional and Essayistic Literature and its Audience in the Last Third of the 18th Century*], Moscow: Moskovskii gosudarstvennyi universitet imeni Lomonosova, <http://www.dissercat.com/images/1page_diss/3431826.png?8.815072011833102> (last accessed 31 July 2016).

Sevast'ianov, Aleksandr (1995), 'Reparatsii ne vozvrashchaiut' [War reparations will not be returned], sevastianov.ru, <http://www.sevastianov.ru/content/view/75/115> (last accessed 19 January 2016).

Sevast'ianov, Aleksandr (1997), 'Bitva za trofei kak epizod tret'ei mirovoi voiny' [The battle over the trophies as an episode in the third world war], sevastianov.ru, <http://www.sevastianov.ru/problema-peremeschennyh-tsennostey/bitva-za-trofei-kak-epizod-tretjey-mirovoy-voyny.html> (last accessed 25 January 2016).

Sevast'ianov, Aleksandr (2000), 'Pamiati KRO ili kar'era komsomol'tsa' [In memory of KRO, or the career of a Komsomol], *Natsional'naia gazeta*, 10, <http://sevastianov.ru/kuklovody-nyneshney-rossii/pamyati-kro-ili-karjera-komsomoljtsa.html> (last accessed 15 January 2016).

Sevast'ianov, Aleksandr (2003), 'Interv'iu sopredsedatelia Natsional'no-derzhavnoi partii Rossii A.N. Sevast'ianova gazete "Russkaia Pravda"' [Interview with co-chair of the National Great-Power Party of Russia A. Sevastianov with the newspaper *Russkaia Pravda*], *Natsional'naia gazeta*, June, <http://www.nationalka.ru/2003-6-68-/intervjyu-sopredse-datelya-natsionaljno-derzhavnoy-partii-rossii-a.n.-sevastjyanova-gazete-russkaya-prav.html> (last accessed 9 February 2016).

Sevast'ianov, Aleksandr (2004a), 'S pochinom, druz'ia!' [On the first step, friends!], Russkoe delo, June, <http://www.russkoedelo.org/novosti/archive.php?ayear=2004&amonth=june#21_06_2004_S> (last accessed 16 February 2016).

Sevast'ianov Aleksandr (2004b), 'Spisok 49-ti "nedruzei"' [List of 49 'non-friends'], *Natsional'naia gazeta*, August, <http://web.archive.org/web/20120404021829/http://anticompromat.org//naziki/s_sevastyan.html> (last accessed 15 March 2016).

Sevast'ianov, Aleksandr (2005), 'Pis'mo A.N. Sevast'ianova v gazetu "Izvestiia"' [Letter of A. Sevastianov to the newspaper *Izvestiia*], 3 May, <http://beloyar.livejournal.com/105586.html> (last accessed 12 March 2016).

Sevast'ianov, Aleksandr (2008), 'Zaiavlenie A.N. Sevast'ianova "O prekrashchenii chlenstva v NDPR"' [A. Sevastianov's declaration 'about ending his membership in the NDPR'], NDPR, 30 November, <http://ndpr.ru/index.php/2011-07-25-15-59-35/263-2011-07-28-18-34-54> (last accessed 20 February 2016).

Sevast'ianov, Aleksandr (2009a), 'Tufta pod kislo-sladkim sousom' [Bullshit in sweet and sour sauce], March, sevastianov.ru, <http://www.sevastianov.ru/novosti/tufta-pod-kislo-sladkim-sousom.html> (last accessed 19 April 2016).

Sevast'ianov, Aleksandr (2009b), 'Russkoe podpol'e. Real'nost', mif, pers-pektiva' [The Russian underground: reality, myths, prospects], APN, 13 March, <http://web.archive.org/web/20160203043816/http://www.apn.ru/publications/article21441.htm> (last accessed 5 October 2015).

Sevast'ianov, Aleksandr (2011a), 'Delo Tikhonova-Khasis: voskhozhdenie v legendu' [The case of Tikhonov and Khasis: ascent into legend], APN, 11 May, <http://www.apn.ru/publications/article24127.htm> (last accessed 15 April 2013).

Sevast'ianov, Aleksandr (2011b), 'Predvybornyi rasklad' [Election alignment], APN, 1 November, <http://www.apn.ru/publications/article25234.htm> (last accessed 17 April 2016).

Sevast'ianov, Aleksandr (2011c), 'Boloto imeni Sakharova' [A bog named after Sakharov], *Livejournal*, 23 December, <http://a-sevastianov.livejournal.com/7391.html> (last accessed 10 April 2016).

Sevast'ianov, Aleksandr (2011d), 'Podvodia itogi – 2011' [Summarising 2011], APN, 30 December, <http://www.apn.ru/publications/article 25669.htm> (last accessed 18 April 2016).
Sevast'ianov, Aleksandr (2012a), 'O prekrasnodushnykh i doverchivykh russkikh liudiakh' [About starry-eyed and credulous Russian people], Livejournal, 4 January, <http://a-sevastianov.livejournal.com/9176.html> (last accessed 15 April 2016).
Sevast'ianov, Aleksandr (2012b), 'Revoliutsiia sislibov versus natsional'naia revoliutsiia' [The revolution of systemic liberals versus a national revolution], APN, 7 January, <http://www.apn.ru/publications/article25685.htm> (last accessed 13 April 2016).
Sevast'ianov, Aleksandr (2012c), 'Putin i natsional'nyi vopros' [Putin and the national question], Livejournal, 24 January, <http://a-sevastianov.livejournal.com/10113.html> (last accessed 15 March 2016).
Sevast'ianov, Aleksandr (2012d), 'Slepye vedut slepykh. . . v revoliutsiiu' [The blind leading the blind. . . into revolution], Livejournal, 29 January, <http://a-sevastianov.livejournal.com/10863.html> (last accessed 26 September 2016).
Sevast'ianov, Aleksandr (2012e), 'Otnositel'no obyska v moem dome' [Regarding the search of my house], Livejournal, 8 April, <http://a-sevastianov.livejournal.com/14991.html> (last accessed 13 November 2016).
Sevast'ianov, Aleksandr (2012f), 'Byl u sledovatelia' [I was at the investigator's], Livejournal, 12 April, <http://a-sevastianov.livejournal.com/15341.html> (last accessed 16 March 2016).
Sevast'ianov, Aleksandr (2013), Delo Tikhonov-Khasis Palachi ili zhertvy? [*The Case of Tikhonov and Khasis: Executioners or Victims?*], Moscow: Knizhnyi Mir.
Sevast'ianov, Aleksandr (2014a), 'Piataia kolonna' [Fifth column], sevastianov.ru, <http://www.sevastianov.ru/novosti/pyataya-kolonna.html> (last accessed 14 November 2016).
Sevast'ianov, Aleksandr (2014b), 'Sud'ba russkogo naroda reshaetsia v Donetske i Luganske' [The fate of the Russian people is decided in Donetsk and Luhansk], APN, 11 June, <http://www.apn.ru/publications/article31762.htm> (last accessed 26 September 2016).
Sh., K. (1997), 'Eskadrony smerti: khoziaeva v svoem dome' [Death squads: masters in our own house], Natsional'naia gazeta, 4, <http://web.archive.org/web/20050214082222/http://www.ndpr.ru/publication/?pid=716&part=101> (last accessed 20 March 2016).
Shnirel'man, Viktor (2007), '"Tsepnoi pes rasy": divannaia rasologiia kak zashchitnitsa "belogo cheloveka"' ['Watchdog of race': armchair raciology as defender of 'the white man'], SOVA Center, 3 October, <http://www.sova-center.ru/racism-xenophobia/publications/2007/10/d11692> (last accessed 11 February 2016).

Shnirel'man, Viktor (2011), *Porog tolerantnosti: ideologiia i praktika novogo rasizma* [*Threshold of Tolerance: Ideology and Practice of the New Racism*], Moscow: Novoe literaturnoe obozrenie.

Soiuz ofitserov (2001), 'Ob"edinitel'naia platforma novogo russkogo dvizheniia s tsel'iu sozdaniia Natsional'no-derzhavnoi partii Rossii' [Unification platform of the new Russian movement aimed at establishing the National Great-Power Party of Russia], June, <http://agso.narod.ru/docs/ofiz/platf.htm> (last accessed 24 September 2016).

Sokopov, Maksim (2014), 'Obraz BORN' [Image of BORN], Russkaia Planeta, 17 June, <http://rusplt.ru/society/obraz-born-10493.html> (last accessed 18 September 2015).

Spas (1999), 'Kopiia spiska zaverena Tsentral'noi izbiratel'noi komissiei Rossiiskoi Federatsii 18 oktiabria 1999 goda' [Copy of list certified by the Central Election Commission 18 October 1999], <http://web.archive.org/web/20030511010928/http://socarchive.narod.ru/bibl/bloki/par/spas-spisok-f.htm> (last accessed 28 January 2016).

Stepenin, Maksim (2007), 'V Kondopoge k nebol'shim srokam lisheniia svobody prigovoreny initsiatory poboishcha v letnem kafe' [In Kondopoga the initiators of the bloody battle at the summer café are sentenced to short prison sentences], *New Times*, 2 April, <http://web.archive.org/web/20110207075008/http://newtimes.ru/articles/detail/13102/> (last accessed 4 February 2016).

Strategiia-2020 (n.d.[a]), <http://news.nswap.info/?p=26265&page=2> (last accessed 5 February 2013).

Strategiia-2020 (n.d.[b]), <http://news.nswap.info/?p=26265&page=7> (last accessed 5 February 2013).

Sukhova, Svetlana (1999), 'Minus "Spas"' [Minus 'Spas'], *Segodnia*, 25 November.

Tsygankov, Valerii (2003), 'Net takikh partii' [There are no such parties], *Nezavisimaia gazeta*, 18 April, 2.

Vasil'ev, Iurii (2002), 'Ne fashist v zakone' [A fascist, but not according to the law], *Moskovskie Novosti*, 10 December, 2.

Verkhovskii, Aleksandr and Galina Kozhevnikova (2009), *Radikal'nyi russkii natsionalizm: struktury, idei, litsa* [*Radical Russian Nationalism: Structures, Ideas, Persons*], Moscow: SOVA Center.

Vyzhutovich, Valerii (2002), 'Povtorenie neusvoennogo' [Repetition of the undigested], *Vremia MN*, 2 October, 3.

Yanov, Alexander (2014), 'The mystery of Veche's demise', Institute of Modern Russia, 3 November, <http://imrussia.org/en/analysis/nation/2073-the-mystery-of-veche%E2%80%99s-demise> (last accessed 11 February 2016).

Zuev, Dennis (2011), 'The Russian ultranationalist movement on the Internet: actors, communities, and organization of joint actions', *Post-Soviet Affairs*, 27, 2: 121–57.

8

The extreme right fringe of Russian nationalism and the Ukraine conflict: The National Socialist Initiative

Sofia Tipaldou

The annexation of Crimea and the war in Donbas transformed Russia's ever-changing nationalist scene. Up to that point, Russian nationalist organisations had practised a peculiar form of division of labour, with each organisation specialising in certain issues – for example, the rights of ethnic Russians, or immigration. In this way, the nationalist organisations were not competing for the same followers, but complemented each other. Despite constant internal conflicts, Russian nationalists could be said to have formed an integrated network that had many leaders and that made possible multiple affiliations. This strategy granted them a measure of flexibility and enabled them to survive under Russia's hybrid regime,[1] which since the 2011–12 wave of protests has taken an increasingly authoritarian turn (Hale 2015; Gel'man 2016).

The events in Ukraine, however, posed new challenges to the Russian nationalists. A major dividing line soon became evident within the moderate segment of the nationalist opposition: national democrats supported Putin's policies, whereas national liberals saw such support as a betrayal. This chapter explores how Russian nationalist organisations located on the *extreme right* of the political spectrum responded to the Euromaidan events, the annexation of Crimea and the armed conflict in Donbas, as well as the Kremlin's strategies towards them. My focus is on Dmitrii Bobrov's National (People's) Socialist Initiative (*Natsional'naia (narodnaia) sotsialisticheskaia initsiativa*, NSI), an organisation clearly inspired by Hitler's German National Socialist Worker's Party (NSDAP). In addition, I examine the NSI's closest ideological allies, including the Movement Against Illegal Immigration (*Dvizhenie protiv nelegal'noi immigratsii*, DPNI) and the Slavic Union (*Slavianskii soiuz*, SS), and the circles around these organisations. My aim is to uncover the main ideological positions of the nationalists who flirt with totalitarianism, and thereby contribute to a better understanding of the internal dynamics of the Russian nationalist scene today.

I begin by presenting my conceptualisation of Russian nationalist organisations as a social movement with a multifaceted network that includes 'uncivil society' groups, as well as the concept of an internal 'division of labour' within this movement. Then I turn to the NSI and a presentation of its leader, far-right activist Dmitrii Bobrov, and the organisation's ideological lineage, its strategies and the role it has played within the 'ethno-nationalist network'. Finally, I discuss how the extreme right fringe of Russian nationalism positioned itself towards the events in Ukraine from 2013 onwards, with particular attention to the internal division between supporters and opponents of Russia's involvement in Ukraine.

Russian nationalists as a social movement: The network principle and division of labour

In the mid-1990s, rising levels of violence targeting foreigners and asylum seekers led German sociologists to acknowledge the need to introduce a 'social movement approach' in the study of right-wing extremism (Koopmans 1995: 96). Until then, scholars had held that the only serious threats to established democratic regimes came from subversive political parties (Pedahzur and Weinberg 2001: 53). For the study of right-wing extremism as a social movement, Dieter Rucht (1995: 11) proposed a broad definition of 'social movements' as a 'specific type of collectives, namely groups and organisations that function on a continuing basis and aim to bring, stop or reverse social change through protest'. Such a definition draws on perspectives borrowed from social psychology: that these social milieus and associations share a common worldview and understand each other as representatives of the same drive for social change (Frindte et al. 2013: 42).

In their seminal work, Ruud Koopmans and Dieter Rucht (1996) set out the basis for 'the sociological turn' in the study of the far right. They maintain that as long as scholars approach rightist groups and movements as if they were only loosely connected, or not connected at all, they will fail to recognise right-wing extremism as a social movement. Koopmans and Rucht identified at least six varieties of right-wing extremism: (i) radical right parties, (ii) (neo-Nazi) extra-parliamentary organisations, (iii) new right intellectual circles, newspapers and publishing houses, (iv) radical right and xenophobic subcultures (for example, skinheads), (v) violent attacks on foreigners and asylum seekers, and (vi) xenophobic and radical rightist attitudes in society. When some such groups or milieus are connected to each other, we can speak of a *radical right social movement* (Koopmans and Rucht 1996: 272).

As I understand the Russian nationalist scene, having interviewed several Russian nationalist leaders, it indeed fits the definition of a social movement: it is composed mostly of extra-parliamentary organisations with varying ideologies – ranging from democratic to authoritarian – but with a common understanding of belonging to the opposition to the current regime. These organisations form what Mario Diani refers to as a *network*: 'informal interactions between a plurality of individuals, groups and/or organisations, engaged in a political or cultural conflict, on the basis of a shared collective identity' (Diani 1992: 13). The network is constituted by ties of varying strength among the groups and organisations that form the movement (Koopmans and Rucht 1996: 271). Within a social movement, the microlevel may take various organisational forms, from informal circles to political parties and associations. In other words, movements have organisation, but they are not organisations (ibid.).

In the early 2000s, the term 'uncivil society' was introduced to describe the 'dark side' of civil society: far-right organisations and groups with varied organisational structures and strategies, ranging from lobbying to terrorism. Since then, uncivil society and far-right parties have been studied as a double danger to democratic stability, posing a threat from within parliaments as well as from the surrounding environment (Pedahzur and Weinberg 2001: 53–62). Petr Kopecký and Cas Mudde (2003: 4) apply the term 'uncivil society' to groups that espouse non-democratic or right-wing extremist ideas and use violence as a means to achieve their goals, or that lack the spirit of 'civility'.

There have been few sociological or ethnographic studies of Russian organisations belonging to this 'uncivil society' (for some exceptions, see Sokolov 2008; Varga 2008; Pilkington 2010; Zuev 2010; 2011; 2013; Shnirel'man 2011; Zakharov 2013; Tipaldou and Uba 2014; Tipaldou 2015), even though the literature on far-right mobilisation in Russia is continuously growing (Arnold 2009; Laruelle 2009; 2010; Alexseev 2011; Laryš and Mareš 2011; Kolstø and Blakkisrud 2016). If, however, we conceptualise Russian nationalist organisations as a multifaceted social movement which includes organisations and individuals that belong to 'uncivil society' (or did so in the past), this allows for a study that better captures the dynamics within the Russian nationalist scene, with its patterns of continuity and change, and can contribute to a better understanding of the factors that shape this movement.

We know little about the role of skinheads in this 'uncivil society'. According to Hilary Pilkington and colleagues (2013), who have undertaken one of the most detailed ethnographic studies of Russian skinheads thus far, the majority of skinhead gangs, at least in smaller locations, tend to remain independent. Others have come to the same conclusion (Verkhovsky 2009: 92–93). Aleksandr Tarasov (1999), on the other hand, has argued that many Russian right-wing parties are rooted in the skinhead subculture, whereas Mihai Varga (2008: 568–70) demonstrates how skinheads engage with other far-right organisations as specialists on violence. Such 'groupuscules', to use Roger Griffin's term (Griffin 2003: 30), matter, as they can transform individual personal needs and emotions (for example hatred) into real action. And they have become 'the dominant manifestation of revolutionary nationalism' in contemporary Russia (Pilkington et al. 2013: 100–2).

In examining the extreme right fringe of the Russian nationalist movement, the main focus of this chapter is on the NSI and its most immediate network. The NSI is a totalitarian group that advocates what Pål Kolstø and Helge Blakkisrud have defined as 'supremacist nationalism' in the two-by-two matrix presented in the introductory chapter (see Table I.1). For analytical purposes, Kolstø and Blakkisrud divide Russian nationalism into four ideal types, depending on their territorial orientation and on the primacy of ethnic versus statist characteristics (in reality, all nationalisms include a mix of these elements). The NSI's closest allies also fall into the 'primarily ethnically oriented' category: the Slavic Union belonged to the 'supremacist' type while the DPNI, for which Russianness had mostly to do with bloodlines, can be classified under 'ethnic core nationalism'.

That is not to say that cooperation among different organisations within the nationalist movement takes place only along the vertical axis of this typology (that is, according to whether they base their nationalism on the primacy of ethnicity or state). On the contrary, after taking the strategic decision to put aside their ideological differences and work together to accomplish their common goal – the establishment of an ethnic Russian *(russkii)* nation-state – nationalist organisations of all ideological backgrounds adopted a division of labour (Tipaldou 2015). While, for example, the NSI offered an ideological platform for developing contemporary national socialism, the Slavic Union promoted Russian ethnic superiority mainly through sports and military training. Among the 'Russian ethnic core' nationalist organisations, the DPNI focused on combating illegal migration, whereas Konstantin Krylov's Russian Public Movement (*Russkoe obshchestvennoe dvizhenie*, ROD), which later evolved into the National Democratic Party (*Natsional'no-demokraticheskaia partiia*, NDP) has emphasised protection of the 'human rights' of ethnic Russians. However, we tend to see closer alliances forming along the vertical axes between organisations with either primarily statist or primarily ethnic orientation, rather than along the horizontal ones (along the empire- or core-oriented axes).

The organisations that form this ethno-nationalist network may seem to be undergoing constant transformation: new names are always popping up. However, these frequent name changes are not necessarily indicative of the level of actual change. Organisations that adopt a new name may have been banned (and thus change their name in order to be able to function as before); they may have shifted their structure from a movement to a party, or entered into coalitions with other organisations. In the latter case, this is usually a strategic alliance for achieving a specific goal, with each participating organisation representing a specific tendency of Russian nationalism. In other words, the emergence of a new coalition does not mean that the organisations that join hands have themselves been transformed internally, by changing their ideology, goals and/or leadership. Given the frequent reorganisations and transformations, the best way to understand what the various organisations within the ethno-nationalist network stand for is to focus on their leaders: what are their organisational backgrounds, their ideological convictions? Arguably, the original organisations they set up or joined will frequently offer the most authentic manifestation of their political vision.

National socialism à la russe: **Ideological pedigree**

The seedbed of contemporary Russian ethno-nationalism is Aleksandr Barkashov's Russian National Unity (*Russkoe natsional'noe edinstvo*, RNE), founded in 1990. In the 1990s, RNE was the largest and most successful of 'the unequivocally fascist organisations' in Russia (Shenfield 2001: 115); and, according to some surveys, Barkashov was among the country's top ten most influential politicians (Sokolov 2008: 75). RNE ideology was based on a racial understanding of Russianness, anti-Semitism, Orthodoxy and German Nazism (slightly modified Nazi symbols were also employed). The number of RNE followers was estimated to be in the range of 5,000 to 10,000, although Barkashov himself held that his organisation had 15,000 *soratniki* (comrades-in-arms). The RNE appealed particularly to youth (Dunlop 1996: 522; Shenfield 2001: 136).

Barkashov's RNE adopted a totally new pattern of collective action: the RNE proved to be a cross between a small political organisation, a medium-sized security firm and a criminal enterprise. The RNE was organised like a military unit: its members received military training, wore black uniforms and were often employed in the network of the RNE's security firms. Many of them allegedly fought in Transnistria, in Abkhazia and in the former Yugoslavia on the Serbian side. During the 1993 stand-off between Boris Eltsin and the Supreme Soviet, some 100–300 RNE militants, including Barkashov, took up arms to defend the parliamentary building against Eltsin's forces (the rebels declared the RNE fighters to be a 'special military section of the Ministry of Security') (Shenfield 2001: 146; Likhachev 2002; Sokolov 2008: 68–69; Laryš and Mareš 2011: 142).

The RNE was very active in the streets and made frequent use of political violence. The 'favourite collective action' of its members involved patrolling the streets in cooperation with the police. Skinheads, by contrast, engaged in systematic night-time hunts for lone victims, usually people from different ethnic minority groups hailing from the Caucasus, Africa, or Central and South Asia; or youths belonging to different music subcultures, anarchists, homeless people or skinheads who identified with other football teams (Sokolov 2008: 68–72). Many RNE members, including regional leaders, were prosecuted for criminal activities ranging from illegal arms trade to murder. In the early 2000s, the RNE disintegrated and split into various groups – Barkashov founded a movement named after himself in 2006 – but none of them has been able to restore the RNE's old glory (Likhachev 2002: 22–41; Tipaldou 2015: 78–91).

The leaders of both the NSI and the Slavic Union had originally joined the RNE, as 'that was very popular in the 1990s' according to Bobrov.[2] Both of these RNE-inspired organisations came into being when the RNE itself was already in decline.

Dmitrii Demushkin's Slavic Union emerged as an intra-party structure within the RNE's security service before it seceded in 2001 to become the 'best known Russian neo-Nazi organisation' (Laryš and Mareš 2011: 143). By 2005 it had around 5,000 members. The

Slavic Union promoted national socialist ideals of racial purity and – even though its leader publicly condemned violence – a cult of force. In 2001, it was one of very few organisations to have permanent training camps, and Demushkin himself functioned as a combat instructor (Laryš and Mareš 2011: 142; Pilkington 2013 et al.: 244).[3] Many Slavic Union members, including Demushkin, were arrested on charges of violence. The infamous neo-Nazi serial killers Artur Ryno and Pavel Skachevskii, who in 2008 were convicted for the murder of twenty non-Russians (in fact, Ryno pleaded guilty to thirty-seven killings), were members of the Slavic Union – although Demushkin denied knowing them personally, and condemned their extremist actions (Pravda.ru 2007; Harding 2008). In 2010 the Slavic Union, as well as its successor organisation Slavic Force (*Slavianskaia sila*) were banned, and Demushkin went over to the broad ethno-nationalist coalition *Russkie* (Russians) (Verkhovsky 2012: 4) (for more on the latter, see below).

Dmitrii Bobrov, the future leader of the NSI, founded his first own organisation, Schultz-88 (*Shul'ts-88*), in 2001, when he felt that the ideology of the RNE was no longer sufficiently represented in St Petersburg, where he is based (in fact, 'Shul'ts' remains Bobrov's nickname to this day). The most notorious members of Schultz-88 were Dmitrii Borovikov and Aleksei Voevodin, who later became leaders of the neo-Nazi skinhead gangs Mad Crowd (*Med Kraud*) and the Combat Terrorist Organisation (*Boevaia terroristicheskaia organizatsia*) (Laryš and Mareš 2011: 145). In a 2006 wave of arrests, the police detained five members of the Combat Terrorist Organisation and fatally injured Borovikov. The arrested were accused of armed robberies, of hate crimes, including killing ten persons, as well as of the murder of two members of their own gang who were suspected of collaborating with the police (SOVA Center 2006). In 2011, Voevodin was sentenced to life imprisonment together with gang member Artem Prokhorenko (Titova 2011). In September 2016, Voevodin again made the headlines, this time for killing his cellmate in jail (Fontanka.ru 2016). Both Borovikov and Voevodin have become heroes for the Russian and international far-right scene, forming part of a pantheon later joined by among others the Norwegian far-right terrorist Anders Behring Breivik (Enstad 2017).[4]

Schultz-88 was officially founded on Adolf Hitler's birthday and the '88' in its name stands for '*Heil Hitler*', based on H being the eighth letter in the Latin alphabet. According to the SOVA Center, the main activity of Schultz-88 consisted of attacking non-Slavic-looking persons, and publishing the journals *Made in St-Petersburg* and *Gnev Peruna* (*Perun's Anger*) (Al'perovich 2011; Samoilov and Donskov 2005). In 2003, Bobrov was arrested, and in 2005, sentenced to six years in prison on charges of founding an extremist community (of teenagers) and inciting ethnic hatred against Jews, Africans and Caucasians (Nurnberg 2005; Samoilov and Donskov 2005). While in jail, Bobrov wrote the book *Notes from a Prisoner of War* (*Zapiski voennoplennogo*), which was banned immediately after it was published and therefore never distributed, although it is still available online. In his biographical note, Bobrov writes that he was the first person in Russia to be sentenced under Article 282 of the Russian criminal code (on inciting racial hatred or enmity). After being released in 2009, he started a solidarity campaign for other 'political prisoners'; he claims to have raised more than one million roubles to help imprisoned Russian nationalists (Bobrov n.d.).

National Socialist Initiative

After his release, in December 2009 Bobrov founded the NSI, a much more moderate organisation than the old Schultz-88. The St Petersburg-based NSI, together with the Moscow-based Slavic Union, have been the most prominent representatives of organisations with a national-socialist orientation in today's Russia. Both drew inspiration from the RNE. The NSI, for example, adopted a Nazi-inspired emblem in black and white with a red laurel wreath and, while it existed, employed white power rhetoric. Bobrov's influence, however, extended beyond the NSI: as an active blogger and writer, Bobrov exerted – and continues to exert – an ideological influence across the Russian nationalist movement, especially across its extreme fringe.

The framing of the NSI was far more cautious than that of Schultz-88: officially, the NSI supported the preservation of Russia's democratic foundations, and it took care to avoid formulations that might provoke new charges against its leader. Especially in his public performances, Bobrov's main criticisms have been targeted at the government and the corrupt state apparatus, paralleled with attacks on neo-liberalism and 'racial enemies'. The words of the NSI leader are indicative:

> We are not bourgeois nationalists, since we oppose the political omnipotence of capital. We are in favour of a gradual displacement of private and other forms of property, for social guarantees for workers, for a progressive income tax, for the socialisation of the capital of the oligarchs and for the implementation of other anti-capitalist measures. (Bobrov 2013)

Bobrov holds that a confrontation is taking place between the 'crooks' in Washington and 'their puppets in the Kremlin', but this he sees as a conflict within a single system. Although Putin has had confrontations with the West, Bobrov does not regard him as a patriot, but as a neo-liberal. He finds corroboration in the fact that Putin has destroyed a few oligarchs, but left the capitalist system as such intact (Bobrov 2015a). He has also compared Putin to Turkey's Recep Erdogan, as – again, in Boborov's view – both have been trying to Islamise their countries and both are dictators who throw members of the opposition into prison (Bobrov 2016a).

Bobrov does not personally define himself as a fascist, but he openly stands for national-socialist ideals, for 'social justice' and for 'the people' (*narod*). His proclaimed goal is to protect the interests of the Russian (*russkii*) people (Vyshenkov 2009), and xenophobia lies at the very foundation of the NSI's ideology. This xenophobia is framed in terms of the alleged biological hatred on the part of the 'Other' (for example, people hailing from North Caucasus) against Russians. And although the NSI does not openly promote violence, those who commit crimes against such 'Others' have been lauded as heroes (Al'perovich 2011).

In June 2015, a new criminal case was opened against Bobrov under Article 282, part 1, of the criminal code, this time for publishing the article 'NSI's racial doctrine' (SOVA Center 2015a; Yudina and Alperovich 2015b). The article claims that globalisation produces a systemic crisis in the states traditionally inhabited by white people and contributes to the loss of racial identity, the destruction of family life and social values, deliberate childlessness and the spread of extreme individualism and anti-social behaviour patterns (like alcoholism, various perversions and hedonism). This negatively affects the reproduction rates of the white race and leads to the inevitable erosion of its spirit, creativity and ability to progress – and, in the worst case, to its extinction. The article goes on to contrast the Western European nations, which have already entered the phase of decay, disorientation and loss of ethnic identity, with the great Russian people, who are managing to overcome this 'phase of rupture' (*faza nadloma*) and ethnic degradation. Russians thus represent the 'most promising White people' to safeguard white identity. Accordingly, the struggle of the Russian national socialists becomes of global importance (*Narodnaia sotsialisticheskaia initsiativa* 2013).

In parallel to the case against Bobrov, in September 2015 the NSI was banned by the St Petersburg City Court (Bobrov 2015b). Bobrov did not appeal the decision, and the NSI then suspended its activity. Unlike some other leaders of banned organisations, Bobrov did not proceed to found a new organisation under a different name (Yudina and Alperovich 2016). Instead he created an eponymous website which he frequently updates with news articles and postings.[5]

Bobrov has also been included in the list of active terrorists and extremists compiled by the Federal Financial Monitoring Service (*Rosfinmonitoring*), and denied the right to work or to leave the country. He remains politically active, however, especially through social media (Vkontakte, Twitter); and despite the regime's 'systematic repression', as he writes on his webpage, in August 2016 he published a second volume of his book, *Notes from a Prisoner of War: Part 2*. He describes this book as 'first-class Russian prose' within the genre of 'prison memoirs' that 'continues the tradition of Dostoevskii's *House of the Dead*' (Bobrov 2016b).

The National Socialist Initiative within Russia's broader ethno-nationalist network

The NSI has, together with the similarly banned Slavic Union, been among the leading organisations of national socialist orientation in contemporary Russia. Another prominent member of the extreme fringe of the Russian ethno-nationalist network – and a close partner of the NSI – has been the earlier-mentioned DPNI. The DPNI was set up in 2002 by Aleksandr Belov and Vladimir Basmanov to undertake actions against 'illegal immigrants'. The movement soon drew the attention of the wider public as a 'broker' between skinheads and Cossacks (Varga 2008: 569), and proceeded to stage some of the most significant nationalist mobilisations in recent years (in Kondopoga, 2006; in Manezhnaia Square, 2011). In 2006, the DPNI also took control over the Russian March – a nationwide nationalist event which had been introduced in 2005 by the DPNI, Aleksandr Dugin's Eurasian Youth Union (*Evraziiskii soiuz molodezhi*) and Aleksandr Sevastianov's National Great-Power Party of Russia (*Natsional'no-derzhavnaia partiia Rossii*) to mark 4 October, the new public holiday of National Unity Day (Tipaldou and Uba 2014: 1085–86).

The DPNI challenged the organisational and strategic style which had dominated among nationalist organisations up to that point by adopting a catch-all ideology, mixed membership with other nationalist organisations, and new communication technologies for mobilising its followers (Zuev 2010: 269; Tipaldou and Uba 2014: 1084). It was the DPNI that popularised the slogan 'Russia for Russians' (*Rossiia dlia russkikh*) in Russian society, a slogan that came to be supported by a majority of the population throughout the decade (Laruelle 2009: 74). In 2007, the SOVA Center classified the DPNI as 'the most dangerous' ultranationalist group, together with the Slavic Union and some other offshoots of the RNE (RFE/ RL 2007). In the course of that same year, however, DPNI went into decline. In 2009, Belov resigned as leader; then, in 2011, the organisation was banned, probably because it had become increasingly aggressively nationalist and anti-Semitic, taking a clear stance against the Kremlin (Tipaldou and Uba 2014: 1084).

After Bobrov had set up the NSI in 2009, this organisation quickly became one of the DPNI's closest allies. The NSI assumed a leading role in the Russian March, was one of its main organisers in St Petersburg, and participated in several notorious nationalist public actions, such as the Russian March of Labour (1 May) and the Day of Remembrance for the Victims of Ethnic Crime (1 October). In these actions the NSI collaborated with Belov's DPNI and other prominent nationalist organisations such as Konstantin Krylov's ROD (Yudina and Alperovich 2011; Tipaldou 2015: 111–12; author's personal communication with Bobrov).

In 2011, Bobrov joined a wide ethno-nationalist coalition initiated by Belov and Demushkin, *Russkie* (Russians), and became head of its regional branch in St Petersburg. The coalition was soon joined by several other nationalist organisations: the Russian Imperial Movement (*Russkoe imperskoe dvizhenie*), the Union of the Russian People (*Soiuz russkogo naroda*), the Russian Liberation Front 'Pamiat'' (*Russkii front osvobozhdeniia 'Pamiat''*) and the National Democratic Party (*Natsional'no-demokraticheskaia partiia*). As declared in its manifesto, the coalition strives for the protection of the ethnic Russians (*russkii narod*) in the wake of the nation's loss of statehood in 1917, and will fight against the constant oppression of the Russian people, oppression that in the past has often taken the form of 'genocide' (as evidence of such genocide, the manifesto's authors note the decreasing size of the population). The short-term objective is announced as being to promote 'ethnic and political solidarity of the Russians', whereas the ultimate goal is 'to establish the power of a national government and the proclamation of a Russian national state'. The manifesto ends with the slogans 'For a free Russia and Russian power! All forces to the national struggle! We are

Russians! We will win!' (Russkie 2011; Newsru.com 2011; Yudina and Alperovich 2011; Tipaldou 2015: 111–14).

On 20 April 2012, the leaders of the *Russkie* movement announced the formation of a new party, the Party of Nationalists (*Partiia natsionalistov*). The founding congress was held in Belarus, so that Russian authorities would not be able to prohibit or disperse it. Demushkin was elected chairman of the organising committee. The Party of Nationalists aimed to function as an umbrella structure that would draw support from three broad tendencies of contemporary Russian nationalism under a common emblem – the Russian imperial flag, a symbol with which all Russians nationalists identify. Orthodox nationalists and monarchists would be represented by the Russian Imperial Movement; moderate nationalists by Semen Pikhtelev's National Democrats (*Natsional'nye demokraty*); and the most radical segment of the Russian nationalists by the NSI (Yudina and Alperovich 2012).

Some members of Boborov's NSI criticised him for this collaboration with other nationalist organisations, such as the national monarchists (with whom Bobrov maintains close relations) and the national democrats. In 2013 Bobrov responded to this criticism in an open letter, arguing that at this juncture, a broad front of nationalists was necessary, for two reasons: first, it was essential to join ranks in order to win the struggle for 'national liberation' against the antinational policies of the Russian government; and second, a common front was needed in order to establish national statehood for ethnic Russians. For this reason, Bobrov argued, even if the NSI was anticapitalist, it should be willing to pact with 'national-bourgeois fellow travellers' who wanted to achieve the same goal: the creation of a nation-state for the Russian nation (Bobrov 2013).

From 2014 onwards, the authorities stepped up pressure against Russian nationalists, with a wave of arrests of nationalist leaders and bans on their organisations. In October 2014, Belov was arrested on charges of laundering money for a Kazakhstani banker in order to fund extremist activities (in August 2016, he was sentenced to 7.5 years in prison). Hence the entire leadership of the coalition fell on Demushkin's shoulders. Consequently, Demushkin also came under the authorities' spotlight. He was detained several times in 2015 and was not allowed to participate in the Russian March that year. One month after the banning of the NSI, the Moscow City Court in October 2015 likewise banned the *Russkie* movement on the grounds of its manifesto being extremist. The Court found that the call for 'the creation of a national state and the struggle for national liberation by any means' could be interpreted as incitement to ethnic hatred (Yudina and Alperovich 2016). In December 2015, a criminal case was opened against Demushkin under Article 282, citing a slogan that had been used in the 2014 Russian March (SOVA Center 2015b), and Demushkin was placed under house arrest.

Ethnic nationalists and the events in Ukraine

The Euromaidan was initially positively received by Russian nationalists – indeed, enthusiastically so. Bobrov himself visited Ukraine in early February 2014 to 'learn from his more successful colleagues' and met with leaders of various groups that took part in the protests, as well as with *Svoboda* deputy Ruslan Zelik (Horvath 2015). He was not alone: according to Russian law enforcement officers, at least thirty-two other leaders and activists of various Russian organisations (for example, from Eduard Limonov's Other Russia, the National Democratic Party and the Russian Imperial Movement) travelled to Ukraine during the Euromaidan revolution.

As soon as Bobrov returned to St Petersburg, he organised a seminar to inform his colleagues about what he had experienced (Life. ru 2014). The seminar was not open to the public, but soon afterwards, on 31 March 2014, on the occasion of Orthodox mourning ceremonies for those massacred by snipers, Bobrov paid public tribute to the demonstrators. For Bobrov, these people were martyrs who would serve as models for all who struggle against repressive regimes (Bobrov 2014; Horvath 2015).

Basmanov and Demushkin from the Party of Nationalists followed the same line. Demushkin described the Euromaidan events as a positive grassroots uprising against a corrupt government ruled by oligarchs, and he compared the revolution in Kiev with the Russian Bolotnaia protests two years prior. For him, the only difference was the degree of success as regards mobilisation (Horvath 2015: 831). Former DPNI leader Basmanov praised the Euromaidan protests for giving more freedom to the people; he also supported the demands for self-determination of Crimean Russians. He was highly critical of the Russian annexation of Crimea, however, warning against what he referred to as the 'propagandist myths' peddled by pro-Kremlin nationalists. This criticism was based on his fears that Russia's military involvement in Ukraine might threaten the Russian population there, and inflict more suffering on them than they had experienced under the previous regime (ibid.: 830–31).

As the situation was escalating and the protests in Donetsk and Luhansk turned into an armed conflict, there came a parting of the ways for the Russian nationalists. The NSI, along with some groups of national-democratic orientation, such as Krylov's National Democratic Party, the New Force (*Novaia sila*), Russia Will be Freed by Our Forces (*Rossiia osvoboditsia nashimi silami*, RONS) and others, supported the 'Russian Spring' in southeast Ukraine (Yudina 2014). However, within this group of supporters of the armed uprising there were also internal divisions. First, while some do not recognise the Ukrainians as a separate nation, others cast the conflict as one between 'Banderite' Ukrainians from central and western Ukraine and Russians from the southeast. Second, supporters of the uprising in Donbas were divided as to what the Kremlin's motivations were. The majority believed that Putin's policy was driven by his will to protect the interests of ethnic Russians in the territory. Valerii Solovei, leader of New Force, for instance, believed that while Putin was no nationalist – on the contrary, Putin regarded Russians as his enemies, according to Solovei – he was in fact building a nation-state. Also Krylov supported the protection of ethnic Russians by military means, but had serious doubts as to whether the Russian population of Ukraine would be better off under Putin's regime (Kolstø 2014: 131–32). Yet others held that Putin was using the Ukrainian crisis either for curtailing political freedoms in Russia itself, or in order to create negative images of the nationalists and the *Russkie* movement inside Russia (Yudina and Alperovich 2014).

Opponents of the Russian Spring include former DPNI leaders Belov and Basmanov as well as Demushkin. They are fewer in number, but hold more consistent views – and, paradoxically, in their assessments, they are closer to the views of the national liberals. They believe that the polarisation along ethnic lines was an artificial construct invented by the Russian government in order to keep Ukrainians from overthrowing the corrupt regime of Viktor Yanukovych. In the view of this segment of the nationalist movement, Ukrainians would be better off under Kiev's pro-Western post-Euromaidan government than under Putin. The antipathy this part of the nationalist movement feels to the Russian government thus seems to be much stronger than their identification with other Slavic nations (Yudina 2014; Yudina and Alperovich 2014).

Disagreements over how to respond to the armed uprising in Donbas prompted Bobrov to accuse Belov and Demushkin of holding an 'anti-Russian and openly Russophobic' position. Soon thereafter he left the *Russkie* coalition. The Russian Imperial Movement followed suit, marking the beginning of the end for this broad coalition that, instead of uniting Russian nationalists of various stripes, was now reduced to an alliance between the officially banned DPNI and the Slavic Union (Yudina and Alperovich 2015a).

Polarisation was smoothed out in 2015 after many nationalist-patriotic organisations began to refocus on their traditional activities. By then, the war in Ukraine had lost its novelty and was no longer so politically expedient. Most supporters of the Russian Spring had stopped openly supporting the militants in Donbas, while at the same time they were turning against the Kremlin for betraying the idea of 'Novorossiia'. The *Russkie* and some other organisations that did not initially support the Russian Spring also toned down their focus on the topic in 2015 and no longer called for an 'anti-war' mobilisation. Bobrov, an ardent supporter of Novorossiia throughout the previous year went so far as to avoid any mention whatsoever of the issue. He announced that he and his organisation would take a neutral position with regard to the Ukrainian conflict and even prohibited NSI members from taking part in any actions. On his webpages Bobrov commented on internal affairs only (Yudina and Alperovich 2015b). However, as has been noted, this realignment was not enough to prevent a crackdown on the part of the authorities: by the end of the year 2015, the NSI was banned and the radical fringe in total disarray.

Conclusions

This chapter has presented the extreme right fringe of current Russian nationalism: its origins, development and how the events in Ukraine 2013–15 have affected it. We have noted the network structure of the ethno-nationalist movement and the internal division of labour that has characterised it. At the centre of the analysis has been a case study of the NSI and its leader. A dynamic analysis of the organisation – describing not only the NSI, but also its organisational seedbed, the RNE, and the organisations the NSI has been working closely together with, including the Slavic Union and the DPNI – has made clear the recent dynamics of the extreme fringe of Russian nationalism. The analysis presented in this chapter has also shown how the political activism of NSI leader Dmitrii Bobrov, a national socialist, has evolved over the years. Bobrov's discourse has become more moderate – as have the coalitions that his various organisations have been involved with. Gradually, as we have seen, the NSI became a constituent part of Russian ethno-nationalism.

Virtually all Russian nationalists welcomed the Euromaidan events, finding in them hopes for reinvigorating the opportunity lost with the failure of the Bolotnaia protests. Then, however, the armed conflict in Donetsk and Luhansk divided them. With events unfolding rapidly, nationalists soon found themselves divided into supporters and opponents of the Russian Spring and Novorossiya – and likewise, into supporters and opponents of Putin's approach. These dividing lines cut across the entire nationalist movement, from the most moderate parts to the most extremist factions.

The war in Ukraine is a clear example of how an external event can serve as a catalyst for dividing a movement. The subsequent crisis allows for a more thorough analysis of movement dynamics. Opposition in Russia, and not least the nationalist opposition, is a complicated issue to study as such, especially the segments belonging to 'uncivil society'. Closer study of the developments within the nationalist movement that were triggered by the Euromaidan protests and the war in Donbas can help to shed light on some aspects of the internal dynamics of the nationalist movement – while at the same time giving rise to new questions. The recent events have helped illuminate who supports whom in the turbulent – in terms of high organisational turnover and frequent name changes – nationalist environment. To some extent, the events in Ukraine have also made clear the balance of power within the movement, and which leaders are sufficiently confident and influential to initiate new ideas and to form new organisations, coalitions or parties – or to leave them.

More questions remain. Will these newly formed coalitions hold together, or are they just another stage in a larger transformation, a transformation that may signify political maturity and readiness for electoral competition? Is what we see a case of 'mainstreamisation' of fringe organisations? Has the NSI now become more democratic – and if so, can we expect this trend to last? And what can be expected of the other – similarly banned – organisations of the ethno-nationalist fringe, the Slavic Union and the DPNI? Will their current legal status push them further towards the margins? Or is the fact that Belov decided to compete for a top slot on the party list of the liberal opposition PARNAS party for the 2016 State Duma elections (RFE/RL 2016) a sign of the radical fringe reorienting itself towards the centre and becoming more democratic? Further qualitative, actor-based research is needed to help us recognise and understand evolving trends within the nationalist movement in today's Russia.

Notes

1. 'Hybrid regimes' combine nominally democratic institutions with persistent authoritarian patterns of governance; they are located in the grey zone between democracy and dictatorship (see Diamond 2002; Levitsky and Way 2002; Colton and Hale 2009).
2. Personal communication with Bobrov, 13 December 2011.
3. Demushkin is shown instructing classes on knife-fighting in a Reggie Yates' BBC documentary on the Russian far right (BBC 2015).
4. In 2010, the neo-Nazi National Socialism–White Power (NS-WP) gang from St Petersburg published a video recording of the murder of a Ghanaian citizen by its members. The video shows a masked man saying: 'The Nazis have lost their best warriors', and ends with a poster depicting Borovikov (RT 2010).
5. The personal website of Dmitrii Bobrov is <http://dbobrov.info/> (last accessed 10 October 2016).

Bibliography

Alexseev, Mikhail A. (2011), 'Societal security, the security dilemma, and extreme anti-migrant hostility in Russia', *Journal of Peace Research*, 48, 4: 509–23.

Al'perovich, Vera (2011), '"Myslit' sprava": kratkii obzor sovremennoi pravoradikal'noi ideologii' [Thinking from the right: a brief overview of current right wing ideology], SOVA Center, 31 October, <http://www.sova-center.ru/racism-xenophobia/publications/2011/10/d22894> (last accessed 15 August 2016).

Arnold, Richard (2009), '"Thugs with guns": disaggregating "ethnic violence" in the Russian Federation', *Nationalities Papers*, 37, 5: 641–64.

BBC (2015), 'Reggie Yates' extreme Russia: far right & proud', <http://www.bbc.co.uk/programmes/b05r844j> (last accessed 19 October 2016).

Bobrov, Dmitrii (n.d.), 'Biografiia Dmitriia Bobrova' [Dmitrii Bobrov's biography], *Sait, posviashchennyi Dmitriiu Bobrovu, grazhdanskomu aktivistu, ideologu, pisateliu*, <http://dbobrov.info/bio> (last accessed 15 August 2016).

Bobrov, Dmitrii (2013), 'Dmitrii Bobrov: O edinstve natsionalistov v bor'be za Russkoe gosudarstvo' [Dmitrii Bobrov: on the nationalists' unity in the struggle for a Russian state], Personal'nyi sait Alekseia

Kolegova, 22 February, <http://rubsev.ru/2013/02/dmitrij-bobrov-o-edinstve-nacionalistov-v-borbe-za-russkoe-gosudarstvo/> (last accessed 15 August 2015).

Bobrov, Dmitrii (2014), 'Pobeda i traur (40 dnei tragicheskim sobytiiam v Kieve)' [Victory and mourning (40 days of tragic events in Kiev)], NS_Dima_Schultz, 31 March, <http://ns-dima-schultz.livejournal.com/140825.html> (last accessed 12 August 2016).

Bobrov, Dmitrii (2015a), 'Putin byl i ostaetsia liberalom' [Putin was and remains a liberal], Art Polit Info, 24 February, <http://artpolitinfo.ru/dmitriy-bobrov-putin-byil-ostayotsya-liberalom-vmesto-berezovskogo-hodorkovskogo-gusinskogo-teper-na-podyome-abramovich-fridman-rottenberg-chto-u-putina-proizoshyol-konflikt-s-zapa/> (last accessed 14 August 2016).

Bobrov, Dmitrii (2015b), 'Gorodskoi sud Sankt-Peterburga zapretil NSI' [St Petersburg city court bans NSI], Sait, posviashchennyi Dmitriiu Bobrovu, grazhdanskomu aktivistu, ideologu, pisateliu, 10 August, <http://dbobrov.info/news/item/115> (last accessed 15 August 2016).

Bobrov, Dmitrii (2016a), 'Dva diktatora, otpravliaiushchikh oppozitsiiu v tiur'my, nashli obshchii iazyk' [Two dictators, sending the opposition to prison, have found a common language], Sait, posviashchennyi Dmitriiu Bobrovu, grazhdanskomu aktivistu, ideologu, pisateliu, 10 August, <http://dbobrov.info/my-articles/item/203> (last accessed 14 August 2016).

Bobrov, Dmitrii (2016b), 'Vtoraia chast' knigi "Zapiski voennoplennogo/Tiuremnye vospominaniia lidera organizatsii Shul'ts88"' [Second part of the book *Notes from a Prisoner of War/Prison Memoires of the Leader of the Organisation Shultz88*], *Sait, Posviashchennyi Dmitriiu Bobrovu, Grazhdanskomu Aktivistu, Ideologu, Pisateliu*, 11 August, <http://dbobrov.info/my-articles/item/205> (last accessed 15 August 2016).

Colton, Timothy J. and Henry E. Hale (2009), 'The Putin vote: presidential electorates in a hybrid regime', *Slavic Review*, 68, 3: 473–503.

Diamond, Larry (2002), 'Thinking about hybrid regimes', *Journal of Democracy*, 13, 2: 21–35.

Diani, Mario (1992), 'The concept of social movement', *The Sociological Review*, 40, 1: 1–25.

Dunlop, John (1996), 'Alexander Barkashov and the rise of national socialism in Russia', *Demokratizatsiya*, 4, 4: 519–30.

Enstad, Johannes D. (2017), 'Glory to Breivik! The Russian far right and the 2011 Norway attacks', *Terrorism and Political Violence*, 29, 5: 773–92.

Fontanka.ru (2016), 'V kolonii v kamere pozhiznenno prigovorennykh Voevodin ubil sokamernika' [In prison Voevodin kills cellmate in cell for life-timers], 24 September, <http://www.fontanka.ru/2016/09/24/022/> (last accessed 12 October 2016).

Frindte, Wolfgang, Daniel Geschke, Nicole Haußecker and Franziska Schmidtke (2013), 'Ein systematisierender Überblick über Entwicklungslinien der Rechtsextremismusforschung von 1990 bis 2013' [A systematic overview of the development of right-wing extremism research from 1990 to 2013], in Wolfgang Frindte, Daniel Geschke, Nicole Haußecker and Franziska Schmidtke, eds, *Rechtsextremismus und 'Nationalsozialistischer Untergrund'* [*Right-wing Extremism and the 'National-Socialist Underground'*], Wiesbaden: Springer, 25–96.

Gel'man, Vladimir (2016), 'Correction of errors: how the Kremlin re-equilibrated authoritarian elections in 2016', *Ponars Eurasia Policy Memo*, 437, <http://www.ponarseurasia.org/memo/correction-errors-how-kremlin-re-equilibrated-authoritarian-elections-2016> (last accessed 13 October 2016).

Griffin, Roger (2003), 'From slime mould to rhizome: an introduction to the groupuscular right', *Patterns of Prejudice*, 37, 1: 27–50.

Hale, Henry E. (2015), *Patronal Politics: Eurasian Regime Dynamics in Comparative Perspective*, Cambridge: Cambridge University Press.

Harding, Luke (2008), 'Russian skinhead gang jailed for murder of 20 migrants', *The Guardian*, 16 December, <https://www.theguardian.com/world/2008/dec/16/russia-trial-gang-murder> (last accessed 20 October 2016).

Horvath, Robert (2015), 'The Euromaidan and the crisis of Russian nationalism', *Nationalities Papers*, 43, 6: 819–39.

Kolstø, Pål (2014), 'Russia's nationalists flirt with democracy', *Journal of Democracy*, 25, 3: 120–34.

Kolstø, Pål and Helge Blakkisrud (2016), *The New Russian Nationalism: Imperialism, Ethnicity and Authoritarianism, 2000–15*, Edinburgh: Edinburgh University Press.

Koopmans, Ruud (1995), 'Bewegung oder Erstarrung? Bestandsaufnahme der deutschen Bewegungsforschung in den letzten zehn Jahren' [Movement or paralysis? Review of German research on social movements in the last ten years], *Neue Soziale Bewegungen*, 8, 1: 90–96.

Koopmans, Ruud and Dieter Rucht (1996), 'Rechtsradikalismus als soziale Bewegung?' [The radical right as a social movement?], in Jürgen W. Falter, Hans-Gerd Jaschke and Jürgen R. Winkler, eds, *Rechtsextremismus: Ergebnisse und Perspektiven der Forschung* [*Right-wing Extremism: Findings and Research Perspectives*], Opladen: Westdeutscher Verlag, 265–87.

Kopecký, Petr and Cas Mudde, eds (2003), *Uncivil Society? Contentious Politics in Post-Communist Europe*, London: Routledge.

Laruelle, Marlene (2009), *In the Name of the Nation: Nationalism and Politics in Contemporary Russia*, Basingstoke: Palgrave Macmillan.

Laruelle, Marlene (2010), 'The ideological shift on the Russian radical right: from demonizing the West to fear of migrants', *Problems of Post-Communism*, 57, 6: 19–31.

Laryš, Martin and Miroslav Mareš (2011), 'Right-wing extremist violence in the Russian Federation', *Europe–Asia Studies*, 63, 1: 129–54.

Levitsky, Steven and Lucan Way (2002), 'The rise of competitive authoritarianism', *Journal of Democracy*, 13, 2: 51–65.
Life.ru (2014), 'Natsionalisty iz Rossii vyekhali v Kiev, chtoby pereniat' opyt Maidana' [Nationalists from Russia went to Kiev to learn from Maidan], 21 February, <https://life.ru/t/%D0%BD%D0%BE%D0%B2%D0%BE%D1%81%D1%82%D0%B8/127661> (last accessed 20 October 2016).
Likhachev, Viacheslav (2002), *Natsizm v Rossii* [*Nazism in Russia*], Moscow: Panorama.
Newsru.com (2011), 'Rossiiskie natsionalisty ob"edinilis' v organizatsiiu "Russkie", pravozashchitniki obespokoeny' [Russian nationalists unite in the organisation 'Russkie', human rights activists are concerned], 5 May, <http://www.newsru.com/russia/05may2011/russkie.html> (last accessed 12 October 2016.)
Narodnaia sotsialisticheskaia initsiativa (2013), 'Rasovaia doktrina NSI' [NSI's racial doctrine], 5 May, <http://ns-initiative.livejournal.com/179619.html> (last accessed 12 October 2016).
Nurnberg, Alexander (2005), 'Russia: 6 years for neo-Nazi', *New York Times*, 10 December, <http://www.nytimes.com/2005/12/10/world/world-briefing-europe-russia-6-years-for-neonazi.html?_r=0> (last accessed 15 August 2016).
Pedahzur, Ami and Leonard Weinberg (2001), 'Modern European democracy and its enemies: the threat of the extreme right', *Totalitarian Movements and Political Religions*, 2, 1: 52–72.
Pilkington, Hilary (2010), 'No longer "on parade": style and the performance of skinhead in the Russian Far North', *The Russian Review*, 69, 2: 187–209.
Pilkington, Hilary, Elena Omel'chenko and Al'bina Garifzianova (2013) *Russia's Skinheads: Exploring and Rethinking Subcultural Lives*, London: Routledge.
Pravda.ru (2007), 'Young Russian skinhead pleads guilty to killing 37 people', 28 May, <http://www.pravdareport.com/hotspots/crimes/28-05-2007/92265-russian_skinhead-0/> (last accessed 20 October 2016).
RFE/RL (2007), 'Neo-Nazi numbers continue to grow', 21 November, <http://www.rferl.org/content/article/1143999.html> (last accessed 10 October 2013).
RFE/RL (2016), 'Natsionalist Potkin (Belov) mozhet poiti na vybory ot partii PARNAS' [Nationalist Potkin (Belov) can run for elections with the party PARNAS], 9 June, <http://www.svoboda.org/a/27789175.html> (last accessed 13 October 2016).
RT (2010), 'New wave of neo-Nazi violence hits St. Petersburg?', 16 January, <https://www.rt.com/news/nazis-russia-internet-confession/> (last accessed 13 October 2016).
Rucht, Dieter (1995), 'Kollektive Identität: Konzeptionelle Überlegungen zu einem Desiderat der Bewegungsforschung' [Collective identity:

conceptual considerations on a desideratum of social movement research]', *Neue Soziale Bewegungen*, 8, 1: 9–23.
Russkie (2011) 'Manifest etnopoliticheskogo ob"edineniia Russkie' [Manifesto of the Ethno-Political Association Russkie], <http://basmanov.livejournal.com/911770.html> (last accessed 31 December 2016)
Samoilov, Aleksandr and Nikolai Donskov (2005), 'Zub drakona vypal' [The dragon's tooth fell], *Novaia gazeta*, 12 December, <http://2005.novayagazeta.ru/nomer/2005/93n/n93n-s15.shtml> (last accessed 14 August 2016).
Shenfield, Stephen D. (2001), *Russian Fascism: Traditions, Tendencies, Movements*, New York: M. E. Sharpe.
Shnirel'man, Viktor (2011), *Porog tolerantnosti. Ideologiia i praktika novogo rasizma* [*The Threshold of Tolerance: Ideology and Practice of the New Racism*], Moscow: Novoe literaturnoe obozrenie.
Sokolov, Mikhail (2008), 'Russian National Unity: an analysis of the political style of a radical-nationalist organization', *Russian Politics and Law*, 46, 4: 66–79.
SOVA Center (2006), 'In St Petersburg, a group suspected of a series of racist killings and assaults were arrested', 26 May, <http://www.sova-center.ru/en/xenophobia/news-releases/2006/05/d8325/> (last accessed 10 October 2016).
SOVA Center (2015a), 'Vozbuzhdeno ugolovnoe delo protiv rukovoditelia NSI D. Bobrova' [Criminal case opened against head of NSI D. Bobrov], 23 June, <http://www.sova-center.ru/racism-xenophobia/news/counteraction/2015/06/d32256/> (last accessed 13 October 2016).
SOVA Center (2015b), 'Vozbuzhdeno ugolovnoe delo protiv Dmitriia Demushkina' [Criminal case opened against Dmitrii Demushkin], 4 December, <http://www.sova-center.ru/racism-xenophobia/news/counteraction/2015/12/d33371/> (last accessed 13 October 2016).
Tarasov, Aleksandr (1999), 'Skinheads ou naturel' [Skinheads or natural], *Neprikosnovennyi zapas*, 5, <http://magazines.russ.ru/nz/1999/5/taras.html> (last accessed 12 October 2016).
Tipaldou, Sofia (2015), *Russia's Nationalist-Patriotic Opposition: The Shifting Politics of Right-Wing Contention during Post-Communist Transition*, PhD Thesis, Barcelona: Universidad Autónoma de Barcelona.
Tipaldou, Sofia and Katrin Uba (2014), 'The Russian radical right movement and immigration policy: do they just make noise or do they have an impact as well?', *Europe–Asia Studies*, 66, 7: 1080–101.
Titova, Irina (2011), '2 Russian neo-Nazi leaders get life in jail', cnsnews.com, 14 June, <http://www.cnsnews.com/news/article/2-russian-neo-nazi-leaders-get-life-jail> (last accessed 10 October 2016).
Varga, Mihai (2008), 'How political opportunities strengthen the far right: understanding the rise in far-right militancy in Russia', *Europe–Asia Studies*, 60, 4: 561–79.

Verkhovsky, Alexander (2009), 'Future prospects of contemporary Russian nationalism', in Marlene Laruelle, ed., *Russian Nationalism and the National Reassertion of Russia*, London: Routledge, 89–103.

Verkhovsky, Alexander (2012), *The Ultra-right in Russia in 2012*, Berlin: Friedrich-Ebert-Stiftung.

Vyshenkov, Evgenii (2009), 'Shul'ts: "My poidem drugim putem"' [Shultz: 'We will go another way'], *Fontanka*, 2 November, <http://www.fontanka.ru/2009/11/02/031/> (last accessed 12 October 2016).

Yudina, Natalia (2014), 'Beware the rise of the Russian ultra-right', SOVA Center, 14 September, <http://www.sova-center.ru/en/xenophobia/reports-analyses/2014/09/d30212/> (last accessed 19 October 2015).

Yudina, Natalia and Vera Alperovich (2011), 'Spring 2011: causes célèbres and new ultra-right formations', SOVA Center, 12 July, <http://www.sova-center.ru/en/xenophobia/reports-analyses/2011/07/d22101/> (last accessed 13 October 2016).

Yudina, Natalia and Vera Alperovich (2012), 'Spring 2012: ultra-right on the streets, law enforcement on the web', SOVA Center, 27 July, <http://www.sova-center.ru/en/xenophobia/reports-analyses/2012/07/d24976/> (last accessed 12 October 2016).

Yudina, Natalia and Vera Alperovich (2014), 'Ukraine upsets the nationalist apple-cart: xenophobia, radical nationalism and efforts to counteract it in Russia during the first half of 2014', SOVA Center, 6 August, <http://www.sova-center.ru/en/xenophobia/reports-analyses/2014/08/d30003/#ultr006> (last accessed 20 October 2015).

Yudina, Natalia and Vera Alperovich (2015a), 'Calm before the storm? Xenophobia and radical nationalism in Russia and efforts to counteract them in 2014', in Alexander Verkhovsky, ed., *Xenophobia, Freedom of Conscience and Anti-extremism in Russia in 2015*, Moscow: SOVA Center, 5–66.

Yudina, Natalia and Vera Alperovich (2015b), 'Pro-Kremlin and oppositional – with the shield and on it: xenophobia, radical nationalism and efforts to counteract them in Russia during the first half of 2015', SOVA Center, 31 August, <http://www.sova-center.ru/en/xenophobia/reports-analyses/2015/08/d32675/> (last accessed 18 October 2015).

Yudina, Natalia and Vera Alperovich (2016), 'The ultra-right movement under pressure: xenophobia and radical nationalism in Russia, and efforts to counteract them in 2015', in Alexander Verkhovsky, ed., *Xenophobia, Freedom of Conscience and Anti-extremism in Russia in 2015*, Moscow: SOVA Center, 7–66.

Zakharov, Nikolay (2013), 'The social movement against immigration as the vehicle and the agent of racialization in Russia', in Kerstin Jacobsson and Steven Saxonberg, eds, *Beyond NGO-ization: The Development of Social Movements in Central and Eastern Europe*, Abingdon: Routledge, 169–89.

Zuev, Denis (2010), 'The Movement Against Illegal Immigration: analysis of the central node in the Russian extreme-right movement', *Nations and Nationalism*, 16, 2: 261–84.

Zuev, Denis (2011), 'The Russian ultranationalist movement on the Internet: actors, communities, and organization of joint actions', *Post-Soviet Affairs*, 27, 2: 121–57.

Zuev, Denis (2013), 'The Russian March: investigating the symbolic dimension of political performance in modern Russia', *Europe–Asia Studies*, 65, 1: 102–26.

Part III

Identities and otherings

9

'Restore Moscow to the Muscovites': Othering 'the migrants' in the 2013 Moscow mayoral elections

Helge Blakkisrud and Pål Kolstø

In June 2013, Moscow Mayor Sergei Sobianin unexpectedly announced that, after a hiatus of ten years, Muscovites would again be allowed to choose their head of executive power through direct elections. Since the turn of the millennium, Russian elections had gradually shifted from being more or less open contests for voter support, to closely managed referenda over the political line set by the Kremlin (Sakwa 2011). The decision to make the Moscow mayoral elections semi-competitive by allowing candidates other than the regime's own hand-picked, 'controllable', sparring partners to run turned this into an interesting experiment (Orttung 2013; Waller 2013).

In this chapter, we focus on one aspect of this campaign, the topic that ordinary Muscovites identified as *the* most important: the large numbers of labour migrants in the capital. We explore how the decision to open up the elections into a more genuine contest compelled the regime candidate, incumbent mayor Sobianin, to adopt a more aggressive rhetoric on migration than that officially endorsed by the Kremlin. This, we hold, was due to at least two reasons. For one, Sobianin faced stiff competition from the rising star of the non-systemic opposition, liberal-nationalist Aleksei Navalnyi, and had to find a way to outbid him on the migrant issue.[1] Second, in a more competitive environment, Sobianin could not rely solely on administrative resources: he had to respond to popular demands in order to ensure an acceptable win.[2] Thus, the Moscow experiment contributed to pushing the borders of what mainstream politicians saw as acceptable positions on migrants and migration policy – and, implicitly, we argue, to a further strengthening of the image of migrants as a new 'Other' in Russian identity discourse (see Kolstø and Blakkisrud 2016).

We begin by outlining the position of 'the migrant' in contemporary Russian identity discourse. Then we provide a brief overview of the background for the Moscow mayoral campaign, before examining how the candidates approached the migrant issue: what images did they present of 'the migrants'? How did they assess migrants' prospects of successful integration into Russian society? And how should the flow of new migrants be regulated? Next, we turn to the Muscovites themselves, to see whether campaign promises reflected the positions of the electorate on the same issues. In conclusion, we argue that the experiment with semi-competitive elections in Moscow in 2013 demonstrated the limits of the Kremlin's ability to control Russian nationalist discourse *and* contributed to cementing the idea of 'the migrants' as the new 'Other'.

Who is 'the migrant' in Russian identity discourse?

In the run-up to the 2012 Russian presidential elections, Vladimir Putin presented his political programme for the next six-year period in a series of newspaper articles. One of these, published in *Nezavisimaia gazeta*, was titled 'Russia: the national question' (Putin 2012). Here Putin argued that Russia's process of state formation was unique in that 'we have a multinational society, but a united people'. However, he went on to say, ethnic Russians constitute 'the state-forming nation' (*gosudarstvoobrazuiushchii narod*) within this community: 'What has woven the fabric of this unique civilisation is the [ethnic] Russian people, Russian culture.' Hence, while retaining a traditional state-centred orientation in line with an imperial and Soviet as well as post-Soviet civic *rossiiane* understanding of the nation (Tishkov 1995; Tolz 2001), Putin signalled an ethnic turn by explicitly declaring 'Russianness' to be the ethno-cultural core of the national identity (Kolstø 2016; Teper 2016).

The question of whom to include in such a core or in-group is always linked to the question of where to draw the outer borders: who is the constitutive 'Other'? In the Russian debate in recent years, this role has been filled by 'the migrants' (*migranty*) (Pain 2007; Mukomel' 2011; Kolstø and Blakkisrud 2016).[3] In the above-mentioned article Putin devoted considerable space to the migration issue, acknowledging that many people were seriously concerned about current trends, and also noting the need to combat illegal immigration. Nevertheless, his main message concerned the need for 'civilised integration and socialisation' of migrants: 'It is important that the migrants can adapt (*adaptirovats'ia*) normally in society', he argued. In line with his new, more openly Russo-centric approach, he concluded that, as a minimum, migrants should be expected to learn to speak Russian and adapt to Russian culture (Putin 2012).

In that article, Putin underlined the differences between legal and illegal as well as external and internal migration. However, in the everyday Russian identity debate, the term 'migrant' is often used to refer to members of certain ethnic and regional communities. As Emil Pain, a leading expert on Russian nationalism, has noted: 'In Moscow no one calls someone from St Petersburg, Oryol or Tyumen a "migrant", nor Tatars or Bashkiris from their republics' – in fact, even people from Ukraine and Belarus may escape this epithet (Pain 2013a). The term 'migrant' is reserved predominantly for people arriving from the Caucasus – both North and South – and from Central Asia (ibid.).

This new 'Other' is thus not necessarily a foreigner: he or she may just as well be a Russian citizen whose forefathers have lived on the territory of today's Russian Federation since time immemorial. The term is more culturally defined: in Russian identity discourse, a 'migrant' is a bearer of a cultural identity seen as alien, and difficult – perhaps impossible – to integrate into the Russo-centric understanding of who belongs in the Russian in-group (Tolz and Harding 2015; Blakkisrud 2016). In the following, we examine how 'the migrant' came to play a major role when the capital experimented with semi-competitive elections in 2013.

The Moscow mayoral elections: Background

The September 2013 mayoral elections represented the first time in almost a decade that the Muscovites themselves were allowed to influence who was to hold top executive power in the city. Long-term mayor Iurii Luzhkov (in power 1992–2010) had been elected for a fourth consecutive term back in December 2003; but in the following year, in the wake of the Beslan terrorist attack, direct elections were abolished and replaced by a centralised appointment regime. In October 2010, after a bitter row with Luzhkov, President Dmitrii Medvedev appointed deputy prime minister and former head of the presidential administration Sergei Sobianin as new mayor of Moscow; and although public elections were reinstated in 2012, Sobianin could in principle have served until 2015 without testing his public support. However, in June 2013, he decided to cut his term short and call snap elections.

The most likely reason for this was the perceived need for strengthening the authority of the mayor's office with a popular mandate (Waller 2013; see also Blakkisrud 2015). In an interview with *Moskovskie novosti* just prior to the announcement, Sobianin explained, 'a person who has been supported by the voters, who enjoys a mandate based on trust, can realise his plans and programmes faster and more efficiently' (Nikolaeva and Bogomolov 2013). Moreover, the timing seemed right: in the wake of the flawed December 2011 State Duma elections, Moscow had seen a wave of large-scale public demonstrations against the powers-that-be. By June 2013, however, the protests were clearly losing steam, whereas the non-systemic opposition was struggling to hold their shaky coalition together.[4]

On 5 June, Sobianin made a formal request to President Putin to be relieved of his duties, so as to pave the way for early elections. Putin responded by appointing Sobianin acting mayor and wishing him 'the best of luck' (Latukhina 2013), leaving no doubt about whom the Kremlin wanted to see as the future mayor of the nation's capital. Two days later, the Moscow City Duma formally decided to hold mayoral elections on 8 September 2013. The die was cast.

Who were the contenders?

With only three months till election day, the campaign kicked off immediately. Local legislation allowed candidates to register as party candidates or as independents. To be registered, mayoral hopefuls had to prove that they enjoyed the backing of at least 6 per cent of the representatives in the Moscow City Duma and/or municipal councils (110 representatives). Independents had to collect signatures of support from at least 1 per cent of the registered voters (approximately 120,000 signatures). With United Russia's near-total dominance in the legislative bodies – in the Moscow City Duma, for example, United Russia then controlled thirty-two out of thirty-five seats – Sobianin's potential challengers faced a formidable obstacle.

In the end, six candidates nevertheless passed the threshold and were allowed to run for the office of Moscow mayor. As expected, Sobianin was among these. He had not opted for the easiest way, though. As an incumbent – and indeed, as a centrally placed member of United Russia – he could have relied on the backing of the 'party of power'.[5] Instead, he chose to run as an independent.

His challengers were all nominated by political parties. Among these, the most interesting name – and for many observers the most surprising one – was that of Aleksei Navalnyi, who had risen to prominence as a key opposition leader on the back of the 2011–12 protest movement. Although not a party member himself, Navalnyi had been promoted by one of the key members of the non-systemic opposition, the liberal-democratic party Republican Party of Russia–People's Freedom Party (*Respublikanskaia partiia Rossii–Partiia narodnoi svobody*, RPR-PARNAS).

While RPR-PARNAS was seen to embrace Western-style liberalism, Navalnyi presented more of a political Janus face (Coalson 2013). His relentless anti-corruption crusade had won him the support of many liberals, but Navalnyi was also embraced by the nationalists. The latter could point to his role in setting up the nationalist-oriented organisation NAROD back in 2007, his active backing of the 'Stop feeding the Caucasus' campaign, as well as his outspoken support for the now-banned Movement against Illegal Migration (*Dvizhenie protiv nelegal'noi immigratsii*, DPNI) (Kolstø 2014; Laruelle 2014; Moen-Larsen 2014). Moreover, on several occasions Navalnyi had participated in the 'Russian March', which on 4 November each year gathered thousands of nationalists in the streets of Moscow.

Navalnyi himself has defended his participation in these marches by claiming that, if one disregards those individuals who shout '*Sieg Heil!*', the agenda promoted by the Russian March reflects the real concerns of many ordinary, conservative-minded citizens (Naval'nyi 2013b). According to Navalnyi's authorised biography, he is a liberal with nationalist convictions rather than a nationalist with democratic ideas (Voronkov 2012). To what extent he is actually a proponent of nationalism and xenophobia has been a matter of considerable controversy. Grigorii Golosov, for one, claims that Navalnyi's alleged nationalism was always 'fairly dubious', amounting to 'not much more than a stance on individual issues, such as illegal immigration and inter-budgetary relations' – the latter a reference to the slogan 'Stop feeding the Caucasus' (Golosov 2013). Also the earlier-mentioned Emil Pain gives Navalnyi a basically clean bill of health. Together with his team of assistants, Pain had examined more than 1,300 of Navalnyi's postings on *LiveJournal* over the three years prior to the Moscow elections and found that only forty of them focused on ethno-political issues (Pain 2013b). Still, as we will return to below, for ethno-nationalistically inclined voters, Navalnyi was the obvious choice.

Clearly, it was Navalnyi's participation in the Moscow mayoral elections that made them one of the most talked-about political events in Russia in 2013: the charismatic oppositionist represented a fresh face, someone not tainted with the mistakes of the past. His registration, however, was fraught with uncertainty until the last moment: since April 2013, Navalnyi had been involved in a court case, accused of embezzlement from the state-owned Kirovles timber company; if convicted, he would automatically have been barred from running.[6] Moreover, while the support of RPR-PARNAS meant that he was exempted from having to collect voter signatures, the party could not provide Navalnyi with anything near the necessary 110 signatures from Moscow municipal representatives. In the end, Navalnyi was saved by his main opponent. In order to win a convincing victory, Sobianin needed Navalnyi's participation – a simple walkover victory, running against candidates from parties belonging to the pro-regime/loyal opposition (LDPR, the Communist Party, and A Just Russia) would not do. Hence, Sobianin ordered United Russia representatives to assist in securing a multicandidate field, and in particular, to ensure the necessary number of signatures in support of Navalnyi's candidature (Ignatova and Protsenko 2013).

The remainder of the field was made up of a rather motley crew of party-nominated candidates. LDPR opted for youthfulness and a fresh face and nominated thirty-two-year-old Mikhail Degtiarev, a State Duma representative from Samara. The Communist Party placed their bets on the experienced but rather colourless Ivan Melnikov, a professor at the Moscow State University and a member of five consecutive State Dumas, at the time holding the position as Duma first deputy speaker. A Just Russia and Iabloko both chose to file their party leaders – Nikolai Levichev and Sergei Mitrokhin, respectively. Mitrokhin had been a party leader since 2008 and had previously served in the State Duma (1993–2003) and the Moscow City Duma (2005–9), while Levichev, who was from St Petersburg and had been a member of the Party of Life, had become leader of A Just Russia in 2011. With the field of candidates in place, the stage was set for the mayoral campaign to commence.

'Migrants' in the mayoral campaign

Obviously, there were several problems that voters in the capital were concerned about. In the four rounds of official TV debates, issues like the chronic difficulties in the transport sector, pressure on the housing market, and the quality and availability of healthcare services were highlighted. However, the large numbers of migrants in the capital also appeared to worry many Muscovites.

Vera Tolz and Sue-Ann Harding have shown how during the spring of 2013, the two main state-aligned TV channels, Channel One and Rossiia, were brimming over with programmes with a strong anti-immigration bias. Just as the mayoral campaign was about to kick off, this concerted drive came to a halt, as a series of ethnic riots across Russia prompted a return to more cautious reporting (Tolz and Harding 2015). Even so, the Moscow public had been 'warmed up' to the migration issue. According to a July 2013 Levada poll, 'migrants' constituted the main problem facing the city (Levada 2013b); and as the mayoral campaign evolved, this further 'fanned the flames of migrant phobia' (Pain 2013a).

Before we turn to the campaign rhetoric, a few words about the ethnic composition and scope of migration to the Russian capital are in order. Officially, in ethnic terms, Moscow is an overwhelmingly 'Russian' city. According to the 2010 census, no less than 91.7 per cent of the Muscovites self-identified as *'russkie'* (Vserossiiskaia perepis'... 2010). This makes Moscow one of the most ethnically homogeneous big cities in Europe – in fact, one of the few capitals in the world that is more ethnically homogeneous than the rest of the country: nationwide, the share of ethnic Russians stood at 80.9 per cent. Official figures do not tell the whole story, however. The *migranty* and *gastarbaitery* (guest workers), not least those living in the capital without proper registration, may have gone undetected by the census takers. Their exact numbers are unknown; Sobianin has estimated that as many as 300,000 illegal migrants are living in Moscow (*Izvestiia* 2013).

MIGRANTS AS A SOURCE OF CRIME; SAFETY CONCERNS

Although Sobianin was obviously running as the regime candidate, in the mayoral campaign he opted for a much tougher and more populist stance on migration issues than the official Kremlin line; in fact it has been claimed that he was exploiting the migration issue more actively than any of the other candidates (Pain 2014). As soon as the campaign got started, Sobianin began playing up an image of the migrants as a threat to the safety and well-being of the Moscow populace. Previously Sobianin had gone on record as claiming that up to 80 per cent of the labour migrants in Moscow were 'illegal' in the sense that they did not have proper work permits (APN 2011). During the campaign he followed up by arguing that migrants were heavily overrepresented in the crime statistics: 'If we take away crimes committed by non-locals (*priezzhie*),

Moscow would be the most law-abiding city in the world' (*Izvestiia* 2013). In his election platform, Sobianin promised to make Moscow 'a safe city'. And the way to ensure this was to implement 'an effective immigration policy' (Sobianin 2013).

Several of the candidates excelled in xenophobic statements and ethnic slurs. Unsurprisingly, LDPR's Degtiarev took the lead:

> It is important that we have a Russian (*russkii*) mayor in Moscow; that we have fewer illegal immigrants, whom we will return home peacefully. Moscow does not need gay pride parades, but 'Russian Marches'. . . . There is nothing wrong with strolling through the capital of Russia and saying: 'We, the Russians (*russkie*), are opposed to having our rights infringed upon!' (quoted in Tsoi and Subbotina 2013)

In his election platform Degtiarev announced that, if elected, he would 'fight ethnic criminality until its eradication' (Degtiarev 2013). As for A Just Russia's Levichev, he caused a minor scandal when it was discovered that his campaign material contained crosswords with the words *zhid* (a derogatory term for Jew) and *niger* (nigger) (Pertsev 2013). In his programme, Levichev claimed that 50 per cent of all crime in Moscow was committed by non-locals: 30 per cent by people from other parts of Russia and 20 per cent by migrants from 'the Near Abroad' (Levichev 2013). Without differentiating between legal and illegal, internal or external migrants, Levichev throughout the campaign repeatedly called on the Moscow police to clamp down on 'ethnic criminality' (Pain 2013a).

Melnikov, the Communist Party candidate, probably felt somewhat constrained by his party's official internationalist ideology, but on his platform, the approach to migration policy was summed up in the slogan 'toughness and efficiency' (Mel'nikov 2013). After praising the traditional hospitality of the residents of the capital, he immediately switched to pointing out the negative aspects of current migration trends: migration contributed to crime (over the last few months, crime committed by migrants had allegedly risen by 40 per cent), to undercutting the labour market (providing 'cheap slave labour, raising the profit of dirty business') and to 'an assault on the tradition, culture, language and the spirit of Moscow, on the security of Muscovites' (ibid.).

As expected, Navalnyi joined the xenophobic chorus. Given his reputation as a Russian ethno-nationalist, his campaign appeared surprisingly subdued, however. In the *Moscow Times* Victor Davidoff pointed out that Navalnyi was the only candidate who openly stated that a provisional detention camp for illegal immigrants set up in Moscow in July 2013 was in itself illegal (Davidoff 2013). And although Navalnyi used anti-immigrant rhetoric in meetings with voters, Pain opines that 'nothing particularly shocking' seeped through to the press (Pain 2013a). Navalnyi did, however, single out illegal migration as a 'breeding ground for violence and crime' and called for 'monitoring of places where migrants live compactly, and the prevention of the formation of ethnic criminal ghettos' (Naval'nyi 2013a).

Iabloko's Mitrokhin professed to be the only candidate who did not exploit latent xenophobia, although some observers held that his campaign slogan 'I will restore Moscow to the Muscovites' had been deliberately kept ambiguous.[7] Arguing that the other candidates approached the issue of fighting illegal immigration based on an understanding of migrants as 'dangerous and disgusting', Mitrokhin defined the problem quite differently: 'What is disgusting is not the immigrants, but the racist attitude towards them, they are treated like cattle' (Mitrokhin 2013c). While his election platform made Mitrokhin stand out from the pack, he nevertheless pointed to the 'enormous numbers of migrants' as a source of 'growing nationalist sentiment and an aggravated crime situation' (Mitrokhin 2013a).

Thus, all six mayoral candidates associated migration with increased crime rates and/or social tension. Even more worrisome, most candidates tended to blur the distinction between legal and illegal immigration, simply lumping all migrants into a single category.

WHAT IS TO BE DONE? INTEGRATION VS REPATRIATION

How, then, to resolve the challenges associated with the presence of a large migrant community in Moscow? Rather than discussing how to integrate the migrants, the mayoral hopefuls focused on how to repatriate them. In fact, the only candidate to include specific proposals for facilitating integration was the nationalist Navalnyi, who called for the establishment of special centres where the children of migrant families could learn Russian (Ul'ianova 2013; Naval'nyi 2013a). However, Navalnyi strongly opposed granting citizenship to migrants – be they legal or illegal – and warned that, unless this practice was discontinued, 'it will, within the next 10–15 years, lead us into some very problematic issues' (Ekho Moskvy 2013a). There were limits to the integration: the children of migrants should adapt to Russian culture, but they were not to become future citizens (Osharov 2013).

Sobianin opted for a more selective approach. In an interview with *Moskovskie novosti* immediately prior to announcing his decision to call snap elections, he bluntly declared that he wanted most migrants to return home:

> If anyone should stay, it should first and foremost be Russophones with a culture that adequately meets our traditions. The compatriots, as we often call them. For people who speak Russian poorly, who have a very different culture, it is better to live in their own country. Therefore, we do not welcome their adaptation (*adaptatsiia*) in Moscow. (quoted in Nikolaeva and Bogomolov 2013)

According to Sobianin, 'Russophone' was thus not merely a linguistic category, but a wider cultural one. Migrants who did not belong to this cultural category – and here he singled out 'seasonal workers' from Central Asia – were unwelcome to stay beyond their current work contracts. If a migrant was not a bearer of Russophone culture in the first place, he or she should not even try to integrate: 'I believe ... they should return to their families, their homes, their own countries', Sobianin concluded (Nikolaeva and Bogomolov 2013).

Melnikov expressed his plans in rather general terms, proposing that the new administration 'together with representatives of the ethnic diasporas develop an action plan for the normalisation of inter-ethnic relations' (Mel'nikov 2013). However, this should be accompanied by 'a drastic reduction in the number of migrants' (ibid.). Integration was an option for the few: the vast majority of migrants should return home.

As to the remaining three candidates, in their programmes none of them explicitly addressed how to integrate the migrants. On the contrary, Degtiarev, following in the populist footsteps of LDPR leader Vladimir Zhirinovskii, in one TV debate flatly declared that 'there should be no migrants in Moscow, neither legal, nor illegal': 'All should be removed from Moscow ... Moscow needs a Russian mayor. Moscow is the Russian capital of the Russian state (*russkaia stolitsa russkogo gosudarstva*) (*Moskva doverie* 2013).

Levichev and Mitrokhin adopted a more law-and-order based approach, pledging to fight illegal migration, but also to strike down hard on those who employed illegal labour (Levichev 2013; Mitrokhin 2013c). Under the heading 'From a megapolis of migrants to a city of citizens', Levichev argued that the current situation was 'intolerable' and that it was 'necessary to tighten the criminal liability of federal and city officials, entrepreneurs and contractors for the employment of illegal immigrants, as well as of law enforcement officers who provide a cover for this arbitrariness (*proizvol*)' (Levichev 2013). Mitrokhin promised to punish all who hired illegal 'slave labour', beginning with the city administration itself (Mitrokhin 2013c).

Among all six candidates there was thus general agreement on the need for a radical reduction in the number of migrants in the capital; they all held that Moscow did not need anything near the existing number of labour migrants in order to keep the economy running. Sobianin, for one, refuted the idea that Moscow was dependent on migrants from Central Asia to do menial, low-paid jobs: 'Officially, Moscow needs just 200,000 migrants from abroad', he declared, 'in reality, there are two or three times more' (Interfax 2013).

How to curb the influx of new migrants?

To reduce the number of migrants, repatriation was not a solution unless accompanied by parallel efforts to curb the influx of new entrants. To achieve this, the candidates proposed tightening the entry regime, and making it less attractive to hire migrant labour.

At the time, citizens of other CIS states were exempt from having to get a visa in order to visit Russia; in fact they did not even have to hold a regular passport – they could stay for up to ninety days travelling on a national ID document (e.g. an internal passport). In order to battle illegal migration, this practice would have to be halted, Sobianin averred: '. . . as soon as possible, we should switch to foreign passports, so that people do not turn up at the border with a piece of paper, but with real passports, making it possible to identify these citizens' (quoted in Protsenko 2013).

Navalnyi took the issue one step further: Not only should prospective migrants be required to obtain passports from their respective state authorities before seeking entry into Russia, they should also have to get a visa. Passports can easily be purchased or falsified, Navalnyi argued, and the only way to control the flow of immigrants was therefore by introducing a visa regime for the countries that provided most of the labour migrants (Ekho Moskvy 2013a; Osharov 2013).

Melnikov adopted a somewhat intermediary position. He categorically dismissed the need for a general visa regime for travel between former Soviet republics, arguing that 'this will create a completely abnormal situation' (Ekho Moskvy 2013b). Instead he suggested that the solution could be found in introducing work visas for CIS citizens. He also proposed launching a 'comprehensive programme for replacing foreign labour with Russian citizens', arguing that some three million Russian citizens in the European part of the country were ready to take on the work now performed by migrants (Mel'nikov 2013). To facilitate a reorientation towards local labour, employers should be required to pay higher social insurance fees when hiring migrant labour than when employing Russian citizens, he proposed (Ekho Moskvy 2013b).

Once again, it was Degtiarev who espoused the most radical views: he proposed to introduce a ban on foreign nationals working in the retail trade (Degtiarev 2013), an employment niche where migrants have traditionally been overrepresented.

'Migrants' and the voters: Popular attitudes

As noted, Muscovites identified 'migrants' as the main problem facing their city. To gauge the sentiments among ordinary Muscovites in greater detail, we conducted a survey in spring 2013, just prior to Sobianin's announcement about calling early elections. The survey included 600 respondents in Moscow as well as 1,000 respondents in a parallel nationwide sample.

MIGRANTS AND SOCIAL STABILITY

Although Moscow is quite homogeneous in ethnic terms, 38.2 per cent of the Muscovites surveyed were of the opinion that, when walking about in the city, they now encountered 'Russian faces' less often than before. And even though Moscow's population is overwhelmingly Russian, almost half of the respondents considered inter-ethnic relations in the capital to be 'bad' or 'very bad' (37.8 per cent and 10.0 per cent, respectively).

The presence of migrants clearly contributed to these perceptions. When asked about the main threat that migration posed to society, only 13.8 per cent referred directly to a rise in 'interethnic and religious hostility or violence'; but migrants were openly associated with crime and heightened security threats: one in four Muscovites (25.0 per cent) held that migrants contributed to an increase in the threat of 'terrorism and banditry'. Another 24.0 per cent were concerned about 'illegal residents', while 15.7 per cent feared that immigration would undermine the Russian economy. Only 7.8 per cent felt that migration as such did not constitute a threat to society. Moreover, when later presented with the statement 'Migrants represent a major source of violent crime in Russia', 72.4 per cent of the respondents concurred.

These anti-immigrant sentiments were combined with ethnocentric attitudes and open hostility toward Islam. More than two thirds of the Muscovites surveyed (69.8 per cent) supported the slogan 'Russia for Russians' (*Rossiia dlia russkikh*)[8] and 95.3 per cent opined that ethnic Russians (*russkie*) should play 'a leading role in the Russian state'. In our parallel national sample, the averages were significantly lower: 59.3 per cent supported 'Russia for Russians', whereas 82.1 per cent held that ethnic Russians ought to play the leading role in Russia. Moreover, 73.8 per cent of the Muscovites agreed, fully or to some degree, that Islam represented 'a threat to Russian culture and social stability' – as compared to 60.4 per cent in the national sample.

Prospects for integration

The negative assessment of migrants was also reflected in the evaluation of the potential for their future integration in Russian society. More than half of the Moscow respondents (53.3 per cent) supported sending all migrants, legal as well as illegal, back to their former place of residence. Similarly, when asked whether migrants and their children should be granted permanent residence permits in Russia, 79.0 per cent came out against such a policy.[9]

And yet, while in principle preferring the migrants to return home and refusing them permanent residence, respondents still expected the migrants to adapt to their new environment: Only 4.8 per cent agreed that 'migrants in Russia should have the right to maintain and develop their own culture'. A slim majority, 50.3 per cent, held that the migrants 'must adapt to Russian culture, but should have the right to preserve their own'. Somewhat surprisingly, given the reluctance to grant permanent residence to migrants, 39.8 per cent of the Muscovites surveyed held that migrants ought to 'blend into Russian culture'. Thus, migrants were apparently expected to adapt to Russian society, or even become assimilated – but should not enjoy the same rights as the rest of the population.

How to tackle the influx?

Given the rather xenophobic attitudes noted above, it comes as no surprise that survey respondents were overwhelmingly against lifting the current quota restrictions on the hiring of migrant workers: as many as 82.2 per cent were fully or partly opposed to such a liberalisation of the migration regime. Once again, the attitudes of the Muscovite sample emerge as far more negative than what we find in the national sample: in the latter, 'only' 58.6 per cent said they were opposed to such a move. When asked how the authorities should deal with the issue of migrants from the Caucasus and Central Asia in the capital, 36.5 per cent called for the imposition of tougher restrictions, while an additional 25.2 per cent were in favour of outright deportation. Only about a quarter of the respondents (26.3 per cent) appeared satisfied with the current situation, expressing support for the status quo.[10]

Overall, our survey documented not only widespread ethno-nationalist and xenophobic attitudes in the Russian capital, but also that such attitudes were more common there than elsewhere in Russia. That was not expected: xenophobia is commonly assumed to be more frequent among groups with low levels of income and education, whereas Muscovites have higher education and considerably more money than the average Russian. Moreover, as pointed out, Moscow is ethnically more homogeneous than the country as a whole. However, the levels of perceived threats associated with migrants do not necessarily correspond to actual levels of immigration (Alexseev 2006). And while there are proportionally more (ethnically) non-Russians in other parts of the country than in the capital, they are frequently members of ethnic minority groups with deep historical roots in Russia. In Moscow, by contrast, the non-Russians are to a much larger degree non-citizens, *gastarbaitery* and relative newcomers.

Hitting each other over the head with the migration stick

The mayoral candidates appear to have been in step with popular attitudes when they advocated introducing drastic measures for regulating further migration. In our interviews with politicians and activists in the aftermath of the elections, we were repeatedly told that 'the migration question' had been 'number one' for the Muscovites, and that candidates that could be accused of being 'soft on migration' were at a disadvantage. Incumbent mayor Sobianin appeared particularly vulnerable in this respect. Having served as mayor for close to three years already, he could be held responsible for the city's handling of migration-related matters. Thus, in a widely circulated campaign paper, the national-liberal Democratic Choice party – which did not field its own candidate, but called on voters to support either Navalnyi or Mitrokhin – lashed out against Sobianin's inept migration policy. Allegedly, during his years in power, the number of migrants in Moscow had increased by 50 per cent. These newcomers contributed to the high crime levels, the spread of infectious diseases, and to corruption among city employees and house owners who exploited the hapless jobseekers; they had transformed the Moscow suburbs into Central Asian villages (*auly*), it was argued (Stepanov 2013).

Sobianin therefore had to work hard to present himself as 'tough on migrants'. To achieve this within the field of candidates, he had to stretch the boundaries for what had traditionally been perceived as politically correct by the Kremlin. One such example of Sobianin moving the goalposts in the migration debate was his statement on not welcoming the future integration of migrants who had poor knowledge of Russian, a message that flew in the face of the position Putin had expressed during the election campaign the year before (Putin 2012).

Not everyone bought into this new image of Sobianin, however. During the campaign, when Moscow police arrested 1,200 Vietnamese citizens who had been working in an underground garment factory, Mitrokhin dismissed the whole operation as a pathetic attempt on the part of Sobianin to exhibit some resolve: 'Very convenient, isn't it? With minimal effort, move 1,200 Vietnamese from an illegal dormitory into a tent camp nearby and turn this into a gigantic public relations stunt in Sobianin's fight against illegal migration!' (Mitrokhin 2013b). In Mitrokhin's view, the deportation of a few thousand illegal migrants was a mere drop in the ocean; furthermore, it failed to address the real issue: exposing the people who hire illegal labour migrants or help them to get into Moscow without the necessary documents. The main reason why no investigation was conducted into the affairs of such people was clear, Mitrokhin maintained: the 'migration mafia' had deeply rooted connections in the corridors of power. 'The main breeding grounds of illegal migration in Moscow is the city administration itself' (ibid.).

While Mitrokhin accused Sobianin of engaging in empty rhetoric and meaningless PR stunts, he also tried to play the migration card against Navalnyi. After all, Mitrokhin and Navalnyi were fighting to control the same political landscape: the liberal intelligentsia/creative class. Navalnyi had already established his nationalist credentials and could now focus on polishing his image as a democrat and a liberal. Mitrokhin therefore opted to expose Navalnyi the nationalist. In his blog, he attacked Navalnyi for blatant misuse of statistical data: while Navalnyi in an interview with Ekho Moskvy (2013a) had insisted that 50 per cent of all crime in Moscow was committed by 'migrants from abroad', official statistics showed that no more than 20 per cent of the perpetrators were foreign nationals. 'What is this but populist and irresponsible flirting with xenophobic sentiments?' Mitrokhin asked (Mitrokhin 2013d). The blog posting was illustrated with a photo of Navalnyi posing together with several organisers of the Russian March, including Aleksandr Belov (Potkin), a former DPNI leader who was anathema to most of the liberal intelligentsia.

For Navalnyi, on the other hand, it was essential to be able to appeal to both the nationalist and the liberal constituencies without losing the support of either. His credentials as a nationalist were solid; and even if some nationalists had certain misgivings about him, they viewed all the other candidates as being worse. The nationalist news agency NSN (*Natsional'naia sluzhba novostei*), for instance, carried an article that declared:

> it is no secret that the candidates take their cues from public opinion polls. Therefore, Sobianin's words about the need to curb migration, which he himself has encouraged and could stop at any moment, sound like a cruel mockery of the Muscovites. And about Melnikov and Mitrokhin there is nothing good to say: both the Communists and the Iabloko people curse the nationalists and nationalism. (NSN 2013)

Levichev and Degtiarev were dismissed as spoilers. According to NSN, Navalnyi was the only candidate who passed the test. He could therefore reap the nationalist vote almost by walkover. The liberals, however, needed more cajoling and reassurance. If Navalnyi pressed the anti-immigration issue too hard, he might easily push these voters into Mitrokhin's embrace. Masha Gessen holds that 'Navalny's lapses into xenophobic rhetoric have alienated a small part of the opposition but have probably won him many more supporters' (Gessen 2013). While this is basically correct, closer examination of his campaign statements suggests that he was fully aware of this situation and made a deliberate (and rather successful) bid to present a message that was palatable to liberals as well. Tellingly, on several campaign issues Sobianin came across as pursuing a more xenophobic stance than the putative nationalist Navalnyi.

Mitrokhin's strategy for capturing the liberal middle-class vote had its inevitable cost in the anti-immigrant atmosphere that prevailed during the campaign. In an apparent attempt to compensate for that, some of Mitrokhin's attacks on Sobianin were themselves formulated in rather xenophobic language, as when he accused the city authorities of having 'opened the "floodgates" to Moscow, allowing the influx of huge waves of illegal migration' that had led to 'Moscow being transformed from the capital of Russia to a Central Asian province' (Mitrokhin 2013a).

Mitrokhin's somewhat half-hearted jump onto the already crowded anti-migration bandwagon failed to sway the voters, though. On election day, Mitrokhin ended up with 3.5 per cent of the vote – less than half of what Iabloko had polled in Moscow in the 2011 State Duma elections. The candidates from the systemic opposition did not fare any better: Melnikov won 10.7 per cent (the Communist Party had polled 19.3 per cent in 2011), Degtiarev 2.9 per cent (the LDPR, 9.4 per cent in 2011) and Levichev 2.8 per cent (A Just Russia, 12.1 per cent in 2011). All the established parties lost voters to the newcomer Navalnyi. The latter's mix of liberal and nationalist credentials and, by Russian standards, sophisticated electoral campaign (Orttung 2013) clearly resonated with the Moscow electorate; Navalnyi won a respectable 27.2 per cent. Nevertheless, Sobianin managed to scrape through: with 51.4 per cent, he picked up just enough votes to avoid an embarrassing run-off, and thus saw his mayoral mandate confirmed by popular vote.

Conclusions

What lessons can be drawn from the Kremlin's 2013 experiment with semi-competitive elections in Moscow and Sobianin's flirt with anti-migrant sentiments? First, it is clear that opening up the political field for more genuine competition, albeit under close control and the threat of sanctions, proved to be a not entirely risk-free undertaking. Sobianin got his popular mandate – but with a slim margin that did not give him the political boost he had hoped for. Moreover, the experiment had the unwanted side effect of making Sobianin's main opponent, Navalnyi, a household name in Russian politics. The outcome thus probably served to discourage the Kremlin from repeating such experiments except in situations where some element of competitiveness was deemed essential in order to legitimise the outcome.

Second, the campaign showed that the Kremlin was not able to control the way in which the anti-migration/nationalist debate evolved. While the Presidential Administration was trying to strike a balance between popular attitudes, the need to attract additional labour, and Russian great-power ambitions with plans for a Eurasian Economic Union, Sobianin was forced to adopt a more populist stance on questions of entry regulations, quotas and return. This finding challenges the conventional understanding of Russian policymaking as hyper-centralised and top down, but dovetails with Vera Tolz and Sue-Ann

Harding's conclusion that in the anti-migration debate, the Kremlin during Putin's third term has been predominantly reactive, riding on the currents from below rather setting the agenda itself (Tolz and Harding 2015).

In the heat of the race for the office of Moscow mayor, 'the migrants', as a visible and vulnerable group, proved to be a readily available scapegoat for whatever was wrong – from the rising crime rates to the overcrowded public transport system and pressures on the capital's health and educational infrastructure. By collapsing internal and external as well as legal and illegal migrants into one category, Sobianin and the other mayoral contenders contributed to cementing the idea of this mythical 'migrant' as the new 'Other' in Russian identity discourse.

Notes

1. We base our discussion of the migrant issue in the campaign on an analysis of the political platforms of the candidates, TV debates and media coverage. While ultimately drawing on a wide range of media reports, we have made a systematic search in seventy-one federal print media available through the EastView Database for the period 5 June–8 September 2013, using a search string that included the name of the mayoral candidates and 'migra*'. This returned 263 hits for Sobianin, 136 for Navalnyi, 89 for Mitrokhin, 65 for Melnikov, 49 for Degtiarev and 37 for Levichev.
2. To examine public attitudes to migrants and migration, we organised a survey in May 2013 conducted by Russian Public Opinion and Market Research (*Rossiiskoe obshchestvennoe mnenie i issledovanie rynka*, ROMIR). The survey data were followed up and supplemented by fieldwork and interviews in Moscow in October 2013.
3. After the 2014 annexation of Crimea, 'the West' surged in the polls as a constitutive 'Other'; however, continued stable support for the nationalist slogan 'Russia for Russians' indicates that 'migrants' have remained central to this process (Levada 2016).
4. Following the 2011 State Duma elections, various parts of the non-systemic opposition – parties not represented in the State Duma – had tried to coordinate opposition to the Putin regime by establishing a Coordination Council. The Council included quotas for nationalists, liberals and leftists, as well as for civic activists in general. By the time of the mayoral elections, however, the efficacy of the Council was being questioned even by Council members themselves (authors' interviews with members of the Coordination Council: Gennadii Gudkov, Konstantin Krylov and Vladimir Tor, Moscow, October 2013).

5. Sobianin had been a member of United Russia's Supreme Council ever since the party was first established in 2001 and had also been the leader of the party's Moscow chapter 2011–12.
6. On 18 July, the day after he had officially been registered as a candidate running for Moscow mayor, Navalnyi was sentenced to five years' imprisonment, but subsequently, based on an appeal from the prosecutor's office, released pending a hearing in a higher court. In October 2013, the sentence was suspended.
7. Mitrokhin had lived his whole life in Moscow. On his platform, he accused Sobianin of being a *variag*, an outsider who had been imposed on Moscow, and therefore in charge of an administration that did not really care about the well-being of the Muscovites. According to Mitrokhin, it was now time to return the city to one of its own (Mitrokhin 2013a).
8. When asked about how they understood 'Russian' (*russkii*) in this context, one third of the respondents allowed for other ethnic groups to be subsumed under this category. In fact, 16.8 per cent were willing to include *all* ethnic groups residing in the Russian Federation (i.e. a full merger of the categories of *russkii* and *rossiianin*). A plurality (43.2 per cent) nevertheless espoused a purely ethnic approach.
9. Once again, respondents in the national sample appeared less hostile to migrants: 43.0 per cent favoured sending all migrants home, whereas on the question of granting them permanent residence permits, 60.9 per cent were against.
10. We did not ask respondents whether they supported the introduction of a visa regime for South Caucasus and Central Asia, but this has been done by the Levada Centre. According to their national survey in July 2013, 84 per cent of the respondents fully or partly supported the introduction of such a policy (Levada 2013a).

Bibliography

Alexseev, Mikhail (2006), *Immigration Phobia and the Security Dilemma*, Cambridge: Cambridge University Press.

APN (2011), 'Sobianin: trudovaia migratsiia v Moskva na 80% sostoit iz nelagalov' [Sobianin: 80% of labour migration to Moscow consists of illegals], 5 August, <www.apn.ru/news/article24638.htm> (last accessed 26 March 2014).

Blakkisrud, Helge (2015), 'Governing the governors: legitimacy vs. control in the reform of the Russian regional executive', *East European Politics*, 31, 1: 104–21.

Blakkisrud, Helge (2016), 'Blurring the boundary between civic and ethnic: the Kremlin's new approach to national identity under Putin's third term', in Pål Kolstø and Helge Blakkisrud, eds, *The New Russian*

Nationalism: Imperialism, Ethnicity and Authoritarianism, 2000–15, Edinburgh: Edinburgh University Press, 249–74.

Coalson, Robert (2013), 'Russia's Aleksei Navalny: hope of the nation – or the nationalists?' RFE/RL, 28 July, <www.rferl.org/content/russia-navalny-nationalist-fears/25059277.html> (last accessed 1 April 2014).

Davidoff, Victor (2013), 'The many myths about Navalny', *Moscow Times*, 11 August, <www.themoscowtimes.com/opinion/article/the-many-myths-about-navalny/484711.html> (last accessed 10 August 2014).

Degtiarev, Mikhail (2013), 'Poriadok. Komfort. Dostatok. Predvybornaia programma kandidata na post Mera Moskvy ot LDPR' [Order. Comfort. Prosperity. Electoral programme of the candidate for the position of mayor of Moscow from the LDPR], <http://degtyarev.info/document/raznoe/138480> (last accessed 2 April 2014).

Ekho Moskvy (2013a), 'Interv'iu: Migratsiia. Aleksei Naval'nyi' [Interview: migration. Aleksei Navalnyi], 23 August, <www.echo.msk.ru/programs/beseda/1139878-echo> (last accessed 2 April 2014).

Ekho Moskvy (2013b), 'Interv'iu: Migratsiia. Ivan Mel'nikov' [Interview: migration. Ivan Melnikov], 4 September, <http://echo.msk.ru/programs/beseda/1148686-echo> (last accessed 3 April 2014).

Gessen, Masha (2013), 'Mad race for Moscow mayor', *New York Times*, 12 August, <http://latitude.blogs.nytimes.com/2013/08/12/the-mad-race-for-moscow-mayor/?_php=true&_type=blogs&_r=0> (last accessed 13 August 2014).

Golosov, Grigorii (2013), 'Navalny steps into the ring', OpenDemocracy, 19 July, <www.opendemocracy.net/od-russia/grigorii-golosov/navalny-steps-into-ring> (last accessed 10 August 2014).

Ignatova, Ol'ga and Liubov' Protsenko (2013), 'Kazhdomu svoi kandidat' [Each has its own candidate], *Rossiiskaia gazeta*, 4 July, <www.rg.ru/2013/07/04/kandidati.html> (last accessed 25 March 2014).

Interfax (2013), 'Sobianin podschital, kakoe kolichestvo trudovykh migrantov nuzhno Moskve' [Sobianin has calculated how many migrant workers Moscow needs], 22 August, <www.interfax.ru/324732> (last accessed 25 March 2014).

Izvestiia (2013), 'Sergei Sobianin: "Rabota mera interesnee premerstva"' [Sobianin: 'Job as mayor more interesting than the premiership'], 13 June, <http://izvestia.ru/news/551895#> (last accessed 2 April 2014).

Kolstø, Pål (2014), 'Russia's nationalists flirt with democracy', *Journal of Democracy*, 25, 3: 120–34.

Kolstø, Pål (2016), 'The ethnification of Russian nationalism', in Pål Kolstø and Helge Blakkisrud, eds, *The New Russian Nationalism: Imperialism, Ethnicity and Authoritarianism, 2000–15*, Edinburgh: Edinburgh University Press, 18–45.

Kolstø, Pål and Helge Blakkisrud, eds (2016), *The New Russian Nationalism: Imperialism, Ethnicity and Authoritarianism, 2000–15*, Edinburgh: Edinburgh University Press.

Laruelle, Marlene (2014), 'Alexei Navalny and challenges in reconciling "nationalism" and "liberalism"', *Post-Soviet Affairs*, 30, 4: 276–97.

Latukhina, Kira (2013), 'Moskve na vybor' [Moscow to choose], *Rossiiskaia gazeta*, 6 June, <www.rg.ru/2013/06/05/kadry-site.html> (last accessed 25 March 2014).

Levada (2013a), 'Otnoshenie k migrantam' [Attitude toward migrants], 3 July, <www.levada.ru/03-07-2013/otnoshenie-k-migrantam> (last accessed 4 April 2014).

Levada (2013b), 'Moskva nakanune vyborov mera: polnoe issledovanie' [Moscow on the eve of the mayoral elections: a complete study], 17 July, <www.levada.ru/17-07-2013/moskva-nakanune-vyborov-mera-polnoe-issledovanie> (last accessed 1 April 2014).

Levada (2016), 'Intolerantnost' i ksenofobiia' [Intolerance and xenophobia], 11 October, <http://www.levada.ru/2016/10/11/intolerantnost-i-ksenofobiya> (last accessed 18 October 2016).

Levichev, Nikolai (2013), 'Programma kandidata na dolzhnost' Mera Moskvy: Gorod spravedlivosti' [Programme of the candidate for the position of Moscow mayor: city of justice], <www.levichev.info/5_50332.htm> (last accessed 31 March 2014).

Mel'nikov, Ivan (2013), 'Predvybornaia programma kandidata v Mery Moskvy Ivana Mel'nikova' [Election programme of the candidate for mayor of Moscow Ivan Melnikov], <http://ivan-melnikov.ru/elections> (last accessed 2 April 2014).

Mitrokhin, Sergei (2013a), 'Nachnem peremeny s Moskvy! Programma Sergeia Mitrokhina na vyborakh mera Moskvy' [Let us start the changes from Moscow! Sergei Mitrokhin's programme for the Moscow mayoral elections], 15 June, <www.yabloko.ru/programm2013> (last accessed 27 March 2014).

Mitrokhin, Sergei (2013b), 'Sergei Mitrokhin: Migratsionnyi piar Sobianina' [Sergei Mitrokhin: Sobianin's migration PR], 13 August, <www.yabloko.ru/blog/2013/08/13> (last accessed 12 August 2014).

Mitrokhin, Sergei (2013c), '2 podkhoda k bor'be s nelegal'noi migratsiei' [Two approaches to the fight against illegal migration], Ekho Moskvy, 27 August, <www.echo.msk.ru/blog/sergei_mitrohin/1144292-echo> (last accessed 27 March 2014).

Mitrokhin, Sergei (2013d), 'Chem ia otlichaius' ot drugikh kandidatov' [Where I differ from the other candidates], Ekho Moskvy, 5 September, <www.echo.msk.ru/blog/sergei_mitrohin/1150774-echo> (last accessed 12 August 2014).

Moen-Larsen, Natalia (2014), '"Normal nationalism": Alexei Navalny, LiveJournal and "the Other"', *East European Politics*, 30, 4: 548–67.

Moskva Doverie (2013), 'Deviatyi raund debatov kandidatov na post mera Moskvy' [Ninth round of debates between candidates for Moscow mayor], 30 August, <www.m24.ru/articles/24645> (last accessed 27 March 2014).

Mukomel', Vladimir (2011), 'Integratsiia migrantov: vyzovy, politika, sotsial'nye praktiki' [Integration of migrants: challenges, policies, social practices], *Mir Rossii. Sotsiologiia.Etnologiia*, 1: 34–50.

Naval'nyi, Aleksei (2013a), 'Programma kandidata v Mery Moskvy Alekseia Naval'nogo: Izmeni Rossiiu, nachni s Moskvy' [Programme of candidate for Moscow mayor Aleksei Navalnyi: Change Russia, starting with Moscow], <http://navalny.ru/platform/Navalny_Program.pdf> (last accessed 2 April 2014).

Naval'nyi, Aleksei (2013b), 'Russkii marsh' [The Russian March], 2 November, <http://navalny.livejournal.com/877154.html> (last accessed 10 August 2014).

Nikolaeva, Anna and Aleksandr Bogomolov (2013), 'Nuzhny i demokratiia, i vlast" [Both democracy and power are needed], *Moskovskie novosti*, 30 May, <www.mn.ru/moscow_authority/20130530/347635870.html> (last accessed 26 March 2014).

NSN (2013), 'Stoit li natsionalistam golosovat' za Naval'nogo? Pliusy i minusy Naval'nogo [Is it worth it for nationalists to vote for Navalnyi? Pros and cons of Navalnyi], 30 July, <http://ru-nsn.livejournal.com/3229171.html> (last accessed 13 August 2014).

Orttung, Robert W. (2013), 'Navalny's campaign to be Moscow mayor', *Russian Analytical Digest*, 136, <https://www.files.ethz.ch/isn/170649/RAD-136.pdf> (last accessed 16 October 2016).

Osharov, Roman (2013), 'Naval'nyi obeshchaet sokratit' kolichestvo migrantov na 70%' [Navalnyi promises to cut the number of migrants by 70%], *Golos Ameriki*, 31 August, <www.golos-ameriki.ru/content/moscow-election/1740986.html> (last accessed 3 April 2014).

Pain, Emil (2007), 'Xenophobia and ethnopolitical extremism in post-Soviet Russia: dynamics and growth factors', *Nationalities Papers*, 35, 5: 895–911.

Pain, Emil (2013a), 'From protests to pogroms', OpenDemocracy, 27 August, <www.opendemocracy.net/od-russia/emil-pain/from-protests-to-pogroms> (last accessed 1 April 2014).

Pain, Emil' (2013b), 'Rossiiskoe ideologicheskoe bezvremen'e' v zerkale Runeta' [Russian ideological stagnation in the mirror of Runet], *Vestnik Instituta Kennana v Rossii*, 24: 62–72.

Pain, Emil' (2014), 'Ksenofobiia i natsionalizm v epokhu rossiiskogo bezvremen'ia' [Xenophobia and nationalism in the era of Russian stagnation], *Pro et contra*, 18, 1/2: 34–53.

Pertsev, Andrei (2013), 'Slovo "zhid" est' v slovare' [The word 'yid' is found in the dictionary], Gazeta.ru, 6 August, <www.gazeta.ru/politics/2013/08/06_a_5543917.shtml> (last accessed 27 March 2014).

Protsenko, Liubov' (2013), 'Vesti ot Sergeia Sobianina' [News from Sergei Sobianin], *Rossiiskaia gazeta*, 7 July, <www.rg.ru/2013/07/07/intervie-site.html> (last accessed 30 March 2014).

Putin, Vladimir (2012), 'Rossiia: natsional'nyi vopros' [Russia: the national question], *Nezavisimaia gazeta*, 23 January, <www.ng.ru/politics/2012-01-23/1_national.html> (last accessed 25 March 2014).

Sakwa, Richard (2011), *The Crisis of Russian Democracy: The Dual State, Factionalism and the Medvedev Succession*, Cambridge: Cambridge University Press.

Sobianin, Sergei (2013), 'Predvybornaia programma kandidata v mery Moskvy S. Sobianina, vybory 2013 god' [Election programme for the candidate for mayor of Moscow S. Sobianin, the elections of 2013]. <http://yavibral.ru/?page=3&news_id=15> (last accessed 3 April 2014).

Stepanov, Oleg (2013), 'Immigratsionnoe bessilie' [Immigration impotence], *Svobodnaia rech'*, 3 September, <http://demvybor.ru/gazeta_svobodnaia_rech.html> (last accessed 12 August 2014).

Teper, Yuri. 2016, 'Official Russian identity discourse in light of the annexation of Crimea: national or imperial?' *Post-Soviet Affairs*, 32, 4: 378–96.

Tishkov, Valery A. (1995), 'What is Rossia? Prospects for nation-building', *Security Dialogue*, 26, 1: 41–54.

Tolz, Vera (2001), *Inventing the Nation: Russia*, London: Arnold.

Tolz, Vera and Sue-Ann Harding (2015), 'From "compatriots" to "aliens": the changing coverage of migration on Russian television', *Russian Review*, 74, 3: 452–77.

Tsoi, Iuliia and Svetlana Subbotina (2013), 'Mikhail Degtiarev: "Razreshu gei-parad, no noch'iu i tikho"' [Mikhail Degtiarev: 'I will allow a gay parade, but at night, and quietly'], *Izvestiia*, 6 September, <http://izvestia.ru/news/556596> (last accessed 31 March 2014).

Ul'ianova, Zhanna (2013), 'Personal'naia programma Naval'nogo' [The personal programme of Navalnyi], Gazeta.ru, 1 July, <www.gazeta.ru/politics/2013/07/01_a_5402685.shtml> (last accessed 26 March 2014).

Voronkov, Konstantin (2012), *Aleksei Naval'nyi: Groza zhulikov i vorov* [*Aleksei Navalnyi: A Thunderbolt against Crooks and Thieves*], Moscow: Eksmo.

Vserossiiskaia perepis' naseleniia (2010), 'Natsional'nyi sostav i vladenie iazykami, grazhdanstvo' [Ethnic composition and language skills, citizenship], <www.gks.ru/free_doc/new_site/perepis2010/croc/perepis_itogi1612.htm> (last accessed 25 March 2013).

Waller, Julian G. (2013) 'Re-setting the game: the logic and practice of official support for Alexei Navalny's mayoral run', *Russian Analytical Digest*, 136, <https://www.files.ethz.ch/isn/170649/RAD-136.pdf> (last accessed 16 October 2016).

10

Anti-migrant, but not nationalist: Pursuing statist legitimacy through immigration discourse and policy

Caress Schenk

Putin's return for a third term as president spurred the active development of increasingly securitised migration policy. Parallel changes to migration law and the administrative code that have made violations of basic migration rules punishable by deportation and an entry ban of five or more years are indicative of this trend. But do these changes reflect an increasingly overt nationalist campaign directed by the Kremlin?

Several of the contributors to the original *New Russian Nationalism* volume (Kolstø and Blakkisrud 2016) argued that even prior to Putin's return to the presidency a new phase of national fervour had begun, in which nationalist ideas became more mainstream and were utilised more strategically by the regime. A parallel upsurge in anti-migrant media rhetoric has also been noted (Tolz and Harding 2015; Hutchings and Tolz 2016). Putin began laying the groundwork for key migration-related policy projects, such as reforming registration and work permits, language exams for labour migrants and stricter control over migrant entry, even during his re-election campaign in 2011. Many of the migration policies adopted since 2012 can be said to be compatible with major strains of nationalist ideology. However, this chapter questions whether the Kremlin's migration rhetoric actively taps into available nationalist frames.

Here I analyse three common migration myths as a framework for evaluating the nationalist content of the Kremlin's rhetoric. Migration myths take the form of populist slogans that are utilised by politicians and the media to blame various problems on migrants. These myths gain power through their resonance with the public, rather than as a function of their veracity. Slogans claiming that migrants take jobs, are culturally incompatible with the host society, and represent a threat to security are played up in the media and by some politicians as populist rhetoric. Populist rhetoric is often consistent with public opinion, as shown in the NEORUSS survey results. However, as I will show through an analysis of Vladimir Putin's policy speeches and public statements, migration myths are not actively utilised by the Kremlin.[1]

A migration crisis?

Russia has been among the three largest immigrant-receiving countries (along with the United States and Germany) since the fall of the Soviet Union. The first wave of migrants coming to Russia after 1991 consisted primarily of Russian-ethnic repatriates from other former Soviet republics. After the turn of the century, there came a fundamental shift from permanent migrants to temporary labour migrants (Mukomel' 2005). Several factors contributed to this shift, including structural features like geographic proximity and a history of colonial linkages that contributed to shared language and culture, political factors like the visa-free regime between former Soviet countries of the Commonwealth of Independent States (CIS), and economic and demographic factors in both Russia and sending countries. Economic decline in many Caucasian and Central Asian countries at the same time as Russia was experiencing the prosperity of the oil boom in the early 2000s contributed to an increased supply of workers, especially from Uzbekistan, Tajikistan and Kyrgyzstan (Korobkov 2008). The demographic crisis in Russia, with an acute decline in the working-age population, has also contributed to greater demand in all sectors of the labour market (Ioffe and Zayonchkovskaya 2010).

The influx of temporary labour migrants has created various tensions in the labour market and society, as policymakers are well aware. The desire to strike a balance is palpable in Putin's 2005 address to the Security Council:

> The migration and demographic situation in the country dictate the necessity of taking deliberate measures for the large-scale attraction of foreign workers to the Russian economy. It should be borne in mind the possibility of highly sensitive social, ethnic and confessional changes this could bring to the structure of society. That is, it will be necessary to effectively protect the national labour market, and special attention should be given to the native (*korennoe*) population of Russia, so they are not exposed to unjustified challenges or costs. (Putin 2005)

Tensions between labour-market demand and the social pressures created by rising numbers of visible minorities are not uncommon elsewhere, though most traditional migrant-receiving countries take these challenges as issues of integration and adaptation. By contrast, the Russian policy approach has focused on boosting the labour capacity of citizens and screening out migrants seen as less desirable or less likely to integrate (Schenk 2010; 2016). Though Russian migration policy has developed a complex and nuanced set of programmes and regulations, anything that could be called an integration policy is almost completely absent, and the relationship between migration and national identity remains vaguely defined.

The migration–nationalism nexus

As nationalism always seeks to define the 'rightful' group (an ethnic group or nation) entitled to certain material or ideational resources (membership, identity, state benefits), migrants inevitably put pressure on the bounds of the community. Nationalism as a theory has various iterations, including those that highlight gaining power over a state (Breuilly 1993), legitimising a state (Hechter 2000), competition for resources (Olzak and Nagel 1986; Brass 1991), or group homogeneity (Gellner 1983; Connor 1993). Russian nationalism is diverse, as reflected in the many strains that have developed throughout its history (Tolz 2001). Even in the current period, there is no singular ideologically cohesive idea of Russian nationalism (Gerber 2014), which in turn leads to nationalist sentiment having a range of targets depending on the view of the 'nation' and how open it is to outsiders (Schenk 2012; Herrera and Kraus 2016).

The editors of this volume define the new Russian nationalism as an ethnic turn in nationalist sentiment, spurred in part as a result of the influx of non-Slavic migrants in Russia (Kolstø 2016a). In other words, they argue that a version of Russian nationalism is gaining ground, one with especial importance for the country's migration situation. Supporting this general observation are several recent studies that have sought the roots of increasing anti-immigrant and xenophobic sentiment in society, though no consensus has emerged on the relative importance of economic or cultural variables.[2]

The nationalism–migration connection has been far less explored than that between nationalism and ethnic minority groups, which involves questions such as why there are differences between nations (or ethnic groups) and how states can navigate those differences.[3] In the nationalism literature, when migration is addressed, the focus is often on long-term or permanent migrants related to issues of their integration and eventual citizenship (Portes and Manning 1986; Favell 1998). On some level this focus on long-term processes of social change and its impact on national identity might be seen as logical: temporary labour migrants could be perceived as an advantageous influx of needed labour that rarely organises or demands group rights, thus requiring little response from the host state and posing little threat to the nation. However, temporary labour migrants in Russia have been increasingly framed as a threat to national identity. The new influxes of low-skilled, low-wage labour migrants tend to work in high-turnover jobs and have non-traditional lifestyles, not only in religion and culture, but also in migrant-specific practices such as sharing living quarters with many people (Reeves 2013).

The practices that set migrants apart make them a visible minority ripe for easy (albeit clichéd) scapegoating. The migration myths analysed here are examples of the type of discourse that provokes alarm while also identifying the main cause of the threat. These myths are consistent with deeper nationalist discourses in Russia (and more generally in migrant-receiving states), which focus on economic performance, a single ethnic group within a multi-ethnic state and a strong state as the basis for the nation.

One of the most common immigration myths is that migrants take jobs away from the native workforce. Despite ample evidence that any negative impact of immigrants on the labour market is minimal (Orrenius and Zavodny 2012), this myth has retained its populist appeal and is utilised by politicians throughout the migrant-receiving world. Labour protectionism is a concrete manifestation of an instrumental or rational interest-based approach to ethnic and nationalist politics, where the resources of the state (in this case the labour market) are seen as the main driver of ethnic politics and even the preferential entitlement of insiders (Semenenko 2015). For example, Iurii Luzhkov, mayor of Moscow from 1992 to 2010, frequently declared: 'we need to preserve jobs for Muscovites!' (BBC Russia 2008).

The myth that migrants are incompatible with the host-country culture focuses on the potential for ethnic conflict triggered by increased migration (Shnirelman 2009; Tsygankov 2016). At its core, this view relies on emotional appeals to the symbolic aspects of nationalism, and is thus distinct from the rationalist tinges of the unemployment myth (Connor 1993). The view that ethnic Russians and Russian culture constitute the core of Russian national identity is a central theme in nationalist discourse, which acknowledges the multi-ethnic realities of the population yet privileges Slavs and is variously open to immigrants of different origins (Panov 2010; March 2012).[4] However, rhetoric that 'others' migrants, pointing out how they are different, serves to further the sense that migrants threaten the very core of the host country's culture. Current Moscow mayor Sergei Sobianin (2010–) has been vocal in his opposition to the construction of new mosques in Moscow, declaring that if mosque attendance were limited to Muscovites or other legal residents in the city, nobody would be attending services (RBK 2012). These comments imply that migrants change the appearance and cultural practices of the city.

The security myth that portrays migrants as a risk to the physical health and survival of residents is related to state capacity and sovereignty.[5] Given the centrality of the state in modern nationalism, weaknesses of state capacity can also be seen as threats to the nation. The securitisation of migration is common in many immigrant-receiving countries (Alexseev 2006). However, despite public sentiments, research has shown that the links between immigration and increases in criminality and other security threats are dubious (Bianchi et al. 2012).

Portrayals of immigration and immigrants in security-related frames have been common in the Russian media (Kozhevnikova 2007; Tolz and Harding 2015). Russian officials below the Kremlin level also use security language when discussing immigrants. Mayor Sobianin, for example, has said that 'we understand that half of all crimes in the city are committed by migrants: if we remove migrant crime from the statistics – not only international, but also interregional migration – then Moscow would be the safest city in the world' (quoted in Lysova et al. 2013).

While all of these myths are active in the Russian discourse, none of them is embraced directly by the Kremlin, leaving the migration arena without a unifying ideological framework defined by the executive. Putin's careful language surrounding the migration myths, combined with comparatively resolute policy reform, indicates an effort to solve migration-related problems through efforts besides anti-migrant ethnic nationalism.

Nationalism is often seen as a tool of mobilisation; another essential trait is its function of legitimating political rule (Gellner 1983; Goode and Stroup 2015). Populist myths that frame migration as an acute threat to the state and society could be a further tool for producing legitimacy, when linked to dominant nationalist discourses and when the state is seen as able to solve relevant problems. However, in Russia these strategies must be balanced with the main legitimation discourses of the Putin administration, which focus on a strong state that can produce stability and prosperity. By adopting a technocratic focus, the state can balance the tensions created by migration through policy solutions that pursue economic prosperity parallel to social stability and security. That leaves the state free to follow various migration policy trajectories without creating an overarching nationalist framework that might contradict some policy goals.

In the following, I trace Putin's public statements across the three migration myths, finding that he only very rarely engages the migration myths. Further, he treats migration in a differentiated way depending on the goals of the state. In the economic arena, migration is seen as not merely an economic opportunity, but a necessity. Policies for marketising immigrant labour are consistent with this rhetoric. Culturally, Putin's rhetoric focuses on the need for migrants to integrate, and key statements are followed by policies aimed at selecting migrants on the basis of their integration potential. Regarding security issues, Putin emphasises the need for improved regulation and control, which in turn has led to policies that sharpen the penalties for violations of migration procedures. In practice, the mentality of managing migration through control mechanisms has permeated policy reforms in all three arenas, leading to policies that do not meet the stated goals and that can be interpreted as broadly anti-migrant. However, even the anti-migrant direction of policy should not be seen as overtly nationalist, both because it lacks an overarching ideological framework and because policies do not discriminate against any particular ethnic group.

'Migrants take our jobs!'

The 2013 NEORUSS study shows mixed results on views of migrants in the Russian labour market. A majority of those surveyed agree that migrant workers are needed in Russia to fill gaps in the labour market, but nearly 49 per cent believe that migrants do not work honestly and are a threat to society (see Table 10.1).[6] When migrants are framed as an economic solution to permanent population loss, less than a third of respondents support increasing migration.

The Kremlin has overtly played to the unemployment myth on only one occasion, which predated Putin's third term. Amid the 2008 global financial crisis and fears of rising unemployment, Putin agreed with a caller during his annual call-in show that new migrant quotas should be decreased by a minimum of 50 per cent (Putin 2008). As

Table 10.1 Public opinion on migrants in the labour market

	Fully or mostly agree
Migrants are very much needed in Russia, because they work in low-paying (but important) jobs that Russians are reluctant to do	52.8%
Many migrants come to Russia not for honest wages, but in order to steal from Russians and make the Russian people weak	48.7%
Given the declining population in Russia, more migrants are needed, to prevent labour shortages that could threaten the country's security	31.8%
Restrictions on hiring migrants should be lifted	28.9%

Source: NEORUSS 2013 nationwide survey, available at <http://www.hf.uio.no/ilos/english/research/projects/neoruss/> (last accessed 3 November 2016).

Russians are particularly worried about unemployment (Gimpelson and Oshchepkov 2012; Gorshkov 2016), this has become a repeated theme in Putin's annual call-in shows. Typically, Putin's statements have been limited to reporting unemployment figures and casting them in comparative terms (for example, improving since the previous period, or better than in Europe). Unemployment is rarely linked specifically to immigration, though occasionally the priority of protecting the local labour market is emphasised. In general, Putin has taken care to stress that migrants can make important contributions to the Russian economy.

In his third term, Putin has given more attention to migration issues than ever before. Speeches, especially in 2012–13, tackled the issue of migration head-on yet remained somewhat circumscribed in their language, never directly engaging the unemployment myth:

> Another difficult problem related to the condition of the labour market is international labour migration. The lack of proper order not only deforms the structure of employment, but it causes imbalances in the social sphere, provokes ethnic conflict, and leads to higher crime rates. We need to streamline the employment of foreign citizens coming to Russia under the visa-free regime, and strengthen the responsibility of employers who use foreign labour. And of course, if they live and work in Russia, use the education and health care systems, they must comply with obligations to pay taxes and other payments. (Putin 2013)

Putin is careful to avoid attributing the problems of the labour market to migrants. In this statement, it is not migrants themselves that are the problem, but the lack of order in the system. The solutions Putin offers in this speech are regulation (of labour migrants), coordination (with employers) and control (over migrants' entry and stay in Russia). While coordination with employers gets only passing attention, the issues of improving regulation of labour migrants and increasing control over entry and stay receive detailed treatment. Putin's comments on these issues could be called technocratic in their level of detail about specific policies. He goes on to call for reform of 'patents' (a type of labour permit for CIS workers), indicating in detail whom migrants should be allowed to work for, in which regions and who should be responsible for setting the costs of the permits. Most important for this discussion of the economic impact of migrants are the directives he gives to policymakers initiating reforms:

> The system of patents should differentiate and stimulate the flow of migrants to Russia who are above all professional, educated specialists, who know the Russian language and are close to our culture . . . I expect that if the work of migrants is organised competently, it will be an economic instrument for regulating migration flows. Do you understand me? An economic instrument – taking into account the cost of patents in different regions of the Russian Federation. (Putin 2013)

Putin's comments foreshadowed a new phase in migration policies where labour patents have become both marketised and monetised. As with previous statements on migration, Putin focused on the economic potential of migrant workers, and not their threat to the labour market. Even the 2014 economic crisis failed to provoke populist language about protecting the labour market.

Overall, migration policies enacted during Putin's third term reflect liberalisation in the sense of increased marketisation of migration regulation. On 1 January 2015, two important pieces of legislation entered into force. One was an amendment to the migration laws, reforming the patent system along the lines Putin indicated above. The second was the Eurasian Economic Union (EEU) agreement, which created an open labour market for citizens of member states. Both reforms marked a liberalisation of the rules for labour migrants in Russia.

The reform of the patent system created a new set of procedures for labour migrants from CIS countries. Prior to 2015, these migrants could obtain either a work permit or patent, depending on the type of employer in question. The reforms made patents the only labour permit available for CIS citizens and allowed them to work for any type of employer, but increased the requirements and expense involved in obtaining the proper documents. These patents represent a monetisation of the migration system, bringing profits from the migration process into the state coffers in the guise of a liberalisation of policy. The result has been an increase in revenues from the sales of patents and associated collection of taxes, but a decrease in the number of patents issued.[7]

For citizens of EEU countries, access to the labour market has been simplified dramatically. The EEU agreement gives workers access to the labour markets of other member states on par with citizens, without the need for a work permit or patent. This is an especially attractive arrangement for EEU member countries (and potential member countries) who are major migrant donors (Uzbekistan, Tajikistan and Kyrgyzstan). Despite the opening of the labour market, early evidence indicates that Kyrgyz citizens (the largest population of low-skilled labour migrants among EEU member states) cannot fully realise the advantages of the agreement – primarily because, in order for a migrant to work legally, a labour contract must be submitted to the migration services. Labour contracts have not traditionally been a part of the migrant experience, and are usually considered unnecessary or even undesirable.[8]

While reforms in the patent system have increased the bureaucratic burden on migrants and can be framed as anti-migrant, they cannot necessarily be called nationalistic. The policies do not discriminate against a specific group of migrants, and offer advantages to migrants from CIS countries compared with migrants from the 'far abroad'. The EEU takes these advantages even further. Because reforms are implemented in a manner that emphasises mechanisms of control, the role of the state as the main actor in migration management contributes to the statist legitimacy discourse pursued by the Kremlin even though it does not frame labour migration in nationalist terms.

'Migrants destroy our culture!'

Opinion polls in Russia in 2012–13 showed that 46 per cent of respondents believed that migrants destroy Russian culture (Levada 2013). However, public opinion also shows a bent toward multiculturalism as well as other nuances. For example, a majority of respondents in the NEORUSS survey take a moderate view on migrant integration,

Table 10.2 Commitment to multiculturalism

	Fully or mostly agree
Migrants in Russia should have the right to preserve and develop their own cultures	12.2%
Migrants in Russia should adapt to Russian culture, but they should have the right to preserve their own culture	53.2%
Migrants in Russia should assimilate to Russian culture	26.1%

Source: NEORUSS 2013 nationwide survey, available at <http://www.hf.uio.no/ilos/english/research/projects/neoruss/> (last accessed 3 November 2016).

agreeing that while migrants should adapt to Russian culture, they should also be able to retain their own culture (see Table 10.2).

Furthermore, once respondents are given a chance to differentiate between different minorities, certain groups are seen as more compatible (Belarussian and Ukrainian) than others (Chechen, Gypsy and Chinese). These results do not necessarily shed light on how Russians view international migrants compared with national minorities and internal migrants – since, for example, all Central Asian groups (international migrants in many cases) are seen as more compatible with Russian culture than Chechens, who are Russian citizens. Nevertheless, the sometimes contradictory opinions of the public show how xenophobia and multiculturalism can coexist.

Many experts agree that the Kremlin was generally reticent on the question of national identity until just before Putin's third term (Kolstø and Blakkisrud 2016). Despite a greater willingness to discuss national issues beginning in 2011 and 2012, the Kremlin has remained evasive on the issue of migrants and the potential for ethnic conflict. Although in his discussions Putin has noted the need to create tolerance and inter-ethnic conciliation, most of his comments are directed at Russia's multi-ethnic population. Comments on international migrants tend to focus on integration and adaptation and are far fewer in number. Nevertheless, he has been resolute in his call for migrants to adapt, linking the rise of xenophobia in Europe to migrants who refuse to adapt to their host societies. In his election campaign article 'Russia: the national question', Putin called for a policy approach to address migrant integration:

> For us it is important that migrants can adapt to society. It is elementary that people who want to live and work in Russia should be willing to learn

the Russian language and culture. Exams in Russian language, Russian history, Russian literature and the basics of Russian law should be made compulsory for the granting or extension of migrant status. (Putin 2012a)

Rather than indicating migration as such as the cause of ethnic conflict, in his article, Putin firmly placed the blame on flaws in the state institutions as the source of the highly publicised ethnic clashes in Kondopoga (Karelia), Sagra (Sverdlovsk) and on Moscow's Manezhnaia Square. These statements echo comments cited above, with Putin placing the onus for ethnic tensions on the lack of order in the migration sphere, and further the rhetoric that migration can be managed by the state through proper policies.

Putin has been more resolute in his comments linking migration and cultural destruction when he discusses global processes and migration in Western societies. His language evokes several migration myths at once as a warning that Russia should take measures to avoid becoming like those societies:

> In many countries, closed national and religious communities are forming, which not only refuse to assimilate, but will not even adapt. There are neighbourhoods and entire cities where generations of immigrants are living on welfare and do not speak the language of the host country. The response to this situation has been a rise of xenophobia among indigenous populations seeking to protect their interests, jobs and social benefits in the face of 'foreign competitors'. People are shocked by the aggressive pressure on their traditions and way of life, and are seriously threatened by the possibility of losing their national identity. (Putin 2012a)

Perhaps Putin's most 'nationalist' statements on the migration issue concern his definitions of 'compatriots', and whether Central Asian migrants qualify as compatriots. Compatriots are unequivocally seen as 'good' migrants who 'are culturally and spiritually close to Russia' (Putin 2012b). However, Putin has outlined the criteria for being a compatriot differently, even in the course of a single speech to the Federal Assembly in 2013. At one point, he includes CIS citizens in the category of compatriot: 'foreign citizens and our compatriots, especially from CIS states' (Putin 2013). Elsewhere in the same text, he seems to exclude them: in discussing distance education, he refers to 'our compatriots *and* citizens of the CIS' (Putin 2013, emphasis added). As in the following statement, Putin often leaves room for interpretation as to whether CIS citizens may or may not be considered compatriots:

> Russia needs an inflow of new [labour] force, without question. They should be smart, educated, hardworking people, who do not simply want to come here to make some money and then leave, but who want to move here, to settle in Russia and consider Russia their home (*rodina*). However, current regulations do not facilitate this process. Rather, they do the opposite. The process for our compatriots, those who are culturally and spiritually close to Russia, to obtain citizenship is complicated and ridiculously bureaucratic. But to import unskilled labour, including illegal workers, is relatively simple. I charge you to develop an accelerated procedure for granting Russian citizenship to our compatriots, the bearers of Russian language and culture, direct descendants of those born in the Russian empire and Soviet Union. (Putin 2012b)

Since most temporary labour migrants and illegal migrants come from Central Asian states of the former Soviet Union, these statements imply separation between Central Asian migrants and compatriots. However, the language is indirect, and cannot be taken to mean that migrants from Central Asia are necessarily excluded as compatriots if they have some core affinity with Russian culture, speak Russian and are willing to integrate.

Two important reforms in 2012 and 2014 reinforce the centrality of integration in the migration process, focusing primarily on language. The Russian language and history/culture exams required of labour migrants are consistently framed as a tool for integration, but their implementation shows limits to that potential. Undoubtedly, migrants who speak Russian are seen as better able to adapt to life in Russia, but a second reform that aims to simplify access to residence and citizenship for the 'bearers of Russian language' remains out of reach for many migrants.

Soon after Putin took office in 2012, he set a target date of November that year for instituting obligatory exams for labour migrants that would cover Russian language, history and basic legislation. In January 2015, the exams were concretely linked to labour patents, and thereby became common practice. However, the period allotted to migrants for completing the exams and submitting all necessary work documents was thirty days, showing its limited potential as an integration project that could assist migrants in adapting to Russian society.

Reforms in 2014 simplified the procedure for 'Russian speakers' to obtain residence status and citizenship. The mechanism used for determining language ability (an interview) would indicate that far fewer people are expected to utilise this option than the more standardised language exams. Furthermore, the timing of the reform is important as it enabled refugees from Ukraine to gain simplified access to migration and citizenship status in Russia (Schenk 2016).

These policy reforms also reflect a focus on state control through screening migrants out who are less likely to adapt. In reality, the reforms discriminate against those who do not speak Russian, yet without targeting any specific ethnic group. Perhaps it could be argued that migrants from Central Asia are most disadvantaged by these policies – but that argument focuses on the sheer number of migrants coming from that area, and ignores the fact that they already have preferential access to the labour market through the visa-free regime and patent regulations. Furthermore, migrants from EEU countries are exempt from language exam requirements.

'Migrants are a security threat!'

Many Russians do not distinguish between legal and illegal migrants, leading to the widespread perception of *all* migrants as criminals.[9] The NEORUSS survey results show that the majority of respondents are concerned with security issues (see Table 10.3) – especially terrorism, banditry and inter-ethnic conflicts.

Much like the Kremlin's stance on welcoming economic migrants, securitising migration rhetoric is handled delicately, without overt use of the populist rhetoric of migration myths. Even in relation to Putin's key projects, such as registration reform, which has disproportionately severe consequences for international migrants, Putin's rhetoric has focused on internal migrants. Moreover, whereas many migrants are registered in 'rubber apartments' where they do not actually reside, Putin places the blame squarely on property owners and corrupt officials, not on migrants (whether internal or international) themselves. When Putin proposed introducing administrative

Table 10.3 What kinds of threat do migrants pose?

Terrorism and banditry	30.3%
Illegal stay (registration violations)	13.5%
Territorial threat (territorial claims on Russian land)	7.8%
Interethnic and religious hostility and violence	23.6%
Undermining the Russian economy	8.1%
Damage to the environment	10.2%

Source: NEORUSS 2013 nationwide survey, available at <http://www.hf.uio.no/ilos/english/research/projects/neoruss/> (last accessed 3 November 2016).

and criminal penalties for violations of registration in his pre-election 'Russia: the national question', he did so after noting that at times (internal) migrant behaviour is 'inappropriate, aggressive, outrageous or disdainful' (some of his strongest language against migrants), but without linking migrant behaviour to any specific violations (Putin 2012a).

On the few occasions Putin mentions illegal immigration, his language has been measured and policy-focused, avoiding inflammatory declarations of the populist sort.

> I think it is reasonable and necessary to strengthen the punishments for illegal immigration, for violations in the sphere of registration. The relevant laws are already being discussed in the Duma. I ask the deputies to pass these laws. (Putin 2012b)

> We need to strengthen control over the purpose of entry of foreign citizens. This is what all civilised countries do. The government should know why and for what period foreigners are coming to Russia. At the same time, we need to solve the question of visa-free foreigners coming for long periods without a defined purpose. Certainly, they have a purpose, but the state knows nothing about it. The period of their stay in Russia should be limited, and those who violate the rules of stay should be prohibited from re-entering Russia. Depending on the severity of the violation, for a period of 3 to 10 years. These measures will act as additional barriers for foreign citizens, who, frankly, are engaged in the shadows, either in criminal activities or working illegally, often in inhumane conditions, and unfortunately themselves become victims of crime. (Putin 2013)

As with the discussion of patents, Putin's statements about regulating entry both reflects laws already in place, and paves the way for policies yet to be adopted. Moreover, it defines the political context of migration using technocratic, not populist, methods. At the same time, Putin engages in various crosscutting discourses, particularly apparent in the second quote, where he appeals to modernisation (what 'civilised countries' do), human rights (migrants who become victims of crime) and securitisation, all of which create an underlying dissonance in this set of statements. Nevertheless, this is a dissonance without nationalist or populist shadings.

In many cases, Putin seeks to de-link migration from criminality and terrorism. During Putin's call-in shows, a caller may occasionally attribute terrorism and crime to migrants, but Putin has consistently minimised these threats. When in 2015 a caller queried Putin about the threat from migrants involved with IS, Putin downplayed both the potential threat and any links between migrants and terrorist threats (Putin 2015). Furthermore, in the 2016 call-in show, he argued that qualified specialists and students should find Russia a viable alternative for work and study where they are safer from terrorist threats than in Europe (Putin 2016b).

Only in 2016 did Putin begin to directly address security issues related to international migrants.[10] For the first time, we can note rhetoric typical of the populist security myth:

> Criminal gangs, drug traffickers, foreign intelligence agencies and the emissaries of international extremist and terrorist organisations are all trying to use illegal migration channels to their advantage. These attempts must be stopped. . . . Of serious concern is the continuing level of crime among foreign citizens. . . . Such crimes have resonance. They often cause a surge of xenophobic and nationalist moods, and give rise to propaganda attacks. (Putin 2016a)

These statements mark the first real effort by the Kremlin to portray international migration in overt security terms, and give credence to policies that had already been adopted: unlike the fairly circumscribed language of the Kremlin, the policies enacted during the first part of Putin's third term have served to securitise the migration regime and have made obtaining legal entry and stay in Russia significantly more difficult for migrants from CIS countries. In addition to the criminalisation of fictitious registration, several changes to the administrative code and migration laws have made it easier to deport migrants and prevent them from entering Russia for lengthy periods.

On 23 July 2013 Putin signed six migration-related laws, two of them dealing with securitising mechanisms: administrative expulsion and entry bans (sometimes referred to as 'blacklists'). The laws expanded the list of possible grounds for denying migrants entry, including violations at the border (the use of false documents) or violations on previous visits (for example non-payment of taxes).

Further, on 21 December 2013 Putin signed the law widely known as 'On Rubber Apartments', making it a crime for citizens or foreigners to register at an address where they do not actually stay. For Russian citizens, penalties include fines and potential prison time. For foreigners, there is the additional possibility of administrative expulsion[11] and a re-entry ban for five years.

The legal activity and its high-level endorsement by Putin, through his repeated pledges to reform the registration system and other key aspects of the migration system, have marked a turn in migration

Table 10.4 Blacklists and deportations

	2011	2012	2013	2014	2015
Blacklisted migrants*	64,933	88,748	459,337	644,918	490,893
Migrants barred entry**	n/a	73,816	456,434	682,893	481,404
Migrants expelled or deported	28,585	35,115	82,413	139,034	117,493

* Decisions made about barring the future entry of a foreign citizen
** Number of migrants physically prevented from entering Russia, either as a result of the person's name appearing on a blacklist, or due to the various circumstances whereby a foreign citizen can be denied entry at the border (violation of migration rules, health factors, etc.).
Source: Data from the now defunct database of the Glavnoe upravlenie po voprosam migratsii MVD Rossii for the period 2012–15.

enforcement. Table 10.4 shows a sharp increase in the number of migrants who have been administratively expelled and blacklisted.

Though there have been no explicit instructions (in the public record) from the Kremlin to enforce new and existing laws in an increasingly securitised way, the legal amendments and their framing in the media have served to heighten the awareness of local and regional government agencies to migration and the mechanisms that can be used to regulate it. In this context, conservative interpretations and applications of the law can help regional leaders to avoid reprimand for any migration-related unrest, and to ingratiate themselves with their superiors and the public by appearing tough on immigration.

Undoubtedly, migration policies have become more securitised during Putin's third term in office than in previous periods, but this does not necessarily mean greater nationalisation of migration issues in the security sphere in a way that favours one ethnic group over another. Because Putin's rhetoric has not explicitly embraced populist or nationalist rhetoric linking migration to security threats, it is difficult to establish any direct nationalising intent. The focus seems to be on greater control and coordination, aimed at creating a more 'civilised' migration system.

Conclusions

Migration policy has seen significant reforms during Putin's third term as president. The reform of the patent system, registration rules, procedures for entry and language exams mark important changes in the procedures for international migrants to legalise their status in Russia. While changes to the patent system, for example, have in some ways liberalised access to Russia's labour market, the overall direction of the new policies is towards greater governmental control through onerous bureaucratic procedures and hefty penalties for violation. And while the general direction of the policy reforms can certainly be seen as anti-migrant, the Kremlin's rhetoric has not actively utilised nationalist frames in discussing policy-related problems. Instead, Putin has appealed to statist legitimacy through technocratic approaches to policy.

Is the recent anti-migrant policy direction explicitly adopted by the Kremlin as a part of a broader nationalist agenda? From the discussion above we can conclude that if a nationalist agenda can be identified in the Kremlin's migration strategy, it is a firmly statist rather than ethnic type of nationalism – a technocratic migration strategy which shores up the dominant legitimacy frames of a strong state that can produce stability and prosperity.

In the three migration myths assessed in this chapter, we find that Putin has eschewed a populist course, instead pursuing a migration discourse that looks to utilise migration for the benefit of the state. Economically, migrants are framed as a tool for development rather than a threat to the labour market, taking jobs away from the native workforce. Culturally, migrants are not framed as incompatible, as there is always the possibility of integrating into Russian society (though it is acknowledged that those with previous cultural affinity can do this more easily). Even after numerous efforts to attract the 'right' kind of migrants (that is, compatriots and Russian speakers), Putin does not brand CIS migrants in general or any sub-group within them as being the 'wrong' kind of migrants. Indeed, such a move would be counterproductive, given the establishment of the EEU and the commitment to a free labour market.

As regards security, the goal is always law and order, furthering the strong state discourse that has marked Putin's strategy throughout his presidential tenure. Only in 2016 has Putin's language approached the type of populism embraced by the migration myths – and even then, only in the sphere of security. Moreover, this turn toward stronger language has not invoked anti-migrant frames, nor has it singled out any specific ethnic group within the migration population.

Putin's goal seems to be to address the potential problems associated with migration through policy solutions before the situation becomes untenable. There is an underlying sense that if the right policies are found, if loopholes are closed and the state can manage migration in a civilised way, then Russia will never experience the migration problems common in Europe and the West in general. Thus, Putin has framed his policies as preventative in nature even though they concern long-standing issues like the informal labour market and registration procedures.

The technocratic strategy pursued by the Kremlin allows for liberalising policies in the economic sphere, screening policies in the cultural sphere and punitive reforms in the security sphere. By focusing on policy, the Kremlin can pursue these different strategies without contradicting the unifying ideology of a strong state. While the discourse focuses on the development potential of migration, policies prioritise security and control, creating an anti-migrant bias. And although the policies and their framing fail to take full advantage of the economic and demographic development potentials of migration, they cannot be said to be overtly nationalist.

Notes

1. Using a qualitative discourse analytical approach, I analyse migration-related statements made by Putin during and immediately preceding his third presidential term. I analysed these texts with a view to how Putin framed international migration in general, and specifically how he approached the economic place of migrants (related to the unemployment myth), issues of immigrant integration (related to the cultural incompatibility myth), and security concerns related to migration.
2. See for example Gerber 2014; Gorodzeisky et al. 2015; Bahry 2016; Bessudnov 2016; Herrera and Kraus 2016.
3. There is a sizable literature on ethnic conflict and ethnic secessionism that focuses on cleavages between groups with long-term relationships to territory within the bounds of a state (Horowitz 1981; Fearon and Laitin 2003; Hale 2008).
4. For an overview of various nationalisms and their views on core identity, as well as how open they are to immigration, see Kolstø 2016b and Schenk 2012.
5. Specifically, migrants are often associated with increases in crime and a range of illegal practices including drug trafficking, organised crime and terrorism. Migrants are also associated with health risks that jeopardise the physical security of the local population.
6. There is surprisingly little overlap between those who answered positively to the first question and negatively to the second question in Table 10.1. Only 26.8 per cent of the sample fully or mostly agreed with the first question and fully or mostly disagreed with the second question; 23.1 per cent of the sample agreed fully or mostly with both questions. This indicates a certain amount of ambivalence in people's views on the migration issue.
7. This is particularly striking in view of the fact that 3 million work permits and patents were issued to CIS citizens in 2014, whereas only

1.8 million patents were issued in 2015 after patents became the only option for CIS migrants. Though this period coincides with economic crisis resulting from low oil prices and sanctions related to the 2014 conflict with Ukraine, experts cite increasing difficulties in obtaining patents as the main driver, arguing that any decrease in migrant flows as a result of the economic situation was short-lived.
8. This observation was made by several interview respondents during field research in Moscow and Kazan in 2015.
9. Author interview with a migrant rights organisation, Moscow, 2009.
10. In his election campaign article on the national question Putin noted security issues related to inter-ethnic relations, though these were linked to internal migrants rather than international migrants. On the issue of international migrants, Putin limited his framing of the threat as a 'concern' or 'annoyance' (Putin 2012a).
11. Violations of entry and the terms of stay in Russia (including registration) committed in Moscow, Moscow oblast, St Petersburg and Leningrad oblast require automatic administrative expulsion.

Bibliography

Alexseev, Mikhail (2006), *Immigration Phobia and the Security Dilemma: Russia, Europe and the United States*, New York: Cambridge University Press.

Bahry, Donna (2016), 'Opposition to immigration, economic insecurity and individual values: evidence from Russia', *Europe–Asia Studies*, 68, 5: 893–916.

BBC Russia (2008), 'Luzhkov podderzhal sokrashchenie kvot na migrantov' [Luzhkov supported the reduction of quota for migrants], 10 December, <http://news.bbc.co.uk/hi/russian/russia/newsid_7776000/7776470.stm> (last accessed 27 July 2016).

Bessudnov, Alexey (2016), 'Ethnic hierarchy and public attitudes towards immigrants in Russia', *European Sociological Review*, 32, 5: 1–14.

Bianchi, Milo, Paolo Buonanno and Paolo Pinotti (2012), 'Do immigrants cause crime?', *Journal of the European Economic Association*, 10, 6: 1318–47.

Brass, Paul R. (1991), *Ethnicity and Nationalism: Theory and Comparison*, New Delhi: Sage.

Breuilly, John (1993), *Nationalism and the State*, Manchester: Manchester University Press.

Connor, Walker (1993), 'Beyond reason: the nature of the ethnonational bond', *Ethnic and Racial Studies*, 16, 3: 373–89.

Favell, Adrian (1998), *Philosophies of Integration: Immigration and the Idea of Citizenship in France and Britain*, New York: St Martin's Press.

Fearon, James D. and David D. Laitin (2003), 'Ethnicity, insurgency, and civil war', *American Political Science Review*, 97, 1: 75–90.

Gellner, Ernest (1983), *Nations and Nationalism*, Ithaca, NY: Cornell University Press.

Gerber, Theodore P. (2014), 'Beyond Putin? Nationalism and xenophobia in Russian public opinion', *The Washington Quarterly*, 37, 3: 113–34.

Gimpelson, Vladimir and Aleksey Oshchepkov (2012), 'Does more unemployment cause more fear of unemployment?' *IZA Journal of Labor and Development*, 1, 6: 1–26.

Goode, J. Paul and David R. Stroup (2015), 'Everyday nationalism: constructivism for the masses', *Social Science Quarterly*, 96, 3: 717–39.

Gorodzeisky, Anastasia, Anya Glikman and Dina Maskileyson (2015), 'The nature of anti-immigrant sentiment in post-socialist Russia', *Post-Soviet Affairs*, 31, 2: 115–35.

Gorshkov, Mikhail (2016), 'Twenty years that shook Russia: public opinion on the reforms', in Piotr Dutkiewicz, Richard Sakwa and Vladimir Kulikov, eds, *The Social History of Post-Communist Russia*, New York: Routledge, 90–129.

Hale, Henry (2008) *The Foundations of Ethnic Politics: Separatism of States and Nations in Eurasia and the World*, Cambridge: Cambridge University Press.

Hechter, Michael (2000), *Containing Nationalism*, Oxford: Oxford University Press.

Herrera, Yoshiko M. and Nicole M. Butkovich Kraus (2016), 'Pride versus prejudice: ethnicity, national identity, and xenophobia in Russia', *Comparative Politics*, 48, 3: 293–312.

Horowitz, Donald L. (1981), 'Patterns of ethnic separatism', *Comparative Studies in Society and History*, 23, 2: 165–95.

Hutchings, Stephen and Vera Tolz (2016), 'Ethnicity and nationhood on Russian state-aligned television: contextualising geopolitical crisis', in Pål Kolstø and Helge Blakkisrud, eds, *The New Russian Nationalism: Imperialism, Ethnicity and Authoritarianism, 2000–15*, Edinburgh: Edinburgh University Press, 298–335.

Ioffe, Grigory and Zhanna Zayonchkovskaya (2010), 'Immigration to Russia: why it is inevitable, and how large it may have to be to provide the workforce Russia needs', NCEEER Working Paper, Seattle, WA: National Council for Eurasian and East European Research.

Kolstø, Pål (2016a), 'Introduction: Russian nationalism is back – but precisely what does that mean?', in Pål Kolstø and Helge Blakkisrud, eds, *The New Russian Nationalism: Imperialism, Ethnicity and Authoritarianism, 2000–15*, Edinburgh: Edinburgh University Press, 1–17.

Kolstø, Pål (2016b), 'The ethnification of Russian nationalism', in Pål Kolstø and Helge Blakkisrud, eds, *The New Russian Nationalism:*

Imperialism, Ethnicity and Authoritarianism, 2000–15, Edinburgh: Edinburgh University Press, 18–45.

Kolstø, Pål and Helge Blakkisrud, eds (2016), *The New Russian Nationalism: Imperialism, Ethnicity and Authoritarianism, 2000–15*, Edinburgh: Edinburgh University Press.

Korobkov, Andrei V. (2008), 'Post-Soviet migration: new trends in the twenty-first century', in Cynthia J. Buckley, Blair A. Ruble and Erin Trouth Hofmann, eds, *Migration, Homeland, and Belonging in Eurasia*, Baltimore, MD: Johns Hopkins University Press, 69–98.

Kozhevnikova, Galina (2007), 'Iazyk vrazhdy posli Kondopogi' [Hate speech after Kondopoga], in Aleksandr Verkhovskii, *Iazyk vrazhdy protiv obshchestva* [*Hate Speech against Society*], Moscow: SOVA Center, 10–71.

Levada (2013), *Russian Public Opinion 2012–2013, Yearbook*, Moscow, <http://www.levada.ru/books/obshchestvennoe-mnenie-2012-eng> (last accessed 26 January 2015).

Lysova, Tat'iana, Bela Liauv and Mariia Zheleznova (2013), 'Interv'iu: Sergei Sobianin, vrio mera Moskvy' [Interview: Sergei Sobianin, Acting Mayor of Moscow], *Vedomosti*, 6 August, <http://www.vedomosti.ru/library/articles/2013/08/06/intervyu-sergej-sobyanin-vrio-mera-moskvy> (last accessed 3 October 2016).

March, Luke (2012), 'Nationalism for export? The domestic and foreign-policy implications of the new "Russian Idea"', *Europe–Asia Studies*, 64, 3: 401–25.

Mukomel', Vladimir (2005), *Migratsionnaia politika Rossii* [*Migration Policy of Russia*], Moscow: Institute of Sociology, Russian Academy of Sciences.

Olzak, Susan and Joane Nagel (1986), *Competitive Ethnic Relations*, New York: Academic Press.

Orrenius, Pia M. and Madeline Zavodny (2012), 'Economic effects of migration: receiving states', in Marc R. Rosenblum and Daniel J. Tichenor, eds, *Oxford Handbook of the Politics of International Migration*, New York: Oxford University Press, 105–31.

Panov, Petr (2010), 'Nation-building in post-Soviet Russia: what kind of nationalism is produced by the Kremlin?', *Journal of Eurasian Studies*, 1, 2: 85–94.

Portes, Alejandro and Robert D. Manning (1986), 'The immigrant enclave: theory and empirical examples', in Susan Olzak and Joane Nagel, eds, *Competitive Ethnic Relations*, New York: Academic Press, 47–68.

Putin, Vladimir (2005), 'Vstupitel'noe slovo na zasedanii Soveta Bezopasnosti po migratsionnoi politike' [Opening remarks at the Security Council meeting on migration policy], Kremlin.ru, 17 March, <http://kremlin.ru/events/president/transcripts/22861> (last accessed 30 September 2016).

Putin, Vladimir (2008), 'Razgovor s Vladimirom Putinym' [Conversation with Vladimir Putin], 4 December, <http://2008.moskva-putinu.ru> (last accessed 21 July 2016).

Putin, Vladimir (2012a), 'Rossiia: Natsional'nyi Vopros' [Russia: the national question], *Nezavisimaia gazeta*, 23 January, <http://www.ng.ru/politics/2012-01-23/1_national.html> (last accessed 30 September 2016).

Putin, Vladimir (2012b), 'Poslanie Prezidenta Federal'nomu Sobraniiu' [President's Address to the Federal Assembly], Kremlin.ru, 12 December, <http://kremlin.ru/events/president/transcripts/messages/17118> (last accessed 16 July 2016).

Putin, Vladimir (2013), 'Poslanie Prezidenta Federal'nomu Sobraniiu' [President's Address to the Federal Assembly], Kremlin.ru, 12 December, <http://kremlin.ru/events/president/transcripts/messages/19825> (last accessed 16 July 2016).

Putin, Vladimir (2015), 'Priamaia liniia s Vladimirom Putinym' [Direct line with Vladimir Putin], Kremlin.ru, 14 April, <http://kremlin.ru/events/president/news/49261> (last accessed 16 July 2016).

Putin, Vladimir (2016a), 'Zasedanie Soveta Bezopasnosti' [Meeting of the Security Council], Kremlin.ru, 31 March, <http://kremlin.ru/events/president/news/51618> (last accessed 16 July 2016).

Putin, Vladimir (2016b), 'Priamaia liniia s Vladimirom Putinym' [Direct line with Vladimir Putin], Kremlin.ru, 14 April, <http://kremlin.ru/events/president/news/51716/work> (last accessed 14 July 2016).

RBK (2012), 'S. Sobianin: Ne fakt, chto Moskve nuzhny eshche mecheti [S. Sobianin: it is not the fact that Moscow needs more mosques], 11 October, <http://www.rbc.ru/society/11/10/2012/5703fdfd9a7947fcbd44153e> (last accessed 30 September 2016).

Reeves, Madeleine (2013), 'Clean fake: authenticating documents and persons in migrant Moscow', *American Ethnologist*, 40, 3: 508–24.

Schenk, Caress (2010), 'Open borders, closed minds: Russia's changing migration policies: liberalization or xenophobia?', *Demokratizatsiya*, 18, 2: 101–21.

Schenk, Caress (2012), 'Nationalism in the Russian media: content analysis of newspaper coverage surrounding conflict in Stavropol, 24 May–7 June 2007', *Nationalities Papers*, 40, 5: 783–805.

Schenk, Caress (2016), 'Assessing foreign policy commitment through Russia's migration policy', *Demokratizatsiya*, 24, 4: 475–500.

Semenenko, Irina (2015), 'Ethnicities, nationalism and the politics of identity: shaping the nation in Russia', *Europe–Asia Studies*, 67, 2: 306–26.

Shnirelman, Victor (2009), 'New racism, "clash of civilizations", and Russia', in Marlene Laruelle, ed., *Russian Nationalism and the National Reassertion of Russia*, New York: Routledge, 125–44.

Tolz, Vera (2001), *Inventing the Nation*, New York: Oxford University Press.

Tolz, Vera and Sue-Ann Harding (2015), 'From "compatriots" to "aliens": the changing coverage of migration on Russian television', *The Russian Review*, 74, 3: 452–77.

Tsygankov, Andrei (2016), 'Crafting the state-civilization: Vladimir Putin's turn to distinct values', *Problems of Post-Communism*, 63, 1: 146–58.

11
Everyday patriotism and ethnicity in today's Russia

J. Paul Goode

When does patriotism turn into nationalism?[1] The rapid social mobilisation in support of Russia's annexation of Crimea in 2014 caught many observers off-guard and spurred a lively debate about the influence of nationalism in domestic and foreign policy. Surprisingly, observers paid little attention to the Kremlin's promotion of patriotism, focusing instead on the attitudinal or intellectual sources of the 'new Russian nationalism'. For over a decade, the Kremlin had invested significant resources in patriotism through the media, education and policy, seeking to unify society around the themes of shared statehood, sacrifice and achievement. However, as patriotic programmes grew in complexity, they also created the space, opportunity and infrastructure for the populace to use patriotic observance to celebrate dominant ethnicity. This chapter argues that the emergence of nationalism in Russia may be understood in terms of the ethnicisation of everyday patriotic practices.

I begin with a brief discussion of the divergent ways that scholars have analysed patriotism and nationalism. Next I examine the historical relationship of patriotism and nationalism in Russia and the Kremlin's recent articulation of patriotism as state doctrine. I then consider vernacular understandings of the relationship of patriotism to nationalism, scrutinising how patriotism is understood and infused with ethnic meaning in the daily lives of Russians. Recognition of the place of dominant ethnicity in discussions of patriotism can shed light on the extent to which Russians' sense of patriotism is (to paraphrase Stalin) patriotic in form, but nationalist in content.

Thinking theoretically about patriotism and nationalism

Despite considerable disagreement about the nature of the relationship of patriotism to nationalism, most scholars agree that the two concepts are closely related. Constructivist theories of nationalism see the relationship between concepts as relational and continuous. For Benedict Anderson, patriotism is the opposite of racism (rather than nationalism), observing that 'nations inspire love, and often profoundly self-sacrificing love' (Anderson 2006: 141). Michael Billig took the point further in suggesting that patriots are but nationalists who perceive their own nationalism as quintessential, beneficial and necessary (Billig 1995: 55). In Rogers Brubaker's formulation, patriotism and nationalism are overlapping and flexible political languages, encompassing 'ways of framing political arguments by appealing to the *patria*, the fatherland, the country, the nation' (Brubaker 2004: 120). The practical consequence of this approach is that constructivist studies of nationalism often treat patriotism as related yet conceptually indistinct. While this approach sacrifices theoretical parsimony, it provides a good understanding of the meanings and utility of patriotic and nationalist appeals from actors' perspectives, and the implications for social and political action.

By contrast, studies from the fields of sociology, social psychology and political science treat the positive and negative connotations of patriotism and nationalism as signifying differences in kind rather than differences of degree. In other words, the difference between patriotism and nationalism is taken to be fixed and categorical: patriotism involves positive emotions towards one's country and co-nationals, and is more cooperative and compatible with cosmopolitan values, whereas nationalism is militaristic and intolerant (Kosterman and Feshbach 1989; Druckman 1994; Martynov 2009). However, social psychologists note that these orientations are two sides of the same coin, insofar as nationalism concerns negative orientations towards intergroup differentiation, while patriotism involves positive in-group evaluations (Mummendey et al. 2001). Similar dualities emerge in the respective literatures concerning nationalism and patriotism: 'civic' nationalism is inclusive and tolerant, while 'ethnic' nationalism is discriminatory and coercive (Ignatieff 1993; Yack 1996; Kohn 2005); 'constructive' patriotism is critical and peaceful, while 'blind' patriotism is chauvinistic and bellicose (Adorno 1950; Schatz et al. 1999; Parker 2010).

In practice, policymakers and members of the public regularly blur the distinction between patriotism and nationalism (and between varieties of patriotism and nationalism) in daily life. Oxana Shevel's (2011) study of Russia's nationality policy since the 1990s reveals a 'purposeful ambiguity' in the ways that 'ethnic' and 'civic' appeals serve tactical political purposes in lieu of consistent policy.

Since coming to power, Vladimir Putin has promoted a vision of state patriotism as the glue to bind state and society (Sperling 2003), though the content of this vision has been varied and sometimes contradictory. The ambiguity in policy and daily usage of patriotism and nationalism may persist *precisely* because the terms are considered categorically distinct. In this regard, it is telling that the wave of popular enthusiasm for the annexation of Crimea in 2014 is usually referred to as a 'burst of patriotism' (*vsplesk patriotizma*) in Russia, whereas 'nationalism' is reserved for extremists and separatists. However, official representations of patriotism in the media and government propaganda may conceal the ways in which it is meaningful or contested in people's daily lives (Laruelle 2015; Le Huérou 2015; Goode 2016).

This chapter adopts a constructivist approach, focusing on the ways the state has attempted to shape the meaning of patriotism and on the micro-processes whereby the boundaries between patriotism and nationalism are elaborated and maintained in Russians' everyday lives. In studying how social identities are practised and activated in daily life, scholars often utilise a combination of ethnographic (participant) observation and indirect interviewing (Fox and Miller-Idriss 2008; Goode and Stroup 2015; Bonikowski 2016). The rationale for this approach is that surveys and direct observation run the risk of confirming the researcher's assumptions, expectations and experiences, rather than revealing the actual salience of ethnicity or other forms of group identity in daily life (Dwyer and Buckle 2009). It is further possible that survey responses may repeat or confirm hegemonic social narratives rather than reflecting individual opinions. Surveys concerning, say, Russians' support for the slogan 'Russia for Russians' convey the impression that the slogan is constantly meaningful in the same way for a given portion of the population (or, conversely, that the meaning is given by that percentage of the population that supports it). However, the question may not be an adequate guide for understanding how respondents understand and act on ethnicity, aside from the moment of selecting a survey response. Moreover, such questions evade various thornier issues, not least the meaning of national identity. As a Russian colleague once exclaimed to me in exasperation, 'if Russia is not for Russians, then whom is it for?'

A similar problem arises when observers treat nationalised space or elite claims regarding ethnicity as representative of societal sentiment. Simply put, just because governments and leaders promote or talk about ethnicity or the nation does not mean that it resonates with the populace (Hobsbawm 1992: 11), though elites shape discursive space and create opportunities for its articulation on a quotidian level (Whitmeyer 2002). In their examinations of everyday ethnicity in the Romanian city of Cluj, Rogers Brubaker and colleagues (2006) and Jon E. Fox (2004) found it striking how *little* politicians' nationalist rhetoric mattered to residents and students. Steve Fenton (2007) similarly uncovered a surprising ambivalence towards national identity among English youth in Britain, while Michael Skey (2012) discovered a relationship between devolution in public politics and the activation of Englishness in response. And, despite rising *migrantophobia* in Moscow, Natalya Kosmarskaya and Igor Savin (2016) found that Muscovites who had regular contact with migrants in their daily lives tended to be more tolerant.

My own research focuses on everyday practices associated with social identity – in this case, patriotism. By 'practices' I mean the regularised, daily, practical acts that people undertake in the context of durable social dispositions – or what Pierre Bourdieu (2007) refers to as *habitus*. While states proffer their own versions of patriotism and patriotic identification, recirculated through institutions like education and mass media, what members of the public actually *do* with these official narratives in their daily lives is quite a different matter (see de Certeau 1984; Palmer 1998). Whereas indirect methods of observation are possible during 'quiet' or 'settled' times (Goode 2012; Bonikowski 2016) when people are not politically mobilised and the scholar's own identity is not at issue, they are impractical (if not impossible) during 'noisier' periods. Moreover, indirect observation may be risky in non-democratic regimes where state security organs might view it as potential grounds for deportation (Ahram and Goode 2016).

Since my research was principally concerned with understanding patriotism, I was able to observe ways that ethnicity and ethnicising practices co-occurred with discussions of patriotism, without specifically pressing respondents on the subject.[2] In more than sixty interviews in Russian regions in 2014–16, respondents were asked to explain what it means to be a patriot in today's Russia, what it means to 'love the motherland', what they think about nostalgia for the Soviet era and the 1990s, and how they understand the difference between patriotism and nationalism.[3] In every instance, respondents were pressed for concrete illustrations from their daily lives to support their answers. Having analysed the interviews to identify the practices associated with being a patriot, I then turned to focus groups to see whether participants would arrive at the same repertoire of practices without my prompting.[4]

Patriotism and nationalism in Russian history and today

The complicated relationship between patriotism and nationalism in contemporary Russia has a lengthy history.[5] In tsarist times, the term 'patriot' was rarely used; devotion to one's homeland was taken to mean the same thing as loyalty to the monarch. While patriotism in the American and French revolutions pointedly differentiated the interests of the homeland from that of the monarch, such usage in Russia was never popular except among intellectual elites familiar with the Enlightenment. In the time of Petr I, the organic sense of belonging to the Russian imperium (as a 'son of the Fatherland') was more likely to be understood as patriotism, although it would later be construed as mediated by Russian ethnicity such that it became difficult to distinguish from nationalism (Il'in 2015: 10). After falling into disrepute for its Western connotations during the war with Napoleon, the term 'patriot' was rehabilitated under Nikolai I as meaning 'loyal subject' in accordance with the doctrine of 'Orthodoxy, autocracy and nationality' as the pillars of tsarist rule. The basis of this unity was understood in terms of the 'true faith' (*istinnaia vera*), positing the tsar as the ultimate defender of that faith. Before long, the 'true' faith came to be ethnicised as 'Russian' faith, and all things Russian were axiomatically recognised as superior (Odesskii and Fel'dman 2008: 112). Through to the early twentieth century, official patriotism was weaponised in the battle with dissidence and the search for internal enemies, satirised by the liberal intelligentsia as 'bureaucratic patriotism' (*kazennyi patriotizm*) – a term conveying a sense of artificiality and hypocrisy of a patriotism subsidised by the state to defend the interests of the motherland, but more often invoked by the state's agents to oppress ethnic, religious and intellectual opponents of the regime (ibid.: 115).

If Russians' relatively weak sense of national identity and patriotism at the start of the First World War are commonly seen by historians as liabilities, they became powerfully entwined by the experience of war and its commemoration of the soldier as the symbol of patriotism, citizenship and national belonging. As Melissa Stockdale observes, 'Active patriotism became, at least rhetorically, the determinant of membership in the national community: love of the motherland, expressed in willingness to serve and sacrifice, characterised patriots and the genuine members of the nation' (Stockdale 2006: 484). After the Revolution, the Bolsheviks attempted to graft patriotism onto defence of the Socialist International, but after the Second World War (in Russian referred to as the 'Great Patriotic War'),[6] it returned to military themes, joining celebration of the Soviet people's decisive contribution to victory with the pre-revolutionary formula of equating loyalty to the regime with defending the motherland's interests against foreign and domestic foes (Magaril 2016: 144–45). In doctrinal terms, Soviet patriotism was understood to mean devotion to the socialist motherland and the Communist Party. Significantly, this form of patriotism reinforced the ideological claim that the USSR was a historically novel political entity defined by citizenship rather than ethnicity, language, culture or history (Kolstø 1984: 5–6). By the late twentieth century, this form of military patriotism had become deeply bureaucratised and ritualistic in ways that allowed Russian nationalists to drive a wedge between patriotism and national membership.

In the 1990s, the government of Boris Eltsin sought to advance a civic definition of nationality and then to define a new Russian idea through an ill-fated national competition (Smith 2002). Moreover, Eltsin was unable to secure the agreement of the State Duma on new national symbols, and found himself forced to adopt them by presidential decree. For many Russians, the 1990s were the most unpatriotic time in Russian history. The collapse of the Soviet state and the absence of unifying national institutions to replace it meant that collective practices of grief and discourses of bereavement served as a defining basis of belonging, manifesting itself in what Serguei Oushakine (2009) describes as a 'patriotism of despair'. Real movement on officially adopting state symbols came only after Putin's Unity faction shared leadership of the State Duma with the Communist Party after the 1999 parliamentary elections. With the Communists' support, Eltsin's wordless and unfamiliar national anthem was replaced by the Soviet-era melody with new lyrics penned by one of its original authors (Kolstø 2006: 686–88).

Soon after assuming the presidency in 2000, Putin launched a series of political and economic reforms intended to strengthen the hand of central government over Russia's regions, to consolidate presidential executive control over parliament and to restore state solvency. While these various moves attracted considerable scholarly and journalistic attention, less noticed was the simultaneous initiative to consolidate society behind a patriotic ideal. Starting with the first State Programme for Patriotic Education (SPPE) in 2001 (Gosudarstvennaia programma 2001), the Kremlin steadily moved to promote patriotism in public life. The bulk of funding for the SPPE was allocated to the ministries of education and culture (in Figure 11.1 subsumed under the category 'Socio-economic ministries'),

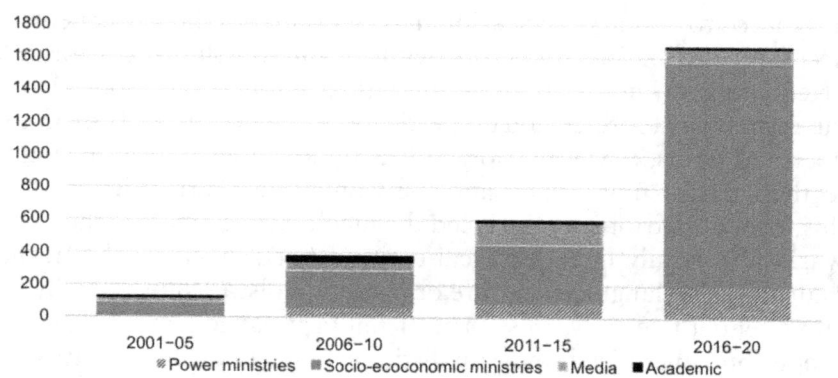

Figure 11.1 Budget for State Programme for Patriotic Education, 2001–20 (millions of roubles)

though with significant amounts dedicated to the power ministries. Accompanying this steady progression in the promotion of patriotism, the SPPE served as a foil for attracting various sectors to participate and become involved in the promotion of patriotism through central funding for academic conferences, business fairs, and especially sporting events and competitions.

During Putin's two first terms, the Kremlin sought to foster social consensus around 'the rehabilitation of fatherland symbols and institutionalized historical memory, the instrumentalisation of Orthodoxy for symbolic capital, and the development of militarized patriotism based on Soviet nostalgia' (Laruelle 2009: 154). Early on, the state promoted the creation of traditional military-patriotic entertainment, particularly in film and broadcast media (Gillespie 2005; Norris 2012). In primary and secondary education, Soviet history was rehabilitated, with particular emphasis on the Second World War, the modernising achievements of the Soviet state under Leonid Brezhnev, and the USSR's role and status as a world power. One of the most visible manifestations of this rehabilitation of Soviet history and military patriotism was Putin's revival of the use of military vehicles in the Victory Day (9 May) parade in 2008. In the social sector, the government promoted the creation of patriotic organisations at the local and regional levels, although these groups sometimes appropriated 'patriotism' as a brand to legitimate their own activities (Laruelle 2015; Le Huérou 2015).

A critical juncture in the development of patriotism as state doctrine occurred with the back-to-back spectacles of the Sochi

Olympics and the annexation of Crimea in 2014. The Sochi games (and particularly the opening ceremonies) presented an opportunity for the Kremlin to establish the present regime on equal footing with the USSR. However, the games were soon overshadowed by Russia's undeclared intervention in Crimea and then its annexation of the peninsula on 18 March. The political consequences are now well known: in domestic politics, the regime achieved record levels of support and a chilling of dissent (Suslov 2014; Teper 2016). Euromaidan, the annexation of Crimea and the subsequent war in eastern Ukraine have further divided Russian nationalists (Horvath 2015; Kolstø 2016), who now must choose between clinging to Putin's line and opposing 'the overwhelming patriotic majority' (Verkhovsky 2016: 99).

Patriotism became the only game in town – and patriotism increasingly came to mean loyalty to Putin's regime and anti-Westernism. With the Russian economy faltering and relations with the West worsening, the Kremlin doubled down on patriotism as a unifying force that would see it through troubled times. In a widely reported meeting with the leaders of small businesses on 3 February 2016, Putin declared, 'We do not and cannot have any other unifying idea but patriotism' (Kremlin.ru 2016). Whereas the 130 million rouble budget for the SPPE in 2001 was so meagre that it amounted to a symbolic commitment (Blum 2006), the new budget for the SPPE in 2016 rose to 1.67 billion roubles despite the ongoing recession and the imposition of austerity measures in other sectors. While previous plans emphasised historical celebrations (especially Victory Day) and propaganda, the 2016 plan allocated more than a third of its budget (628.2 million roubles) for 'youth military preparation' (see Table 11.1).

The shift in focus in state patriotism is further evident in the kinds of activities funded by the SPPE: budgets for commemorative activities and traditional propaganda declined steadily, while mobilisational and competitive activities increased nearly four-fold (see Table 11.2). The programme also significantly increased funding for activities with ethnic themes, allocating 133 million roubles – more than the entire 2001 State Programme – for activities related to Cossacks and a further 53.4 million roubles for activities promoting inter-ethnic tolerance.

With the official sanction of patriotism and the potential for converting patriotism into patronage, political innovators found new ways to adapt patriotic themes to movements and organisations.[7]

Table 11.1 State Programme for Patriotic Education – budget breakdown (millions of roubles)

2001*		2006		2011		2016	
Events		Historical celebrations	187.1	Events	226.8	Academic conferences	31.3
Organisational		Propaganda	167.9	Historical celebrations	12.4	Civic events	40.1
Propaganda		Scientific-technical	110	Military service	38.4	Cossacks	133
Scientific-technical		Social coordination	31.9	Organisational	123.7	Cultural events	226.7
Social coordination		State symbols	39	Propaganda	225.5	Film, TV, radio	78.4
		Victory Day	27.9	State symbols	6	Historical events	25.3
				Victory Day	131.5	Informational	50
						Journalism	25.4
						Memorial events	11.5
						Research and training	28.2
						Sporting events	117.6
						Symbolic events	3.3
						Training	97.5
						Veterans	6.8
						Volunteerism	2.7
						Youth military preparation	628.2

*The 2001 programme does not specify individual programme budgets

Table 11.2 State Programme for Patriotic Education – activity budgets (millions of roubles)

	2006	2011	2016
Award	14.6	12.9	0
Broadcast	48.7	45	63
Commemoration	14.9	15.8	10.4
Competition	180.5	217.6	654.9
Computer games	3.6	0	2
Conference/seminar	36.7	38.4	88.9
Coordination	10.2	65.8	3
Exhibition	19.9	55.7	105
Festival	40.1	97.7	127.6
Film	9	35	8
Internet	16.2	23	50
Mobilisation	73.5	120.4	427.9
Publication	52.2	25.8	21.8
Research	3.4	0	0
Training	4.1	4	45

Presidential grants for non-commercial organisations in 2016 awarded millions of roubles to patriotic proposals, including a 3.1 million rouble grant to promote Slavic unity for the pro-Kremlin biker group Night Wolves, 3 million roubles to stage a patriotic cross-country motor rally for the veterans group Combat Brotherhood (*Boevoe bratstvo*), and a further 3 million roubles to the Immortal Regiment movement to create a hotline to counteract 'information warfare and manipulative technologies' that suggest negative interpretations of the events and outcomes of the Second World War (Kozlov 2016).[8] Even pro-business environmentalists called for 'ecological patriotism to form the basis for a new national idea' and wryly suggested the Kremlin apply 'import substitution' (that is, to create domestic alternatives) to groups like the World Wildlife Foundation and Greenpeace (Chernykh 2016). More than ever before in post-Soviet Russia, patriotism has become a form of symbolic capital that is produced, monitored and regulated by the state.

If patriotism is now an unavoidable feature of Russian politics, what is it supposed to mean for ordinary members of the public? In the SPPE's original formulation in 2001, patriotic education was oriented towards 'the formation and development of an identity, possessing the qualities of a patriot of the Motherland and readiness to fulfil one's civic duties in times of peace and war' (Gosudarstvennaia programma 2001). With the programme's most recent incarnation, the government's ambitions expanded to include fostering civic accountability for the fate of the country, consolidating society behind national security and development goals, strengthening attachment to the history and culture of Russia, facilitating generational continuity, and educating citizens who love their motherland and family (Gosudarstvennaia programma 2015).

Before proceeding to the fieldwork analysis, a few points are worth making about this definition of patriotism. First, the programme is aimed at *citizens* rather than ethnic Russians. The 2006 state programme acknowledges the importance of Russia's multinational character and the mutual influence of national cultures for patriotic upbringing and social progress (Gosudarstvennaia programma 2005), while later programmes include activities that celebrate multi-ethnicity and tolerance. This fits broadly with Helge Blakkisrud's (2016) analysis of Putin's speeches as stopping short of pursuing 'clear-cut ethnonationalism' while maximising the Kremlin's room for manoeuvre. Second, the *state* is conspicuous by its absence – indeed, funding for programmes related to state symbols and state history declined precipitously after 2006–10. The text of the programme makes individual interests and duties appear subordinate to society, motherland and family, though these themes are not prioritised in the programme budget. Third, patriotic participation in the life of the country is envisioned in terms of ensuring its security and development. Political participation of citizens is not addressed or encouraged.

In sum, state patriotism after Crimea differs from the kind of patriotism that was propagandised immediately after the turn of the millennium. It moved from a relatively minor background goal during the initial stages of state centralisation to becoming a state doctrine, such that it now potentially touches on all aspects of public politics and life. Compared to the more commemorative forms of patriotism that dominated the previous decade, the Kremlin prefers mobilisational and competitive activities that provide opportunities to demonstrate loyalty and readiness to defend the state. And though the state largely avoids openly addressing ethnicity in the context of patriotism, ethnicity may still be found in Soviet-style celebrations of inter-ethnic tolerance (the 'friendship of peoples' trope), the emphasis on unity with other Slavic states, or the promotion of Cossack military traditions.

From everyday patriotism to everyday ethnicity

Observing the ways that patriotism matters in people's everyday lives is somewhat more complicated than evaluating state patriotism. All vernacular understandings of patriotism in Russia begin with the commonplace definition or patriotism as 'love for the motherland' (*liubov' k rodine*). Beyond this throwaway phrase, we find a whole range of actions and activities associated with patriotism. For most people, patriotism is individual and local. They feel an intense attachment to their *malaia rodina* (little motherland)[9] and they enjoy visiting and learning about different parts of their home regions – but the motherland as a whole is felt to be too abstract and distant to be meaningful. In daily life, Russians associate patriotism with clean living, raising one's children properly, not making trouble for others, doing one's job and improving one's surroundings. While these associations cropped up regularly in interviews and focus groups, participants commonly worried that they differed from 'real patriots' – that is, those who support the government and come closer to the state media's portrayal of patriots.

In interviews and focus group discussions, it became clear that participants felt that patriotism *ought* to be easy to understand, though defining it proved contentious. In both contexts, participants sought ways first to elaborate and then to simplify the concept. This movement towards simplifying the notion of patriotism holds part of the key for understanding its transformation into nationalism – because, in both settings, ethnicity and *ethnicising* (attributing ethnic meaning or significance) emerged as important for reducing conceptual complexity and patrolling social boundaries (see Barth 1969; Wimmer 2013).

Ethnicising is a persistent practice that is common, though not ubiquitous, in discussions of patriotism in Russia. Out of sixty-three in-depth interviews, ethnicising was observed in twenty-five cases (39 per cent), occurring most frequently with reference to Russian ethnicity. By contrast, migrants were mentioned only once, while multi-ethnicity and religion each were mentioned just three times.

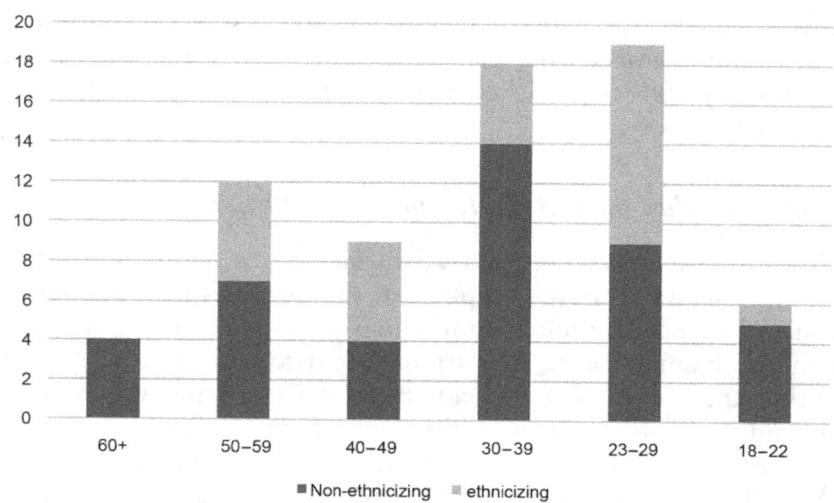

Figure 11.2 Ethnicising by age group (number of respondents)

The correspondence between patriotism and dominant ethnicity was not incidental. As one respondent put it, 'if you call yourself a Russian (*russkii*), then that is already to be a patriot. I think that these words aren't even differentiated' (Respondent 154217). Among all categories of respondents, ethnicising was observed predominantly among youth (twenty-three to twenty-nine years) – the generation targeted by the SPPE since its inception in 2001, even though respondents in this age group generally considered themselves unaffected by it (see Figure 11.2).

Differentiating patriotism from nationalism

Ethnicising plays a subtle role in bridging vernacular conceptions of patriotism and nationalism. In popular usage, patriotism and nationalism appear to be categorically opposed: 'nationalism' is used in reference to chauvinism, extremism or separatism, whereas 'patriotism' is unifying, tolerant and pluralistic. Almost all respondents noted this sharp difference in connotations:

> Patriotism has a 'plus' sign, nationalism has a 'minus'. Nationalism assumes that one nation is higher, one is lower. Patriotism does not. We simply love our motherland and our people, but it doesn't mean that other countries and peoples are worse. (Respondent 112556)

However, the ways in which Russians differentiate patriotism and nationalism belie an ethnic understanding of the nation as essentially related to both concepts. More specifically, the categorical difference claimed between the concepts obscures the extent to which they share an ethnic core.

At a fundamental level, ethnicising mediates and simplifies understandings of patriotism. This is especially relevant in the context of the SPPE's call for people to embrace their belonging to a single 'great history and culture', as the meaning of this single history and culture is something of a cipher. The extent to which this single culture is unambiguously assumed to be ethnic rather than civic or multinational finds expression in how respondents perceive the relationship between nationalism and patriotism:

> Ours is a large, multinational country, *so it is easy to confuse love for the motherland with love for one's nation, one's ethnicity* . . . And here it is very easy to hop over the line from loving the motherland to loving [ethnic Russians] and then we have the problem of nationalism and patriotism. (Respondent 115924)[10]

> A country's patriots can only be people of different nations, and nationalism is the expression of one nation. . . . Right now we have a kind of 'patriotic nationalism'. As if [ethnic Russians] are praising themselves. As yet it hasn't crossed the line into nationalism. But it's a very thin boundary. (Respondent 154510)

Thus, distinguishing 'good' (or 'patriotic') nationalism from 'bad' nationalism emerges as more important than differentiating patriotism from nationalism. The salient difference between 'good' and 'bad' nationalism lies in the extent to which one's goals or motivations are viewed as extremist or chauvinistic, while the categorical distinction between patriotism and nationalism is secondary.

> I understand that nationalism on its own is not bad. Its extreme forms are bad, when it declares that we are better than the rest. Up to that point, in itself love for being *russkii*, pride that I'm Russian – this is good and this is nationalism, in principle. (Respondent 122134)

Respondents made similar distinctions between 'correct' and 'incorrect' patriotism, in which the former involves love and respect while the latter involves xenophobia. What distinguishes good nationalism from patriotism? While nationalism is about one's own nation or ethnicity, patriotism is about the motherland – and yet the motherland is understood in essentially ethnic terms.

The ethnicisation of everyday patriotism

Patriotism is defined almost universally as 'love for the motherland', while the motherland, in turn, is principally associated with one's place of birth, family, culture and history. In practice, Russian ethnicity (and, more precisely, ways of being Russian) and loving the motherland are indistinguishable:

> It's interesting to me that people say that loving the motherland means sacrifice. That is, for example, I love the Russian language very much, I love Russian literature, I love Russian culture . . . cinema, music, everything connected with literature – [I love them] unconditionally. Russian is my native tongue and I really like it, I like to speak it, I like to hear it, but I also like to study other languages and I feel myself 100 per cent Russian in that way, in a cultural sense. That is, I am never embarrassed to say in other countries that I am from Russia, that is, I don't have any problems. That is for me, given my Slavic appearance. (Respondent 182619)

By contrast, few respondents drew a connection between patriotism and citizenship – and even then, they did so in order to explain how they are fundamentally different. Citizenship is treated as little more than a legal category, conferring no benefits or obligations (other than military service). In other words, it is the boundaries of the motherland rather than the state that determine membership in the *patria* in the collective imagination. That is not surprising: the boundaries and institutions of the state have changed over time (sometimes radically), while one's connection to the notion of motherland provides a sense of its endurance.

Ethnicising works in distinctly different ways, depending upon the nature of co-occurrence. It is not imposed 'from above', as state patriotism rarely emphasises ethnic themes and generally promotes inter-ethnic tolerance. Nevertheless, Russians make sense of complex international conditions and especially the conflict in Ukraine in terms of ethnicity as a powerful, unifying force – whether in terms of Russian ethnic peculiarities, Slavic ethnic unity (rarely), or in terms of defining essential differences between Russia and the (seemingly non-ethnic) West. In recounting the effects of the conflict in Ukraine on social ties, one respondent related a now-familiar story of patriotism as activated along ethnic cleavages even within families:

> ... we have friends, a younger married couple. She's Ukrainian but hasn't lived there for years. He's Russian, though his surname is also Ukrainian. I met with her literally two weeks ago and she told me that when these events [in Ukraine] arose, when everything started up, 'what didn't I hear from my warring husband?' ... And you understand, this is just one family, but she says 'this is my husband, see, *he's a patriot. For him everything is black or white, there are no shades of grey.*' (Respondent 143359)[11]

It is important to note that ethnicising practices do not emerge solely in support of regime policy. For instance, opposition to the government's activation of patriotism in the war with Ukraine may similarly provoke ethnicisation:

> ... despite all the recent events in Ukraine, we have a great many relatives in Ukraine with whom we stay in touch, and we worry about them because, all the same, it's a tie. That is, regardless of whatever their political agitation, [their] government's attempt to turn everything negative, and here maybe there's something similar ... *all the same, it is the blood ties. Historical ties. They're still there, though all politicians are trying to change it.* (Respondent 122134)[12]

In these cases, ethnicising reduces the patriotic complexities surrounding events in Ukraine's domestic politics and Russia's intervention, interpreting politics in terms of ethnicity and suppressing dissent even within the family. Ethnicity thus becomes bound up with political loyalty in the sense of both defining and demanding it: being *russkii* requires one to be a patriot, and vice versa.

In other aspects of daily life unrelated to the ongoing conflict in Ukraine, instances of state patriotism emerge – whether activated via educational institutions, the workplace or domestic politics – that provide opportunities for celebrating the dominant ethnicity:

> ... for example, our department is developing a textbook on the history of *russkaia* [ethnic Russian] culture. In fact, it deals not just with *russkaia* culture, but with general culture and history. And when I agreed to work on the project, I had exactly this sort of feeling. Possibly it was patriotism, to propagandise certain *russkaia* culture ... I had literature, so maybe my patriotism was for this propaganda: to show this is *russkii* – *russkaia* culture, *russkaia* literature, music. (Respondent 103302)

Here, ethnicising both expresses and simplifies patriotism by distilling its essence in ethnic terms. Notably, it departs from the government's encouragement to celebrate the history and achievements of the Russian state and its multinational people, substituting the dominant ethnicity in their place.

Ethnicising also featured in respondents' comparisons of Russian and Western varieties of patriotism. In general, respondents used comparisons with the West to document Russia's normality. For example,

> The concept of patriotism for us hasn't changed its meaning, not in pre-revolutionary Russia, not in the Soviet era, not now. That is, it always signifies love for the motherland, for one's fatherland, but if we take other states for example, you can see similar cases. For instance, you could look at the war for independence of the US, the conflict between Great Britain and its North American colonies. You've probably seen the Mel Gibson movie, *The Patriot*? (Respondent 145058)

> In any case, Russia is a multinational country. There is ... a widely shared opinion that the USSR was a 'prison of nations'. This is because it united peoples by force, one has to admit, including small nations. It was the same in your country's history, as in the history of any large state. (Respondent 145822)

But when non-Russian ethnicity is brought into focus, comparisons shift from accounting for Russia's normality to explaining its exceptionality. Consider the following interview excerpts:

> I cannot call myself a patriot of Russia. That is, I can't in the same way an American citizen considers himself to be a patriot of America. Because there, losing his ethnic identity, he becomes simply an American – well, conditionally. . . . But the situation is different here. We have 120 peoples at a minimum, of which 15–20 are fully developed ethnic groups with their own history and culture. See, I myself belong to one of these ethnic groups, the Tatars, one of the largest after Russians. For them, let's say, I do not fully identify myself with Russian culture and history. (Respondent 110526)

> Russia is a multinational country. People love their country but they don't love *russkie* [ethnic Russians] in this country. All the same, the culture in this country is connected with the culture of one nation. Though we have a lot of nations, Russia is associated with *bliny*, crosses – the culture of the Russian nation. . . . They say 'I'm from Russia, I'm *russkii*', even if one is a Tatar or Azeri. But by mentality he is *russkii*. (Respondent 112556)

At first glance, these comparisons show very different orientations to majority and minority ethnicity in Russia. In the first, the respondent worries that ethnicising is what separates Russian from American patriotism insofar as one cannot be anything but ethnic in Russia. In the second, the respondent claims that non-Russians are Russified by association with the state (and ethnic Russians as representatives of the state-bearing culture). Despite their differing perspectives, both respondents proceed from a common starting point: that ethnicity fundamentally defines the individual's (inevitable) identification with the state. This is a classic example of the ways in which dominant ethnicities enshrine ethnic values and attributes in the trappings of civic nationality, as ethno-cultural membership, citizenship and identification with the state are bound together. Russianness is thus 'unmarked' (Brubaker et al. 2006: 214), but its activation goes some way towards indicating how patriotism in Russia is converted into nationalism in daily life.

Conclusions

All states draw upon relatively similar repertoires to cultivate national identification and legitimacy. Russia's repertoires of state patriotism are no different, though bounded by tsarist- and Soviet-era traditions. While everyday understandings of patriotism are far more varied and apolitical than the state's version (Goode 2016), people also feel that state patriotism ought to be simple and intuitive. When state patriotism gets complex, many Russians – over a third of the respondents in this study – turn to ethnicity to simplify and articulate the relationship between loyalty and motherland.

In this regard, the fact that ethnicisation is not imposed 'from above' makes it especially powerful. The Russian state advances a version of patriotism premised upon multi-ethnic citizenship that nationalists criticise for neglecting ethnic Russians as a state-bearing people. Nevertheless, the Kremlin occasionally signals when ethnic appeals are appropriate, as with Putin's invoking of ethnic and historical ties to justify the annexation of Crimea. Similarly, citizens individually may carry apolitical and idealistic notions of patriotism, but they draw upon dominant ethnicity to fill in the affective gaps in state patriotism and to simplify otherwise complex orientations towards state and nation: ethnicising construes loyalty and citizenship in terms of ethnic membership, while patriotism binds ethnicity to the state by way of the motherland. 'Loving the motherland' thus allows ethnic Russians to celebrate dominant ethnicity without being labelled nationalists. This way of differentiating between patriotism and nationalism further means that the state is categorically excluded from being considered as nationalist. What really distinguishes a patriot from a nationalist in practice is loyalty to regime rather than ethnic sentiment.

This finding has two important implications. First, public displays of patriotism are inevitably associated with regime loyalty rather than civic participation – meaning that the difference between patriotism and nationalism in Russia is political and coercive in the sense of being binding and not open to choice. This may explain the broad public consensus behind state patriotism despite private doubts, in which even homeless people and State Duma deputies share common views and emotions regarding Russia's leaders, the country's status as a great power, its domestic challenges and its future prospects (Kasamara and Sorokina 2011). Moreover, it may account for how nationalist support for the annexation of Crimea could arise 'suddenly' from within shared observance and participation in state patriotism.

A second implication is that scholars of nationalism may have missed (or mis-identified) potential nationalisms by treating patriotism as distinct from, or opposed to, nationalism. By problematising the relationship between patriotism and nationalism at the intersection of state policies and everyday lives, the constructivist approach adopted in this study reveals the manner in which overtly patriotic mobilisation could become ethnicised and nationalist in content, even if nationalist actors failed to declare themselves as such. This insight has potentially broad relevance for the comparative study of post-Soviet politics. Given the shared legacy of territorialised nationality and the modularity of state patriotic practices across the post-Soviet space, re-evaluating instances of popular mobilisation like the post-Soviet 'colour revolutions' in Georgia, Ukraine and Kyrgyzstan as forms of nationalist mobilisation may help to explain divergent paths of political development after regime change. Examining shared patriotic repertoires and ethnicised patriotism may further shed light on the nature of authoritarian legitimacy among post-Soviet states, as well as the appeal of public diplomacy and the success of soft-power projection across post-Soviet Eurasia. Thus, further study of everyday patriotism promises not just to explain instances of nationalist mobilisation, but to provide an ideational basis for comparing and explaining the trajectories of post-Soviet politics.

Notes

1. A previous version of this chapter was presented at the conference 'Nation-building and Nationalism in Today's Russia', Tallinn University, Estonia, 28 April 2016. My thanks to conference participants, and especially to Pål Kolstø, Helge Blakkisrud, David Stroup and Jesko Schmoller, for helpful comments on earlier drafts.

2. Co-occurrence is used here to mean that a patriotic practice is discussed in close proximity to ethnicisation during an interview. In other words, co-occurrence marks actions and ideas that contextualise conversation, even if respondents do not specifically discuss them as causally related to one another. In this sense, observing and measuring co-occurrence may be understood as a form of indirect observation.
3. Fieldwork funding for this research was provided by a Fulbright FLEX grant. All interviews were conducted by me, transcribed by an assistant, and entered into Nvivo for coding and analysis. My thanks to Ekaterina Semushkina (Tiumen) and Valeriia Umanets (Perm) for their valuable research assistance.
4. I am grateful to Oleg Lysenko and his team at Perm State Pedagogical University for facilitating and conducting these focus groups.
5. A full discussion of this relationship would go well beyond the confines of this chapter. For an authoritative examination, see Valerii Zhuravlev (2015).
6. It is perhaps worth noting that this common translation is derived from patria or fatherland (*otechestvennyi*) rather than being a direct translation of *patrioticheskii*.
7. For a discussion of nationalist innovation as a response to regime signals, see Goode (2012).
8. For the full list of presidential grants awarded to support non-governmental organisations (NGOs) since 2013, see <https://grants.oprf.ru/competitions> (last accessed 11 April 2017).
9. Interview respondents most often spoke of the 'little motherland' in referring to their place of birth, though it sometimes simply meant where they were living at present.
10. Emphasis added.
11. Emphasis added.
12. Emphasis added.

Bibliography

Adorno, Theodor W. (1950), *The Authoritarian Personality*, New York: Harper.
Ahram, Ariel I. and J. Paul Goode (2016), 'Researching authoritarianism in the discipline of democracy', *Social Science Quarterly*, 97, 4: 834–49.
Anderson, Benedict (2006), *Imagined Communities: Reflections on the Origin and Spread of Nationalism*, London: Verso.
Barth, Frederik (1969), *Ethnic Groups and Boundaries*, Boston, MA: Little, Brown & Co.
Billig, Michael (1995), *Banal Nationalism*, London: Sage.
Blakkisrud, Helge (2016), 'Blurring the boundary between civic and ethnic: the Kremlin's new approach to national identity under Putin's third term', in Pål Kolstø and Helge Blakkisrud, eds, *The New Russian*

Nationalism: Imperialism, Ethnicity and Authoritarianism, 2000–15, Edinburgh: Edinburgh University Press, 249–74.

Blum, Douglas W. (2006), 'Official patriotism in Russia: its essence and implications', PONARS Policy Memo, 420, <http://www.ponarseurasia.org/memo/official-patriotism-russia-its-essence-and-implications> (last accessed 17 March 2017).

Bonikowski, Bart (2016), 'Nationalism in settled times', *Annual Review of Sociology*, 42, 1: 427–49.

Bourdieu, Pierre (2007), *Outline of a Theory of Practice*, New York: Cambridge University Press.

Brubaker, Rogers (2004), 'In the name of the nation: reflections on nationalism and patriotism', *Citizenship Studies*, 8, 2: 115–27.

Brubaker, Rogers, Margit Feischmidt, Jon Fox and Liana Grancea (2006), *Nationalist Politics and Everyday Ethnicity in a Transylvanian Town*, Princeton, NJ: Princeton University Press.

Chernykh, Aleksandr (2016), 'Patriotizm – poslednee pribezhishche ekologii' [Patriotism: the last refuge of ecology], *Kommersant*, 7 April, <http://www.kommersant.ru/gallery/2957238> (last accessed 7 April 2016).

de Certeau, Michel (1984), *The Practice of Everyday Life*, Berkeley, CA: University of California Press.

Druckman, Daniel (1994), 'Nationalism, patriotism, and group loyalty: a social psychological perspective', *Mershon International Studies Review*, 38, 1: 43–68.

Dwyer, Sonya Corbin and Jennifer L. Buckle (2009), 'The space between: on being an insider-outsider in qualitative research', *International Journal of Qualitative Methods*, 8, 1: 54–63.

Fenton, Steve (2007), 'Indifference towards national identity: what young adults think about being English and British', *Nations and Nationalism*, 13, 2: 321–39.

Fox, Jon E. (2004), 'Missing the mark: nationalist politics and student apathy', *East European Politics and Societies*, 18, 3: 363–93.

Fox, Jon E. and Cynthia Miller-Idriss (2008), 'Everyday nationhood', *Ethnicities*, 8, 4: 536–63.

Gillespie, David (2005), 'Defence of the realm: the "new" Russian patriotism on screen', *The Journal of Power Institutions in Post-Soviet Societies*, 3, <http://pipss.revues.org/369> (last accessed 25 October 2014).

Goode, J. Paul (2012), 'Nationalism in quiet times: ideational power and post-Soviet electoral authoritarianism', *Problems of Post-Communism*, 59, 3: 6–16.

Goode, J. Paul (2016). 'Love for the motherland (or why cheese is more patriotic than Crimea)', *Russian Politics*, 1, 4: 418–49.

Goode, J. Paul and David R. Stroup (2015), 'Everyday nationalism: constructivism for the masses', *Social Science Quarterly*, 96, 3: 717–39.

Gosudarstvennaia programma (2001), 'Patrioticheskoe vospitanie grazhdan Rossiiskoi Federatsii na 2001–2005 gody' [State programme 'Patriotic Education of Citizens of the Russian Federation for 2001–2005'], 16

February, <http://gospatriotprogramma.ru/previous-first-and-second-of-the-state-program/the-first-state-programme-of-patriotic-education-2001-2005-.php> (last accessed 8 August 2016).

Gosudarstvennaia programma (2005), 'Patrioticheskoe vospitanie grazhdan Rossiiskoi Federatsii na 2006–2010 gody' [State programme 'Patriotic Education of Citizens of the Russian Federation for 2006–2010'], 11 July, <http://gospatriotprogramma.ru/previous-first-and-second-of-the-state-program/the-second-state-programme-of-patriotic-education-in-2006-2010.php> (last accessed 8 August 2016).

Gosudarstvennaia programma (2015), 'Patrioticheskoe vospitanie grazhdan Rossiiskoi Federatsii na 2016–2020 gody' [State programme 'Patriotic Education of Citizens of the Russian Federation for 2016–2020'], 30 December, <http://gospatriotprogramma.ru/upload/gospotriot_2016_2020.pdf> (last accessed 8 August 2016).

Hobsbawm, Eric J. (1992), *Nations and Nationalism since 1780: Programme, Myth, Reality*, New York: Cambridge University Press.

Horvath, Robert (2015), 'The Euromaidan and the crisis of Russian nationalism', *Nationalities Papers*, 43, 6: 819–39.

Ignatieff, Michael (1993), *Blood and Belonging: Journeys into the New Nationalism*, New York: Farrar, Straus and Giroux.

Il'in, Nikolai (2015), 'Formirovanie osnovnykh tipov natsional'noi ideologii ot M. V. Lomonosova do N. Ia. Danilevskogo' [Formation of basic types of national ideology from Mikhail Lomonosov to Nikolai Danilevskii], in Valerii Zhuravlev, ed., *Patriotizm i natsionalizm kak faktory Rossiiskoi istorii (konets XVIII v.–1991 g.)* [*Patriotism and Nationalism as Factors in Russian History (from the End of the 18th Century to 1991)*], Moscow: Rosspen, 9–112.

Kasamara, Valerii and Anna Sorokina (2011), 'Obraz Rossii v diskurse politicheskoi elity i rossiiskikh bezdomnykh' [Images of Russia in the discourse of political elites and Russian homeless], *POLIS: Politicheskie issledovaniia*, 4: 171–84.

Kohn, Hans (2005), *The Idea of Nationalism: A Study in Its Origins and Background*, New Brunswick, NJ: Transaction Publishers.

Kolstø, Pål (1984), 'The concept of "patriotic internationalism": a contribution to the understanding of Soviet ideology', *Nordic Journal of Soviet and East European Studies*, 1, 4: 1–29.

Kolstø, Pål (2006), 'National symbols as signs of unity and division', *Ethnic and Racial Studies*, 29, 4: 676–701.

Kolstø, Pål (2016), 'Crimea vs. Donbas: how Putin won Russian nationalist support – and lost it again', *Slavic Review*, 75, 3: 702–25.

Kosmarskaya, Natalya and Igor Savin (2016), 'Everyday nationalism in Russia in European context: Moscow residents' perceptions of ethnic minority migrants and migration', in Pål Kolstø and Helge Blakkisrud, eds., *The New Russian Nationalism: Imperialism, Ethnicity and Authoritarianism, 2000–15*, Edinburgh: Edinburgh University Press, 132–59.

Kosterman, Rick and Seymour Feshbach (1989), 'Toward a measure of patriotic and nationalistic attitudes', *Political Psychology*, 10, 2: 257–74.

Kozlov, Viacheslav (2016), 'Prezidentskie granty dostalis' tserkvi, veteranam i baikeram' [Presidential grants won by churches, veterans and bikers], RBK, 5 July, <http://www.rbc.ru/politics/05/07/2016/576fe0ea9a7 9473c15c0fda5> (last accessed 21 March 2017).

Kremlin.ru (2016), 'Vstrecha s aktivom Kluba liderov' [Meeting with members of the Club of Leaders], 3 February, <http://kremlin.ru/events/president/news/51263> (last accessed 8 August 2016).

Laruelle, Marlene (2009), *In the Name of the Nation: Nationalism and Politics in Contemporary Russia*, New York: Palgrave Macmillan.

Laruelle, Marlene (2015), 'Patriotic youth clubs in Russia: professional niches, cultural capital and narratives of social engagement', *Europe–Asia Studies*, 67, 1: 8–27.

Le Huérou, Anne (2015), 'Where does the motherland begin? Private and public dimensions of contemporary Russian patriotism in schools and youth organisations: a view from the field', *Europe–Asia Studies*, 67, 1: 28–48.

Magaril, Sergei (2016), 'Smysly patriotizma – istoricheskie transformatsii' [Meanings of patriotism: historical transformations], *Sotsis: Sotsiologicheskie issledovaniia*, 1: 142–51.

Martynov, Mikhail (2009), 'Zametki o poniatiiakh "natsionalizm" i "patriotizm"' [Notes on the concepts of 'nationalism' and 'patriotism'], *Sotsis: Sotsiologicheskie issledovaniia*, 11: 138–41.

Mummendey, Amélie, Andreas Klink and Rupert Brown (2001), 'Nationalism and patriotism: national identification and out-group rejection', *British Journal of Social Psychology*, 40, 2: 159–72.

Norris, Stephen M. (2012), *Blockbuster History in the New Russia: Movies, Memory, and Patriotism*, Bloomington, IN: Indiana University Press.

Odesskii, Mikhail and Dmitrii Fel'dman (2008), 'Ideologema "patriot" v russkoi, sovetskoi i postsovetskoi kul'ture: lozung i rugatel'stvo' [The ideologeme 'patriot' in Russian, Soviet and post-Soviet culture], *Obshchestvennye nauki i sovremennost'*, 1: 109–23.

Oushakine, Serguei (2009), *The Patriotism of Despair: Nation, War, and Loss in Russia*, Ithaca, NY: Cornell University Press.

Palmer, Catherine (1998), 'From theory to practice: experiencing the nation in everyday life', *Journal of Material Culture*, 3, 2: 175–99.

Parker, Christopher S. (2010), 'Symbolic versus blind patriotism: distinction without difference?' *Political Research Quarterly*, 63, 1: 97–114.

Schatz, Robert T., Ervin Staub and Howard Lavine (1999), 'On the varieties of national attachment: blind versus constructive patriotism', *Political Psychology*, 20, 1: 151–74.

Shevel, Oxana (2011), 'Russian nation-building from Yel'tsin to Medvedev: ethnic, civic or purposefully ambiguous?' *Europe–Asia Studies*, 63, 2: 179–202.

Skey, Michael (2012), '"Sod them, I'm English": the changing status of the "majority" English in post-devolution Britain', *Ethnicities*, 12, 1: 106–25.
Smith, Kathleen E. (2002), *Mythmaking in the New Russia: Politics and Memory during the Yeltsin Era*, Ithaca, NY: Cornell University Press.
Sperling, Valerie (2003), 'The last refuge of a scoundrel: patriotism, militarism and the Russian national idea', *Nations and Nationalism*, 9, 2: 235–53.
Stockdale, Melissa K. (2006), 'United in gratitude: honoring soldiers and defining the nation in Russia's Great War', *Kritika: Explorations in Russian and Eurasian History*, 7, 3: 459–85.
Suslov, Mikhail D. (2014), '"Crimea is ours!" Russian popular geopolitics in the new media age', *Eurasian Geography and Economics*, 55, 6: 588–609.
Teper, Yuri (2016), 'Official Russian identity discourse in light of the annexation of Crimea: national or imperial?' *Post-Soviet Affairs*, 32, 4: 378–96.
Verkhovsky, Alexander (2016), 'Radical nationalists from the start of Medvedev's presidency to the war in Donbas: true till death?', in Pål Kolstø and Helge Blakkisrud, eds., *The New Russian Nationalism: Imperialism, Ethnicity and Authoritarianism, 2000–15*, Edinburgh: Edinburgh University Press, 75–103.
Whitmeyer, Joseph M. (2002), 'Elites and popular nationalism', *British Journal of Sociology*, 53, 3: 321–41.
Wimmer, Andreas (2013), *Ethnic Boundary Making: Institutions, Power, Networks*, Oxford: Oxford University Press.
Yack, Bernard (1996), 'The myth of the civic nation', *Critical Review*, 10, 2: 193–211.
Zhuravlev, Valerii, ed. (2015), *Patriotizm i natsionalizm kak faktory rossiiskoi istorii (konets XVIII v. –1991 g.)* [*Patriotism and Nationalism as Factors in Russian History (from the End of the 18th Century to 1991)*], Moscow: Rosspen.

12

Identity in Crimea before annexation: A bottom-up perspective

Eleanor Knott

Whatever the case, Russia will have to deal with the effects of Crimea being part of an independent Ukraine for 23 years. . . . Russia is not the motherland of an entire generation of Russian-speaking youth who are coming of age, but the motherland of their ancestors. (Andrei Malgin 2014)

Beyond Perekop, there is no land for us. (Vasilii Zaitsev 1981)

What is the lived experience of Russian identity and nationalism beyond Russia? In this chapter, I aim to complement existing research which examines the contemporary salience, if not resurgence, of nationalism within Russia from the top down and the bottom up (Kolstø and Blakkisrud 2016) with a case study of Crimea, a region where the majority of residents are assumed to identify as ethnically Russian. I use the approach of everyday nationalism to examine the meanings of identifying as ethnically Russian in Crimea to unpack how, prior to the 2014 annexation, being Russian was articulated, experienced, negotiated and subverted, and opposed to, or combined with, being Ukrainian and/or Crimean.

Throughout the chapter, I argue for a more nuanced understanding of Crimea. I challenge the dominant framing of Crimea that sees the peninsula as populated by a majority who identify strongly and uniformly as ethnically Russian and express pro-Russian sentiments and support of separatism. Similarly, I challenge the assumption that identity and territorial preferences are associated: that being Russian determines and explains territorial preferences (here: support for separatism). Such a framing would argue that Crimea's de facto secession from Ukraine – and annexation by Russia – has a simple explanation: a belligerent kin-state (Russia) and a supportive populace (Crimean society) finally got what they had been wanting ever since the collapse of the Soviet Union. Instead, I argue that, in the period immediately prior to the annexation (2012–13), separatism was framed as impossible and undesirable, even by the minority who were most vociferously and actively pro-Russian.

To support this argument, I use interview data to examine questions of identity from the bottom up to problematise a simplistic and homogenising understanding of the experiences and meanings of Russian identity in Crimea prior to annexation. In particular, I argue for conceptually and empirically disentangling the often-elided ideas of identification *as* ethnically Russian (*russkii*) and identification *with* Russia, and consider different ways of being Russian (politically, culturally, territorially, linguistically and ethnically) vis-à-vis being Ukrainian and/or Crimean. To do this, I briefly discuss different ways of conceptualising identity in Crimea, using data I gathered before annexation (in 2012 and 2013) to construct inductive categories of identity. This enables a more systematic discussion of the multiplicity of identities in Crimea in terms of identifying *as* Russian, Ukrainian and Crimean, and *with* Russia, Ukraine and Crimea, by constructing five inductively derived identification categories (Knott 2015b).

Next, I consider each inductive category in turn in terms of territorial preferences and imaginings vis-à-vis Ukraine (support for status quo) and Russia (support for separatism). Here, irrespective of Russian identification and support of Russia, I find backing for the status quo and a lack of support for separatism. Most importantly, I identify opposition to separatism even among members of organisations such as Russian Unity (*Russkoe edinstvo*, RE) and the Russian Community of Crimea (*Russkaia obshchina Kryma*, ROK), organisations that supported, if not facilitated, Russia's annexation of Crimea in 2014. Overall, I argue, the majority of interlocutors saw Crimea as a legitimate part of Ukraine. Even the minority that questioned Ukraine's legitimacy were supportive of a 'bad peace' over a 'good war' (Laitin 1998: 8), and thus did not back the kind of bloody conflict they thought secession/annexation might require. I conclude by discussing the theoretical implications of my findings, assessing the value of an everyday nationalism perspective on Russian identity and nationalism beyond Russia before and during a time of crisis.

Identity debates in post-Soviet Crimea

Identity in Crimea has frequently been conceived in mutually exclusive terms. Census data, for example, show Crimea (with Sevastopol) to be an ethnic outlier within Ukraine: the only region where the majority, according to the 2001 census, identified ethnically as Russian (see Figures 12.1 and 12.2). Hence, in Crimea, the otherwise Ukrainian majority is a minority, while the otherwise Russian minority is a majority – and moreover, the Ukrainian minority overwhelmingly speak Russian as their everyday language (see Figure 12.3).

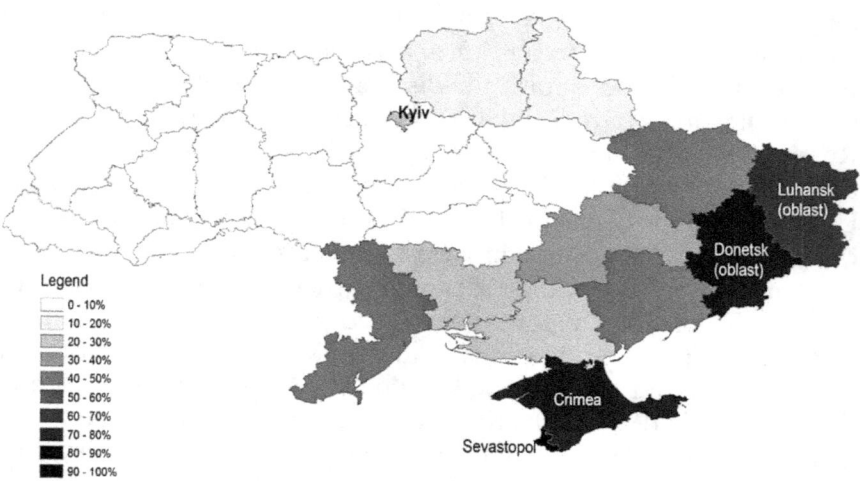

Figure 12.1 Russian language use in Ukraine according to the 2001 Ukrainian census (State Statistics Committee of Ukraine 2001)

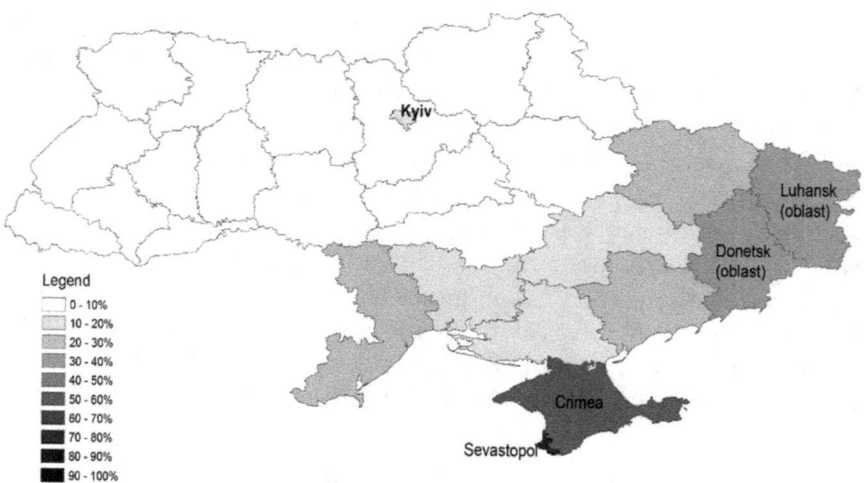

Figure 12.2 Russian ethnicity in Ukraine according to the 2001 Ukrainian census (State Statistics Committee of Ukraine 2001)

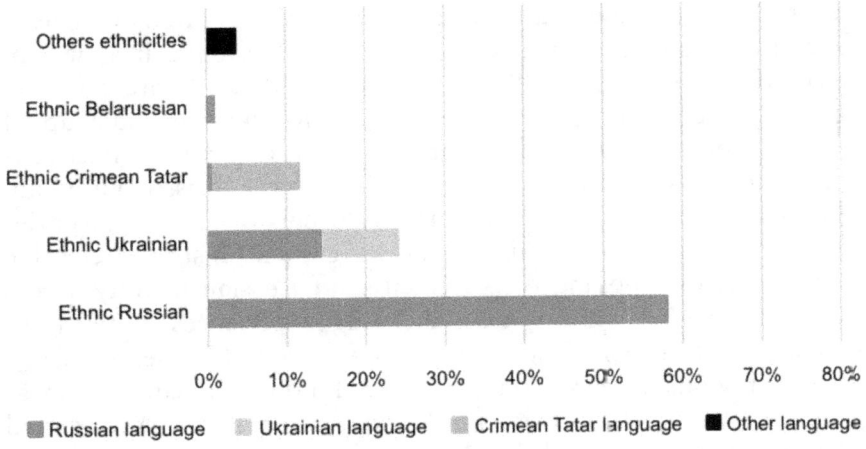

Figure 12.3 Language and ethnicity in the 2001 Ukrainian census (State Statistics Committee of Ukraine 2001)
Note: Percentages add up to 100: 58 per cent identify as ethnic Russian and speak Russian, 14.5 per cent identify as ethnic Ukrainian and speak Russian, 9.8 per cent speak Ukrainian and identify as Ukrainian, etc.

Surveys frequently adopted such a mutually exclusive approach when collecting data about how people identify (see, for example, Razumkov Centre 2009; International Republican Institute 2013). This approach offers little insight into *how* and *why* individuals choose and interpret certain categories, and experience, negotiate and subvert these categories in their everyday lives. For example, a Razumkov survey asked respondents to choose between different homelands (Ukraine, the USSR, Russia or their local region) (Pop-Eleches and Robertson 2014), assuming that respondents had mutually exclusive notions of 'homeland', rather than an overlapping one where it would be possible to belong to – and identify with – both Ukraine and Russia at the same time (see Kolstø 1996). In this context, Crimea appears to be a region that is 'hegemonically' an ethnic and linguistic Russian 'zone' (Arel 2002: 243). Analytically, therefore, Crimea appears 'Other' to Ukraine. This status was institutionally buttressed by a (notional) status of autonomy vis-à-vis Kyiv that allowed for regional de facto and *de jure* rights supporting Russian language and culture in the peninsula, and that offered a means to dissipate – and institutionalise – tensions between Kyiv and Crimea after Crimea's failed secession attempt in 1994 (Sasse 2007).

This sense of being 'Other' to Ukraine was also important for how Crimea was researched – or at least how being Russian was researched in Ukraine and Crimea. For example, research on identity debates in Ukraine often overlooked Crimea, framing it as unrepresentative of the rest of Ukraine (Fournier 2002). Andrew Wilson (2002) conceptualised a 'middle ground' in Ukraine made up of Russian speakers who hold mixed views of their ethnic self-identification, and who prefer to identify with the 'Russo-Ukrainian' category rather than with the mutually exclusive census categories of either 'Russian' or 'Ukrainian'. However, Wilson studied Ukraine as a whole, overlooking the specificities of Russian identity across Ukraine's diverse regions, with differing experiences in terms of language, culture and history (see, for example, Narvselius 2012). While previous research has considered how Russian identification functions in other regions of Ukraine, such as the Donbas, and how this interrelates with local/regional economic and social practices (Narvselius 2012; Osipian and Osipian 2012), these debates in Crimea have remained largely untouched.

In this gap, where Crimea was framed as not representative of the rest of Ukraine, the notion of Crimea as a region populated by ethnic Russians promulgated an idea that this majority was necessarily and uncritically pro-Russian and pro-Russia (see, for example, Hedenskog 2008; Maigre 2008; Barrington and Faranda 2009; Kuzio 2010). This was based on the assumption that this (Russian) majority was cohesive in terms of its identification and preferences. Likewise, the fact that many people in Crimea held Russian passports was, according to this perspective, taken as indicating lack of loyalty to Ukraine and loyalty towards Russia instead, which in turn determined support for Russian irredentism (Shevchuk 1996; Maigre 2008). With Crimea being framed as a pro-Russian Trojan horse of pro-Russian fifth columnists, the peninsula was presented as a region of potential instability and insecurity (Krushelnycky 2008; Kuzio 2010).

Such perspectives could appear validated by the annexation of Crimea in 2014. Here, however, I am not going to problematise this argument. Rather I will try to unpack the meaning of being Russian in Crimea, and the existence of support for Russia within Crimea. Thus, I engage with the potential internal heterogeneity and dynamic politics and social relations within Crimea vis-à-vis Ukraine and Russia. This approach is supported by more nuanced, albeit top-down, analysis such as that of Tetyana Malyarenko and David J. Galbreath (2013: 917), who argue for a perspective that can contradict the notion of mutually exclusive 'ethnic Russian' and 'ethnic Ukrainian' communities in Crimea. Malyarenko and Galbreath make the case that Russians and Ukrainians in Crimea 'consistently behave as one actor' (that is, collapse mutually exclusive categories) and identify overwhelmingly as 'Crimeans'. They argue that Crimean residents have preferred this Crimean multi-ethnic identification because of their 'greater sense of regional difference from the rest of Ukraine', cementing Crimean as the dominant identity and thus a cleavage vis-à-vis Ukraine, rather than an ethnic Russian/Ukrainian cleavage (ibid.: 918). Hence, we see that not only was Crimea framed as different to other Ukrainian regions, if not to Ukraine itself, Crimean residents also framed themselves as different to the rest of the population of Ukraine – in part because of a lack of differentiation between different ethnic 'groups' in Crimea.

Other studies, such as a 2009 Razumkov Centre survey, identify a large 'Slavic community' in Crimea (Razumkov Centre 2009). They describe this as a 'pan-ethnic group' made up of ethnic Russians and Ukrainians. Like Wilson's 'middle ground', members of this category speak Russian at home, consider Russian their native language, affiliate with a Russian 'ethnic cultural tradition' and see no difference between ethnic Russians and Ukrainians in Crimea. They thus challenge research in Crimea from the early 1990s that pitted ethnic Ukrainians and ethnic Russians, as separate categories, against each other, or at least as expressing different political preferences (see, for example, Bremmer 1994).

A further contradictory, if not counter-intuitive, trend discussed by Malyarenko and Galbreath (2013) is that, up to 2014, elite and popular support for separatism had consistently decreased since its apex in the mid-1990s. Before 2014, then, separatism could no longer 'represent a serious threat to Ukraine's territorial integrity' (Mizrokhi 2009: 2; see also Figure 12.4). Rather, it was in Russia's interest to 'exaggerate the danger and potency' of pro-Russian sentiment and the support of pro-Russian political and cultural organisations within Crimea. In that way, Moscow could bolster its interests within Crimea (for example, the stationing of Russia's Black Sea Fleet) and hinder Ukrainian political projects (like NATO integration) (ibid.).

Overall, these varying perspectives present an interesting, if not confounding, picture of ethnic identification and territorial preferences in Crimea. They point to a gap in understanding, from the bottom up and in terms of lived experience, of what it means (or meant) to be Russian in Crimea, and how this idea of being Russian interacted with ideas of being Ukrainian and Crimean, and with identifying with Russia, Ukraine or Crimea. Everyday nationalism

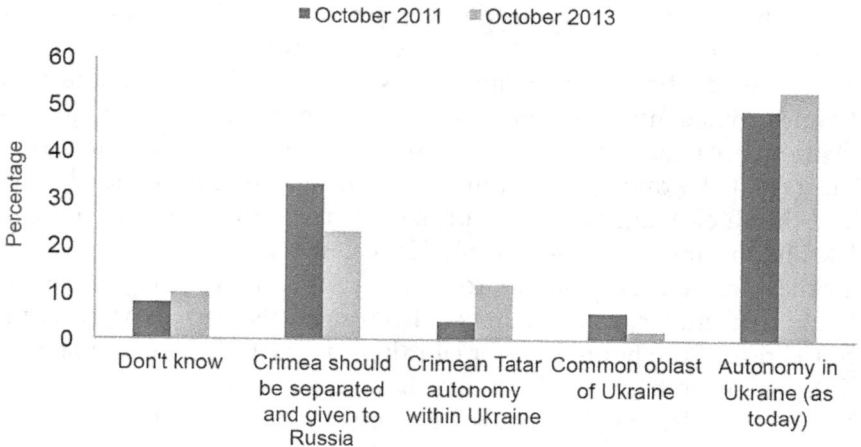

Figure 12.4 'In your opinion, what should the status of Crimea be?' (International Republican Institute 2014)

(see Brubaker et al. 2006; Fox and Miller-Idriss 2008), as the approach of this chapter, offers a way to analyse – and unpack – how being Russian was articulated, experienced, negotiated and subverted, and opposed to, or combined with, being Ukrainian and/or Crimean.

A second gap concerns territorial preferences – support for different territorial configurations from the bottom up – and how these preferences intersect with identification as ethnically Russian and with Russia. Such potential territorial preferences include status quo (remaining within Ukraine), separatism (Crimean independence) and irredentism (unification with Russia). The question – and explanation – of territorial preferences has become more potent since annexation. The data discussed here, collected in 2012 and 2013, present a window for analysing these aspirations in the period preceding the Russian annexation.

Using everyday nationalism to study Crimea from the bottom up

To address these two gaps, I apply the approach of 'everyday nationalism' to consider bottom-up perspectives on questions of nationalism and ethnicity (de Cillia et al. 1999; Brubaker et al. 2006; Fox and Miller-Idriss 2008; Kosmarskaya and Savin 2016). As I have argued elsewhere, this approach is useful for dealing with questions of cross-border co-ethnic identification, that is, kin-state politics, as in the case of the relationship between Crimea and Russia (Knott 2015a).

Everyday nationalism builds on Rogers Brubaker and Frederick Cooper's argument that we should move away from categories of *analysis*, such as census categories, or at least problematise these, and instead consider categories of *practice* – that is, 'lay' categories of 'everyday social experience' used by 'ordinary social actors' (Brubaker and Cooper 2000: 4). The aim here is to gather data which can explore how individuals 'appropriate, internalise, subvert, evade or transform' categories such as mutually exclusive census categories 'that are imposed upon them' (Brubaker et al. 2006: 12; see also Fox and Miller-Idriss 2008: 537), as well as to address issues of how far ethnicity is salient in everyday life (Brubaker et al. 2006).

Methodologically, there is a difference between scholars who use indirect and direct approaches to study nationalism as a category of practice (that is, everyday nationalism). John E. Fox and Cynthia Miller-Idriss (2008) use an indirect approach, studying how nationhood is practised by observing how individuals talk about, choose, perform and consume the nation. Other scholars use a more direct approach, such as interviews (Fenton 2007) and focus groups/group interviews (de Cillia et al. 1999; Skey 2011), while maintaining the focus on the meanings and lived experience of ethnic identification. Following the latter, I adopted a more direct approach, using interviews to ask about how and why individuals identify in certain ways, with what territorial entities, and how they envisage future relations between Crimea, Ukraine and Russia. This maintains the experience-near focus of everyday nationalism (see Knott 2015b) even if it differs, methodologically and in terms of the data derived, from the more indirect approach used by Fox and Miller-Idriss (2008).

To complement existing research, which recognises the importance, if not resurgence, of nationalism within Russia (Kolstø and Blakkisrud 2016), this chapter focuses on everyday Russian nationalism *beyond* Russia, in the case of Crimea. Crimea is a significant case for analysing everyday nationalism because of the intersection of a period of increasing nationalism within Russia with a period that predated crisis in Ukraine but culminated in Russia's annexation of the peninsula in February–March 2014. Using the everyday nationalism approach is also useful for studying Russians abroad within debates concerning the politics of Russia's 'beached diaspora', debates that have focused either on the potential for mobilisation and separatism (Kolstø 1996) or the lack of mobilisation capacity

(Smith and Wilson 1997). Here, however, I do not limit my study to the organisational capacity of Russians abroad to mobilise as a diaspora, as that would have focused on only the most pro-Russian elements within Crimea. Rather, I seek to explore the variation and spectrum of identification as 'Russian' and 'with Russia', and to what extent this has consequences (or not) for territorial preferences such as separatism or status quo.

The study is based on fifty-three interviews that I conducted in 2012 and 2013, with the final interviews being collected just eight months prior to Crimea's annexation. I interviewed everyday social actors representing a variety of perspectives across the political spectrum, in particular from the post-Soviet generation (for example, representatives of the youth wings of political parties and student organisations as well as non-politically involved youth). This research did not begin as a deliberate study of the post-Soviet generation, but it became evident that these individuals were both more accessible for initial contact (via the Internet and snowballing) and easier to build rapport with, perhaps because they were less suspicious of my being a 'spy'. I made initial contact with large numbers of people, by phone or email, either by cold calling (based on Internet sources of organisations) or snowballing (using the recommendation of previous respondent).

The interlocutors discussed here represent a diversity of ages – from eighteen to sixty+, but with around half being in their twenties – and of places of birth (in Crimea, elsewhere in Ukraine/the Ukrainian Soviet Socialist Republic, and Russia/the RSFSR). As residents of Simferopol, Crimea's administrative centre, most respondents were university educated. I do not argue that this sample of interlocutors is representative of Crimea: the size is too small to warrant this claim or evaluation (see Small 2009). Rather, following Peregrine Schwartz-Shea and Dvora Yanow (2012), I sought a diversity and richness of perspectives to allow for analysis and critique of the existing literature on Crimea.

In the first empirical section below, I analyse discussions of what it meant to be Russian in Crimea in 2012–13, conceptualised by constructing inductively derived identification categories. The second section uses these categories to analyse my interlocutors' territorial aspirations. This analysis is employed to demonstrate the lack of association between identity and territorial aspirations, or at least lack of support for territorial reconfiguration (separatism or unification) irrespective of identification.

Identity in pre-annexation Crimea

To demonstrate the fractures evident in notions of identifying *as* Russian and *with* Russia, I present five inductively derived identification categories that show areas of agreement between interlocutors (within categories) as well as disagreement (across categories).

DISCRIMINATED RUSSIANS

The category of 'discriminated Russians' is made up of those who identified most strongly as ethnically Russian and, as a counterpoint, were anti-Ukrainian, identifying themselves primarily in terms of feeling victimised and discriminated by the state which Ukraine had become after 1991. Many of these interlocutors were affiliated with local Russian and compatriot organisations based in Simferopol, such as the ROK and its political affiliate, RE, organisations that, as mentioned, were central in supporting Crimea's annexation in 2014.

The defining characteristic of these interlocutors was their strong identification as Russians and with Russia. For the 'discriminated Russians', Crimea was a legitimate (cultural) part of Russia, a 'Russian cultural enclave' (C-19a, C-48a, C-48). They saw themselves as victims of Ukraine's 'forced' policy of Ukrainisation (*ukrainizatsiia*), which they believed was designed to 'assimilate Russians' (C-25, C-24) and to erase Russian perspectives and the Russian language from Crimea as well as from the rest of Ukraine. As such, these 'discriminated Russians' lacked attachment to Ukraine, feeling themselves to be unwanted 'stepchildren' in the Ukrainian state which was, according to one interlocutor, 'against me as a citizen' (C-24).

The category of 'discriminated Russians' is a 'category of practice' as opposed to a 'category of analysis' (see Brubaker and Cooper 2000). That is to say, I conceive of them as 'discriminated Russians' because this is how they conceived of themselves: as ethnic Russian and as discriminated by the Ukrainian state. The point is not to make a judgment as to their objective or actual discrimination but rather to focus on how this was a key, and distinguishing, trope of these individuals in terms of their identification (as well as of the pro-Russian organisations many of them were affiliated with, which served to reinforce this sense of discrimination). There was thus a cleavage between ethnic Russians who felt victimised and marginalised by Ukraine's post-Soviet policies, and ethnic Russians who identified with the Ukrainian state (categorised here as 'ethnic Russians').

Ethnic Russians

The 'ethnic Russians' identified primarily as ethnically Russian and saw Russia as their cultural homeland. However, they felt less culturally threatened by the Ukrainian state than did the 'discriminated Russians' and did not see problems in identifying as ethnically Russian and residing in Ukraine. The 'ethnic Russians' identified Russian culture as 'native' (C-14b, C-15, C-34). Being ethnically Russian was not a choice: 'every culture is transmitted through blood and mother's milk' – or, as some interlocutors put it: 'I think in Russian so I am Russian' (C-21, C-3, C-22). Crimea too was, historically, 'Russian land' and a 'Russian enclave' (C-8, C-9, C-14b, C-53) and Russia remained the 'big motherland' (*bol'shaia rodina*) and 'historical motherland', whereas Crimea was the 'little motherland' (*malaia rodina*) (C-3, C-15, C-34, C-53). However, this was counter-balanced by less favourable attitudes to Russia as a political entity, as Russia was perceived as 'not understanding' Crimea: Putin merely wanted to undermine and disrespect Ukrainian politicians (C-22). Equally, the same interlocutor explained, Ukraine did not understand that identifying as Russian and speaking Russian were not the same as being a 'patriot of Putin' (C-22).

This sense of being Russian was also balanced by the legitimacy this category gave to being part of Ukraine as 'my state' (C-21, C-8, C-22, C-46). Thus, the 'ethnic Russians' managed to reconcile being Russian with residing in Ukraine. They challenged the claims advanced by the 'discriminated Russians' that Russian language and culture were threatened in Crimea, and in Ukraine more broadly. For example, they did not see language as an 'acute issue' and did not observe a 'strangulation of Russian culture' (C-21, C-22). Rather, disputes over language were 'at the political level, the establishment level'– at the everyday level, there were no differences, as people could speak the language they wished (C-22, C-53).

Crimeans

The 'Crimeans' problematised two mutually exclusive ethnic categories, by identifying 'firstly' as Crimean. They justified this identification because of where they lived (in Crimea) and because they identified being Crimean as an inter-territorial and inter-ethnic category that reflected how they situated themselves between Ukraine and Russia, and between Ukrainian and Russian (C-2a).

Identifying as Crimean allowed this group of interlocutors to negotiate their sense of complexity in having mixed parents and experiences of Ukraine, Crimea and Russia. As they explained, Crimea itself was 'partly Russian, partly Ukrainian' (C-36, C-38). The 'Crimeans' reconciled their confusion and hybridity by identifying as 'more Crimean' (C-38), which allowed them to remain connected to the peninsula and to identify as simultaneously, but not fully, Ukrainian as well as Russian.

In general, this category included relatively few interlocutors compared to the larger categories of 'ethnic Russians' and 'political Ukrainians' (see Table 12.1). What is significant is that they *did* identify themselves, in their own words, as Crimean (*krymchan*) as a way of negotiating the hybrid meanings of what it meant to be from Crimea – territorially, culturally and personally.

POLITICAL UKRAINIANS

The 'political Ukrainians' also resisted ethnic identification categories and instead identified as being Ukrainian citizens first. This category is interesting, as it demonstrates resistance to subscribing to mutually exclusive and ethnic categories (ethnic Ukrainian vs ethnic Russian). For the interlocutors in this category what was considered important was *political* membership as Ukrainian. It was their common experiences of being part of Ukraine, rather than ethnic divisions, which mattered because, as one interlocutor claimed, 'citizens live badly, irrespective of ethnicity' (C-23).

Several 'political Ukrainians' explained how 'I feel myself as a citizen [of Ukraine], regardless of ethnicity' (C-23, C-47), because Ukraine is 'my home' (C-59). They did not identify as Russian because they were 'not born in Russia', but in Crimea, which 'is Ukraine'. Also significant was the fact that many of this group had been born, or had grown up, when Ukraine was an 'independent state' (C-31), that is, after 1991, meaning that Russia was somewhere foreign, and somewhere they felt foreign (C-28, C-59).

Crucially, the 'political Ukrainians' signalled the dynamism of identity in Crimea by pointing out the sense of difference they felt from their parents, who identified as ethnic Russians. They also signalled how, in post-Soviet Crimea, it was possible to be Ukrainian without being ethnically Ukrainian. They were the generation that had *become* Ukrainian, in a political sense. This demonstrates the contingency of ethnic identification where identity is not necessarily

Table 12.1 Conceptualising identity in Crimea

	Number of interlocutors	Native language	Identify as ...			Identify with ...		
			Russian	Ukrainian	Crimean	Russia	Ukraine	Crimea
Discriminated Russians	9	Russian	X		X	X		X
Ethnic Russians	18	Russian	X		X	partially	X	X
Crimeans	5	Russian	X	X	X		X	X
Political Ukrainians	15	Russian		X	X	X	X	X
Ethnic Ukrainians	6	Ukrainian		X			X	

experienced in terms of common descent, but has been modified and produced by political experiences.

Ethnic Ukrainians

Finally, respondents in the last category, 'ethnic Ukrainians', did not identify with Russian culture or language: they demonstrated a strong attachment to Ukraine, speaking Ukrainian as their 'native' language and being part of Ukrainian culture. These 'ethnic Ukrainians' identified as Ukrainian 'by birth' – incidentally, all of them were born outside Crimea – and expressed 'love' for Ukraine and Ukrainian culture (C-45, C-26). This was a diverse group, made of respondents who were not born on the peninsula, but who had arrived in Crimea during the Soviet or post-Soviet period as children, to study or for work. As contemporary residents of Crimea, they recognised that Russian was the 'dominant' language in Crimea, even if 'Ukrainian is the state language' (C-13, C-26, C-45).

While the 'ethnic Ukrainians' recognised the practicality of speaking Russian in Crimea, they considered the identity component of *being* Russian in Crimea as a false consciousness: Soviet policies had made everyone 'Russian-speaking', hence 'many have become pro-Russian' even though 'they are not identical to the Russians' (C-49). These 'ethnic Ukrainians' believed 'ethnic Russians' held misguided and nostalgic views about Russia, that Russia was taken to represent 'something ideal, beautiful' (C-27), even though many had 'never been to Russia' (C-49).

The 'ethnic Ukrainians' are included in this analysis of Russian identity because the category demonstrates an interesting generational and regional contrast to the 'political Ukrainians'. For 'ethnic Ukrainians', identifying as Ukrainian and being from Crimea were mutually exclusive. Their identification as Ukrainian was territorial, linguistic and cultural as opposed to political, and they saw Ukraine and Crimea as conceptually and culturally distinct, not as overlapping concepts.

Fractured Meanings of Identifying as Russian in Pre-annexation Crimea

As summarised in Table 12.1, this analysis has highlighted different ways of being Russian and how being Russian is appropriated, negotiated and hybridised with ideas of being Ukrainian, belonging to Ukraine, and being Crimean. As we have seen, the idea of being

Russian in Crimea was highly complex and contested, accompanied by notions of feeling threatened and victimised by Ukraine (the 'discriminated Russians'), of reconciling being Russian with belonging to Ukraine, at least politically (the 'ethnic Russians') or of hybridising with being Ukrainian (the 'Crimeans'). Being Russian – and moreover, being defined by ethnicity – was also rejected by some interlocutors, who preferred to focus more on their political sense of belonging to Ukraine (the 'political Ukrainians). Being Russian was, therefore, far from an accepted or homogenising idea in Crimea, at least in the period preceding the Russian annexation.

Following this logic, it is important to contest the view of Crimea as a region populated by a 'Russian majority'. That being said, in line with the methodological approach of this chapter, it is also important to recognise the contingency and context specificity of identity debates in Crimea. Identity debates are not only dynamic during 'peaceful' periods (as was the case between 1994 and 2014), but also can be profoundly affected by extreme political events, such as the fall of the Soviet Union in 1991 and the 2014 annexation of Crimea.

Territorial aspirations in pre-annexation Crimea

In the following I draw on the five categories developed above, examining the territorial aspirations of each category by analysing interlocutors' preferences for territorial status quo or reconfiguration, and their justification of these preferences. Addressing these issues has become increasingly important due to Crimea's secession from Ukraine and its annexation by Russia in 2014. As will be shown, the 2014 events contrast to the data considered here, with both the secession and the annexation being framed as undesirable and unlikely by most interlocutors, irrespective of how they identified as Russian and with Russia.

DISCRIMINATED RUSSIANS

The 'discriminated Russians' felt part of the 'fraternity of Russian people' that had been divided by 'artificial' post-Soviet borders, a process in which they had no agency because 'we did not leave Russia' (C-20, C-55, C-46, C-19b, C-20). Moreover, the organisational ties of these 'discriminated Russians' demonstrated how far this identity was politicised, and how identifying as Russian and engaging in pro-Russian organisational activities were mutually reinforcing. As such, these individuals might be expected to be the most likely within

Crimea to support territorial revision in the form of separatism and/or unification with Russia (see Kolstø 1996).

However, these symbolic ties did not determine their territorial preferences: it emerged that the 'discriminated Russians' neither supported nor promoted territorial change. As C-19b argued:

> We're not talking about the fact that Crimea in this situation should secede from Ukraine, we understand that it is impossible to make this happen without bloodshed, without a cataclysm. We want to live peacefully, we here are sensible people who want to continue living here.

Thus, from these interviews conducted in 2012 and 2013, it was evident that individuals associated with pro-Russian organisations such as ROK and RE (as C-19b was) saw neither themselves nor their organisations as backing territorial reconfiguration – although these same organisations would come to support Russian annexation of Crimea in 2014.

Fundamental to their rejection of territorial change was their belief that separatism would incur costs of conflict and bloodshed that they were unwilling to bear; they preferred the territorial status quo as a peaceful option (C-24). This speaks to observations concerning early post-Soviet Latvia made by David Laitin (1998: 8) of the preference for a 'bad peace' over a 'good war'. In situating themselves as peaceful and law-abiding, the 'discriminated Russians' also framed Crimean Tatars as the 'main source of separatism', whereas they themselves were constructively wanting to 'develop' Ukraine, rather than dismantle it (C-24, C-25, C-19b). Overall, the 'discriminated Russians' demonstrated a lack of support for territorial reconfiguration that can be explained by their support for peace and a path-dependent vision of the future, with Crimea's divorce from Russia – and Russia's unwillingness to intervene – as signifying a future within Ukraine.

Ethnic Russians

Most of the 'ethnic Russians', like the 'discriminated Russians', supported Crimea's territorial status quo vis-à-vis Russia and Ukraine. Thus, C-34 emerges as an outlier among all interlocutors in revering Russia and supporting Crimea's (re)unification with Russia, framing the fact that Crimea was part of Ukraine and not of Russia as 'historical error' (C-34). By contrast, most 'ethnic Russians' rejected separatism because they saw it as leading to 'conflict' (C-9,

C-53). They referred to those who had championed separatism in the 1990s as 'political losers' – and those who currently supported separatism as motivated by self-interest in reaping 'some kind of political, economic and financial benefits' from this project (C-3, C-21).

Hence, the 'ethnic Russians' criticised the fixation of the *'rossiiane'* (Russian citizens in Russia) on the 'return' of the 'gold mine', that is, of Crimea (C-22). They described how Russia and Russian citizens conceived of Crimea as Russia's rightful property, to be consumed and enjoyed by the *rossiiane* (C-51). For example, C-51 parodied a conversation with a Russian citizen who asked 'When will Crimea go to Russia? How is it there? And who ate our *salo* [salted lard]?' C-51's imagined response was that 'I say, you know, I don't know who ate your salo or when Crimea will join Russia – probably it will never happen.'

In contrast to the *rossiiane*, who were seen as holding onto the idea of Crimea's unification with Russia, for these 'ethnic Russians', separatism/unification was a failed and undesirable project (C-53). Instead, they generally supported the integration of Crimea within an independent Ukraine and felt a 'solidarity' with Ukraine that was absent among the 'discriminated Russians' (C-57b). Pragmatically they wanted good relations with Russia as 'two states' – like, for example, Germany and Austria today: as two separate but culturally and linguistically similar states. They felt spiritual closeness to Russia rather than loyalty (*vernost'*) to the Russian state, and this closeness did not undermine their ability to be a 'patriot' of Ukraine at the same time (C-53, C-8, C-21, C-7, C-22).

Crimeans

Like members of the two previous categories, the 'Crimeans' in this study framed Crimea as 'stable', 'normal' and a 'part of Ukraine' (C-36, C-38). Separatism was depicted as a historical movement, supported 'only in the 1990s' (C-38). Now this was undesirable: the 'Crimeans' associated separatism with negative outcomes in other post-Soviet states, a fate that Crimea had been spared:

> Yes, the political situation is calm. After all, Crimea is now completely dependent on Kyiv. . . . it was unstable, because there was talk that Crimea might separate from Ukraine [but this was] only in the 90s, when Ukraine became independent . . . in 1991–92, and so on . . . But thank God, that did not happen. . . . If Crimea had separated from Ukraine, in Crimea there would have been about the same as what happened in

Transnistria, what happened in Georgia, Azerbajan ... In Crimea there would have been great nationalist clashes ... (C-38)

This interlocutor explained how this was a positive outcome not only for Ukraine and Crimea, but also for Russia, which was not 'ready' to support Crimean secession (and annexation), in view of the financial costs of providing material resources, such as pensions, to 'two and a half million people' (C-38).

Only C-57a supported a more Russian-focused solution. This was not something he would 'speak about aloud' or campaign for, because he was happy to remain part of Ukraine (C-57a). However, he believed that Crimea was already cognitively 'separate' and could be 'perfectly self-reliant', if not 'better in Russia' (even though he admitted he had 'never been there [in Russia]') (C-57a).

POLITICAL UKRAINIANS

Identifying as 'patriots' of Ukraine, the 'political Ukrainians' supported Ukraine's independence and separation from Russia. They resisted both Russification (*russifikatsiia*) within Ukraine as well as Ukraine's policy of a single state language, as they wanted both Ukrainian and Russian to be recognised as official languages (C-12, C-31, C-30, C-11a, C-11b, C-18). Moreover, they welcomed a strengthening of Ukraine's borders and sense of independence vis-à-vis Russia (C-23).

The 'political Ukrainians' rejected separatism, framing it as a first step towards Russian annexation, as Crimea could not exist by itself (C-18). However, they also framed separatism as 'impossible', because constitutionally, any decisions on the status of Crimea would require an 'all-Ukrainian referendum' (C-18).[1] In this climate, Crimea appeared as 'stable' and 'very loyal, calm' – there was 'no desire' for separatism any longer (C-28, C-32).

ETHNIC UKRAINIANS

The 'ethnic Ukrainians' described Crimea as 'a single whole' with Ukraine and framed this as 'very important' (C-49, C-45). They were pleased that the 'attractiveness of Russia' had weakened for Crimean society; this led them to believe that since independence Ukraine was 'developing quite peacefully' with 'no bloody conflict' (C-26, C-27, C-49). However, unlike the other categories, the 'ethnic Ukrainians' saw growing 'insecurity' in Crimea (C-49). While support for

Russia was 'decreasing every year', they lacked faith in Crimean society, believing that 'tomorrow' there could be a referendum in which '63–70 per cent might vote' in support of separatism (C-49).

This sense of personal contrast to the imagined majority in Crimea reinforced the often-assumed association between identity and territorial preferences. Whereas I have sought to challenge this assumption here, it is important to recognise that it was a salient association for those of my interlocutors who identified as 'ethnic Ukrainians', serving as a cultural identification linked to not being 'from' Crimea.

Meanings vs territorial preferences: support for the status quo

As with identity, territorial preferences can be contingent, responding to and affected by political changes. Yet, it remains an important empirical finding that, in the period preceding Russia's 2014 annexation of Crimea, interlocutors in this study were supportive of the territorial status quo, as opposed to separatism or unification with Russia (Table 12.2).

Significantly, regardless of the various ways in which my interlocutors identified (or not) as Russian, all but one individual supported the territorial status quo, seeing Crimea as a legitimate part of post-Soviet Ukraine. Whereas there was variation as regards the meanings of ethnic identification *as* Russian and *with* Russia, this variation converged when it came to support for Crimea as being a legitimate part of Ukraine: how my interlocutors identified did thus not determine their territorial aspirations concerning the peninsula.

The 'discriminated Russians', in particular, were a surprise in terms of their support for territorial status quo. This support can be explained by their preference for peace over a conflict that might lead to bloodshed, even if peace left them feeling discriminated. This

Table 12.2 Territorial aspirations, by inductively derived identification category

	Support separatism?	Reason
Discriminated Russians	No	Support peace
Ethnic Russians	No	Crimea as legitimate part of Ukraine
Crimeans	No	Crimea as legitimate part of Ukraine
Political Ukrainians	No	Crimea as legitimate part of Ukraine
Ethnic Ukrainians	No	Crimea as legitimate part of Ukraine

discourse of a 'discriminated' and victimised ethnic Russian majority aligned with the views of pro-Russian political and cultural organisations within Crimea, which used the notion of marginalisation and victimisation vis-à-vis Ukraine to engage with – and mobilise – their core supporters, notably the elderly. Still, separatism was not on the agenda of the 'discriminated Russians' in this study.

Conclusions

In this chapter I have applied the 'everyday nationalism' approach in examining questions of Russian nationalism beyond Russia, more specifically issues of Russian identity and territorial preferences in Crimea, and the relationship between identity and territorial preferences. Drawing on data collected in 2012 and 2013, only months before the 2014 annexation of Crimea, I have scrutinised and problematised assumptions that Crimea – in contrast to elsewhere in Ukraine – was a territory populated by an ethnic Russian majority, and that ethnicity was what determined the people's support – culturally, politically and territorially – for Russia. In the wake of Russia's annexation of Crimea, this logic has been used to argue *as if* Crimea were a region characterised by popular support for separatism and weak consent for Crimea remaining part of Ukraine. By contrast, I have demonstrated the varying meanings of Russian identification in Crimea. The chapter has examined how being Russian was experienced and associated (or not) with preferences for secession/unification with Russia, and has shown the different ways of being Russian and Ukrainian, identifying with Russia, Crimea and Ukraine. A major finding is that many members of the post-Soviet generation identified politically as Ukrainian, even if their parents considered themselves ethnically Russian.

I also found that these identity cleavages, in terms of strength and different assemblages of identification, neither determined nor mapped onto territorial preferences. Rather, most of my respondents supported the territorial status quo with Crimea remaining as a legitimate and peaceful part of Ukraine: they held that reconfiguration would entail uncertainties that were unappealing or directly negative. This finding is crucial, as it shows that even the most pro-Russian elements within Crimea (politically, organisationally and in terms of identification) did not support territorial change in the period immediately prior to the annexation, as they perceived the costs to be too high. That is not to say they did not aspire for stronger relations with Russia – but these aspirations were not territorially framed, as they came to be by 2014.

This reveals a different empirical picture of Crimea from the dominant discourse, in particular around the Russian annexation of Crimea *as if* the majority at least passively endorsed such reconfiguration. While recognising the fluidity and contingency of identity and territorial preferences, I agree with Malyarenko and Galbreath's observation that secessionist sentiment was decreasing. As we have seen, separatists were seen as failures of the 1990s that were now out of place in the contemporary political scene. The explanation for why support for separatism and unification was decreasing in Crimea is premised on a path-dependent notion of Russia's relationship to Crimea and Ukraine, as well as Ukraine's relationship to Crimea. The situation changed with the departure of Ukrainian President Viktor Yanukovych in February 2014. The ensuing securitisation and militarisation of Russia's relations with Ukraine is certain to have affected contemporary, post-annexation forms of identification and territorial preferences.

However, as this chapter shows, the case of Crimea and annexation remains a puzzle, and cannot be explained away by alleged pre-existing territorial preferences. After twenty-three years, Russian authorities shifted their stance politically and militarily, albeit perhaps not discursively, towards legitimising their right to intervene in Ukraine. But, how did the organisations which seemed not to support secession up to 2014 come to support, if not facilitate, annexation? One possible explanation lies in the ascent to power of the leaders of these organisations, such as Sergei Aksenov, leader of Russian Unity 2008–14, who became head of the Republic of Crimea, and the ability of these leaders to empower their friends and family members[2] in the midst of Ukraine's Euromaidan revolution.

Overall, the everyday nationalism approach offers important analytical leverage for studies of Russian nationalism in Russia as well as within ethnic Russian communities abroad – and for studies of nationalism in general. It can provide a voice and sense of nuance to debates of nationalism, complementing analysis of state-based forms of imperial or ethnic nationalism (Kolstø 2016; Pain 2016). It focuses attention on sentiments of nationalism and ethnic identity from the bottom up and in everyday terms, in order to examine how ethnic and kin-state identification are given meaning through everyday life, whether in terms of ethnic relations vis-à-vis migrants within Russia (Kosmarskaya and Savin 2016), or what it means to be Russian abroad, as this chapter has discussed.

This everyday perspective offers an important counterpoint to top-down studies of Russian nationalism which focus on elites and nationalism in moments of crisis (like the conflict in Ukraine) for understanding how identity functions in the banality of everyday life. It also points to the contingency of identity, nationalism and territorial preference in response to the dynamics of political contexts. This provides evidence that can contest simplistic explanations, like seeing the Russian annexation of Crimea *as if* this were a post-Soviet inevitability to be explained by the combined lack of support for the Ukrainian state and the backing of unification with Russia. In this chapter I have emphasised the heterogeneity of meanings concerning what it meant to be Russian in Crimea prior to 2014 as well as the homogeneity of territorial preferences: widespread support for a known 'bad peace', as opposed to the potentially destabilising unknowns of a 'good war'.

Notes

1. This requirement was flagrantly flouted in Crimea's 2014 status referendum, which was held only in Crimea and Sevastopol.
2. For example, Aksenov's father Valerii Aksenov and his sister-in-law Evgeniia Dobrynia were given places on the United Russia list for the Crimean parliamentary elections in 2014.

Bibliography

Arel, Dominique (2002), 'Interpreting "nationality" and "language" in the 2001 Ukrainian census', *Post-Soviet Affairs*, 18, 3: 213–49.
Barrington, Lowell and Regina Faranda (2009), 'Reexamining region, ethnicity, and language in Ukraine', *Post-Soviet Affairs*, 25, 3: 232–56.
Bremmer, Ian (1994), 'The politics of ethnicity: Russians in the new Ukraine', *Europe–Asia Studies*, 46, 2: 261–83.
Brubaker, Rogers and Frederick Cooper (2000), 'Beyond "identity"', *Theory and Society*, 29, 1: 1–47.
Brubaker, Rogers, Margit Feischmidt, Jon Fox and Liana Grancea (2006), *Nationalist Politics and Everyday Ethnicity in a Transylvanian Town*, Princeton, NJ: Princeton University Press.
de Cillia, Rudolf, Martin Reisigl and Ruth Wodak (1999), 'The discursive construction of national identities', *Discourse and Society*, 10, 2: 149–73.
Fenton, Steve (2007), 'Indifference towards national identity: what young adults think about being English and British', *Nations and Nationalism*, 13, 2: 321–39.
Fournier, Anna (2002), 'Mapping identities: Russian resistance to linguistic Ukrainisation in Central and Eastern Ukraine', *Europe–Asia Studies*, 54, 3: 415–33.

Fox, Jon E. and Cynthia Miller-Idriss (2008), 'Everyday nationhood', *Ethnicities*, 8, 4: 536–63.
Hedenskog, Jakob (2008), *Crimea: After the Georgian Crisis*, Stockholm: FOI, Swedish Defence Research Agency.
International Republican Institute (2013), *Public Opinion Survey Residents of the Autonomous Republic of Crimea May 16–30, 2013*, <http://www.iri.org/sites/default/files/2013 October 7 Survey of Crimean Public Opinion%2C May 16-30%2C 2013.pdf> (last accessed 17 April 2014).
Knott, Eleanor (2015a), 'Generating data studying identity politics from a bottom-up approach in Crimea and Moldova', *East European Politics and Societies*, 29, 2: 467–86.
Knott, Eleanor (2015b), 'What does it mean to be a kin majority? Analyzing Romanian identity in Moldova and Russian identity in Crimea from below', *Social Science Quarterly*, 96, 3: 830–59.
Kolstø, Pål (1996), 'The new Russian diaspora – an identity of its own? Possible identity trajectories for Russians in the former Soviet republic', *Ethnic and Racial Studies*, 19, 3: 609–39.
Kolstø, Pål (2016), 'The ethnification of Russian nationalism', in Pål Kolstø and Helge Blakkisrud, eds, *The New Russian Nationalism: Imperialism, Ethnicity and Authoritarianism, 2000–15*, Edinburgh: Edinburgh University Press, 18–45.
Kolstø, Pål and Helge Blakkisrud (2016), *The New Russian Nationalism: Imperialism, Ethnicity and Authoritarianism, 2000–15*, Edinburgh: Edinburgh University Press.
Kosmarskaya, Natalya and Igor Savin (2016), 'Everyday nationalism in Russia in European context: Moscow residents' perceptions of ethnic minority migrants and migration', in Pål Kolstø and Helge Blakkisrud, eds, *The New Russian Nationalism: Imperialism, Ethnicity and Authoritarianism, 2000–15*, Edinburgh: Edinburgh University Press, 132–59.
Krushelnycky, Askold (2008), 'Crimean peninsula could be the next South Ossetia', *The Independent*, 28 August, <http://www.independent.co.uk/news/world/europe/crimean-peninsula-could-be-the-next-south-ossetia-910769.html> (last accessed 3 May 2013).
Kuzio, Taras (2010), *The Crimea: Europe's Next Flashpoint?* Washington, DC: Jamestown Foundation.
Laitin, David D. (1998), *Identity in Formation: The Russian-Speaking Populations in the Near Abroad*, Ithaca, NY: Cornell University Press.
Maigre, Merle (2008), *Crimea – the Achilles Heel of Ukraine*, Tallinn: International Centre for Defence and Security.
Malgin, Andrei (2014), 'Krymskii uzel. Chto privelo k "Russkoi vesne"– 2014?' [The Crimean knot: what led to the 2014 'Russian Spring'?], *Global Affairs*, 27 April, <http://www.globalaffairs.ru/number/Krymskii-uzel-Chto-privelo-k-russkoi-vesne-2014-16591> (last accessed 26 February 2015).

Malyarenko, Tetyana and David J. Galbreath (2013), 'Crimea: competing self-determination movements and the politics at the centre', *Europe–Asia Studies*, 65, 5: 912–28.
Mizrokhi, Elena (2009), *Russian 'Separatism' in Crimea and NATO: Ukraine's Big Hope, Russia's Grand Gamble*, Quebec: Université Laval/Chaier de recherche du Canada sur les conflict identitaires at le terrorisme.
Narvselius, Eleonora (2012), *Ukrainian Intelligentsia in Post-Soviet L'viv: Narratives, Identity, and Power*, Lanham, MD: Lexington Books.
Osipian, Ararat L. and Alexandr L. Osipian (2012), 'Regional diversity and divided memories in Ukraine: contested past as electoral resource, 2004–2010', *East European Politics and Societies*, 26, 3: 616–42.
Pain, Emil (2016), 'The imperial syndrome and its influence on Russian nationalism', in Pål Kolstø and Helge Blakkisrud, eds, *The New Russian Nationalism: Imperialism, Ethnicity and Authoritariansim, 2000–15*, Edinburgh: Edinburgh University Press, 46–74.
Pop-Eleches, Grigore and Graeme Robertson (2014), 'Do Crimeans actually want to join Russia?' Washington Post Monkey Cage, 6 March, <http://www.washingtonpost.com/blogs/monkey-cage/wp/2014/03/06/do-crimeans-actually-want-to-join-russia/> (last accessed 1 May 2014).
Razumkov Centre (2009), 'Dominant communities of Crimea: self-identification, character of relations, prospects of their evolution (in Crimean and pan-Ukrainian contexts)', *National Security and Defence*, 5: 1–72.
Sasse, Gwendolyn (2007), *The Crimea Question: Identity, Transition, and Conflict*, Cambridge, MA: Harvard University Press.
Schwartz-Shea, Peregrine and Dvora Yanow (2012), *Interpretive Research Design: Concepts and Processes*, Abingdon: Routledge.
Shevchuk, Yuri I. (1996), 'Dual citizenship in old and new states', *European Journal of Sociology / Archives Européennes de Sociologie*, 37, 1: 47–73.
Skey, Michael (2011), *National Belonging and Everyday Life*, Basingstoke: Palgrave.
Small, Mario Luis (2009), '"How many cases do I need?" On science and the logic of case selection in field-based research', *Ethnography*, 10, 1: 5–38.
Smith, Graham and Andrew Wilson (1997), 'Rethinking Russia's post-Soviet diaspora: the potential for political mobilisation in Eastern Ukraine and North-East Estonia', *Europe–Asia Studies*, 49, 5: 845–64.
State Statistics Committee of Ukraine (2001), 'All-Ukrainian population census', <http://2001.ukrcensus.gov.ua/eng/> (last accessed 2 June 2011).
Wilson, Andrew (2002), 'Elements of a theory of Ukrainian ethno-national identities', *Nations and Nationalism*, 8, 1: 31–54.
Zaitsev, Vasilii (1981), *Za Volgoi zemli dlia nas ne bylo. Zapiski snaipera* [*Beyond the Volga, There Was No Land for Us. Notes of a Sniper*], <http://lib.ru/MEMUARY/1939-1945/PEHOTA/snaiper1.txt> (last accessed 27 November 2013).

Index

Abdulatipov, Ramazan, 8
Abkhazia, 62
abortion, 106
adoption, 74, 100, 105–6
affirmative action empire, 54
Agamben, Giorgio, 95–96
aggression, theories of, 174;
  see also violence
Agurskii, Mikhail, 31
A Just Russia party, 74, 218,
  220, 229
Aksenov, Sergei, 302
Aleksandr I, Tsar, 24
Aleksandr II, Tsar, 25
Aleksandr III, Tsar, 6–7, 26
All-Russian March for
  Peace, 129
All-Russian National Movement,
  6, 146
All-Russian People's Front, 106
All-Russian Social-Christian
  Union for the Liberation
  of the People (*Vserossiiskii
  sotsial-khristianskii soiuz
  osvobozhdeniia naroda*,
  VSKhON), 30
anarchism, 124, 126–30
Anderson, Benedict, 259

anomie, 52
Anpilov, Viktor, 32, 122
anti-alcohol campaigns, 157
anti-authoritarianism, 128, 135
anti-capitalism, 120, 194, 198
anti-Communism, 32–33, 37–38
anti-corruption, 148, 217
anti-establishmentism, 71,
  76, 81
anti-extremism legislation,
  169, 174
Antifa, 177
anti-fascists, 126, 128, 131, 136
anti-gay sentiments, 74,
  104–5
anti-globalism, 64, 127
anti-government protests, 71,
  73–75; see also For Fair
  Elections movement
anti-immigrant sentiments
  anti-migrant campaigns, 147,
    176, 252
  and biopolitics, 99
  and Crimean annexation,
    75–79
  Kremlin policies, 252
  migrantophobia, 158,
    219, 261

Moscow 2013 mayoral elections,
219, 221, 228
and the patent system, 244
pro-Kremlin nationalist groups,
156–57
rise of, 238
anti-imperialism, 34, 36, 149
anti-Islamic/anti-Muslim
sentiments, 59, 61,
225, 240
anti-liberalism, 23, 30, 35, 38
Anti-Maidan movement,
155–56, 157
anti-Putin activism, 73–75
anti-regime nationalism, 6
anti-Russian Spring nationalism, 6
anti-Semitism
history of Russian nationalism,
26, 29
Movement Against Illegal
Immigration (*Dvizhenie protiv
nelegal'noi immigratsii*), 197
national socialists, 132
neo-Nazis, 164, 165, 167,
168, 170
post-Soviet Russia, 31, 154
RNE (Russian National
Unity), 192
anti-Sovietism, 37
anti-Ukrainian Crimeans, 291
anti-US sentiments, 55–56, 57, 58,
59–61, 63, 80, 82
anti-Westernism
and biopolitics, 99, 109
in the history of Russian
nationalism, 53, 127
ideological backing for, 75
morality politics, 74
and patriotism, 265
popular support for, 158
post-Soviet Russian nationalism,
31, 34, 39, 55, 57, 61, 63, 155

and Syria, 82
Antonov, Rostislav, 37
Article 282 (inciting racial hatred),
194, 195
arts
counter-biopolitical, 108
counterculture activists, 122
'Russian character',
28–29
Soviet period, 30
Arutiunian, Iurii, 40, 41
assassinations, 131, 170, 171–72,
176, 177
assimilation, 78, 225, 244,
246, 291
Attack (*Ataka*), 144, 145
authoritarianism, 37, 101, 121,
124–25, 128, 134, 158
autocracy, 24, 25, 26, 29, 37
Autonomous Action (*Avtonomnoe
deistvie*), 128

Baburin, Sergei, 143,
146, 157
Baburova, Anastasiia, 131, 177
Balkars, 28
ballistic missile defence, 1
Baltics, 54
bannings
as biopolitical tool, 108
of books, 194
of nationalist political groups,
195–96, 198, 201
from political groups, 98
of political movements, 40,
61–62, 146, 153, 157,
169–70
of re-entry of migrants,
236, 250
Banshantsev, Kirill, 127, 128
Barkashov, Aleksandr, 122, 167,
191, 192

Basmanov, Vladimir, 153, 159n, 196, 200
Battle for Donbas (*Bitva za Donbass*), 151, 152
Bazylev, Maksim (Adolf), 132
Beketov, Igor, 160n
Belarus, 54, 79, 245
Belousov, Iaroslav, 135
Belov, Aleksandr (Potkin), 81, 142, 145, 146, 153, 196, 197, 198, 200, 202, 228
Beslan terrorist attack, 215
Billig, Michael, 259
biological racism, 166
biopolitics, 93–116
biopower, 95
birth rates, 94–95, 237
Biriulevo riots, 50, 60, 76
Black Bloc (*Chernyi blok*), 154
Black Hundreds, 3, 26, 31, 122
blacklists, 250, 251
Black Sea Fleet, 287
Blakkisrud, Helge, 78, 190, 268
Blood&Honour/Combat88, 177
Bobrov, Dmitrii, 145, 187, 192, 193, 194, 197, 198, 199, 201–2
Bobrova, Valentina, 152
bodily art, 108
Bolotnaia Square, 103, 125, 135, 199, 202
Bolsheviks, 4, 5, 27, 54–55
bombings, 172–73, 174
Bondarik, Nikolai, 145
borders
  and Crimea, 296–97
  of in-group vs Other, 214–15
  national interests no longer confined to, 57–58
  reinstatement of 1913 borders, 32–33
  of the Russian 'nation', 238
  'Russian World' transcending, 50–51, 62
  Russia's boundaries bigger than Russian Federation, 2
  state boundaries and biopolitics, 102–3
BORN *see* Combat Organisation of Russian Nationalists (*Boevaia organizatsiia russkikh natsionalistov*)
Borovikov, Dmitrii, 175, 193
Borovikov-Voevodin skinhead gang, 170
Bourdieu, Pierre, 261
bourgeoisie, 125, 198
Breivik, Anders Behring, 193
Brezhnev, Leonid, 122, 264
Bright Rus (*Svetlaia Rus'*), 144, 153
Bromlei, Iulian, 25
Brubaker, Rogers, 259, 261, 289
Bunge, Nikolai, 26
bylinas (epic poems), 28

camp mentality, 104
capitalism, 127, 132, 135, 195; *see also* neo-liberalism
Caucasus and Central Asia
  anti-immigrant sentiments, 75–77, 130
  as 'compatriots', 246–47
  ethnic phobias towards, 39, 59–60
  and great-power politics, 64
  migration from, 237
  national democrats, 134
  reducing migration from, 222–23, 226
  seen as migrants, 215
  as 'Significant Other', 59–60

as subjugated territory of Russia 'proper', 54
xenophobia, 195
Celtic cross, 129
censorship, 30
Central Asia *see* Caucasus and Central Asia
Chaika, Iurii, 169
Chaplin, Vsevolod, 104
character, national Russian, 26
chauvinism, 70, 270
Chechnya, 28, 41, 64, 167, 245
Cherkizovskii Market bomb, 172–73, 174
Chesnakov, Aleksei, 85
Chest' i svoboda (Honour and Freedom), 153
China, 245
Chubais, Anatolii, 171–72
Chuev, Feliks, 30
Chuvashov, Eduard, 131–32
Citadel (*Tsitadel'*), 154
citizenship
  for migrants, 221, 247
  and patriotism, 268, 272
  and the USSR, 263
civic consciousness, 43
civic indifference, 45
civic nationalism
  and Eltsin administration, 263
  historical attempts to neutralise, 23, 24
  vs imperial nationalism, 51, 62
  and the national democrats, 149
  and patriotism, 259, 275
  Putin on, 214
civic nations, construction of, 43, 50
civic Russian nation (*rossiiskaia natsiia*), 64, 85
civic vs ethno-cultural understandings of nations, 8–10

civilisational nationalism, 33, 126
civil rights, 125
civil service, non-Russians in, 26
coercive control, 96
Cohen, Stephen F., 69
Cold War rhetoric, 34
collective consciousness, 39, 98
collectivisation, 28
colour revolutions, 276
Combat Brotherhood (*Boevoe bratstvo*), 267
Combat Organisation of Russian Nationalists (*Boevaia organizatsiia russkikh natsionalistov*, BORN), 50, 62, 131–32, 177, 179
Combat Terrorist Organisation (*Boevaia terroristicheskaia organizatsia*), 193
combat training groups, 152–53, 154, 193
Committee of 25 January (*Komitet 25 ianvaria*, K25), 146, 150–51
common descent, myth of, 51
common enemy, 64
Commonwealth of Independent States (CIS)
  as 'compatriots', 246–47
  labour market liberalisation, 243–44
  visas, 76, 223, 237, 243
Communism, 31, 33, 34, 54–55
Communist Party, 27, 30, 32
Communist Party of the Russian Federation (KPRF), 32, 71, 122, 157, 218, 220, 229, 263
compatriot policies, 62, 246, 252
Congress of Russian Communities (*Kongress russkikh obshchin*, KRO), 165–66

conscription, 106
conservatism
  and biopolitics, 97, 98, 99, 100, 104
  conservative revolution movements, 120, 136
  conservative turn in Western politics, 64
  post-Soviet Russia, 31, 74, 79
conspiracy theories, 149
Constitution, Russian, 24, 85, 125
constructivist approaches, 260
consumerist ideologies, 108, 127
contraceptives, 107
corruption, 75, 93–94, 217, 248; see also anti-corruption
cosmopolitanism, 29, 54, 127
Cossacks, Russian, 40, 105, 265, 269
counterculture activists, 108, 122, 124
crime, as concern about migration, 219–21, 224, 240
Crimea
  'Crimea is ours!', 45
  as a cultural part of Russia, 291, 292
  'sacred' nature of, 79
  as subjugated territory of Russia 'proper', 54
Crimean annexation
  Aleksandr Sevastianov on, 179
  effect on nationalist organisations, 187
  ethnic nationalism, 75–79, 80, 199–201
  great-power ideologies, 39
  and identity, 53, 282–305
  imperial nationalism, 61, 63
  mass consciousness, 39

  and the national bolsheviks, 125
  national democrats, 38, 135–36
  patriotism, 260, 265
  public support for, 102, 136, 258, 260, 265, 276
  as re-imperialisation strategy, 62
  and *russkii* identity, 283, 284
Crimean Tatars, 28
cult of the empire, 34
cult of the leader, 45
culture
  assimilation, 78, 225, 244, 246, 291
  and biopolitics, 98
  as core of national identity, 239–40
  Crimea as a cultural part of Russia, 291, 292
  cultural definitions of 'migrant', 215, 222, 245
  cultural identities, 41, 239–40
  cultural style of the national bolsheviks, 122
  cultural superiority, 35
  'migrants destroy our culture', 244–48
  migrants' incompatibility with host-country's, 239–40
  and patriotism, 271, 272

Day of Remembrance for the Victims of Ethnic Crime, 197
Day of the Russian Nation (*Den' russkoi natsii*), 151
death lists, 175
death squads, 166
de Benoist, Alain, 127
Decembrists, 24
Deep and Comprehensive Trade Agreement with EU, 1

Defence of Holy Russia!
  (*Za Rus' sviatuiu!*), 33
Degtiarev, Mikhail, 218, 220, 222,
  224, 228, 229
democracy
  'democratic turn', 37
  national anarchists/national
    revolutionaries, 127
  and the national bolsheviks,
    124–25
  national-democratic nationalism,
    36–40, 133–36
  and national identity, 69
  and the national socialists, 132
  'new' nationalism, 55
  non-imperial nationalism, 71
  threats from the far-right, 189
Democratic Choice
  (*Demokraticheskii vybor*),
  148, 226
demographic crisis, 237
Demushkin, Dmitrii, 6, 81, 143,
  145, 153, 154, 192–93,
  198–99, 200
deportations, 28, 29, 130, 227,
  236, 251
despotism, 25
diaspora, Russian, 134, 222,
  289–90
Dima Iakovlev law, 74, 100, 105
'direct action', 177
Dissenters' Marches, 125
dissident organisations, 29–30,
  31, 33
'divided Russian people'
  ideology, 32
Donbas
  combat training groups, 152–53
  effect on nationalist
    organisations, 187
  and ethnic nationalism,
    200–1, 202

great-power ideologies, 39
  and imperial nationalism, 2, 6,
    34, 63, 81
  media coverage, 17
  nationalism, 200
  Russian identification, 286
Donetsk, 79, 125, 135–36, 144,
  200, 202
Donetsk People's Republic, 78
Donskoi, Dmitrii, 42
Dostoevskii, Fedor, 30, 196
DPNI *see* Movement Against
  Illegal Immigration (*Dvizhenie
  protiv nelegal'noi immigratsii*)
Drobizheva, Leokadiia,
  40, 42
Dugin, Aleksandr, 80, 123, 151,
  155, 164, 196
Dvorkovich, Arkadii, 93
Dzaparidze, Ilia, 131
Dzhibladze, Iurii, 171

economic prosperity, 61, 70, 72,
  84, 265
economic sanctions, 57, 100
egalitarianism, 124
Eisenstadt, Shmuel, 119
Ekaterina II, Tsarina, 42
Ekishev, Iurii, 146
elections
  1990s State Duma, 36
  2011 State Duma, 71, 72
  2016 State Duma, 85, 157,
    158, 202
  electoral fraud, 72
  Moscow 2013 mayoral elections,
    7–8, 76, 213–35
  presidential, 61, 85
  protests for fair, 37, 107, 125,
    135, 147, 178
elites, 53–65, 97, 260–61,
  262, 287

Eltsin, Boris, 8, 9, 34, 35–36, 69, 166, 167, 192, 263
empire, Russian, 3; *see also* imperial nationalism
enemies, perceived, 39, 101
enemies of the Russian people, 171, 178
E.N.O.T Corp, 144, 153
Enteo, Dmitrii (Tsorionov), 74
environmentalism, 267
essentialism, 25, 272
Estonia, 41
ethnically 'clean' communes, 126
ethnic cleansing, 28, 29
ethnic core nationalism, 5, 190–91, 214
ethnicisation of everyday patriotic practices, 269–76
ethnic nihilism, 41
ethnic quotas, 175
ethnic riots, 219, 246
ethnic Russians, history of, 3, 4, 25; *see also russkii* vs *rossiiskii*
ethnic separatism, history of, 25
ethnic turn, 72–75, 214, 238
'ethnic war', 174
ethnocentric non-imperial nationalism, 71
ethnocentrism, 40–41, 225
ethnocide, 78, 179
ethno-conservative turn, 72–75
ethnogenesis, 173, 179
ethnographic studies, 189–90, 260
ethno-nationalism
  Aleksandr Sevastianov, 166
  Aleksei Navalnyi, 217, 220–21
  alliances with other organisations, 191
  and the concept of nationality, 25

ethnic core nationalism, 5, 190–91, 214
  history of, 4, 23–27
  versus imperial nationalism, 51
  Kremlin ethnic policies, 61–63, 75–79, 252
  Motherland (*Rodina*), 156
  national anarchists/national revolutionaries, 126, 129
  national democrats, 133–36, 149
  National Socialist Initiative (*Natsional-sotsialisticheskaia initsiativa*, NSI), 144, 187–209
  and patriotism, 259
  popular attitudes, 226
  post-Soviet Russia, 33
  russkii vs *rossiiskii*, 2, 3, 8–10, 70, 72, 77–78, 231n, 273
ethnonyms, 25
ethnophobias, 39–40, 43
ethno-political upsurge, 42
ethno-sociology, 40
EU (European Union), 1, 62
eugenics, 166
Eurasian Economic Union (EEU), 243–44, 252
Eurasian integration, 61, 80, 229
Eurasian Youth Union (*Evraziiskii soiuz molodezhi*), 151, 196
Euromaidan events, 187, 199–201, 202, 265, 302
Europe; *see also* anti-Westernism; Western models
  conservative turn in Western politics, 64
  European nation model, 10
  freedom of thought, 24
  returning Russia to Europe, 34

as Russia's 'Significant
    Other', 99
everyday nationalism, 282–305
Evtushenko, Dmitrii 'Beshenyi', 145
extraditions, 75
extremists
    arrests for extremist activities,
        80–81
    bannings for, 198–99
    criminal convictions, 145
    nationalism seen as, 40,
        270, 271
    and the Ukraine conflict, 187–209

family
    and biopolitics, 94, 99, 106–7
    family values as security
        priority, 100
    and the national bolsheviks, 124
far-right politics, 170, 187–209;
    see also ultranationalism
fascism, 42, 195
fatherland, 259, 262, 264, 274
Federal Financial Monitoring
    Service (*Rosfinmonitoring*),
    196
Fedorov, Evgenii, 6, 156
feminised 'Russian people', 108
feminism, 107
fifth column, 79
Filatov, Fedor, 131
flags, 34, 73, 198
folk culture, 127
folklore and national identity, 28
Fomenkov, Artem, 29–30
For Fair Elections movement, 37,
    107, 125, 135, 147, 178
For Responsible Power,
    146, 151
Foucault, Michel, 43, 44, 95
Fox, John E., 261, 289
France, 4–5, 9, 43, 51, 53, 149

Free Russia (*Svobodnaia
    Rossiia*), 153
From Under the Rubble, 31

Gaaze, Konstantin, 85
Gagarin, Iurii, 42
Gagauzia, 62
gay culture, 74, 100,
    102–3, 105
gay marriage, 99
Gellner, Ernest, 52
gender representations, 107–8
genocide, 197
geopolitics, 2, 33, 51, 82, 94, 95
Georgia, 1, 41, 56, 59, 62, 64, 75,
    100, 276
German nationalism, 4–5, 9,
    53, 149
German revolution, 119, 120
Gertsenshtein, Mikhail, 26
Gessen, Masha, 228
Girenko, Nikolai, 170–71
Girkin (Strelkov), Igor, 6, 146,
    150, 154
Girs, Nikolai, 26
Glazev, Sergei, 73
Glazunov, Ilia, 73
global financial crisis (2008),
    59, 241
globalisation, 195
global power, Russia as, 82;
    see also great-power ideologies
God's Will (*Bozh'ia volia*), 74
Golosov, Grigorii, 217
Gorbachev, Mikhail, 35, 123
Goriachev, Ilia, 132
grand narratives, 94, 99
grassroots, 23, 27, 29, 31, 35, 36,
    68, 74, 142–62, 199
Great Fatherland Party (*Partiia
    velikoe otechestvo*),
    156, 157

Great Patriotic War, 28, 42, 262, 264, 267
great-power ideologies
  after Syria, 64
  and biopolitics, 99
  and ethnic self-identification, 42
  Eurasian integration, 229
  history of Russian nationalism, 27, 34, 36, 39, 264
  and morality politics, 75
  and national identity, 68, 69
  Putin's, 69–70
  and suppression of nationalist extremism, 81
  and Syria, 82–83
Great Russia (*Velikaia Rossiia*), 4, 27, 28, 54, 55, 151
Greenfeld, Liah, 53
Green Party (*Zelenye*), 152
Greenpeace, 267
Grigas, Agnia, 2, 62
Gubarev, Pavel, 2
Gudkov, Gennadii, 125, 230n
guest workers (*gastarbaitery*), 219, 222, 226
Guliaev, Sergei, 133
Gumilev, Lev, 30, 33
Gushchin, Ilia, 135
Gypsies, 245

habitus, 261
Harding, Sue-Ann, 219, 229–30
hate crimes, 132, 144, 145, 154
health, 93, 94–95, 99, 157
hegemonic masculinity, 94, 107
Herder, Johann Gottfried, 26
heroes, national, 39, 42, 127–28, 178
hierarchy of peoples, 28, 123

high state functionaries, as targets, 171, 175, 176
history
  of revolution, 120–21
  of Russian nationalism, 23–45, 53–55
Hobsbawm, Eric J., 52
homelands, 3, 5, 262, 285, 292; *see also* fatherland; motherland
homophobia, 99, 103, 105, 128
homosexuality, 96, 101, 104–5, 143, 171
Honour and Freedom (*Chest' i svoboda*), 153
hooligans, 40, 156
Hosking, Geoffrey, 44, 54
human rights, 169, 171, 175, 191, 249

Iabloko, 218, 221, 228, 229
Iarovaia, Irina, 74
identity
  and biopolitics, 97, 98, 99
  Crimea pre-annexation, 282–305
  cultural identities, 4, 41
  ethnic identities, 195
  ethnic vs imperial, 61
  against geopolitical rival, 51
  hyphenated identities, 286, 288–89, 293
  identity-based social contract, 68–92
  multi-ethnic identities, 286–87, 288–89, 293
  negative collective identities, 55
  ontological void in post-Soviet Russia, 94
  patriotic identity, 261
  post-Soviet crisis in, 52
  russkii vs *rossiiskii*, 2, 3, 8–10, 70, 72, 77–78, 231n, 273

self-identification of the ethnic majority, 40–44
'Soviet' vs 'Russian', 41
state identity stronger than national, 40–44
illegal immigration
and 'compatriots', 247
in Moscow, 219, 224
and the Moscow 2013 mayoral campaign, 76, 214–15, 219, 221, 227, 228–29
national socialists, 196
neo-Nazis, 168
Putin on, 249
imagined communities, 50, 51, 98
Immortal Regiment movement, 267
imperial eagle symbol, 34
imperial flag, 198
imperialism vs nationalism, 2–3
Imperial Legion (*Imperskii legion*), 153
imperial nationalism, 50–67
and collapse of Soviet Union, 2
ethno-symbolism, 51
imperial consciousness, 45
national bolsheviks, 123
and the national democrats, 149
post-Soviet Russia, 32–33
import bans, 100
import substitution, 267
incitement to racial hatred, 80, 81, 167, 169, 199
inclusive exclusion, 98, 104
In Defence of Holy Russia! (*Za Rus' sviatuiu!*), 33
indigenisation (*korenizatsiia*), 54
information warfare, 62, 177, 267

in-groups/insiders, 4–5, 39, 214, 259
Ingushetians, 28
Institute of Ethnology and Anthropology, 41
intellectuals, 2, 5, 123, 149, 152, 164, 262
  Aleksandr Sevastianov, 163–86
intelligentsia, 29, 30, 165, 227, 228, 262
inter-communal violence, 76, 84
inter-ethnic tensions, 76, 224, 245
inter-ethnic tolerance, spending on, 265, 269
Internationale, The, 28
International Eurasian Movement, 33
internationalism, 27, 28, 29, 120, 127
internet, 37, 195, 196, 290
Iollos, Grigorii, 26
Iraq war, 59
irredentism, 10, 77, 81, 288
Islam, hostility to *see* anti-Islamic/anti-Muslim sentiments
Islamic expansion, 159
Islamic State (IS), 82
Islamisation, 195
Islamist violence, 71
isolationism, 159
Ivanov, Pavel, 170
Ivan the Terrible, 28, 42
Izborsk Club, 157

Jews, 26, 29, 31, 132, 165, 168, 169; *see also* anti-Semitism
jingoism, 136
journals, 194

Just Russia party *see* A Just Russia party
juvenile justice, 107

K25, 146, 150–51
Kadyrov, Ramzan, 64
Kalashnikov, Maksim (Kucherenko, Vladimir), 151
Kaliningrad protests, 135
Kalmyks, 28
Karachais, 28
Karaganov, Sergei, 35
Kara-Murza, Sergei, 32
Karamzin, Nikolai, 53
Karelia, 60
Kasianov, Mikhail, 123
Katasonova, Mariia, 157
Katkov, Mikhail, 26
Kazakhstan, 79
KGB, 30
Khasis, Evgeniia, 131, 132, 177–78
Khirurg (Zadolstanov, Aleksandr), 74
Khodorkovskii, Mikhail, 103, 104
Kholmogorov, Egor, 77, 78, 151
Kholmogorova, Nataliia, 180
Khramov, Aleksandr, 37, 134
Khrushchev thaw, 29, 35
Khutorskoi, Ivan, 131
Kirill, Patriarch, 155
Kisilev, Dmitrii, 83, 155
Kliuchevskii, Vasilii, 53, 54
knife-fighting clubs, 154
Kobzev, Igor, 30
Kohn, Hans, 4
Kolegov, Aleksei, 145
Kolmanovskii, Ilia, 105
Kolstø, Pål, 5, 8, 63, 190
Kondopoga riots, 50, 60, 196, 246

Korchagin, Viktor, 33
korenizatsiia (indigenisation), 54
Korolev, Nikolai, 175
Kosenko, Mikhail, 103
Kosmarskaya, Natalya, 261
Kosovo crisis, 59
Kostin, Konstantin, 159n
Kozhinov, Vadim, 30
Kozyrev, Andrei, 171
Krasovskii, Anton, 105
KRO (Congress of Russian Communities, *Kongress russkikh obshchin*), 165–66
Krylov, Konstantin, 36–37, 40, 71, 134, 146, 147, 151, 191, 197, 200, 230n
Kryshtanovskaia, Olga, 106
Kucherenko, Vladimir (Kalashnikov, Maksim), 151
Kuniaev, Stanislav, 30
Kurekhin, Sergei, 122
Kvachkov, Vladimir, 146
Kyrgyzstan, 237, 244, 276; *see also* Caucasus and Central Asia

labour permits, 223–24, 236, 243–44, 247
Labour Russia (*Trudovaia Rossiia*), 32, 122
Laitin, David, 297
language
    indigenisation (*korenizatsiia*) policy, 54
    migrants and the Russian language, 215, 221, 227, 246, 247–48, 252
    native Russian speakers as community, 78
    as part of ethnic identity, 4, 10
    and patriotism, 272

protection for Russian-speaking minorities, 62, 69
Russian language in Crimea, 284, 287, 291, 292, 295, 299
in Ukraine, 284
Ukrainian language, 285, 295, 299
Laruelle, Marlene, 264
Latvia, 297
Lavrov, Sergei, 35, 79
Lazarenko, Ilia, 37, 133, 148
League for the Defence of the National Heritage of Russia, 165
Lebed, Aleksandr, 166
Left Front, 128
left-wing politics
leftist imperial nationalism, 32
national anarchists/national revolutionaries, 127–28
national democrats, 135
revolutionary nationalism, 120, 167
legislation
anti-extremism legislation, 169, 174
Article 282 (inciting racial hatred), 194, 195
Dima Iakovlev law, 74, 100, 105
migration, 243, 249, 250
profane language laws, 74
restrictive legislation post-Pussy Riot, 74
threats against legislators, 175
Lenin, Vladimir, 27, 28
Levada Centre, 39, 40, 44, 59, 231n, 244
Levichev, Nikolai, 218, 220, 222–23, 228, 229

LGBT (lesbian, gay, bisexual and transgender) issues, 74, 99, 104–5
Liberal Democratic Party of Russia (LDPR), 6, 156, 158, 166, 178, 218, 220, 222, 229
liberalisation, 29–30, 35–36, 243
liberalism
Aleksandr Sevastianov against, 178
alliance with ultra-rightists, 154
and anti-Westernism, 75
and biopolitics, 98, 99, 101, 104, 107
and nationalism, 179
and nationalist movements, 153
non-imperial nationalism, 71
perestroika, 69
pre-Revolution liberals vs conservatives, 3
response to National Great-Power Party, 169
traditionalism as counter to, 73–74
Western models of, 31, 59
Liberal Russian party (*Liberal'naia Rossiia*), 169
life without mediation, 97
Likhachev, Dmitrii, 165
Limonka, 122
Limonov, Eduard (Savenko), 32, 121–26, 135, 146, 151, 199
Lion Against (*Lev protiv*), 157
literary-patriotic circles, 30, 33
'little motherland' (*malaia rodina*), 269, 292
Little Russians (*malorossy*), 4, 54
Lorenz, Konrad, 174

'love for the motherland' (*liubov' k rodine*), 269, 272, 275
Luhansk, 79, 125, 135–36, 144, 202
Luzhkov, Iurii, 36
Lysenko, Nikolai, 122

Mad Crowd, 193
Magnitskii affair, 103
Maidan Square, Kiev, 38, 128, 155–56
Makhno, Nestor, 124
malaia rodina ('little motherland'), 269, 292
Malakhov, Vladimir, 31–32, 33
Malia, Martin, 119
Maltsev, Viacheslav, 153–54
Manezhnaia Square unrest, 60, 71, 196, 246
Markelov, Stanislav, 131, 177
market economies, 135, 243
Markov, Sergei, 82
martial arts training, 154
Martsinkevich, Maksim (Tesak), 145
Martynov, Kirill, 85
Marxism, 29, 127, 132
mass consciousness
  anti-US sentiments, 58–59
  anti-Westernism, 63
  of the Great Patriotic War, 42
  and imperial nationalism, 65
  manipulation of, 34
Matvienko, Valentina, 123
media
  anti-immigrant sentiments, 219, 236
  anti-Westernism, 63–64
  consumerist ideologies, 108
  coverage of Syria, 82
  folklore and national identity, 28
  gender representations, 107–8
  media-based identity campaigns, 84
  and the Moscow 2013 mayoral campaign, 228
  and national identity, 70
  patriotism, 264, 269
  Putin's majority, 79
  sexual representations, 107–8
  and the social contract, 72
  Ukraine coverage, 17, 80
  ultra-rightist, 175
Medinskii, Vladimir, 74
Medvedev, Dmitrii, 36–38, 72, 93, 215
Medvedev, Sergei, 103–4
Melnikov, Ivan, 218, 220, 222, 223–24, 228, 229
Melnikov, Oleg, 135
'melting pot' nation-building strategies, 4
mental hospitals, 103
migration; *see also* anti-immigrant sentiments; illegal immigration
  and crime, 219–21, 224, 240, 248–51
  and the elites, 59
  ethnic phobias towards immigrants, 43
  integration vs repatriation, 221–23, 225
  internal migration, 76
  limiting, 39–40, 225–26
  migrantophobia, 158, 219, 261
  'migrants are a security threat', 248–51
  'migrants destroy our culture', 244–48
  'migrants take our jobs', 239, 241–44
  migration crisis, 237–38

migration myths and Kremlin's nationalist rhetoric, 236–57
migration–nationalism nexus, 238–41, 251
no distinction made between legal and illegal, 221
non-Slav migration to Russian core, 71, 76
Othering of migrants in the 2013 Moscow mayoral elections, 213–35
'raids' on migrants, 143–44
reduction in flow of, 222–24
Mikhailov, Viacheslav, 85
Mikhalkov, Nikita, 123
military force
  anti-Westernism, 57
  combat training groups, 152–53, 154, 193
  and imperial nationalism, 64
  media coverage of, 82
  military patriotism, 263–64
  national anarchists/national revolutionaries, 127
  RNE (Russian National Unity), 192
Miller, Aleksei, 24, 54
Miller-Idriss, Cynthia, 289
Milov, Vladimir, 148
Minin and Pozharskii's People's Militia (*Narodnoe opolchenie imeni Minina i Pozharskogo*, NOMP), 146
Mironov, Boris, 33, 154, 167, 168, 169
Mironov, Ivan, 172
Misanthropic Division, 145
Mitrokhin, Sergei, 218, 221, 222–23, 226, 227, 228, 229
Mizulina, Elena, 74, 100, 106

modernisation, 52, 55, 93, 123, 249
Moldova, 62, 100
Molodaia gvardiia (Young Guard), 30, 33
Molotkov, Lev, 132
monarchists, 122, 151, 198
monarchy, history of, 24–25
moral conservatism, 155
morality politics, 72–75, 79, 93, 102–3, 143–44, 159
Mordovia, 103
Moscow
  2013 mayoral elections, 7–8, 76, 148, 213–35
  Cherkizovskii Market bomb, 172–73, 174
  ethnic homogeneity of, 219, 224, 226
  ethnic unrest in, 60
  Manezhnaia Square unrest, 60, 71, 196, 246
Moscow Bureau for Human Rights, 172
Moscow Patriarchate, 44
motherland, 269, 271–72, 274–75, 292
'little motherland' (*malaia rodina*), 269, 292
Motherland party (*Rodina*), 33, 70, 73, 152, 156, 157–58
Movement Against Illegal Immigration (*Dvizhenie protiv nelegal'noi immigratsii*, DPNI), 50, 81, 127, 134, 142–43, 148, 170, 187, 190–91, 196–99, 200, 201, 202, 217, 228
multi-culturalism, 99, 245
multi-ethnic identities, 286–87, 288–89
multi-ethnic nation, 61, 174, 240, 245, 268

multinational empire, Russia as, 62, 73, 214, 268, 274
Munich speech (Putin, 2007), 34
murders, 26, 131–32, 144, 170, 173, 193
Muromets, Ilia, 28
Muslim ethnic groups, 59, 61, 64, 71, 73, 75; *see also* anti-Islamic/anti-Muslim sentiments
myth of common descent, 51

NAROD (National Russian Liberation Movement, *Natsional'noe russkoe osvoboditel'noe dvizhenie*), 133–36, 148, 217
Narodnaia diplomatiia (People's Diplomacy), 152, 157
Narodnaia Volia (Popular Will), 128–29
narodniki, 128
narodnost' ('Orthodoxy, autocracy, nationality') doctrine, 6, 24, 262
Narodnyi sobor (People's Assembly), 153
Nash sovremennik (Our Contemporary), 30, 33
national anarchists/national revolutionaries, 120, 121, 126–30, 263
national anthem, 28, 263
National Bolshevik Party (*Natsional-bol'shevistskaia partiia*), 32, 120, 121–26, 136
national bolsheviks, 54, 151
National Bolshevist Platform (*Natsional-bol'shevistskaia platforma*), 126, 129

National Conservative Movement 'Russian World' (*Natsional'no-konservativnoe dvizhenie 'Russkii mir'*), 151, 152
National Democratic Alliance (*Natsional-demokraticheskii al'ians*), 37, 38, 133, 148, 153
National Democratic Party (*Natsional'no-demokraticheskaia partiia*, NDP), 37, 134, 146–48, 149, 191, 197, 199, 200
national democrats, 36–40, 120–21, 133–36, 143, 147–50, 187, 198, 200
National Democrats (*Natsional'nye demokraty*), 198
National Front, 133, 151, 156
National Great-Power Party of Russia (*Natsional'no-derzhavnaia partiia Rossii*, NDPR), 33, 167–68, 172, 173, 196
National Great-Power Path of Rus (*Natsional'no-derzhavnyi put' Rusi*, NDPR), 170
nationalism
  bottom-up, 6
  core-oriented vs larger imperial predecessors, 5
  Crimea as watershed moment in, 5–6
  decline of, 142–62
  dynamism of, 17
  between French and German models, 4–5
  imperialism vs nationalism, 2–3
  imperialist vs ethnic, 3, 4–5
  mainstreamisation of, 236

INDEX   321

migration–nationalism nexus,
  238–41, 251
'nationalist turn', 7
negative views of
  'nationalism', 52
and patriotism, 258–61, 262–69,
  270–72, 276
political ideological spectrum,
  5–6
positive views of
  nationalism, 52
post-Crimea, 142–62
prohibition under Soviet
  Union, 27
pro- vs anti-regime, 6
pro- vs anti-Russian Spring, 6
revival of state nationalism, 7–8
russkii vs *rossiiskii*, 8–10
as a social movement, 188–91
sources of, 6–7
as tool to mobilise popular
  support (history), 7
nationality, official, 24, 29, 30,
  34–36, 78
nationality vs nation, 25
national liberals, 187, 200, 213,
  217, 226, 228
National Liberation Movement
  (*Natsional'no-osvoboditel'noe
  dvizhenie*, NOD), 6, 156, 157
national liberation struggles in
  Soviet period, 27
National-Patriotic Front 'Pamiat'
  (*Natsional-patritoticheskii
  front 'Pamiat'*), 35
national pride, 61; *see also*
  patriotism
national provocateurs, 133
'national question', history
  of, 25
national revolutionaries,
  120–41

National Revolutionary Action
  Front (*Front
  natsional-revoliutsionnogo
  deistviia*, FNRD), 133
National Revolutionary Bloc
  (*Natsional-revoliutsionnyi
  blok*), 126, 129
National Russian Liberation
  Movement (*Natsional'noe
  russkoe osvoboditel'noe
  dvizhenie*, NAROD), 133–36,
  148, 217
National Social Initiative, 144
National Socialist Initiative
  (*Natsional-sotsialisticheskaia
  initsiativa*, NSI), 144,
  187–209
national socialists, 120, 130–32,
  191–94
National Socialist Society–North
  (*Natsional-sotsialisticheskoe
  obshchestvo–Sever*,
  NSO–Sever), 132
national traitors, 79
National Unity Day, 196
'Nation and Freedom' Committee
  (*Komitet 'Natsiia i svoboda'*,
  KNS), 153
nation-building
  and biopolitics, 94, 98, 100, 109
  'melting pot' nation-building
    strategies, 4
  and the national
    democrats, 149
  obscured by state-building, 44
  and Putin, 200
  russkii vs *rossiiskii*, 9, 190
nation-states
  civic nations as constructs
    of, 50
  civic vs ethno-cultural
    understandings of, 8–10

nation-states (*cont.*)
  co-ethnic groupings residing outside, 10
  historical evolution of, 23–27
  nineteenth century, 24
  Putin's model, 8–9
NATO (North Atlantic Treaty Organisation), 1, 56, 57, 59, 62, 287
Natsional'naia gazeta, 163–64, 171, 172
Navalnyi, Aleksei, 7–8, 71, 76, 103, 133, 148, 213, 217–18, 220–21, 223, 226, 227, 229
Nazis, 122, 136, 165, 192
Near Abroad, 123, 220
Nemtsov, Boris, 45, 71
neo-Eurasianism, 164
neo-fascists, 5
neo-liberalism, 194, 195
neo-Nazis, 130–32, 163–86
  anti-extremism legislation, 169
  decline of, 154
  decline of traditional nationalism, 142, 144, 145
  and the extreme far-right, 188
  lack of public support for, 147
  revolutionary nationalism, 120, 126, 130–32, 136
  security crackdown on, 173
  skinheads, 193
  Slavic Union (*Slavianskii soiuz*, SS), 143, 146, 173, 187, 190–94, 197, 201–2
neo-pagans, 33
NEORUSS study, xvii, 143, 237, 241, 244, 248
neo-Slavophiles, 78
Nevskii, Aleksandr, 28, 42
New Force (*Novaia sila*), 37, 147–48, 200
'new' nationalism, 36–40, 55–61

New Right, 120, 126
New Russian Barometer (NRB), 58
Nietzsche, Friedrich, 53
Night Wolves, 267
Nikolai I, Tsar, 6, 24, 35, 262
Nikolai II, Tsar, 7
non-systemic opposition, 5
nonviolent action, 123, 135
North Caucasus, 59, 64, 75, 76; *see also* Caucasus and Central Asia
Northern Boundary (*Rubezh severa*), 145
Notes from a Prisoner of War (*Zapiski voennoplennogo*, Bobrov), 194, 196
Novgorod Republic, 129
Novikov, Sergei, 31
Novorossiia (New Russia), 79, 80–81, 125, 136, 146, 150, 151, 152–53, 201, 202
NPSR, *Narodno-patrioticheskii soiuz Rossii* (People's Patriotic Union of Russia), 32

occupation government, 149
official identity, 68–69, 78, 83–84
official nationality, 24, 29, 30, 34–36, 78
offshore capital, 178
Ogurtsov, Igor, 30
Onishchenko, Gennadii, 100
oppositional nationalism, 150–54
Orthodox Christianity
  and familial biopolitics, 106
  history of Russian nationalism, 30
  and national identity, 73–74
  nationalist movements, 153
  and racism, 33
  replaced by Stalinism, 29

Syria, 83
and traditionalism, 34
and Western antagonism, 79
'Orthodoxy, autocracy, nationality'
   (*narodnost'*) doctrine, 6,
   24, 262
OSCE (Organisation for Security
   and Co-operation in
   Europe), 34
Other
   borders of in-group vs Other,
      214–15
   Caucasus and Central Asia as
      'Significant Other', 59–60
   constitutive other, 43
   Crimea as 'Other' to Ukraine,
      285–86
   Europe as 'Significant
      Other', 99
   migrants as 'Other',
      213–35, 240
   and religion, 78
   Ukrainians as, 78
   USA as 'Significant Other',
      55, 61
   'us' and 'them', 43
   West as 'Significant
      Other', 155
   xenophobia, 195
Other Russia (*Drugaia Rossiia*),
   125, 135, 146, 151, 199
Other Russia, The (Limonov,
   2003), 124
Oushakine, Serguei, 263

pagans, 33
Pain, Emil, 3, 6, 8, 62, 84, 171,
   215, 217, 221
Pamiat, 35, 36, 197
paramilitary groups, 102, 105,
   166, 168, 177, 179, 192
Parkhomenko, Sergei, 125

PARNAS (People's Freedom Party,
   Partiia narodnoi svobody),
   153–54, 202
partisans, 174–75, 176–77,
   178, 179
Party of Nationalists (*Partiia
   natsionalistov*), 198, 199
passportisation, 62, 223
patents (work permits), 243–44,
   251–52
paternalism, 23, 24–25, 29
patriarchy, 24–25, 64,
   94, 107
patriotism
   aggressive, 39
   and anti-Westernism, 265
   and biopolitics, 101–2
   and citizenship, 268, 272
   and civic nationalism,
      259, 275
   compatriot policies, 62,
      246, 252
   conservative-patriotic
      values, 74
   'Crimeans', 298, 299
   and culture, 272
   ethnicisation of everyday
      patriotic practices, 270–76
   and ethno-nationalism, 259
   everyday patriotism, 269–70
   following Chechnya war, 167
   great-power ideologies, 70,
      82–83, 84
   growth of, 155
   media, 264, 269
   military patriotism, 263–64
   and nationalism, 258–61,
      262–69, 270–72, 276
   and propaganda, 265
   and Putin, 79, 260, 263–64
   and racism, 259
   and religion, 83

patriotism (*cont.*)
  Soviet period, 29, 55, 263
  statist patriotism (*derzhavnost'*), 70, 83, 149, 268
  and Ukraine conflict, 265, 272–73
  Western models of, 274
  and xenophobia, 271
Patriots of Russia (*Patrioty Rossii*), 152
Patrushev, Nikolai, 100
Pavlenskii, Petr, 108
People's Assembly (*Narodnyi sobor*), 153
People's Diplomacy (*Narodnaia diplomatiia*), 152, 157
People's Freedom Party (*Partiia narodnoi svobody*, PARNAS), 153–54, 202
People's Patriotic Union of Russia (*Narodno-patrioticheskii soiuz Rossii*, NPSR), 32
People's Republican Party (*Respublikanskaia narodnaia partiia*), 122
perestroika, 35, 69
Petr the Great, 53, 262
Pikhtelev, Semen, 198
Pilkington, Hilary, 190
pluralism, 270
pochvennichestvo, 30, 32, 33
Podberezkin, Aleksei, 32
Poland, 24, 54
Polish Independence Day march, 128
Polish uprising (1830–31), 24
Politkovskaia, Anna, 171
Popular Will (*Narodnaia Volia*), 128–29
populism
  and migration, 240–41, 251

Moscow 2013 mayoral elections, 213, 219, 222, 229, 236, 239, 248, 249
  national bolsheviks, 124
  Putin eschewing, 251, 252
  security issues, 250
post-Communists, 32
post-politics, 98
Potkin (Belov, Aleksandr), 81
poverty, 52, 58
Pozner, Vladimir, 169
Prilepin, Zakhar, 101–2
Primakov, Evgenii, 56
prisons, 103–4, 175
Prokhanov, Aleksandr, 2, 32
Prokhorenko, Artem, 193
pro-Kremlin nationalist groups, 151, 152, 154–58
propaganda
  ban on gay propaganda, 74, 104–5
  and the Crimean annexation, 199
  cult of the empire, 34
  folklore and national identity, 28
  fuelling xenophobia (Soviet period), 29
  national identity, 69
  official rhetoric, 155
  and patriotism, 265
  post-Soviet Russia, 32, 34
  Russian culture and history promulgation, 55
Proshechkin, Evgenii, 171
Prosvirnin, Egor, 37–38, 80, 145, 151
psychiatry, 93, 103
Public Chamber, 93
public offices, symbolic takeovers of, 123
Pushilin, Denis, 78
Pussy Riot, 73–75, 103, 108, 109

Putin, Vladimir
  Aleksandr Sevastianov on, 178–79
  and the anti-immigrant agenda, 76
  'beseiged fortress' rhetoric, 34
  biopolitics, 96, 97, 99, 100–1, 106–7
  body of, 100–1
  condemned by national democrats, 136
  on Crimea, 2, 200
  describing collapse of Soviet Union, 2
  disappearance of Ukraine events from speeches, 17
  divorce, 100
  identity issues, 68
  on illegal immigration, 249
  King of Nature/King of the Beasts, 108
  Limonov's approval of, 125
  on migration, 227, 230, 236, 237, 240–51
  Munich speech (2007), 34
  and national identity, 69–70
  nationalism, 7–8, 155
  and the 'national question', 69–70, 72–73, 214–15, 245–46, 249
  nation-state model, 8–9, 61
  on Novorossiia, 80
  on patriotism, 260, 263–64
  popularity of, 38
  portrayed as masculine and virile, 107–8
  power vertical, 97
  and the revival of state nationalism, 7–8
  rossiiskaia natsiia (civic Russian nation), 64
  and Russian imperialism, 2–3
  'Russia: the national question', 214–15, 245–46, 249
  russkii vs *rossiiskii*, 2–3, 70, 72, 77
  and Sergei Sobianin, 216
  on Syria, 82
  and the Ukraine, 292
  Valdai Discussion Club, 72, 74, 79

racism
  Aleksandr Sevastianov, 165, 168, 179
  Article 282 (inciting racial hatred), 194
  biological racism, 166
  decline in street violence, 144
  growth of racially-motivated violence, 70
  and the Moscow 2013 mayoral campaign, 221
  national democrats, 133, 134, 154
  and patriotism, 259
  pochvennichestvo, 33
  racist violence, 163–64
  revolutionary nationalism, 120–21
  skinheads, 130
  surge in xenophobic violence, 172
Radonezhtsy, 30
'raids', 143–44, 156–57
rasologiia ('raciology'), 164
Razin, Stepan, 128
Razumkov Centre, 285, 287
Red Army, 54
red-brown ideologies, 33, 37, 166, 167
redistributive policies, 59

re-ethnicisation, 130
regime of truth, new, 98
re-imperialisation, 62
religion; *see also* Muslim ethnic groups; Orthodox Christianity
   and familial biopolitics, 106
   fundamentalism, 134
   legislation to protect, 74
   morality politics, 73, 74, 75, 79
   and national identity, 73–74
   and otherness, 78
   as part of ethnic identity, 4
   and racism, 33
   Soviet period, 29
   statist patriotism (*derzhavnost'*), 83
   Syria, 83
   and traditionalism, 34
   tsar's right to rule, 25
reproductive behaviour, 94, 99, 100, 106–7
Republican Party of Russia–People's Freedom Party (*Respublikanskaia partiia Rossii–Partiia narodnoi svobody*, RPR-PARNAS), 217–18
Reserve (*Rezerv*), 153
Respublikanskaia narodnaia partiia (People's Republican Party), 122
ressentiment, 53, 57, 121
Restrukt! 144, 145
reunification of Russian people, 32
revolutionary nationalism, 119–41, 176, 190
Revolution of 1917, 3, 262
Right-Conservative Alliance (*Pravo-konservativnyi al'ians*, PKA), 151, 152
Right March, 170
right-wing politics
   far-right politics, 152, 154, 170, 175, 187–209; *see also* ultranationalism
   history of extreme radical Russian nationalism, 26
   national anarchists/national revolutionaries, 126
   national democrats, 148
   New Right, 120, 126
   post-Soviet Russia, 32–33
   racially-motivated violence, 70
   and revolution, 120
riot police, 175
riots, 50, 60, 76, 196, 219, 246
RNE (Russian National Unity, *Russkoe natsional'noe edinstvo*), 35, 36, 40, 121–22, 166, 191–92, 197, 201
ROD (Russian People's Movement, *Russkoe obshchestvennoe dvizhenie*), 191, 197
Rogozin, Dmitrii, 178
ROK (Russian Community of Crimea, *Russkaia obshchina Kryma*), 283, 291, 297
ROS (Russian All-People's Union, *Rossiiskii obshchenarodnyi soiuz*), 143, 146, 157
Rose, Richard, 58
Roshal, Leonid, 105
rossiiane nationalism, 214, 298
rossiiskaia natsiia (civic Russian nation), 64
rossiiskii identity, 2, 8–10, 64, 70
rubber apartments, 248, 250
'Russia for Russians' (*Rossiia dlia russkikh*), 26, 130, 150, 197, 225, 260
'Russian 1 May' (*russkii pervomai*), 151

Russian All-People's Union
  (*Rossiiskii obshchenarodnyi
  soiuz*, ROS), 143, 146,
  157
'Russian character', 28–29
Russian Civic Union (*Russkii
  grazhdanskii soiuz*, RGS),
  134, 135, 148
Russian Cleansing (*Russkaia
  zachistka*), 145
Russian Community of Crimea
  (*Russkaia obshchina
  Kryma*, ROK), 283,
  291, 297
Russian-Georgian war, 59
Russian Image (*Russkii obraz*),
  132, 135, 175
Russian Imperial Movement
  (*Russkoe imperskoe
  dvizhenie*), 151, 153,
  197–99, 201
Russian Joint National Alliance
  (*Russkii ob"edinennyi
  natsional'nyi al'ians*,
  RONA), 153
Russian language
  in Crimea, 284, 287, 291, 292,
    295, 299
  indigenisation (*korenizatsiia*)
    policy, 54
  migrants, 215, 221, 227, 246,
    247–48, 252
  'nationality' in, 8–10, 25
  native Russian speakers as
    community, 78
  and patriotism, 272
  protection for Russian-speaking
    minorities, 62, 69
  in Ukraine, 284
Russian Liberation Front 'Pamiat'
  (*Russkii front osvobozhdeniia
  'Pamiat''*), 197

Russian Marches
  2012, 37
  2014, 199
  2015, 45, 63, 143, 154
  declining numbers attending,
    8, 143
  and the DPNI, 196
  Motherland (*Rodina*), 156
  national socialists, 170, 197
  Navalnyi's participation in,
    217, 228
  social marginalisation, 51
  as symbol of nationalism,
    50, 142
Russian March of Labour, 197
Russian Mothers (*Russkie materi*)
  movement, 105
Russian National Front (*Russkii
  natsional'nyi front*, RNF), 151
Russian National Party, 29
Russian National-Socialist Party, 29
Russian National Unity (*Russkoe
  natsional'noe edinstvo*, RNE),
  35, 36, 40, 122, 166,
  191–92, 197
Russian Opposition Coordination
  Council, 135
Russian Orthodox Church
  and Jewish ancestry of clerics,
    170
  and national identity, 73–74
  and 'official nationality', 44
  on punishment, 104
  and 'traditional values', 159
  and Western antagonism, 79
Russian Party (*Russkaia partiia*), 33
Russian People's Movement
  (*Russkoe obshchestvennoe
  dvizhenie*, ROD),
  191, 197
Russian Popular Party (*Russkaia
  narodnaia partiia*), 29

Russian Public Movement
(*Russkoe obshchestvennoe dvizhenie*), 134, 135
Russian Resistance (*Russkoe soprotivlenie*), 175
Russian Right Party (*Rossiiskaia pravaia partiia*), 153
Russian Socialist Movement (*Russkoe sotsialisticheskoe dvizhenie*, RSD), 129
Russian Soviet Federative Socialist Republic (RSFSR), 3, 28
Russian Spring (*Russkaia vesna*), 6, 63, 200, 201, 202
Russian Union of Youth, 133
Russian Union of Youth–National Revolutionary Action (*Soiuz russkoi molodezhi–Natsional-revoliutsionnoe deistvie*, SRM–NRD), 133
Russian Unity (*Russkoe edinstvo*, RE), 283, 291, 297, 302
Russian Verdict (*Russkii verdikt*), 175
Russian World (*Russkii mir*), 50–51, 62, 99, 109, 151–52
'Russia's special path', 24, 26
Russia Will be Freed by Our Forces (*Rossiia osvoboditsia nashimi silami*, RONS), 200
Russification, 27, 299
Russkie movement
  banning of, 6, 62, 198
  as coalition, 197–98
  Dmitrii Bobrov, 197
  Dmitrii Demushkin, 6, 193, 201
  revolutionary nationalism, 135, 144, 145, 148–49, 150, 153
  and Ukraine, 200

russkie territories, 79
russkii vs *rossiiskii*, 2, 3, 8–10, 70, 72, 77–78, 231n, 273
Russo-centrism, 68, 71, 73–74, 78, 85, 215
Russophobia, 35, 171, 177, 201
Russophone category, 222;
  see also Russian language
Ryno, Artur, 174–75, 193
Ryzhkov, Vladimir, 125

Sagra riots, 246
samizdat, 31
Samokhin, Aleksei, 154
sanitation, 100
Sankia (Prilepin, 2006), 101–2
Saveliev, Andrei, 33, 151
Savenko, Eduard (Limonov), 121
Savin, Igor, 261
Schultz-88 (*Shul'ts-88*), 193–94
secessionist movements, 62, 253n, 282, 285, 297
Second World War see Great Patriotic War
secular racists, 33
securitisation, 240, 249, 251, 252, 302
self-awareness, ethnic, 41–42
self-determination, 54, 68, 199
self-governance, 129
self-identification of the ethnic majority, 40–44, 68
semi-legal nationalist groups, 30
separate ethnic identities, 41–42
separatism, 41–42, 102, 136, 146, 179, 270, 282–83, 287–88, 297–301
SERB (South East Radical Bloc), 156
Serbskii Centre, 103

serial killings, 174, 193
Sevastianov, Aleksandr, 33, 163–86, 196
sexuality, 94–95, 100, 107–8, 124; see also gay culture
Shafarevich, Igor, 30, 31
Shargunov, Sergei, 32
shestidesiatniki ('60's generation'), 29
Shevchenko, Maksim, 155
Shevel, Oxana, 8, 259
Shevtsov, Ivan, 30
Shield of Moscow (*Shchit Moskvy*), 144
Shiropaev, Aleksei, 37, 38, 133, 136, 148
Significant Other, 51, 55, 59–61
Siniavskii, Andrei, 45n
Skachevskii, Pavel, 174, 175, 193
skinheads
  bans on nationalist groups, 40
  collective action, 192
  decline of traditional nationalism, 142, 147, 164
  ethnographic studies, 190
  national anarchists/national revolutionaries, 126
  national socialists, 130–32, 189
  neo-Nazis, 170, 174, 175
  and the right-wing, 190
Skokov, Iurii, 166
Slavic Community (*Slavianskaia obshchina*), 127
Slavic Force (*Slavianskaia sila*), 193
Slavic Union (*Slavianskii soiuz*, SS), 143, 146, 173, 187, 190, 191, 192–93, 194, 197, 201, 202

Slavophiles, 25–26, 78
Slezkine, Yuri, 27
Sober Courtyards (*Trezvye dvory*), 157
Sobianin, Sergei, 76, 213, 215–16, 218, 219, 222–23, 226–27, 229, 230, 240
Sobolev, Rikhard, 135
sobornost' (preference for collectivism), 26
Sochi Olympic Games, 109, 264–65
social and material poverty, 52, 58
social cohesion, 70, 98
social contract, 68–92
Social Darwinism, 124
social engineering, 51–52
socialism, 123, 128, 263
Socialist International, 262
social media, 105, 196
social mobility, 121
social movement approaches, 188–91
social psychology, 259
social solidarity, 52
social stability, 35
societal nationalism, 6, 8, 17
soft power, 62, 94–95
Solidarity movement, 148
Soloukhin, Vladimir, 30
Solovei, Valerii, 2, 3, 37, 79, 85, 133, 148, 149, 200
Solovev, Vladimir, 78, 155
Solzhenitsyn, Aleksandr, 30, 31
Sonderweg, 32
South East Radical Block (SERB), 160n
South Ossetia, 56, 62
SOVA Center, 130–31, 143, 144, 151, 172, 193, 197

sovereignty
  and anti-migrant
    sentiments, 240
  biopolitics, 93–116
  'parade of sovereignties', 41
  principles of popular sovereignty,
    43–44
  Soviet period
    identification with, 55
  and the identity of the Russian
    Federation, 69
  imperialist vs ethnic
    nationalism, 3
  nationalism, 54
  and patriotism, 263
  and Russian identity, 55
  and Russian imperialism, 2
  state nationalism and
    autonomous nationalism,
    27–31
Spain, 42–43
Spas (electoral bloc), 166–67
Spas (military-patriotic club),
  173
Special Purpose Mobility
  Unit (*Otriad mobil'nyi
  osobogo naznacheniia*,
  OMON), 125
Spiritual Heritage (*Dukhovnoe
  nasledie*), 32
Sputnik i Pogrom, 37–38, 80,
  145, 152
spy-mania, 34
Stalin, Iosif, 7, 27–28, 29, 35, 42,
  54–55
Stalinists, 31, 32, 37, 39,
  146, 151
Starikov, Nikolai, 156
state, Russian
  and biopolitical sovereignty,
    101–3
  ideologies, 6–7

national-democratic
  nationalism, 36
Putin on, 214
and societal nationalism, 6–7,
  8, 17
'state-forming nation'
  (*gosudarstvoobrazuiushchii
  narod*), 214
state identity stronger than
  national, 40–44
state ideology, 52
stateless society, 124, 126
State Programme for Patriotic
  Education (SPPE), 263–64,
  265, 266–68
state repression, 144–45,
  146, 196
state symbols, 263–64, 268
state terror, 28
state vs societal nationalism,
  23–49
statism, 45, 80–83, 252
statist patriotism (*derzhavnost'*),
  70, 83, 149
stereotypes, ethnic, 40
Strategiia-2020, 176–77
Strategy-31, 125
Strelkov, Igor (Girkin), 6, 146,
  150, 154
Struve, Petr, 3
suicide, 93
superpower status, 58, 75
Surkov, Vladislav, 171
surrogacy, 100
surveillance, 96, 99, 108
Suslov, Vitalii, 165
Susov, Anton, 134
Svanidze, Nikolai, 171
Svoboda, 199
Syria
  ethnonationalist discourse,
    82–83

great-power ideologies, 39
and imperial nationalism,
    34–35, 64
and Russian identity, 53
Szporluk, Roman, 62

Tajikistan, 237, 244; *see also*
    Caucasus and Central
    Asia
Tatars, 28, 215, 274
technocratic strategies, 97, 241,
    243, 249, 252, 253
Terekhov, Stanislav, 167,
    168, 170
terrorism
    anti-migrant campaigns, 176
    and ethno-national
        identity, 82
    and migrants, 248, 249
    revolutionary nationalism, 163,
        170, 177, 179
    and Russian identity, 53
Third Way, 127
Tigers of the Motherland (*TIGRy
    Rodiny*), 157
Tikhonov, Nikita, 131, 132,
    177–78
Tishkov, Valerii, 8, 171
tolerance, 127, 171, 174, 245,
    265, 268, 270
Tolokonnikova, Nadezhda, 103–4
Tolz, Vera, 219, 229–30
Tor, Vladimir, 37, 71, 230n
Torch of Novorossiia, The
    (Gubarev, 2016), 2
totalitarianism, 34, 188, 190
traditionalism
    history of Russian nationalism,
        28, 34, 41, 42
    and imperial nationalism, 64
    vs modernisation, 159
    moral conservatism, 155
and the national
    bolsheviks, 123
against Western liberalism, 74
'traitor-peoples', 29
trans-ideological politics, 98
Transnistria, 62
trauma, historical, 45
Trofimov, Viktor, 29
'trophy art', repatriation of,
    165, 171
Trudovaia Rossiia (Labour
    Russia), 32, 122
tsarist period, 4, 25, 53–54, 262
Tsorionov (Enteo, Dmitrii), 74
Turkey, 51
Turkic-Muslim peoples, 33;
    see also Caucasus and Central
    Asia
two Russias, 54

UK, 42
Ukraine; *see also* Crimea; Crimean
    annexation; Donbas
    Crimea as 'Other' to, 285–86
    and Crimean identity,
        288–96
    and Crimean separatism,
        297–98
    Donetsk, 78, 79, 125, 135–36,
        144, 200, 202
    ethnic phobias towards, 39
    ethnic Ukrainians seen as
        culturally compatible, 245
    ethno-national appeal, 77–79
    Euromaidan events, 187,
        199–201, 202, 265, 302
    and imperial nationalism, 61
    import bans, 130
    Little Russians (*malorossy*),
        4, 54
    Luhansk, 79, 125, 135–36,
        144, 202

Ukraine (cont.)
    Maidan Square, Kiev, 38, 128, 155–56
    migration and citizen status, 248
    popular mobilisations in, 276
    public support for, 102
    revolutionary nationalism, 128–29
    Russian reaction to, 57
    as Russian re-imperialisation strategy, 62
    as Russia's Other, 78
    seen as backyard, 63–64
    seen as 'ethnic enemy', 179
Ukraine conflict
    Aleksandr Sevastianov on, 179
    and the decline of migrantophobia, 158
    ethnic nationalism, 199–201
    and the national bolsheviks, 125
    and patriotism, 265, 272–73
    radical activists drawn to, 145, 154
Ukrainian language, 285, 295, 299
ultranationalism, 6, 35, 152, 163–64, 166, 197
ultra-rightists, 152, 154, 175
Unappeasable League (*Neprimirimaia liga*), 154
uncivil society, 189–90
underground dissident organisations, 29–30
unemployment, 241–42
unification, Russian, 77
Union of Officers (*Soiuz ofitserov*), 167
Union of Orthodox Banner-Bearers (*Soiuz pravoslavnykh khorugvonostsev*), 33
Union of Orthodox Brotherhoods (*Soiuz pravoslavnykh bratstv*), 33
Union of the Russian People (*Soiuz russkogo naroda*), 26, 122, 197
United Russia Party (*Edinaia Rossiia*), 74, 123, 156, 157–58, 216, 218, 303n
USA
    anti-US sentiments, 55–56, 57, 58, 59–61, 63, 80, 82, 195
    conflict with, 56
    conservative turn in, 64
    as Russia's 'Significant Other', 55, 61
    Russophobia, 35
'us' and 'them', 43
USSR *see* Soviet period
utopianism, 124
Uvarov, Count Sergei, 6, 24, 29
Uzbekistan, 41, 237, 244; *see also* Caucasus and Central Asia

Valdai Discussion Club, 72, 74, 79
Valiaev, Evgenii, 151, 152
Valuev, Count Petr, 25
Vasilev, Dmitrii, 35
Veletskii, Maksim, 136
vengeance, party of, 168–72
Verkhovskii, Aleksandr, 40
Veshniakov, Aleksandr, 123
victimisation, 100
Victory Day (9 May) parades, 264, 265
vigilante groups, 105, 157, 192
violence
    Aleksandr Sevastianov, 170, 174, 179–80
    anti-immigrant, 176, 189
    inter-communal violence, 76, 84

Islamist violence, 71
lack of public support for, 147
linked to migration, 221, 224, 249
and the national socialists, 130, 132
neo-Nazis, 163–86
in pro-Kremlin nationalism, 156–57
'raids', 144
RNE (Russian National Unity), 192
skinheads, 130–31
Slavic Union (*Slavianskii soiuz*), 193
surge in xenophobic violence, 172
theories of aggression, 174
and the ultra-right, 166
virginity promotion, 93
visa regimes, 76, 223, 242
Vitukhnovskaia, Alina, 122
Vladimir, Prince, 79
Vladivostok protests, 135
Voevodin, Aleksei, 193
Volnitsa, 127–28
Vorobev, Stanislav, 151
VSKhON (All-Russian Social-Christian Union for the Liberation of the People, *Vserossiiskii sotsial-khristianskii soiuz osvobozhdeniia naroda*), 30

Weberian ideology, 8, 52
Westernisation of Russia, 59
Western models
 of liberalism, 217
 of masculinity, 107
 of nationality, 24, 25, 31, 53, 155
 of patriotism, 274

White armies, 54
White Memory (*Belaia pamiat'*), 175
white ribbons, 106–7
White Russians (*belarusy*), 4, 54
white supremacists, 133, 164, 190, 194
White Wolves, 131–32
Wilson, Andrew, 286
Working Russia (*Trudovaia Rossiia*), 32, 122
work visas, 223–24, 236, 243–44, 247
world moral leader, Russia as, 75
world revolution, 128
World War II *see* Great Patriotic War
World Wildlife Foundation, 267

xenophobia
 and Aleksei Navalnyi, 217, 220–21
 attitudes of, 189
 co-existence with multiculturalism, 245
 electoral campaigns explicitly condemned, 72
 history of, 26
 in mainstream politics, 76
 in Moscow 2013 mayoral elections, 148, 217, 220, 221, 228
 and nationalism, 147
 national socialists, 195
 and patriotism, 271
 popular anti-migrant views, 225–26
 post-Soviet Russia, 31
 Putin's policies against, 70
 racist violence, 163
 related to economic prosperity, 84

xenophobia (*cont.*)
  and revolutionary nationalism, 121
  rise of, 238
  skinheads, 130
  Soviet period, 28
  and state repression, 145
  subcultures, 189
  surge in xenophobic violence, 172

Yakuts, 42
Yanukovych, Viktor, 1, 200, 302
Yeltsin, Boris *see* Eltsin, Boris
Young Guard (*Molodaia gvardiia*), 30, 33
Young Russia (*Rossiia Molodaia*), 144
youth
  and the national bolsheviks, 121, 124
  nationalism, 142
  neo-Nazis, 174
  post-Soviet generation, 290, 293–94
  RNE (Russian National Unity), 192
  Tigers of the Motherland (*TIGRy Rodiny*), 157
  youth subcultures, 130, 192

Zaldostanov, Aleksandr, 74
Zelik, Ruslan, 199
Zhirinovskii, Vladimir, 5, 6, 32–33, 70, 158, 166, 178, 222
Zhivov, Aleksei, 151, 152
Zhukov, Georgii, 42
Zhuravlev, Aleksei, 157–58
Zimmerman, William, 55–56, 58
Zionism, 31, 168
Ziuganov, Gennadii, 32
Žižek, Slavoj, 52

EU representative:
Easy Access System Europe
Mustamäe tee 50, 10621 Tallinn, Estonia
Gpsr.requests@easproject.com

www.ingramcontent.com/pod-product-compliance
Lightning Source LLC
Chambersburg PA
CBHW061705300426
44115CB00014B/2573